Derrida's *Politics of Friendship*

Derrida's
Politics of Friendship
Amity and Enmity

Edited by Luke Collison,
Cillian Ó Fathaigh and Georgios Tsagdis

EDINBURGH
University Press

Edinburgh University Press is one of the leading university presses in the UK. We publish academic books and journals in our selected subject areas across the humanities and social sciences, combining cutting-edge scholarship with high editorial and production values to produce academic works of lasting importance. For more information visit our website: edinburghuniversitypress.com

Edinburgh University Press Ltd
The Tun – Holyrood Road, 12(2f) Jackson's Entry, Edinburgh EH8 8PJ

Typeset in 10/12 Goudy Old Style by
Cheshire Typesetting Ltd, Cuddington, Cheshire, and
printed and bound by CPI Group (UK) Ltd,
Croydon, CR0 4YY

A CIP record for this book is available from the British Library

ISBN 978 1 4744 8673 6 (hardback)
ISBN 978 1 4744 8675 0 (webready PDF)
ISBN 978 1 4744 8676 7 (epub)

Contents

Part II: Echoes

Part III: Polemics

Acknowledgements

The editors would like to thank Charlotte Thevenet and Sacha Golob for their help at the early stages of this project and Emily Fitzell for her excellent translation work. We are grateful to all those at Edinburgh University Press who assisted us with this volume and especially Carol Macdonald for her encouragement.

The Society for French Studies and the philosophy department of King's College London provided generous financial and institutional backing for the workshop which initiated this text, for which we are very grateful.

Cillian acknowledges that this book forms part of the activities for the following research projects: (1) "Differential Ontology and the Politics of Reason," funded by the Regional Government of Madrid; and (2) "The Politics of Reason" (PID2020-117386GA-I00).

Georgios wishes to acknowledge the Leiden Centre for Continental Philosophy (LCCP) and the research collective Minor Torus, for nourishing thought over the past couple of years. He wishes to thank Cillian and Luke for soldiering through what appeared at times like an interminable war without an enemy. Finally, he wishes to dedicate the labour of his contribution to Ilias Kounelas, who has for a lifetime been friend and friendship.

Finally, we would like to thank our family and friends, near and far, for their care and support throughout this project.

Notes on the Contributors

Isabelle Alfandary is Professor of American literature and critical theory at Sorbonne Nouvelle University. Former President of the International College of Philosophy, her research programme is at the intersection of philosophy and psychoanalysis. A specialist of the relationships between psychoanalysis, philosophy and literature, she is the author of numerous articles and four monographs on these issues, one of which is a reading of Derrida's and Lacan's works considered from the perspective of the question of writing (*Derrida – Lacan: Writing between Psychoanalysis and Deconstruction*, Hermann, 2016). Her latest book is on the epistemology of psychoanalysis: *Science et fiction chez Freud* (Paris, Ithaque, 2021).

Nicole Anderson is Professor in the Department of English, and Director of the Institute for Humanities Research at Arizona State University. She is also Honorary Professor in Cultural Studies at Macquarie University, Sydney. She is co-founder and Editor-in-Chief of the *Derrida Today* journal and the founding Director of the *Derrida Today International Conferences*. She has published numerous book chapters and journal articles and is the author of *Derrida: Ethics Under Erasure* (Bloomsbury 2013), co-author of *Cultural Theory in Everyday Practice* (Oxford 2009), and author of *Culture* (forthcoming, Routledge).

Kit Barton is a Principal Lecturer at Regent's University London. Initially focusing on continental philosophy, Derrida and ethics, with doctoral work supervised by Simon Critchley and examined by Slavoj Žižek, he has now expanded his research to include recent analytic work on population ethics and personal identity. He is a long-standing member of the Society for European philosophy and has published on topics including Derrida, Heidegger, De Beauvoir, Dewey, business ethics and pedagogy.

Cathrine Bjørnholt Michaelsen is Assistant Professor at the Department of Management, Politics and Philosophy, Copenhagen Business School. She holds an MA and a PhD in philosophy from Copenhagen University and Albert-Ludwigs-Universität, Freiburg. Her main research interests are deconstruction, post-structuralism, psychoanalysis and literature. Among her publications are: *Remains of a Self: Solitude in the Aftermath of Psychoanalysis and Deconstruction* (Rowman & Littlefield, 2021); "Auto-Affection and the Curvature of Spacetime: Derrida Reading Heidegger Reading Kant," *International Journal for Philosophical Studies*, Vol. 28:3, 2020; and "On a Language that Does Not Cease Speaking: The Experience of Language in Psychosis and Literature," *Comparative and Continental Philosophy* Vol. 12.2, 2020.

Pheng Cheah is Professor in the Department of Rhetoric at the University of California, Berkeley. He is a specialist in continental philosophy, postcolonial studies, critical theory and cosmopolitanism. He is the author of *Spectral Nationality: Passages of Freedom from Kant to Postcolonial Literatures of Liberation* (Columbia University Press, 2003), *Inhuman Conditions: On Cosmopolitanism and Human Rights* (Harvard University Press, 2006) and most recently *What is a World? On Postcolonial Literature as World Literature* (Duke University Press, 2016). He is also the co-editor (with Suzanne Guerlac) of *Derrida and the Time of the Political* (Duke University Press, 2009). He is presently working on a book on biopower and human rights.

Joseph Cohen is Professor of Philosophy at University College Dublin (Ireland). He has authored *Le spectre juif de Hegel* (Galilée, 2005), *Le sacrifice de Hegel* (Galilée, 2007), *Alternances de la métaphysique. Essais sur E. Levinas* (Galilée, 2009) and co-authored, with Dermot Moran, *The Husserl Dictionary* (Bloomsbury-Continuum, 2012). With Raphael Zagury-Orly, he co-edited *Heidegger et "les juifs"* (Grasset, 2015), *Heidegger. Qu'appelle-t-on le lieu?* (Gallimard, 2008), *Derrida. L'événement déconstruction* (Gallimard, 2012) and *Judéités – questions pour Jacques Derrida* (Galilée, 2003). He has published recently, with Raphael Zagury-Orly, *L'Adversaire privilégié. Heidegger, les juifs et nous* (Galilée, 2021). His areas of scholarship span from German idealism to French and German contemporary philosophy.

Luke Collison is a visiting lecturer at the University of Cologne. He received his PhD from the Centre for Research in Modern European Philosophy, Kingston University London. His doctoral research addressed the intersection of religion and politics in the work of Thomas Hobbes and Carl

Schmitt. His research in political philosophy and political theology is determined by the foci of the early modern formation of the state, and the twentieth-century debate on 'the political'.

Peggy Kamuf is Professor Emerita of French and Comparative Literature at the University of Southern California. She is a major translator of Derrida and an editor of the *Oxford Literary Review*. Her seminal work includes *Signature Pieces: On the Institution of Authorship* (Cornell University Press, 1988), *The Division of Literature, or the University in Deconstruction* (University of Chicago Press, 1997), *Book of Addresses* (Stanford University Press, 2005) and *Literature and the Remains of the Death Penalty* (Fordham University Press, 2019). She is also a co-editor of the series *The Seminars of Jacques Derrida* at the University of Chicago Press.

Rosine Kelz is a research associate in the project 'Politicizing the Future' at the Institute for Advanced Sustainability Studies in Potsdam, Germany. Previously she held an Andrew W. Mellon Postdoctoral Fellowship in the Bio-Humanities at the Illinois Program for Research in the Humanities at the University of Illinois. Publications include the article 'Thinking about Future/Democracy: Towards a Political Theory of Futurity', published in *Sustainability Science* (2019), and the monograph *The Non-Sovereign Self, Responsibility, and Otherness: Hannah Arendt, Judith Butler, and Stanley Cavell on Moral Philosophy and Political Agency* (Palgrave Macmillan, 2016).

Susanna Lindberg is a philosopher, specialised in German idealism, phenomenology and contemporary French philosophy. After earning a PhD at the University of Strasbourg, she has worked as researcher at the University of Helsinki and as lecturer and professor at the University of Tampere. After three years as associate researcher at the Université Paris Ouest Nanterre, she is presently a fellow at the Collegium for Advanced Studies of the University of Helsinki. Her publications include *Techniques en philosophie* (Hermann, 2020), *Le monde défait: L'être au monde aujourd'hui* (Hermann, 2016), *Heidegger contre Hegel: Les irréconciliables* (L'Harmattan, 2010) and *Entre Heidegger et Hegel: L'éclosion et vie de l'être* (L'Harmattan, 2010).

Chris Lloyd is a Senior Lecturer in Law at Oxford Brookes University and has published in the journals *Law Text Culture*, *Australian Feminist Law Journal*, *Social & Legal Studies* and *Information & Communications Technology Law*, as well as in the Routledge edited collections *Graphic Justice: Intersections* *of Comics and Law* (ed. Thom Giddens) and *Synesthetic Legalities: Sensory Dimensions of Law and Jurisprudence* (ed. Sarah Marusek).

Giovanni Menegalle is British Academy Research Fellow in the Department of French at King's College London. Before joining KCL, he completed a PhD on Derrida and Husserl at the University of Cambridge and was Lecteur at the Université de Paris 7 – Denis Diderot. His current project explores critiques of technocracy and technological culture in twentieth-century French philosophy and the human sciences and he is also pursuing research on the reception of cybernetics and information theory in post-war French thought.

Thomas Clément Mercier (ANID FONDECYT/ POSTDOCTORADO/ N° 3200401) is a postdoctoral researcher at Universidad Adolfo Ibañez (Santiago). His work has been published in journals such as *Global Discourse*, *Oxford Literary Review*, *Parallax*, *Derrida Today*, *CR: The New Centennial Review*, *Philosophiques*, *Ostium* and *Revue ITER*. He specialises in twentieth-century philosophy, political thought and international studies, with a particular interest in the multilayered problematics of democracy, violence and political resistance from the perspectives of deconstruction, Marxism and decolonial thinking. He is currently working on the edition and publication of the Derrida–Althusser correspondence.

Cillian Ó Fathaigh is a Postdoctoral Research Fellow in the Department of Logic and Theoretical Philosophy at the Universidad Complutense de Madrid, Spain. A former Gates Cambridge Scholar, he is the co-editor of *#NousSommes: Collectivity and the Digital in French Thought* (Peter Lang, 2019) and has taught previously at the École Normale Supérieure de Lyon. His work has been published in *Derrida Today* and *Paragraph* and his PhD thesis, 'Derrida's Institutions', is currently under preparation for publication.

Allan Parsons teaches theory on the MA Narrative Environments (MANE) course at Central Saint Martins, University of the Arts London, which explores the spatial, temporal and experiential aspects of the design of public, private, performance and communicational spaces, situations and events. For his BA and and MPhil from Middlesex University, he studied the interrelationships among design history, cultural studies and philosophy. For many years he was an external research consultant for the Secretary General's Advisory Unit at the OECD, working on long-term future matters of concern. He maintains several websites including the MANE course compendium and *Poiesis and Prolepsis*.

Gavin Rae is Associate Professor in the Department of Logic and Theoretical Philosophy at the Universidad Complutense de Madrid, Spain. Besides various articles and book chapters on Derrida, he is the author of *Poststructuralist Agency: The Subject in Twentieth-Century Theory* (Edinburgh University Press, 2020), *Critiquing Sovereign Violence: Law, Biopolitics, Bio-Juridicalism* (Edinburgh University Press, 2019), *Evil in the Western Philosophical Tradition* (Edinburgh University Press, 2019), *The Problem of Political Foundations in Carl Schmitt and Emmanuel Levinas* (Palgrave Macmillan, 2016), *Ontology in Heidegger and Deleuze* (Palgrave Macmillan, 2014), *Realizing Freedom: Hegel, Sartre, and the Alienation of Human Being* (Palgrave Macmillan, 2011); and the co-editor (with Emma Ingala) of *Historical Traces and Future Pathways of Poststructuralism: Aesthetics, Ethics, Politics* (Routledge, 2021), *The Meanings of Violence: From Critical Theory to Biopolitics* (Routledge, 2019) and *Subjectivity and the Political: Contemporary Perspectives* (Routledge, 2018).

Jennifer Rushworth is Lecturer in French and Comparative Literature at UCL. She has published two books, *Discourses of Mourning in Dante, Petrarch, and Proust* (Oxford University Press, 2016) and *Petrarch and the Literary Culture of Nineteenth-Century France* (The Boydell Press, 2017). For an article on Proust and Derrida she was awarded the Society for French Studies's Malcolm Bowie Prize 2015; she also received the *Paragraph* Essay Prize 2016, for an article on mourning in Proust and Barthes. Her work is characterised by a consistent engagement with French theory, and by a desire to establish dialogues across temporal and formal boundaries.

Timothy Secret is Head of the Department of Theology, Religion and Philosophy at the University of Winchester. His monograph *The Politics and Pedagogy of Mourning* was published in paperback by Bloomsbury in 2017. Secret has two current main lines of research, one focused on the ethics of singularity and the encounter with particular reference to shame, the gaze, narcissism and contemporary media, the other focused on the borders of reason and madness in Hegel and twentieth-century French thought.

Mauro Senatore is currently on a British Academy Fellowship at Durham University (UK). He a visiting Professor of Philosophy at the Universidad Adolfo Ibáñez (Santiago, Chile). He has been a research fellow and visiting professor in academic institutions of Argentina, Chile, Italy, Mexico, Spain, United Kingdom and United States. His work explores a series of issues at the crossroads of phenomenological tradition and the life sciences, such as animality, self-reference and responsibility. He is the author of the monograph *Germs of Death: The Problem of Genesis in Jacques Derrida* (SUNY Press, 2018) and of several articles published in specialised journals such as *Postmodern Culture*, *Philosophy Today* and *Symposium*.

Georgios Tsagdis teaches at Leiden University, the Erasmus University Rotterdam and the Architectural Association. His work operates across theoretical domains drawing on 20th Century, Contemporary and Ancient Greek Philosophy. His essays have been published in various book collections and international journals, among which *Parallax*, *Philosophy Today* and *Studia Phaenomenologica*. His editorials include special issues for *Azimuth* ('Intersections: at the Technophysics of Space') and the *International Journal of Philosophical Studies* ('Of Times: Arrested, Resigned, Imagined)'. Tsagdis created and convened the Seminar of Neoplatonic Studies at the Warburg Institute in the years 2013-19 and has recently established the cross-border theory network Minor Torus.

Rozemund Uljée is Assistant Professor of European Philosophy at the Institute for Philosophy, Leiden University, the Netherlands. She is interested in the notion of justice as found in phenomenological and post-phenomenological thought. Her research focuses on how this theme calls into question philosophy understood as a concern for truth in favour of a thinking of a difference that cannot be reduced to it. At present, it is her ambition to develop this particular interpretation of the theme of justice towards its political implications. She is the author of *Thinking Difference with Heidegger and Levinas: Truth and Justice* (SUNY, 2020) and co-editor (with Lisa Foran) of *Heidegger, Levinas and Derrida: The Question of Difference* (Springer, 2016).

David Ventura is an Honorary Research Associate at Royal Holloway, University of London, where he recently completed a doctoral thesis on the relation between time and ethics in Bergson, Levinas, and Deleuze. David's work has previously appeared in *The Southern Journal of Philosophy* and *Phenomenological Reviews*. As well as preparing a monograph based on his thesis for publication, David is currently developing a project exploring the relation between race and temporality through the philosophies of Fanon and Glissant.

Naomi Waltham-Smith is Associate Professor in the Centre for Interdisciplinary Methodologies at the University of Warwick. Her work sits at the intersection of continental philosophy and sound studies, and appears in journals including *boundary 2*, *CR: The New Centennial Review*, *diacritics*, *Parrhesia: A Journal of Critical Philosophy*, *Music & Science* and *Music Theory Spectrum*. She is the author of *Music and Belonging Between Revolution and Restoration* (Oxford University Press, 2017) and her second book, *The Sound of Biopolitics: Life, Aurality, Deconstruction*, is forthcoming in Fordham University Press's Commonalities series.

Raphael Zagury-Orly is Invited Professor of Philosophy at Sciences Po – Paris and Directeur de Programme at the Collège International de Philosophie in Paris. He is an affiliated member of the Centre de recherche sur les arts et le langage (EHESS-CNRS) in Paris. He has authored *Questionner encore* (Galilée, 2010) and, with Joseph Cohen, co-edited *Judéités – questions pour Jacques Derrida* (Galilée, 2003) as well as *Heidegger. Qu'appelle-t-on le lieu?* (*Les Temps Modernes*, 2008), *Derrida. L'événement déconstruction* (*Les Temps Modernes*, 2012) and *Heidegger et "les juifs"* (Grasset, 2015). He co-edited, in 2019, with Orietta Ombrosi *Derrida – Levinas. An Alliance Awaiting the Political* (Mimesis, 2020). He has published recently, with Joseph Cohen, *L'Adversaire privilégié. Heidegger, les juifs et nous* (Galilée, 2021).

Welcome Friends: Reading Derrida's *Politics of Friendship*

Luke Collison, Cillian Ó Fathaigh and Georgios Tsagdis

Between amity and enmity, what remains of the *Politics of Friendship* today? This volume seeks to interrogate Derrida's important though still under-appreciated text; to demonstrate its potential for understanding politics, community, fraternity, friendship and our relation to others. Not only, of course, to understand these, but to rethink them and all the figures which they underpin. In this respect, we are repeating the rhythm of Derrida's own work. Yet here each of us, in amity and enmity, applies this rhythm to Derrida's work itself, searching for what new and old forms of politics and friendship remain to be thought.

It is this spirit which motivated a one-day workshop held at King's College London in December 2018. There, a diverse group of scholars, from philosophy, literature, French studies, political theory, gathered for a chapter-by-chapter interrogation of the text, developing its themes and problems, both in the light of Derrida's later works and with respect to the contemporary political context. Almost twenty-five years after its first publication, the relevance of the text in the midst of the twenty-first century's 'crisis of democracy' was unmistakable. Since 2018, the force of these issues has only multiplied: our volume seeks to address these questions by applying the slow, patient pedagogical approach of *Politics of Friendship* to the text itself.

Politics of Friendship Today

In the foreword to *Politics of Friendship*, Derrida tells us that this book is itself 'the foreword to the book I would one day wish to write' and frames this project as 'an introduction', a text that is 'preliminary rather than problematic' (*PF*, vii).[1] There are perhaps two reasons for this. The first concerns the origins of this text, which Derrida explains is but the first session of his 1988–9 seminars, given under the same title of 'Politics of Friendship'.

Indeed, English translations presented in 1988 at both Cornell University and the American Philosophical Association confirm this, in tracing a more concise but analogous trajectory of concepts and philosophers.[2] Moreover, *Politics of Friendship* marks the beginning not only of a seminar, but also a seminar series, with the 'Politics of Friendship' serving as the heading for three seminars from 1988 to 1991.[3] This is no doubt one of the justifications for the 'preliminary' status of the text. Yet there is something curious about presenting a text composed six years earlier as provisional and here we can find another reason for this claim: there is something inherently preliminary, if not provisional, about the style and approach of *Politics of Friendship*. What Derrida describes as the 'hesitant gait' of the text – its slow exposition, patient analysis and marks of careful pedagogy – seems to go hand in hand with this preliminary status. There is at once an acknowledgement of and resistance to the urgency of political action, with each step of the text – just like the citation that it continuously refers to – subject to continuous revaluation, reassessment and reinscription.

Although we should not expect something like a political manifesto from *Politics of Friendship*, the text presents a stubborn and rich resistance even to contextualisation. This is in part because of the distance between its first presentation in 1988, its publication in French in 1994 and its translation into English in 1997, but also because of the notable lack of reference to any contemporary examples. The exclusion of specific indices should not, however, be understood as a denial of the importance of context. Instead, Derrida insists on avoiding specific political examples, since current concerns always already punctuate our reading of the text in advance – an unavoidable and invaluable demarcation.[4]

Derrida justifies this restraint and temperance in three ways. First, the sheer quantity of political issues at stake means that 'the overabundance of such "illustrations" would have swamped the least of our concerns'; second, these very examples could disrupt our ability to rethink the foundations of these problems, 'that which, as it were, *screens out* reflection by projecting itself with the pathetic and "sensational" violence of images onto a too easily mediatizable scene' (272); finally, because there is no need to – 'these examples are in the mind, heart and imagination of anyone who would be interested in the problems we are dealing with here' (272). In this respect, *Politics of Friendship* is a text which also responds to particular contexts, ones so pertinent and present at the time that they did not need to be explicated. While not wholly determined by the socio-political context to which it responds, the silent dialogue that *Politics of Friendship* undertakes was and continues to be of real importance. Among the numerous local, national and transnational developments of the time, the rise of the far right in France and the dissolution of the Soviet Union constitute principal reference points.[5] They offer crucial examples of the friend/enemy logic at work in politics, but are also paralleled in politics today, with the simultaneous return of a nationalist right and a left with openly socialist aspirations.

Within France, perhaps the most important political event of the 1980s was the emergence of the far right as a political force. Indeed, this rise was quite dramatic: in the 1986 legislative elections, the Front National went from zero seats to thirty-five, claiming just under 10 per cent of the vote. This reflected a general change in attitude to migration in France and Europe, marking the end of 'les trente glorieuses', the thirty years of economic growth after the Second World War. In 1988, therefore, Derrida is writing in a political context, where rhetoric of 'fraternity' and the nation becomes increasingly charged. In the early 1990s, this atmosphere would only intensify, with ever more regressive legislation around migration and refugees, as well as the restriction of rights to nationality (particularly *jus solis* or birthright citizenship).

Internationally, the rippling effects of the dissolution of the Soviet Union would not be long in arriving. Already in 1988, there were indications of disruption with organised movements in several states across the Union, many of which were pro-democratic but had also a strong nationalist tendency, themes that resonate throughout *Politics of Friendship*. Derrida had for many decades maintained a strong interest in developments behind the Iron Curtain – most notably demonstrated by his participation in the Jan Hus Educational Foundation and his arrest in Czechoslovakia in 1981.

Politics of Friendship, thus, straddles one of the most important periods in European and international politics of the twentieth century. Indeed, if *Politics of Friendship* has been underappreciated as a text, it is at least in part because at the time of its publication it appeared to have little explicit to say about many of the parameters of the political developments of the day, be it the future of socialism, or 'the clash of civilizations'.[6] Yet, by the same token, and perhaps because it was not framed in these terms, *Politics of Friendship* also offered a chance of rethinking the national and international in a post-bipolar world: in this sense, it responds to the need to reassess the foundations of global politics, precipitated by the end of the Cold War.

Rethinking the political, particularly the binary logic of Cold War politics, points towards one final contextual consideration: the inclusion of Carl Schmitt. Many of the names that we find in *Politics of Friendship* (Aristotle, Nietzsche, Kant, etc.) have travelled with Derrida before. In contrast, Schmitt is a new interlocutor, but his arrival should not be surprising. It is here that the overlap between the friend/enemy logic of the Cold War and the rise of the far right becomes apparent. Schmitt was an influential jurist in Weimar Germany, but his subsequent involvement with the Nazi regime, as legal adviser, political theorist and arguably propagandist, has ensured his disrepute and relative marginalisation within post-war political theory.[7] The echoes of Charles Maurras's extreme right newspaper *Action Française*, of which Schmitt was a regular reader in the 1920s, gives a contemporaneity to Derrida's turn to Schmitt in the context of the rise of the far right in France.[8] Within academia, interest in his work grew significantly following the publication of the translations of *The Concept of the Political* into French in 1972 and English in 1976.[9] Indeed, in the French publication of 1972, both *The Concept of the Political* and *Theory of the Partisan* are included and it is these two texts which represent the focus of Derrida's criticism.[10] Importantly, it is particularly in the former, where Schmitt developed his friend-enemy criteria. If Derrida pays such attention to this issue in Schmitt, it is at least in part because Schmitt provides a prism through which to locate and disrupt, albeit implicitly, the discourse of the Cold War and the rise of the far right.

There are numerous ways in which this political discourse articulates itself today; indeed, it is pervasive in the way we relate to others personally, nationally and internationally. No more than Derrida do we need to resort to illustrations to demonstrate the relevance of the above concerns, both within the global, but also within a specifically occidental political space. Instead, we hope that the reader will keep these concerns in their 'mind, heart and imagination' when passing through the text's chapters (272).

The Text

The ten chapters of *Politics of Friendship* trace the figure of the friend as a ground for politics and political community across a series of canonical philosophical thinkers: Aristotle, Plato, Diogenes Laertius, Cicero, Nietzsche, Schmitt, Montaigne, Augustine, Heidegger, Kant and Blanchot. In addition, the French original text – unlike the English translation – includes a four-chapter text on Heidegger, titled *Heidegger's Ear: Philopolemology (Geschlecht IV)*. Yet such a skeleton summary is misleading, not least because of the ambivalent and somewhat mysterious citation that runs throughout the text: 'O my friends, there is no friend'. This quote, attributed to Aristotle by Diogenes Laertius, serves as a leitmotif through which Derrida demonstrates the shared paradoxes and problems of the concept of friendship in the works of these often-divergent thinkers. It is in the careful turning and returning of this phrase that the text brings out the aporias of friendship. Indeed, what is at stake for Derrida cannot be overstated: an imperative to rethink the ways in which our relation to the other, particularly within a political community, has been defined by fraternity or friendship between men. *Politics of Friendship* thus interrogates the ways in which this paradigm has excluded different others, and in particular women, and how different conceptions of friendship and the political are required to enable inclusion.

In order to situate the text further, three terms deserve emphasis: *aimance* (translated as 'lovence', 'lovance' or 'lovingness'), *teleiopoesis* and the *perhaps*.[11] *Aimance* designates the effort to rethink the relationship between love and amity and particularly to challenge a discourse (pervasive in this canon) that would make a hard distinction and hierarchy between these two.[12] Indeed, the link between friendship and love may itself be stronger in French than in English (the common French verb *aimer*, for instance, having the potential to mean both to love and to like). Moreover, Derrida uses the term to disrupt a distinction between being-loved and loving, to find a 'middle voice' that troubles the distinction of activity and passivity in love. Indeed, through the text, we come to see *aimance* as a structural possibility of a relation to the other, on which all figures and discourses of friendship (*philia*, *eros*, courtly love and so on) necessarily rely (69–70). In this, *aimance* becomes the 'hyperboly' that exceeds any and all determination within these discourses (218). *Aimance* thus represents a crucial resource for deconstructing friendship and for imagining new figures of relationality.

If *aimance* could be said to address the latter part of 'O my friends, there is no friend', then *teleiopoesis* chimes more with the former: the vocative address to the friend. Its translation is complicated, in the first place, by the slippage of the transliteration from Greek to Latin, Latin to French, and finally, French to English.[13] In this passage, *teleiopoesis* is employed to invoke both the imaginative aspect of creation and its very creative act, the act of bringing something into being (*poesis*), where a sense of completion (*telos*) resonates with an undertone of the distant (*tele*). These inflections are simultaneously at work in Derrida's use of the concept as shown in his reading of Nietzsche, where Zarathustra does not address his present readers, but those of the future. This temporal relation – 'the long time of a time that does not belong to time' – is understood as 'messianico-teleiopoetic', that is, as a time 'out of joint', articulating a future promise in a present address (77, 287). This captures a more general structure of the address to the other, one which completes itself outside of the subject's control and ipseity, whose meaning is dependent on the uptake and response of the other. In this, it describes a distance in one's relation to the other; yet, as Derrida also stresses in the *teleio*, 'friendship is implied in advance therein' (32). Each address, therefore, implies and presupposes this possible relation to this other.

Accordingly, the *perhaps* completes this theoretical matrix, by emphasising that this relation to the other is always fundamentally and profoundly unreliable. For if *teleiopoesis* comes from the past to address the subject and the future at once, 'there is no more just category for the future than that of the "perhaps"' (29). This makes evident the development of a central argument in Derrida's thinking of the nature of the event. For there to be a future, worthy of the name, its taking place cannot be certain, lest it be reduced to 'a programme or a causality, a development, a process without an event' (29). What the *perhaps* offers is a way of thinking about a 'friendship to come', but one which may never take place or emerge, one which is promised with no guarantee. Indeed, the *perhaps* does not only provide a way of critiquing a certain view of the future as wholly calculable, but it also suggests a ground to reconsider the very meaning of the possible, 'this other possibility' (67). Appealing to this other experience and thought of the possible, one which cannot be predicted from where we are today, means that we are at an inherent risk of failure. For Derrida, it is the *perhaps* which helps describe this risk of failure, one which must 'not be simply an accidental edge of the condition', but rather fundamental to any event. In this sense, therefore, the *perhaps* is the ground for any rethinking of *aimance* and for any form of *teleiopoetic* address.

Crucial as *aimance*, *teleopoiesis* and the *perhaps* are to *Politics of Friendship*, it must be stressed that removing them from the specific context in which they operate and artificially separating them from each other comes at a price. The ways they complement each other and carry forth the text fashions new possibilities of conceiving the intimate relationship between politics and fraternity. Further, this brief sketch of the explicitly thematised concepts of *Politics of Friendship* says nothing about the style, the experience of reading and the singular use of language that marks all of Derrida's *œuvre*. This rigorous interconnectedness between language and thought entails, as Marian Hobson has brought out expertly, 'a very coherent putting in place at an implicit level, of structures, which can carry the problems and paradoxes thematized and discussed overtly'.[14] Such structures require careful interpretation and the form of patient and 'hesitant gait' that Derrida proposes in *Politics of Friendship* and which this volume seeks to emulate (10).

Finally, a word on 'Heidegger's Ear: Philopolemology (*Geschlecht* IV)', the long essay that was printed alongside *Politics of Friendship* in the original French edition, but which was left out from the English translation, having already been published separately.[15] Constituting a significant part of the

1988–9 lectures, '*Geschlecht* IV' expands the discussion on the friend/enemy distinction in Schmitt, by querying Heidegger's invocation of 'the voice of the friend' in *Being and Time*. Its relation to the main body of the *Politics of Friendship* is also complicated by the fact that it constitutes the fourth and last part of the *Geschlecht* series (notwithstanding the posthumous publication of the third part). The series showcases Derrida's untiring return to Heidegger, on whom the whole connotative spectrum of the German term *Geschlecht* is brought to bear, in the form of a question mark: 'sex, race, family, generation, lineage, species, genre' weave a web of notions that destabilise the Heideggerian text.[16] Thus, in order to appreciate the political purchase of filiation and fraternity, '*Geschlecht* IV' must be read in tandem with the main body of *Politics of Friendship*; the present volume tends to it. A survey of the contributions of the latter will benefit from an overview of the reception of Derrida's text, which it accordingly follows.

Lines of Reception

Between the delivery of the lectures on the themes of politics of friendship in 1988–9 and their publication in book form in 1994,[17] the appearance in 1993 of *Specters of Marx* had a double effect: it gave rise to an intense interest in the ethical and political relevance of deconstruction, which more than three decades later seems hard to imagine ever being in question, but at the same time, it dominated this interest. As such, most of the work in the second half of the 1990s that engaged with the ethico-political in Derrida's thought seemed to relegate *Politics of Friendship* to a secondary, pro-paedeutic place. The urgency of rethinking the legacy of Marxism after the end of the Cold War was far too pressing.

Even among readers of Carl Schmitt, with the exception perhaps of Heinrich Meier, the reception of *Politics of Friendship*, to be examined in more detail below, seems to have taken off only after the work had made its mark in other contexts. Early comparative studies like Chantal Mouffe's *The Return of the Political* (1993), which demonstrated, ahead of the publication of *Politics of Friendship*, a theoretical nexus between Carl Schmitt's conception of the enemy and Derrida's conception of the 'constitutive outside',[18] drew mostly on texts such as the 'Force of Law: The Mystical Foundations of Authority' (1989).[19] Importantly, most of these early studies tended to identify, critically or affirmatively, points of differentiation or divergence between Derrida and Schmitt.[20]

The translation of *Politics of Friendship* into English in 1997 effected a significant acceleration of the reception within the Anglophone world, while a thematic broadening of its importance was advanced by the publication in French the same year of the essay 'On Cosmopolitanism' and of the two essays that comprise *Of Hospitality*. Advancing a politics of alterity, in which the other exceeds the figure of the friend within the history of political theory, these succinct essays made palpable the need for a return to the pivotal place of amity and enmity in this history. Yet, it would take a few years to muster the patience and assume the reticent distance that, as will become apparent, *Politics of Friendship* demands.

Simon Critchley's *Ethics – Politics – Subjectivity* (1999) is indicative of this effort. Drawing on his earlier work in order to address question 'what are the politics of friendship?',[21] Critchley turns to the importance of finitude in Derrida, arguing that 'the precondition for a non-traditional conception of friendship is an acknowledgement of both the ubiquity and ungraspability of finitude'.[22] For Critchley, the idea of friendship that Derrida develops in *Politics of Friendship* is one based on 'an *aimance* for the other *as* mortal'.[23] This finitude is tied to forgetting and memory, becoming political in the notion of the 'passive decision'. '*The other's decision is made in me*, a decision made but with regard to which I am passive', is a result of this 'unconditional priority of the [finite] other'.[24] As others, including Spivak, would emphasise, this 'passive decision' offers no guarantee or certainty: in this sense the *perhaps* and the 'passive decision' are part of the same political matrix for Derrida. For Critchley, the *perhaps* demands a 'non-foundational' ethics and politics, while the mortality of the other makes the relation between ethics and politics 'non-arbitrary'.[25] Nonetheless, Critchley's patience does not extend further; the *Politics of Friendship*, and deconstruction more generally, would be indicted for lacking a 'theory of *hegemonization*' that offers 'an account of the political conceived in terms of strategy and tactics'.[26] In sum, although the import of the 'ethical injunction' of *Politics of Friendship* is recognised as necessary for a repoliticisation of Marxism, the work is also deemed insufficient for carrying out the project by itself.

Gayatri Chakravorty Spivak's 'A Note on the New International' (2001) follows on the same hermeneutic trajectory.[27] Employing the words of *Specters of Marx*, Spivak describes *Politics of Friendship* as effecting 'a powerful-rethinking of "an alliance without an institution"'.[28] The *teleopoiesis* put forward there 'shocks [. . .] the idea of belonging in a collectivity, for it makes a constant and risk-taking effort to affect the distant in a poiesis or imaginative remarking, without guarantees'.[29] This acknowledges the 'curved' nature of social contact, whereby 'no one can be *directly accessed*'.[30] It is this challenge to any thinking of community as in any way evident, certain or guaranteed which marks the political stakes of *Politics of Friendship* and which might provide the ground for more just political community, along the lines that Derrida elaborates under the heading of a 'New International'. Moreover, Derrida provides for Spivak an important political example in his 'plea for slow reading, even at a time of political urgency'.[31] Though Spivak seeks to take this in a different direction, particularly the patient and unguaranteed work of grass-roots activism, she points to this implicit pedagogical model in *Politics of Friendship* – 'citations of citations, indefinitely. Teleopoietic reversals' – which hold out the potential to rethink the future, but also a type of 'non-European "Marxism"'.[32] On this reading, it is the very mode of *Politics of Friendship* which marks its intersection with *Specters of Marx* and the later political themes of the 1990s.

Along the same interpretative thread of extra-institutional and extra-hierarchical alliance, Leela Gandhi's *Affective Communities: Anticolonial Thought, Fin-de-Siecle, and the Politics of Friendship* (2006) showed the potential of Derrida's text for postcolonial studies. Gandhi builds on Derrida's critique of filiation as a ground of political community to complement a study of late Victorian radicalism. Here, Derrida's work becomes a way of thinking 'those invisible affective gestures that refuse alignment along the secure axes of filiation to seek expression outside, if not against, possessive communities of belonging'.[33] Indeed, it is exactly Derrida's constant demonstration and critique of friendship as the 'founding metaphor' of political community in *Politics of Friendship* that clear the space, for Gandhi, to reassess our historical and current understandings of community.[34] Here we can find the grounds to imagine what Gandhi calls *affective cosmopolitanism*: 'the ethico-political practice of a desiring self inexorably drawn towards difference'.[35]

Returning to the early reception of *Politics of Friendship*, it is worth looking at three readings within different disciplinary contexts. First, in the winter of 1998–9, the journal *Eighteenth-Century Studies*, published by Johns Hopkins University Press, brought out an issue simply titled 'Politics of Friendship'. Focusing on themes ranging from the politics of the lesbian relation of Eleanor Butler and Saran Ponsonby, to the poetics of Kleist and the function of friendship in Kant and Jacobi, the issue engages only tangentially with Derrida's work, as a source of inspiration. Peter Fenves's essay 'Politics of Friendship, Once Again', which also functioned as an introduction to the issue, was the most notable exception, bringing Derrida in dialogue with Kant, Lessing and Arendt, but did not move much beyond a rehearsal of the logic of Derrida's critique of fraternal friendship and of the law of the few that determines it.[36]

Second, within a feminist context, Penelope Deutscher examined in 1998 the importance of mourning in *Politics of Friendship*.[37] Paying particular attention to Derrida's reading of Montaigne, and its relationship to his other work on mourning, Deutscher sets the ethical complexities of friendship into relief. She contrasts Luce Irigaray's injunction of a non-appropriation of alterity with Derrida's claim that 'the inability to mourn or incorporate the other is articulated in tandem with an articulation of the inevitability of doing so'.[38] Derrida's grief is as much for the friend as it is for the way in which death 'forces just such a reduction of the friend to the terrain of the self'.[39] In this, Deutscher's text allows us to see how the 'Politics of Friendship' seminars tie closely into the preceding and succeeding seminars which address 'Eating the Other' and 'The Rhetoric of Cannibalism'. Indeed, as Deutscher argues, it is precisely this inescapable appropriation of the other that makes friendship and mourning '*the moral question*'.[40]

Finally, in 2001, Miriam Leonard took it upon herself to assess Derrida's 'appropriations of classical texts in the history of *our* discipline', namely, British classical philology.[41] Writing from Cambridge, less than a decade after the Cambridge affair, which is passed over in silence, Leonard's essay offers a web of insinuations about Derrida's ideological motives. Addressing her fraternal and sororal classicists, Leonard claims confidently that 'it would be possible to analyse how a barely concealed political agenda of rehabilitation of Derrida's disgraced friend and colleague, Paul de Man, operates throughout the PA [*Politiques de l'amitié*]'; but she has no time for such an analysis.[42] This elaborate, albeit broad- and oblique-stroked portraiture of a philologically illiterate ('naive', 'ignorant', 'trite' and 'unoriginal' are some of the marshalled adjectives) apologist of Heidegger's and Schmitt's reactionary politics, ends up being, surprisingly, of value, according to Leonard.[43] Despite conflating past and present and lacking a proper philological methodology, *Politics of Friendship* is redeemed as showcasing how classics can exit their irrelevance and insularity.

Among readers of Derrida, *Politics of Friendship* requires a different kind of introduction at this period. In 'Who is Derrida's Zarathustra? Of Fraternity, Friendship, and a Democracy to Come' (1999) John D. Caputo patiently glosses over the main themes of the 'sibling' of *Specters of Marx*, showing the way in which Derrida, drawing on Blanchot and Levinas, measures up against the fraternal friendship of the Greco-Roman and Judeo-Islamo-Christian tradition, represented in the Western canon by Aristotle, Nietzsche and Schmitt.[44] The appropriation of Nietzsche's Zarathustra showcases, for Caputo, Derrida's effort to foreground the other in the '(br)other', that is to discover infinite alterity within a model of friendship, which the tradition premised on noble equality and a community under the sign of the same. Suffused with messianism, and bereft of any determinate community,

Zarathustra is thus made to speak in fidelity to, *as well as* against, himself; so is Aristotle and all of the Western tradition.[45] For within this tradition, the friend, as brother, calls for his deconstruction, unto a friendship that will no longer be deconstructible.[46]

Caputo takes this reading further, in his 2002 essay 'Good Will and the Hermeneutics of Friendship', which employs the fruitful conception of *teleiopoesis* in order to rethink Derrida's relationship to hermeneutics, and particularly Gadamer.[47] *Teleiopoesis* is here a promise or a prayer of friendship; a way of bringing out 'the irreducibly "intersubjective" character of language' shared by both Derrida and Gadamer. In Derrida's attention to the 'O my friends', the power of this address becomes palpable, making manifest that language is 'always a matter of saying something *to* someone'.[48] Caputo ties this to the notion of the passive decision put forward by Derrida in *Politics of Friendship*. For Derrida, this address *to* the other is not an autonomous one, but rather it pushes 'the notion of the relation with the other beyond the dynamics of good will': this relation, therefore, is no longer 'tainted by the metaphysics of the subjectivity of the subject', but requires, rather, an infinite and ultimately insatiable responsibility. In Caputo's interpretation, therefore, *Politics of Friendship* becomes a means through which to rethink the relationship between Derrida's work and hermeneutics, as well as a ground 'for a justice and a friendship *to come*'.[49]

One could take 2002 as marking a further intensification in the reception of *Politics of Friendship*, which, coupled with the death of Derrida in 2004, would result in numerous dedicated studies in subsequent years. In 2002, an important conference was held at SUNY-Stony Brook in New York. Among its many resonances one finds David Wills's article 'Full Dorsal: Derrida's Politics of Friendship' (2005), subsequently reworked in his book *Dorsality* (2008).[50] Wills traces the 'choreographic' figures of the text, identifying what he labels as its 'torsions' and 'reversals', to demonstrate how *Politics of Friendship* disrupts ideas of symmetry and reciprocity.[51] These concepts are a fundamental part of the matrix of 'classical friendship' but are also presupposed in the Schmittian distinction between friend and enemy. On a methodological as well as thematic level, therefore, *Politics of Friendship* challenges these ideas. Through this 'choreography' Wills develops an idea of *dorsality*, a turning of the back from the symmetrical face-to-face relation, which he considers a more productive ground than the 'posthuman' for rethinking contemporary politics and our relationship to technology and prosthetics.[52]

Another important contribution came from Michael Naas with *Taking on the Tradition* (2003). Emphasising the ambivalence in the constant refrain of *Politics of Friendship*, 'Oh my friends, there are no friends', Naas finds in this 'citation [. . .] of a citation', a crucial ambivalence between the vocative address and a statement about friendship, which reflects 'an essential relationship between friendship and address and [. . .] friendship and mourning'.[53] Naas emphasises how the link between mourning and friendship is developed through the subversions of the traditional values of friendship, such as 'proximity, presence, self-identification'.[54] Yet, like the citation of a citation, Derrida does not simply put forward a position on friendship as 'the withdrawal of [. . .] relations', but it is also a performative address to a friend who is 'perpetually turned to and in withdrawal'.[55] Naas thus gives due emphasis to the performative style of *Politics of Friendship*, arguing that Derrida's iterative approach seeks to acknowledge 'something within this [canonical] tradition that is always in withdrawal [. . .] that cannot be spoken *of* but only *to*'.[56] This speaking *to*, rather than *of*, may be Derrida's unique contribution to a thinking of the friend. In this he resists the temptation to write one final grand text on friendship and instead offers a new approach to the tradition, one which seeks to bring out that which withdraws not through appropriation, but by 'turning like it, repeating or inscribing it as the only way of marking its singularity'.[57] For Naas, therefore, it is not only in Derrida's description of a non-traditional friendship, but also in his enactment of it that *Politics of Friendship* assumes its significance.

William W. Young III, in *The Politics of Praise* (2007), drew on the same distinction between the vocative and the propositional to examine the relation of friendship to the divine in Aquinas and Derrida.[58] For Young, the name of God as well as that of friendship designate singular relations, the latter being premised upon the former.[59] Accordingly, and insofar as the name of God can only be approached in praise, a politics of friendship must give way to a politics of praise.[60] This is a politics of a justice that passes through the singular appellation of the divine; unsurprisingly, Aquinas emerges in Young's analysis as a better champion of such politics than Derrida. In accounting for the impossibility of naming friendship in Derrida, a key component in Young's overall argument, the emphasis is placed on the impossibility of the name, rather than on friendship, making, by default, Young's engagement with *Politics of Friendship* rather nominal.

Young may wish to deduce the possibility and even necessity of a certain kind of politics from the impossibility of the divine name, or of that of the friend, but for David Webb in his 'On Friendship: Derrida, Foucault, and the Practice of Becoming' (2003), the formality of the language of friendship appears phenomenally vague and even inaccurate not only with regard to the experience of friendship, but also in its aporetic recursiveness, politically unproductive.[61] Admitting to a rather 'schematic' treatment of the Derridean text, Webb foregrounds Foucault, in order to articulate an actual ethico-political project, in which 'friends are those with whom we work on the historical conditions of our existence, and those with whom we share the practice of becoming who we are'.[62]

Two years later, Alex J. P. Thomson's monograph, *Deconstruction and Democracy* (2005), engaged with the critique of the pragmatic relevance of the Derridean articulation of friendship, coming from voices such as those of Critchley and Webb, by thematising Spivak's commendation of the patience that *Politics of Friendship* calls for.[63] Thomson's work, itself one of the most sustained engagements with the *Politics of Friendship*, performs this patience, aiming to make central a 'largely neglected text'.[64] *Deconstruction and Democracy* begins by showing that the concepts of decision and responsibility, on which democracy is premised, are also at the heart of deconstruction, the two mutually presupposing each other. This 'hyperbolic' equation of deconstruction and democracy has significant implications, particularly in the face of Derrida's reserve towards ready political programmes. As soon as the political relevance of deconstruction was accepted, critics such as Jürgen Habermas, Thomas McCarthy and Nancy Fraser disparaged it as a 'politics of the ineffable', which dissolved what it claimed to deconstruct, namely politics.[65] Following Geoffrey Bennington and Morag Patrick, Thomson responds by diagnosing in this critique a circularity that presupposes a distinction of theory and practice, as well as a fixed understanding of the political that Derrida does not warrant.[66] Thomson follows the Derridean text in order to articulate a different understanding of the political, one which accommodates uncertainty vis-à-vis the very character of democracy and politics at large and which demands the right to patience in the face of urgency. The *perhaps* means here both that one might not have a definitive answer to the question: 'what is to be done?', but also that there might, in fact, be no answer, nothing to be done.[67] Ultimately, pure patience, just like pure hospitality, justice or forgiveness, is impossible. As soon as one is aware of exercising patience, of waiting for something, this waiting slides into longing or dreading, hope or fear, impatience. Deconstruction is thus the reminder and the demand of a necessary impossibility.

In 2007 the journal *Angelaki* published a dossier on the *Politics of Friendship* edited by Forbes Morlock, whose introduction sets the stage by raising the question of the proximity of a reading, that is, its fraternity and friendship with a text. The time of patient reading seems to have arrived. The dossier brings together a diverse set of responses to the text: a polemical photo-essay from David Bates; a personal letter from Hester Reeve to Petra Von Morstein mentioning the special issue itself; and a few more traditional *essais*, reflecting on the text, its sources and precursors.[68] Graham Allen amplifies the resonances between Derrida's *Politics of Friendship* and the combined works of the family of authors: Mary Wollstonecraft, eighteenth-century advocate for women's rights; William Godwin, the anarchist political philosopher; and Mary Shelley, author of *Frankenstein*.[69] Curiously, Allen does not explicate the *fraternity* within this *familial* response. Shaoling Ma turns to Echo and lets Derrida resonate with Ovid's *Metamorphoses*.[70] Gregg Lambert considers the problem of the 'enemy', drawing parallels between Schmitt and Marx and demonstrating the spectral abstractness that haunts their demands for a concrete enemy. Lambert touches on questions of modality, but they remain, like *Politics of Friendship* itself, marginal to his core argument on the enemy. Instead, Lambert concludes with a turn to Deleuze and Guattari on reading the friend–enemy through the molecular–molar distinction.[71]

Among the dossier's contributions, the closest engagement with Derrida's text is that of John W. P. Phillips, whose essay opens with a lengthy exposition of Aristotelian ethics and the self-presupposing and thus impossible character of virtue.[72] The impossible impasse gives way to action only in being performed, in allowing the passive decision to come forth. The performativity of the passive decision is fragile and often imperceptible: Phillips recognises in the fluidity of the two readings of the omega in the leitmotif 'O, friends' – namely the vocative apostrophe and the dative reference – a return of the alpha, as it enters *différance*.[73] Phillips concludes that a deconstructive algorithm, a mechanised process of reading the text of friendship, will never be able to account for all the silent – or nearly silent – performances between the alpha and the omega of the language of friendship.

Paul Patton describes Derrida's political thought as employing 'two distinct intellectual strategies'.[74] One involves transforming existing concepts through an appeal to an unconditional form of that concept, such as hospitality; the other is a genealogical approach which considers 'the origins of a given concept, its history, interpretations'.[75] *Politics of Friendship* belongs to the second camp, insofar as it studies the aporias of friendship and politics, bringing out the tensions that exist within our inherited conception of politics and democracy. Patton proposes that such an approach can make a significant contribution to political theory by 'open[ing] up new perspectives within contemporary liberal thought'.[76] Yet Patton also takes Derrida to task for his presentation of politics with this genealogical approach, arguing that Derrida relies on 'a very limited textual base and an anachronistic concept of democracy by contemporary standards'.[77] For Patton, this is a necessary step – and one which Derrida does not pursue in *Politics of Friendship* or elsewhere

– to truly critique democracy and one with the potential to create 'novel and important paths for contemporary political philosophy'.[78]

After 2007, direct dialogue with *Politics of Friendship* became incidental – in part because other themes in Derrida's thought, such as animality, would come to the foreground, in part because a certain cycle of reception would have run its course, in part again, because the influence of *Politics of Friendship* would shift into new fields, such as international relations, often in an oblique manner. Undoubtedly, there were exceptions. In 2011, Irving Goh read Derrida as advancing a vital critique of friendship in the face of the 'hyper-gregariousness' of social media.[79] For Goh, such a critique leads inescapably to a rejection of friendship, or rather to the realisation that 'one is always a reject *in* and *of* friendship'.[80] Though such a move is productive for his own conception of the 'reject', in wondering why Derrida should 'stay with the name "friendship"' Goh seems to forget that deconstruction itself is a 'work of love' and to lose sight of the inescapability and the necessity of its *pharmakon*.[81] A diametrically different response came in 2017 from Christopher Elson and Garry Sherbert, whose *In the Name of Friendship: Deguy, Derrida and 'Salut'* celebrates Derrida and Deguy's friendship and dialogue, extending it into an elaborate theorisation of poetic practice.[82] Albeit at the cost of sidelining the political, the work offers a resonant account of the creative and expressive potential of a practice of friendship that passes through Derrida's thought.

In closing this overview, it is worth turning to the reception of *Politics of Friendship* among readers of Schmitt, which constitutes a separate and significant sub-field in the landscape that Derrida's work has formed. In general, commentary from Schmitt scholars has been critical of Derrida's reading. For instance, in a recent essay on the question of rationality, Hugo Herrera defends Schmitt's assertions of a distinctive non-technical 'juridical rationality' against Derrida's objections.[83] Moreover, numerous works that touch upon the *Politics of Friendship* do so only tangentially,[84] while a further handful attempt a moderate engagement with it.[85] We will limit ourselves to the most substantial engagements, namely those of Heinrich Meier, Michael Marder, Gavin Rae and Jacques de Ville.

As mentioned earlier, Heinrich Meier was one of the first among Schmitt scholars to approach *Politics of Friendship*. Although in 1994 he praised the latter as a 'remarkable book', his more detailed commentary, published in the epilogue '*Eine theologische oder eine philosophische Politik der Freundschaft?*', in 1998, is rather circumspect.[86] In the epilogue, Meier reads Derrida through the Schmitt–Strauss antithesis between a theology and a philosophy of the political and asks specifically of the source or origin of the responsibility towards democracy. He notes that the 'question of revelation follows Derrida's considerations on the politics of friendship like a shadow'.[87] What is the epistemological source of our duty to the 'democracy to come'? Only in the closing passages does Meier turn directly and somewhat briefly to Derrida's reading of Schmitt to identify 'three errors': Derrida fails to register the 'development of the conception of the intensity of the political' in Schmitt's work; Derrida misreads the concept of 'total' enmity; finally, Derrida disregards the significance of Lenin for Schmitt.[88] Throughout, Meier emphasises the Levinasian basis of Derrida's thought, implicitly suggesting it falls closer to the side of revelation than reason, a common critique voiced from various quarters, as the above demonstrates.

Another critique of Derrida's engagement with Schmitt came in Michael Marder's *Groundless Existence* (2010), which reads Schmitt's work as 'a series of post-metaphysical interventions'.[89] Marder's idiosyncratic reading of Schmitt emphasises a theoretical heritage shared by Schmitt and Derrida. In addition to the usual parallels with Heidegger, Marder draws attention to the Husserlian dimensions of Schmitt's concept of the political, describing it as a 'clearing away', a 'political-phenomenological reduction'.[90] Marder understands Schmitt's method as a variation of the Husserlian reduction, which forms the basis of both Heidegger's *Destruktion* and Derrida's deconstruction.[91] On *Politics of Friendship*, Marder praises its 'deconstructive sensibility' but notes that Derrida 'misses the non-regional and, in some measure, extra-conceptual determination of the political in Schmitt'. Further, he suggests that Derrida, as a polemical strategy, burdens *The Concept of the Political* with the 'heaviest metaphysical' language in order to cast Schmitt as the 'last great metaphysician of politics' and thereby justify the application of a critique of presence.[92] However, for Marder, Schmitt's use of 'presence' and 'representation' demonstrate his proximity to Derrida. The 'political form' Schmitt aspires to is that of a trace, a 'present absence'.[93] If Marder sides with Derrida against Schmitt, it is only in his reflections on *Rogues*. Since Schmitt, like Spinoza, takes the *conatus* for granted, he fails to account for the self-destructive possibilities of the political entity, its autoimmune response. In agreement with Derrida, Marder contends 'that the concept of the political is itself suicidal'.[94]

An ambitious attempt to grapple with Derrida's reading of Schmitt and its implications is Jacques de Ville's monograph *Constitutional Theory: Schmitt after Derrida* (2017).[95] De Ville reconstructs Derrida's commentary on Schmitt, offering a 'quasi-psychoanalytical' reading of the latter's notion of 'the political', and thus as an exemplar of self-destructive auto-immunity. However, at times, De Ville's interpretation of Schmitt and syntheses of

Derrida's ideas seem questionable. De Ville's difficulties may stem from his *mis*understanding of Schmitt's concept of the political as a 'typical metaphysical' search for an 'essence'[96] – that is, if Marder's post-metaphysical reading is accepted.

Finally, the triangulation of Levinas, Schmitt and Derrida, indicated by Meier, was taken up more recently in Gavin Rae's monograph *The Problem of Political Foundations in Carl Schmitt and Emmanuel Levinas* (2016).[97] Rae, a contributor to this volume, identifies two challenges to Schmitt in Derrida's commentary: one epistemological, the other ontological.[98] The first concerns the nature of the knowledge of the enemy and the friend. Is there an 'epistemic impossibility', as Derrida argues, in Schmitt's criteria of the political insofar as it requires the identification of the enemy and their intentions? Rae defends Schmitt against Derrida's challenge, developing the specificity of the designation of the enemy, demonstrating there is no demand for 'truth' in the determination of the enemy. Derrida's second challenge is related and applies his critique of the ontology of binary opposition to Schmitt's friend–enemy criteria. The criteria appear to demand the impossible purity of all such abstract binaries.[99] Against both challenges Rae insists that Derrida ignores the diachronic and practical nature of Schmitt's criteria. It is not a matter of truth, nor a pure abstraction, that Schmitt demands. Instead, the friend–enemy 'is determined by actual concrete conditions' and actions, and is based on an open and mutable diachronic social relation between the self and others.[100] Interestingly, as noted above, David Webb's contribution to the literature raised the same objection from within a Foucauldian framework. While Rae returns to this theme in the current volume, it is only as a starting point for an alternative line of thought.

The above is intended as an indication, by no means exhaustive, of some of the lines of reception of the *Politics of Friendship* – expressions of critique, allegiance, or both. The present volume wishes to reanimate and carry forward what constitutes undoubtedly a dialogue, albeit one often hidden, oblique or interrupted. Similarly, it intends to sustain and amplify the dialogue of the *Politics of Friendship* with the rest of the Derridean corpus, without making any other work the key, the gate or the gatekeeper of its text.

The Present Volume

In order to accomplish this, the collection at hand offers a series of new readings, reflections, commentaries and critiques of Derrida's *Politics of Friendship*. Reflecting the disparate themes and approaches taken by each author, contributions have been arranged according to three modes of speech or expression. 'Part I: Responses' is unified by a concern with the history of philosophy. Including investigations of the tacit philosophical lineages present in the text, as well as Derrida's explicit engagements, Part I gathers various *responses* to the canon. 'Part II: Echoes' collects contributions on subjectivity, often in dialogue with psychoanalysis, or in a soliloquy in which the subject echoes itself, in the guise of narcissism, mourning and spectrality. Finally, 'Part III: Polemics', assembles chapters on politics and 'the political', bringing together Derrida's polemics with Schmitt, alternative political concepts such as autoimmunity and the hope of a democracy to come.

Opening Part I, a series of responses to the history of philosophy, Georgios Tsagdis follows Derrida's reading of the Aristotelian *tis*, a word upon which converge the determinate 'who' that a friend answers to, and 'what' this friend is, or 'what' it is to be this friend, namely all those conditions and practices that sustain friendship in the figure of the friend. Signifying both 'who' and 'what', *tis* opens a differential that destabilises friendship. Identifying the tremor of this destabilisation with nothing less than the task of deconstruction, Derrida indicts Aristotle for failing to follow the deconstructive gesture he himself set into motion – yet Derrida does not undertake the labour either. Tsagdis reanimates this gesture in order to establish the *who–what* differential at the heart of friendship on a par with the logic of the supplement.

In a 'literary' reading of *Politics of Friendship*, Jennifer Rushworth contrasts the autobiographical character of Montaigne's reflections on friendship with Derrida's philosophical register. Whereas Montaigne's essay 'Of Friendship' is inseparable from his actual friendship with Étienne de La Boétie, Derrida eschews any autobiographical exemplars. Derrida's grounds for this divergence are explored through the lens of temporality: the spectres of the past, the promise of the future and, if only briefly, the simultaneity of the present.

Cillian Ó Fathaigh's essay highlights the prominence of the figure of the couple or pair of friends in Derrida's reading of canonical thinkers, such as Montaigne and Kant. He argues that Derrida uses the figure to demonstrate a double and contradictory desire in traditional conceptions of friendship: on the one hand, the desire to represent the couple as an apolitical or pre-political moment of friendship, and on the other, the desire for it to serve as a ground for and guide to politics. Ó Fathaigh locates in the couple a critical engagement by Derrida with the work of Emmanuel Levinas, suggesting that Levinas also falls foul of this appeal to the pre-political pair of friends. This demonstrates that Derrida views every relation to the other, and every potential moment of friendship and community, as fundamentally and inescapably political.

Exploring the philosophical and phenomenological genealogy of the text itself, Giovanni Menegalle revisits *Politics of Friendship* with an attention to the Husserlian registers at play, detecting in the text a partial methodological fidelity to Husserl, apparent particularly in the analysis of Schmitt and the critique of the phenomenological presence. This presents an opportunity to bring out the continuity between *Politics of Friendship* and Derrida's earlier work on Husserl. In the process, Menegalle teases out Derrida's difference from but also proximity to Husserl and the importance of Derrida's reinterpretation of Husserlian temporality for a 'democracy to come'.

Attentive to a nearby lineage, Susanna Lindberg is the first among the volume's essays to engage with 'Heidegger's Ear: Philopolemology (*Geschlecht* IV)'. In an iconoclastic reading of Hegel and Heidegger, Lindberg identifies an inverted but constitutive role of discord and dispute in philosophy, an existential 'unfriendliness between philosophers', with far-reaching repercussions.

Also tracing Derrida's engagement with Heidegger in '*Geschlecht* IV', Joseph Cohen and Raphael Zagury-Orly focus on the motifs of historicity and recollection of the meaning of Being. They show how Derrida's reading of Heidegger, particularly around the ontology of the gift and the gathering of Being, exposes the omission of singularity within Heidegger's thought. As they demonstrate, the implications extend to questions of truth, history, justice and politics.

Furthering this philosophical lineage, Pheng Cheah's essay opposes *Politics of Friendship* to Hannah Arendt's anthropological understanding of *Mitsein*. Against Arendt's articulation of the political in terms of *bios/zōē*, Cheah argues that Derrida regrounds *Mitsein* in the radical alterity of finite being, itself a figure of autoimmunity, and draws out the implications for political responsibility.

Part II turns to the subjective, spectral and psychoanalytic echoes in the text. Rozemund Uljée probes the temporal disjointedness of friendship. Intertwining past and future, the duration and survival of friendship presupposes loss and mourning. Uljée shows how the spectrality of friendship, embodied in acts of mourning, offers a novel, anachronous way of thinking history. She argues that, in haunting, Derrida's conception of the living present avoids the transcendental tendencies found in Heidegger and Husserl, insofar as it is both condition of possibility and condition of impossibility.

Making an unexpected contrast, Kit Barton draws out the parallels between Derrida and the 'analytic' conception of personal identity developed by Derek Parfit. Barton brings out Derrida's understanding of identity through the cryptic phrase 'I think, therefore I am the other' (*PF*, 224).

Juxtaposing this with Parfit's 'Fission' thought experiment, he argues that an overlap between Derrida and Parfit emerges from their respective critiques of the Cartesian subject.

With explicitly psychoanalytic points of reference, Cathrine Bjørnholt Michaelsen and Isabelle Alfandary take up the question of the other. Bjørnholt Michaelsen explores the two distinct structures of friendship central to the text: the specular and spectral. On the impossibility of overcoming the narcissism inherent in friendship, she productively juxtaposes Lacan and Derrida, exposing the kind of love that is at stake. Alfandary's contribution involves a close analysis of the relation to the other in Derrida's reading of 'Heidegger's Ear' and particularly 'the voice of the friend'. Framing this within some of Derrida's earliest critiques of metaphysics, Alfandary brings out how Derrida's reading emphasises the alterity of this voice and friend, but she also interrogates what type of listening this voice implies. Drawing on the 'third ear' of Theodor Reik, as well as Philippe Lacoue-Labarthe and Jacques Lacan, Alfandary draws out a fruitful intersection for understanding both the alterity of this voice as well as a split/doubled form of listening that it requires.

Returning to the topic of narcissism, Timothy Secret investigates the quasi-transcendental structure that places narcissism at the heart of friendship. In various guises, narcissism is a persistent motif throughout *Politics of Friendship*, but one overlooked in the existing literature. Among the various narcissisms, Secret unearths an 'archi-narcissism' structuring friendship itself. Cicero's dream of survival offers a bridge between narcissism and mourning. Turning to Derrida's eulogies, Secret suggests that dialogue with the dead offers a realisation of this dream with significant political consequences.

Part II closes with two chapters, from David Ventura and Peggy Kamuf, that take as their starting point questions of gender politics raised throughout *Politics of Friendship*. Although Derrida constantly draws attention to and critically exposes the philosophical and historical exclusion of women from the idea of friendship, he does not explicitly break with this tradition, referring nearly exclusively to works of male authors. The contributions of Peggy Kamuf and David Ventura offer different attempts to understand Derrida's ostensible continuity with this masculine bias. David Ventura offers a nuanced, yet critical, commentary on the 'exclusion of the feminine' in *Politics of Friendship*. He draws on the work of Terry Castle and Erin Wunker to suggest that Derrida's implicit evocation of the feminine as a spectre remains inadequate and unsatisfying. In contrast, Peggy Kamuf uncovers the tacit potential of Derrida's recurrent references to Ovid's mythical nymph,

Echo. Kamuf juxtaposes Derrida with Schmitt's superficial remarks on rhyme and draws on subsequent texts in order to argue that Echo offers a complex figure of repetition, not merely a copy, but an inventive response, a lesson and injunction with political parallels in democracy to come.

Political themes of democracy, the enemy and autoimmunity bring together the contributions in Part III. Rosine Kelz, Naomi Waltham-Smith and Allan Parsons survey and extend, in different directions, the deconstruction of democracy that *Politics of Friendship* undertakes. Through an engagement with the temporality of Derrida's conception of 'democracy to come', Rosine Kelz's essay brings Derrida's work to bear on contemporary issues of citizenship, particularly as they pertain to European struggles for migrant rights and the promise of democracy beyond the nation and the community. In contrast, Naomi Waltham-Smith's interest lies in the 'knot between rhythm and democracy' in Derrida's works. Drawing out the syncopation that characterises Derrida's work, Waltham-Smith links the rhythms of democracy to the heartbeat, a syncopated pulsation of blood that eschews the nationalistic and xenoracist rhythms of a politics of tradition and aristocracy. Amplifying often overlooked aspects of the text, Allan Parsons links democracy and justice with questions of design pedagogy, practice and production. Transposing the thrownness of Heidegger's *Dasein* to the space of design and technology, he suggests that extending Derrida opens up the possibility of an active interventionary coexistence beyond thrownness.

Placing *Politics of Friendship* in the broader frame of Derrida's 'political' writings, Chris Lloyd emphasises a juridico-political, rather than medical-biological, interpretation of autoimmunity, in order to stress the link between the latter and self-deconstruction. Turning to the debates in Derridean scholarship on the advent and scope of the autoimmunity, Lloyd identifies the generality and centrality of the concept to Derrida's late work in their first appearance in the lectures of 1988–9.

In contrast to these anthropocentric understanding of politics, Nicole Anderson and Thomas Clément Mercier reach out beyond human politics. Nicole Anderson begins from Derrida's deconstruction of friendship itself. Developing the play of symmetry and dissymmetry as they structure relations of friendship between humans but also between humans and non-humans, Anderson uses the latter to explore our absolute responsibility for the other and subsequently reflects on the place of the animal in 'democracy to come'. In tandem, Thomas Clément Mercier reads the 'question of animality' through the problematic of the trace. Both questions of human kinship and animal companionship lie in a space of representations structured by concepts of culture/nature, that make specific political-juridical demands. Staging the commonalities of Donna Haraway and Derrida on animal companionship, Mercier also shows that Haraway overlooks the possibility of failure and fallibility, which, according to Derrida, haunts kinship and companionship.

The final three essays touch, in varying degrees, on Derrida's engagement with Carl Schmitt, by way of themes of the decision, the foundations of the political, and the modality of the enemy. Mauro Senatore offers a close reading of *Politics of Friendship* focused on decision and the deciding subject. At stake is precisely how subjectivation and decision are articulated according to the unconditionality of the event. As Senatore elaborates, Derrida introduces the 'passive decision', a decision given over to the other, as an alternative that draws together and short-circuits the aporetic determinations he identifies in its classical conception. Linking these questions with those of responsibility and justice, Senatore expands his scope to address the contemporaneous account in 'Force of Law' and reflect on the implications for later works. Revisiting the problem of political foundations through the concept of *différance*, Gavin Rae reconstructs and develops Derrida's engagement with Schmitt. Taking as a starting point Schmitt's appeal to ancient etymology (*hostis/amicus* and *polemios/echthros*), Rae elaborates Derrida's discussion and critique of Schmitt's etymologies. Expanding on these questions of language Rae argues for the foundational role of symbolic fictions in Derrida's conception of the political. With a narrower scope, Luke Collison reads closely Derrida's remarks on real possibility, the unusual modality on which Schmitt's model of the enemy and subsequent conception of the political relies. Collison critiques Derrida's attempted spectral inversion of Schmitt, insofar as it rests on a forced equivocation of the Schmittian exception with the improbable. Collison concludes with an alternative 'energetic' interpretation of this peculiar modality, based on Schmitt's interest in Georges Sorel.

Notes

1. Jacques Derrida, *Politics of Friendship*, trans. George Collins (London: Verso, 1997); Jacques Derrida, *Politiques de l'amitié: suivi de L'Oreille de Heidegger* (Paris: Galilée, 1994). Hereafter, page references to the English translation are given in parenthesis in the text (*PF*).
2. Jacques Derrida, 'The Politics of Friendship', trans. Gabriel Motzkin, *Journal of Philosophy*, 85.11 (1988), 632–44. This was later expanded and published in *American Imago*: Jacques Derrida, 'Politics of Friendship', trans. Gabriel Motzkin, Michael Syrotinski, with Thomas Keenan, *American Imago*, 50.3 (1993), 353–91.

3. The way in which Derrida conceives of these seminars is somewhat confusing, not least because this foreword places the seminars following the 1988–9 session under the heading of 'Questions of Responsibility', when archives suggest that this latter series did not begin until 1991. Indeed, Derrida's presentation of the 'Nationality and Philosophical Nationalism' series in this foreword is also presented a year earlier than the archives. Here is not the place to speculate on the consequences or motives behind this reframing, but for more information see the catalogues at University of California Irvine and *IMEC*: UC Irvine Archives, http://hydra.humanities.uci.edu/derrida/uci.html (accessed 1 March 2021), and the *IMEC* catalogue at Resource 'Jacques Derrida (1930–2004)', https://portail-collections.imec-archives.com/ark:/29414/a011433424761LQUFTQ (accessed 1 March 2021).
4. 'As you will have noticed, we have deliberately refrained from recourse to "illustrations" to "actualize" our analyses or in an attempt to demonstrate their necessity *today*, by delving into the most spectacular "news" on political scenes: local, national, European or worldwide. We have done so through a concern with sobriety [. . .])' (*PF*, 272).
5. To offer a brief list of limited examples in the short span of 1988 to 1994: the end of the apartheid regime in South Africa; the beginning of the Algerian civil war; the creation of the World Trade Organization; the signing of the 1985 Schengen Agreement and the hardening of Europe's external borders.
6. See Samuel P. Huntington, *The Clash of Civilizations and the Remaking of World Order* (New York: Simon & Schuster, 1996), but first proposed in 1992; see also Francis Fukuyama, *The End of History and The Last Man* (New York: Free Press, 1992).
7. For a detailed account of Schmitt's post-war influence, see: Jan-Werner Müller, *A Dangerous Mind: Carl Schmitt in Post-War European Thought* (New Haven, CT: Yale University Press, 2003). On the earlier French reception of Schmitt, see Stefanos Geroulanos, 'Heterogeneities, Slave-Princes, and Marshall Plans: Schmitt's Reception in Hegel's France', *Modern Intellectual History*, 8.3 (2011), 531–60.
8. Reinhard Mehring, *Carl Schmitt: A Biography* (Cambridge: Polity, 2014), p. 125.
9. Although banned from academic posts in Germany after the war, Schmitt was never completely forgotten. Even before the revival of interest signalled by these translations, his work influenced a variety of figures on both the right and left, such as Hans Morgenthau, Reinhardt Kosselleck, Alexandre Kojève and Mario Tronti.

10. Carl Schmitt, *La notion de politique: Théorie du partisan*, trans. Marie-Louise Steinhauser and Julien Freund (Paris: Calmann-Lévy, 1972).
11. The English translation provides 'lovence'. David Wills proposes 'lovingness' as another alternative, see David Wills, *Dorsality: Thinking Back through Technology and Politics* (Minneapolis: University of Minnesota Press, 2008), p. 155.
12. Derrida acknowledges that this is a term that the poet Abdelkebir Khatibi coined (apparently independently) before him in *Dédicace à l'année qui vient* [*Dedication to the Upcoming Year*] (Montpellier: Fata Morgana, 1986).
13. For an excellent article on this and Spivak's usage of the term, see Corinne Scheiner, 'Teleiopoiesis, Telepoesis, and the Practice of Comparative Literature', *Comparative Literature*, 57.3 (2005), 239–45.
14. Marian Hobson, *Jacques Derrida: Opening Lines* (London and New York: Routledge, 1998), p. 3.
15. Published in English as Jacques Derrida, 'Heidegger's Ear: Philopolemology (*Geschlecht* IV)', in *Commemorations: Reading Heidegger*, ed. John Sallis, trans. John P. Leavy Jr (Bloomington and Indianapolis: Indiana University Press, 1993), pp. 163–218.
16. Jacques Derrida, '*Geschlecht* I: Sexual Difference, Ontological Difference', in Derrida, *Psyche 2: Inventions of the Other*, ed. Peggy Kamuf and Elizabeth G. Rottenberg, trans. Ruben Berezdivin and Elizabeth G. Rottenberg (Stanford: Stanford University Press, 2008), pp. 7–12 (p. 7).
17. As noted in different instances above, in the autumn of 1993, aside of '*Geschlecht* IV', the eponymous article 'Politics of Friendship' appeared in the journal *American Imago*.
18. Although Laclau and Mouffe discuss Derrida's work briefly in *Hegemony and Socialist Strategy* (1985) and Mouffe refers to Schmitt's friend–enemy distinction in an essay 1992, the idea of an affinity between Schmitt and Derrida is not raised until 1993. Chantal Mouffe, *The Return of the Political* (London: Verso, 1993), p. 114; Chantal Mouffe, 'Democratic Citizenship and the Political Community', in *Dimensions of Radical Democracy: Pluralism, Citizenship, Community*, ed. Chantal Mouffe (London: Verso, 1992), pp. 225–39 (p. 234).
19. Jacques Derrida, 'Force of Law: The "Mystical Foundation of Authority"', *Cardozo Law Review*, 11.5–6 (1990), 920–1045. The essay's discussion of Benjamin comes from the 1988–9 lectures.
20. William E. Scheuerman, *Carl Schmitt: The End of Law* (Lanham, MD: Rowman & Littlefield, 1999), p. 82; John P. McCormick,

'Poststructuralism Meets Schmitt: Schmittian Positions on Law and Politics?: CLS and Derrida', *Cardozo Law Review*, 21 (2000), 1693–722 (p. 1705); David Bates, 'Crisis between the Wars: Derrida and the Origins of Undecidability', *Representations*, 90.1 (2005), 1–27 (p. 18); Sergei Prozorov, 'The Ethos of Insecure Life: Reading Carl Schmitt's Existential Decisionism as a Foucaultian Ethics', in *The International Political Thought of Carl Schmitt: Terror, Liberal War and the Crisis of Global Order*, ed. Louiza Odysseos and Fabio Petito (Abingdon: Routledge, 2007), pp. 222–41 (p. 232); Matthias Lievens, 'Carl Schmitt's Concept of History', *The Oxford Handbook of Carl Schmitt*, ed. Jens Meierhenrich and Oliver Simons (Oxford: Oxford University Press, 2016), pp. 401–26; Christian J. Emden, 'Theorizing the Political in Germany, 1890–1945: Max Weber, Carl Schmitt, Franz Neumann', *European History Quarterly*, 38.4 (2008), 608–25.

21. See Simon Critchley, *The Ethics of Deconstruction* (Oxford: Blackwell, 1992); 'The Other's Decision in Me (What Are the Politics of Friendship?)', *European Journal of Social Theory*, 2.1 (1998), 259–79.
22. Simon Critchley, *Ethics – Politics – Subjectivity: Essays on Derrida, Levinas & Contemporary French Thought* (London: Verso, 1999), p. 270.
23. Critchley, *Ethics – Politics – Subjectivity*, p. 270.
24. Ibid. p. 277.
25. Ibid. p. 277.
26. Ibid. p. 283.
27. Gayatri Chakravorty Spivak, 'A Note on the New International', *Parallax*, 7.3 (2001), 12–16.
28. Spivak, 'A Note', p. 12. Spivak cites Derrida, *Specters of Marx: The State of the Debt, the Work of Mourning and the New International*, trans. Peggy Kamuf (New York: Routledge, 1994), p. 86.
29. Spivak, 'A Note', p. 12.
30. Ibid. p. 13.
31. Ibid. p. 15.
32. Ibid. pp. 13–14.
33. Leela Gandhi, *Affective Communities: Anticolonial Thought, Fin-de-Siècle Radicalism, and the Politics of Friendship* (Durham, NC: Duke University Press, 2006), p. 10.
34. Gandhi, *Affective Communities*, p. 27.
35. Ibid. p. 17.
36. Peter Fenves, 'Politics of Friendship, Once Again', *Eighteenth-Century Studies*, 32. 2 (1998–9), 133–55.
37. Penelope Deutscher, 'Mourning the Other, Cultural Cannibalism,

and the Politics of Friendship (Jacques Derrida and Luce Irigaray)', *differences: A Journal of Feminist Cultural Studies*, 10.3 (1998), 159–82. Unfortunately, Deutscher's article represents one of only a small number of feminist engagements with *Politics of Friendship*. This is at least in part a result of bad timing, with the important *Feminist Interpretations of Jacques Derrida* being published in the same year as the *Politics of Friendship* translation. See *Feminist Interpretations of Jacques Derrida*, ed. Nancy J. Holland (Philadelphia: Pennsylvania University Press, 1997).

38. Deutscher, 'Mourning the Other', p. 169.
39. Ibid. p. 161.
40. Ibid. p. 182.
41. Miriam Leonard, 'The *Politiques de l'amitié*: Derrida's Greeks and a National Politics of Classical Scholarship', *Proceedings of the Cambridge Philological Society*, 46 (2001), 45–78 (p. 46). Our emphasis; the first plural returns at the end of the essay, p. 73.
42. Leonard, 'The *Politiques de l'amitié*:', p. 63.
43. Ibid. pp. 52, 53, 55.
44. John D. Caputo, 'Who is Derrida's Zarathustra? Of Fraternity, Friendship, and a Democracy to Come', *Research in Phenomenology*, 29 (1999), 184–98 (p. 187).
45. Caputo, 'Who is Derrida's Zarathustra? p. 191.
46. Ibid. p. 191.
47. John D. Caputo, 'Good Will and the Hermeneutics of Friendship: Gadamer and Derrida', *Philosophy & Social Criticism*, 28.5 (2002), 512–22.
48. Caputo, 'Good Will', pp. 512–13.
49. Ibid. pp. 521–22.
50. David Wills, 'Full Dorsal: Derrida's Politics of Friendship', *Postmodern Culture*, 15.3 (2005); Wills, *Dorsality*.
51. Wills, *Dorsality*, p. 140.
52. Ibid. p. 158.
53. Michael Naas, *Taking on the Tradition: Jacques Derrida and the Legacies of Deconstruction* (Stanford: Stanford University Press, 2003), pp. 136, 137.
54. Naas, *Taking on the Tradition*, p. 141.
55. Ibid. pp. 149, 152.
56. Ibid. p. 153.
57. Ibid.
58. William W. Young III, *The Politics of Praise: Naming God and Friendship in Aquinas and Derrida* (Burlington, VA: Ashgate, 2007).

59. Young, *The Politics of Praise*, p. 6.
60. Ibid. p. 7.
61. David Webb, 'On Friendship: Derrida, Foucault, and the Practice of Becoming', *Research in Phenomenology*, 33.1 (2003), 119–40.
62. Webb, 'On Friendship', p. 120.
63. Alex J. P. Thomson, *Deconstruction and Democracy: Derrida's Politics of Friendship* (London: Continuum, 2007).
64. Thomson, *Deconstruction and Democracy*, p. 8. Thomson attributes the neglect to the book's complexity, length and seminar format.
65. Ibid. pp. 1–2. See Jürgen Habermas, *Philosophy and the Discourse of Modernity*, trans. Frederick Lawrence (Oxford: Blackwell, 1990), pp. 161–210; Thomas McCarthy, 'The Politics of the Ineffable: Derrida's Deconstructionism', in McCarthy, *Ideals and Illusions: On Reconstruction and Deconstruction in Critical Theory* (Cambridge, MA: MIT Press, 1991), pp. 91–117; Nancy Fraser, 'The French Derrideans: Politicizing Deconstruction or Deconstructing Politics', *New German Critique*, 33 (1984), 127–54.
66. Thomson, *Deconstruction and Democracy*, p. 3. See Geoffrey Bennington, *Legislations: The Politics of Deconstruction* (London: Verso, 1994); Patrick Morag, *Derrida, Responsibility and Politics* (Aldershot: Ashgate, 1997); Patrick Morag, 'Excess and Responsibility: Derrida's Ethico–Political Thinking', *Journal of the British Society for Phenomenology*, 28.2 (1997), 160–77.
67. Thomson, *Deconstruction and Democracy*, p. 200.
68. 'Dossier: Politics of Friendship', ed. Forbes Morlock, 'Politics of Friendship', *Angelaki*, 12.3 (2007), 1–3; David Bates, 'The Politics of Friendship', *Angelaki*, 12.3 (2007), 107–13; Hester Reeve, 'Letter of Friendship', *Angelaki*, 12.3 (2007), 171–4.
69. Graham Allen, '"Unfashioned Creatures, but Half Made Up"', *Angelaki*, 12.3 (2007), 127–39.
70. Shaoling Ma, 'Echoing the Politics of Friendship', *Angelaki*, 12.3 (2007), 141–53.
71. Gregg Lambert, '"enemy" (*Der Feind*)', *Angelaki*, 12.3 (2007), 123–4.
72. John W. P. Phillips, 'Loving Love or Ethics as Natural Philosophy in Jacques Derrida's *Politiques de L'amitié*', *Angelaki*, 12.3 (2007), 155–70.
73. Phillips, 'Loving Love or Ethics', pp. 164–5.
74. Paul Patton, 'Derrida, Politics and Democracy to Come', *Philosophy Compass*, 2.6 (2007), 766–80 (p. 768).
75. Patton, 'Derrida, Politics and Democracy to Come', p. 768.
76. Ibid. p. 777.

77. Ibid. p. 776.
78. Ibid. p. 777.
79. Irving Goh, 'Rejecting Friendship: Toward a Radical Reading of Derrida's Politics of Friendship for Today', *Cultural Critique*, 79 (2011), 94–124.
80. Goh, 'Rejecting Friendship', p. 116.
81. Ibid. p. 111.
82. Christopher Elson and Garry Sherbert (eds), *In the Name of Friendship: Deguy, Derrida and 'Salut'* (Leiden: Brill Rodopi, 2017).
83. Hugo E. Herrera, 'Schmitt vs. Derrida: The Distinction between the Juridical and the Technical Rationality', *Telos*, 187 (2019), 8–30 (pp. 13–15).
84. Benjamin A. Schupmann, *Carl Schmitt's State and Constitutional Theory: A Critical Analysis* (Oxford: Oxford University Press, 2017), p. 88; Gareth Williams, 'Decontainment: The Collapse of the Katechon and the End of Hegemony', in *The Anomie of the Earth Philosophy, Politics and Autonomy in Europe and the Americas*, ed. Federico Luisetti, John Pickles and Wilson Kaiser (Durham, NC: Duke University Press, 2015), pp. 159–73 (p. 159); William Rasch, *Sovereignty and Its Discontents: On the Primacy of Conflict and the Structure of the Political* (London: Birkbeck Law Press, 2012); Andreas Kalyvas, *Democracy and the Politics of the Extraordinary: Max Weber, Carl Schmitt, Hannah Arendt* (Cambridge: Cambridge University Press, 2008), pp. 5, 94; Kam Shapiro, *Carl Schmitt and the Intensification of Politics* (Lanham, MD: Rowman & Littlefield, 2008).
85. Anne Norton, 'Pentecost: Democratic Sovereignty in Carl Schmitt', *Constellations*, 18.3 (2011), 389–402 (pp. 395, 398); Samir Haddad, 'Friendship', in *Jacques Derrida*, ed. Claire Colebrook (New York: Routledge, 2015), pp. 84–92 (p. 68).
86. Meier's praise in the 1994 preface to the English translation of *The Lesson of Carl Schmitt* can be contrasted with the more critical 1998 epilogue to the second German edition of *The Hidden Dialogue*. Unfortunately, Meier's remarks are not included in the later English editions of the latter text. See Heinrich Meier, *Carl Schmitt, Leo Strauss und 'Der Begriff des Politischen' Zu einem Dialog unter Abwesen* (Stuttgart: J.B. Metzler, 1998), pp. 171–81; Heinrich Meier, *The Lesson of Carl Schmitt: Four Chapters on the Distinction between Political Theology and Political Philosophy, Expanded Edition* (Chicago: University of Chicago Press, 2011), p. xii.
87. Meier, *Carl Schmitt, Leo Strauss*, p. 177.

88. Ibid. p. 179.
89. Michael Marder, *Groundless Existence: The Political Ontology of Carl Schmitt* (New York: Continuum, 2010), pp. 2, 50–1, 68–9, 99.
90. Marder, *Groundless Existence*, pp. 8, 14, 31, 104.
91. Ibid. p. 130.
92. Ibid. pp. 68–9.
93. Ibid. p. 70; Michael Marder, *Energy Dreams: Of Actuality* (New York: Columbia University Press, 2017), p. 143.
94. Marder, *Groundless Existence*, p. 78.
95. Jacques de Ville, *Constitutional Theory: Schmitt after Derrida* (Abingdon: Birkbeck Law Press, 2017).
96. De Ville, *Constitutional Theory*, p. 4.
97. Gavin Rae, *The Problem of Political Foundations in Carl Schmitt and Emmanuel Levinas* (London: Palgrave Macmillan, 2016).
98. Rae, *The Problem of Political Foundations*, pp. 69–74.
99. Ibid. p. 71.
100. Ibid. p. 72. Cillian Ó Fathaigh acknowledges that this chapter forms part of the activities for the research projects: (1) "Differential Ontology and the Politics of Reason," funded by the Government of the Region of Madrid, as part of line 3 of the multi-year agreement with the Universidad Complutense de Madrid: V PRICIT Excellence Program for University Professors (Fifth Regional Plan for Scientific Investigation and Technological Innovation); and (2) "The Politics of Reason" (PID2020-117386GA-I00), financed by the Ministry of Science and Innovation, Government of Spain.

Part I

Responses

1

Who or What: Differential Friendship

Georgios Tsagdis

> This hesitation in the language between the *what* and the *who*, does not seem to make Aristotle tremble [. . .] (*PF*, 6)[1]

Aristotle's question of friendship coalesces around the figure of the friend. The friend forces the question of a determinate 'who' into the fray, while sustaining the question 'what': what it is to be a friend, that is, what traits, conditions and practices are required to discover and sustain friendship in the friend. Derrida's reading locates the measuring up of the *who* of the friend against the *what* of friendship in the Aristotelian word *tis*. Signifying both 'who' and 'what', *tis* opens a differential that destabilises friendship. Identifying the tremor of this destabilisation with nothing less than the task of deconstruction, Derrida indicts Aristotle for failing to follow the deconstructive gesture he has himself set into motion. Yet Derrida does not undertake the labour either: unlike 'Ousia and Grammē' which completes the deconstructive gesture on time on behalf of Aristotle, the *Politics of Friendship* supresses the thematic, or rather relegates it to the margins, where its force remains undiminished.[2] The present essay thematises the *who–what* differential, aiming to establish it on an equal footing with the logic of the supplement. Recovering the *who–what* differential as a key articulation of *différance* opens new terrains of analysis and affinities of thought.

Prelude: the Silent Tremor

A tremble or tremor. The *what* and the *who*. Friendship and the friend. In sum, the tremor between friendship and the friend. How is it to be understood, what is the diagnosis, the pathology of this tremendous tremor, which seems to go unnoticed or at the very least unspoken for Aristotle? And what does this something, if something it is, effect upon Derrida's corpus? Indeed,

Derrida quivers. In the tenor of *différance* a trembling can be heard, a tremor that runs through the history of metaphysics and announces its closure, first as *Destruktion* and then as *déconstruction*.

In his 1964–5 lectures, *Heidegger: The Question of Being and History*, Derrida reads Heidegger as the thinker that makes tremble. *Being and Time* announces *Destruktion* as the task of shaking up, of stirring the dregs that the history of metaphysics, by design or inadvertently, sediments. Importantly, this is neither the first pronouncement, nor the first denouncement of the sedimentation that coalesces into a metaphysical totality. Heidegger draws on and converses here with Hegel, who recognises sedimentation as an essential – one may dare say 'natural' – function of the Spirit, Spirit's nature.[3] In turn, dialectic is understood as the lever that whisks into motion Spirit's idle, geologic nature. This dialectic operation is summed up in the 'recollecting refutation' (*Erinnerung* as *Widerlegung*, *Widerlegung* as *Erinnerung*) that undoes from within Spirit's self-mineralisation.

Yet, insofar as the dialectic labours with and against the deposit of thought in order to recollect and recall the no-longer and the not-yet thought, the difference between Heideggerian *Destruktion* and Hegelian *Erinnerung* appears to dissolve. Derrida is emphatic; what distinguishes the two is

> a nothing, a slight trembling of meaning that we must not overlook, for the whole seriousness of the enterprise sums up in this its fragility and its value. A slight trembling, for Heidegger says *nothing else* after the Hegelian – that is, Western – ontology that he is going to destroy.[4]

Heidegger says nothing, or at least 'as close as possible to *nothing*', after the Hegelian recollection, after the memory of dialectic refutation.[5] Heidegger offers no new propositions after the history of metaphysics and its memory. He merely lets the ontological silence that surrounds Hegel's last philosophy resonate. The silence of *Destruktion* is, however, not the silence of desolate destruction; it is rather the silence in which a ruin reconstructs a world.

Writing after the silence of the memory of the history of metaphysics, Derrida considers translation critical in preserving the clarity of the carefully layered strata of his reading. To achieve this, every translation of *Destruktion* must minimally respect and maximally amplify the silence that makes tremble. Derrida tenders thus with equal commitment the terms 'deconstruction' and 'solicitation'. The fate of the first rendition is well known: 'deconstruction' will achieve a status of ubiquitous incomprehension. 'Solicitation', on the other hand, with its unreputable ring and broad semantic scope, will fade from Derrida's vocabulary. Yet the echo of this second rendition cannot be silenced. Derrida chooses 'solicitation' to allude to the troubling provocation that is heard in the Latin *sollicitare*: the shaking (*ciere*) of the whole (*sollus*). Accordingly, deconstruction emerges as a practice attentive to the silence that shrouds the closure of metaphysics and makes the totality of its history tremble. To announce the closure of metaphysics and expose oneself to the 'absolute danger' of its future, the metaphysical desire must already have been experienced to the breaking point, its history run.[6] The one who deconstructs must tremble in the silence that makes tremble.

Raising the Differential Question

If there is no deconstruction without a tremor and if Aristotle does not tremble, Aristotle does not deconstruct – at least not when it comes to friendship, at least not on the surface of things. For it must be the case that Aristotle can be taken as the ontotheologist par excellence, the paradigm of paradigms of the metaphysics of presence. And yet, a text such as 'Ousia and Grammē' can be adduced as evidence to the contrary, forcefully demonstrating the spuriousness of Heidegger's reading of Aristotelian time as 'vulgar'. For Derrida, Aristotle – along with the history of the metaphysics of time to follow – possesses in the instantaneousness of the now (*nyn*), the organon of his own critique, the mechanism of his self-deconstruction. Aristotle trembles when he thinks time. And since for him there is no friendship and no friends without time (*aneu chronou ou philoi*), and since, moreover, friendship constitutes the principal theme of both the *Eudemian* and the *Nichomachaen Ethics*, it appears inexplicable that thinking of friendship, Aristotle should remain unmoved;[7] that he should pass and establish the passage between the *who* of the friend and the *what* of friendship without flinching, as if the Eleatic *atremes hētor*, the 'untrembling heart' of the being of friendship, came at last to rest in the breast of a friend.

In order to clarify what is presently at stake, the significance of the rift that separates the *who* and the *what* must be established, both with regard to Aristotelian friendship – which in turn elaborates and belabours Platonic friendship – as well as with regard to Derrida's thought as a whole.

One may begin, then, by Derrida's acclamation of Aristotle as 'the first of the maieutic tradition of [the Platonic] *Lysis* [. . .] but beyond him [it]', to ask rigorously what friendship is (*tí esti*), how it is (*poîón esti*) and whether it is said in a single or several senses (*monakhós légetai è pleonakhôs*)' (6). Derrida continues to clarify the crux of the issue:

> It is true that right in the middle of this series of questions, between the one on the being or the being-such of friendship, there is the question which is itself terribly equivocal: *kai tís o phílos*. This question asks *what* the friend is, but also asks *who* he is. This hesitation in the language between the *what* and the *who*, does not seem to make Aristotle tremble, as if it were fundamentally, one and the same interrogation, as if the one enveloped the other, and as if the question 'who?' had to bend or bow in advance before the ontological question 'what?' or 'what is?'. (6)

It comes then, perhaps as a disappointment, that after having localised the *mysterium tremendum* of friendship under the sign of *tis*, Derrida will not attempt to solicit the untrembling Aristotelian text further. While pressing on selfhood and equality, on the modes and the scarcity of friendship, on so many of the inexhaustible themes that proceed from the Aristotelian text, Derrida will set the differential tension between the *who* and the *what* along a subterranean course for the rest of *Politics of Friendship*, allowing it merely to resurface unexpectedly, inconclusively and catalytically in equal measure.

The equivocal *tis* sets up an unfailing, productive perplexity. Aristotle asks first about the what and the how of friendship (*philia*) and then turns to the friend to ask: *tis*.[8] Surely a person is here intended, just as when Plato, in the *Lysis* – the text whence Aristotle departs – has Socrates ask before entering the gymnasium, '*kai tis o kalos*', that is, *who* is the handsome, among the gathered youth.[9] Socrates expects and receives a proper name as answer: Lysis – and in the proper name there is tremor neither for Plato, nor for Aristotle. However, one could collate an equal number of instances across ancient corpora in which *tis* refers directly to the *what*, such as when, for example, the Platonist Hermias asks: '"*tis*" is inspiration?'[10] Aristotle then asks on the *what* and the *how* of friendship and immediately after, on the *what* and the *who* of the friend.

It is as though, in the *who* of the friend a *what* is also uncovered, not friendship simpliciter, but friendship *in the friend* – the conditions, or again the attributes, traits and qualities, that make the friend the recipient, but also perhaps the agent of friendship. In the *Lysis*, Plato calls this *to philon*: the lovable and loved; but also, at one and the same time, the loving. Neither active, nor passive, *to philon* speaks in the middle voice of friendship. Even though Aristotle underutilises the term, *to philon* is the *what* of friendship in the friend, a *what* that acts and suffers without being a person.

Derrida's insistence and celebration of the middle voice is well attested. Indeed, a version of this essay that will remain unwritten would follow the way in which Derrida traces the active and the passive voice of friendship in Aristotle, as well as of the break of their symmetry and equality. For Aristotle wants that loving and being-loved be equally necessary conditions in the constitution of friends, but also wants to privilege the act of love, actively loving, as truer to the meaning and import of friendship, than merely being-loved.

The relation of reciprocity (active/passive) and symmetry (more/less) must be further probed. Importantly here, it is the element of reciprocity that Derrida wants to preserve as he cautions against a quick translation or transposition of the Aristotelian *who* of the *philos*, into the obliterating *what* of love; all the more therefore, Derrida acknowledges the task of such a translation as 'fascinating' (221).[11] It is in turn twice fascinating that Derrida appears oblivious to the occurrence of this transposition in the Platonic *to philon*, the 'friended' and the 'friending' at once, which passes from the *who* of the friend to the *what* of friendship while preserving reciprocity.

The Impasse of *to philon* and *o philos* as Parergon

One step back; one forward. Aristotle will retain, but sideline, the Platonic term. Accordingly, Aristotle claims unequivocally that *to philon* is the good and the pleasant, but desists from theorising the term.[12] For such a theorisation, it is important to return to the *Lysis*. Plato, after the failure of the first three hypotheses of the dialogue to account sufficiently for friendship, tries in the fourth to narrow the focus of *to philon* on the good alone.[13] In order to examine *to philon*, Plato transposes it within his dear medical metaphor. Medically then, *to philon* is both health itself, health as the desired good, as well as the 'neuter' in the body, namely what is neither healthy, nor unhealthy, but seeks health, driven by the evil of sickness.[14] Accordingly, *to philon* is both what is desired and what desires in the middle voice of a field of expansive striving.

The fourth hypothesis of the *Lysis* is then further amended by stipulating that if the neuter is to be truly *to philon*, or, more specifically, the active component of the field that *to philon* constitutes, it cannot be incited by the threat of evil, but only by a congenial desire for the good.[15] As such, *to philon* constitutes an equilibrium which will always break its neutrality from within to reach out for its congenial (*oikeion*) good. *To philon* is thus a movement of the good unto itself, presupposing a point of neutrality for its inception, a point that is taken up in the self-movement of the good. At this gloriously dialectical-ouroboric moment, the fourth hypothesis erupts into an aporia and the dialogue is interrupted. It is beyond the scope of this essay to examine and assess the aporia that cancels the first sustained exploration of friendship in the Western philosophical canon;[16] what follows is – perhaps – more significant.

Having initiated the discussion in casual irony by asking Lysis to help him understand what friendship is, on the basis of the experience (*empereia*) of his friendship with Menexenus, Socrates has overseen the discussion under his steering wreck up against an inescapable impasse.[17] An *ex machina* dramatic interruption saves social grace and Socrates seizes the moment to place himself as third in the friendship of the two young men. Although they have failed to establish *what* a 'friend' is (*ho ti estin o philos*), Menexenus and Lysis may continue addressing each other as friends and Socrates avows to count himself among them.[18] The irony that opened the dialogue redoubles, as Socrates silently, trembling perhaps, exclaims: 'O, dear *whos*, there is no *what*!'

Plato does not allow Socrates the words that Diogenes Laertius placed into the mouth of Aristotle: 'O friends, there is no friend!'[19] Instead, Plato, the master of the parergon, stages a dialogue to examine *to philon*, the field in which friendship shows forth in the reciprocity of the middle voice, and flanks this examination with friends – friends enter and exit, while friendship's holy of holies, *to philon*, remains empty. For Platonism, and for the history of metaphysics insofar as it remains Platonist, this emptiness will be always deemed accidental, provisional. For Derrida, however, the title of the dialogue will retain the trace of a much more ambiguous gesture. *Lysis* is not only the proper name of an existing person, but also a common name that signifies, in Derrida's parataxis, 'unbinding, detachment, emancipation, untangling, the tie undone or dissolved by analysis, solution – indeed, absolution, even solitude' (78). Not only does Socrates, the Silenus, impose his unbearable solitude in the midst of the untroubled youthful exuberance of the friendship of Lysis and Menexenus, but he undertakes a *lysis* of that friendship, the unravelling and unknotting of its presuppositions, its very *what*. And yet, by the same token, at once in perfect irony and perfect honesty, Plato affirms the imperative: one *must* be a friend, without knowing *what* friendship is (155).

Ad Hominem: Plato and Aristotle

To philon will remain elusive for Plato, while Aristotle will employ the term only quasi-technically and in passing. Both will attempt to seek reciprocity and explore questions of symmetry not in the internal logic of this peculiar construct, but externally, in and through the *who* of the *philos*: the former dramatically in the *Lysis*, the latter in a more sustained expository manner in the *Eudemian* and *Nichomachean Ethics*.

At least from this point onwards, the philosophical preoccupation with *philia* will require the *who* and it will require the proper name. The Heideggerian premise that for the Greeks, at least the early Greeks, there is no anthropological subject and no psychology, is for Derrida questionable. Even if, however, Presocratic *philia* could do without the proper name (and even if the latter presupposes subjectivity, although 'nothing seems less assured'), thinking friendship without the proper name presents at present an insurmountable threshold (251). This may be only one more symptom of thought's captivity within the closure of metaphysics, but it is clear that this need is already entrenched in, if not by, Aristotle. Yet, as the latter moves away from the Platonic *to philon* to the *tis* of the *philos*, as he introduces the personhood, albeit perhaps not the humanity, of the *ad hominem* into friendship, he also weaves and thus preserves into it something that is not of the order of the person: a certain silence in the face of the face that can only make the friend tremble.

For the *what* in the *who* of the friend will subsist interminably in the form of a demand. A friend must surely always be *your* friend; not everyone who is good or worthy of friendship will be a friend.[20] However, while Aristotle foregrounds the friend over against friendship, he demands not only that friends be chosen over things (possession repeatedly declared common among friends), but that *certain* friends be chosen over others (17). So, although one must not choose for a *what* over a *who*, one must choose for one *who* over another *on the basis* of a *what* – some *thing*, however concrete or abstract, determines the good from the bad friend, and both from the non-friend.

This *what*, let it be said without further diversion or digression, is virtue, virtue as and in truth. As is well known, in the *pollachōs legomenon* of friendship, Aristotle discovers three species: according to pleasure, usefulness and virtue. The latter, a friendship of reciprocal affection and choice, is understood as primary friendship – not a universal category under which all phenomena and all types of friendship could be subsumed (*kath' hen eidos*), but rather a point of analogic convergence (*pros hen*).[21]

The structural similarity to the prime mover is unmistakable and its implications are vast. For ultimately, the *what* of virtue is the divinity and godliness of the friend.[22] In primary friendship, a friend loves another on the basis of their virtue. One strives to become divine for the sake of the friend's love, the friend, who in a sense, is always already more divine than oneself. This introduces however a double impossibility: until one becomes truly virtuous, that is, truly divine, primary friendship is precluded; up until then, 'there is no friend' (235). Yet, should one become divine, one would find oneself bereft of all need and all drive to seek and relish the other. The *noēsis noēseōs* of the prime mover lacks nothing, expecting from humans their friendship no more than their sacrifices (17, 222). One is thus led to exclaim: 'O friends, should we become true friends, we will no longer be friends.'

The exigencies of such a *what* are devastating. If the *telos* that the friend strives for is true friendship on the basis of true virtue (which is always virtue as truth), this *telos* is an end in both senses of the term: a terminal point for the friend *as* friend. Recognising this, one recognises that there is no friend, either before or after virtue. Neither now, nor in the future, can such a hope be hoped for: friendship is in a perpetual state of *lysis*. In order to *bind* friendship, the *what* must return to the *who*, friendship must be *ad hominem*. Accordingly, the *who* will be nothing but the *katechon* of the *what*, preventing the fulfilment and thus dissolution of human friendship.[23] For just as an adult is not the *friend* (*philos*) of a child, even though he both loves (*philein*) and is being loved (*phileitai*) by it, one cannot be a friend of God. Friends, for Aristotle, must be equal, whereas friendship (*philein* and *antiphilein*) allows, in all its forms, for asymmetry.[24]

Aristotle experiences the asymmetry under Plato's tutelage. He sets upon the path that leads to the equality of friendship, sets out to attain the divinity of the master, and discovers that the path passes through truth. Truth's virtue makes it possible to proclaim and dismiss Plato as a friend with a single blow: 'amicus Plato'. Strangely, Derrida nowhere invokes the proverbial words that echo unmistakably through their own history of transmission, appropriation and transformation, the leitmotif 'O friends'. If, as Patočka believes, it is for Aristotle a 'sacred duty' (*hosion*) to give precedence to truth over his friendship with Plato, two things must be noted of this duty: it is undertaken in perfect fidelity to Plato *and* it undercuts this fidelity by avoiding the Platonic name, by avoiding the proper name as such.[25]

Plato teaches Aristotle that one must prefer the *what* of truth that constitutes the friend as friend, over the friend. Plato has Socrates choose truth over Homer, the master of all tragedians, despite his avowed – however ironic – love (*philia*) and reverence (*aidōs*) for the latter.[26] Similarly, and even more radically perhaps, Plato has Socrates ask Simmias and Cebes to choose truth over himself.[27] At first, a difference appears to set the two instances apart: whereas Simmias and Cebes are personal friends of Socrates, the latter has nothing but two surviving epics on which to ground the proper name 'Homer'. At first, then, it seems that for Socrates no friend can truly be lost in the confrontation between Homeric and absolute truth, since for Socrates there is no Homer outside the text. It takes, however, a single step back to recognise that Socrates, the friend of Simmias and Cebes as much as the repudiator of Homer, is himself a *what* out of whole cloth, nearly nothing but the truth of the Platonic parchment. Cutting hyperbolically along the Platonic page, this is in sum the Platonic lesson: one must prefer the *what* of truth that constitutes the friend as friend, over the friend, because no friend can exist without the *what* of virtue. A *who* bereft of *what*: no such thing can be found.

When, then, Aristotle's turn comes to weigh the master against truth, he performs the task as the most faithful of disciples. In the act, he demonstrates the radical ephemerality of the friend: before confronting Plato with truth, Aristotle, notwithstanding his friendship towards the master, is not yet his friend because he is not yet his equal. After the confrontation, he is his equal no longer, since truth has now left Plato behind. It is perhaps no surprise that the moment of this confrontation, the instant of the friend, is only possible when everything is at stake. Aristotle is in the process of passing judgement on the theory of ideas, when it becomes obvious that there is no sidestepping the issue of his friendship with Plato.[28] Like a true Platonist, Aristotle will choose truth. Yet, at the same instant, Aristotle will also remain subversively committed to *the friend*.

Plato, never an equal and thus never quite a friend, is enough of a friend (this 'enough' is the qualitative recoil of friendship) to evoke tremor and silence. Aristotle condemns Plato's theory of ideas, without pronouncing the master's name. It is neither a matter of tact, nor a matter of fear. Aristotle has already, silently, raised Derrida's question: 'But if one must love truth (this is necessary, is it not?), how will one love anything other than one's own truth, a truth one can appropriate?' (44). Aristotle's answer has been: the friend; the friend who will serve as the *katechon* against the devastating law of friendship, the friend who will keep silent in order to preserve the precariousness that one calls friendship. Friendship speaks, it narrates, praises and condemns, but it needs silence in order to survive: 'friendship does not keep silence, it is preserved by silence' (53) – the silence that the friend keeps, the silence, first and foremost, of the proper name.

The Spectre of *tis* and the Tremor to Come

At the close of *Politics of Friendship* Derrida declares that the 'remaining question' is none other than the question of *Lysis*: *who* is the friend (293–4). The unsettled question will remain deliberately unsettling, the *who–what* differential (*tis*) emerging as the haunting quasi-concept not only of the whole work, but of the Derridean corpus in its totality. It is impossible to follow the acts and effects of this pervasive haunting; a few indications will have to suffice.

Within the *Politics of Friendship*, the major counter-locus of the *tis* is Schmitt's thought. Derrida critiques Schmitt for the unaccounted polemics in his demarcation of 'the political' as a function of the *who*. For Schmitt, 'the political' rests on a 'practical identification' of the friend and the enemy, principally and asymmetrically the enemy, even where theoretical access to 'war, politics, friendship, enmity, hate or love, hostility or peace' remains elusive (116). Knowing the enemy is *sine qua non*. Accordingly, the space of the political as well as all political decisions are determined, neither in advance, nor once and for all, but in the 'concrete' becoming of history on the basis of the question '*who* is the enemy'? (125).

It is possible to argue not only that the sovereign subscribes to the logic of the *tis* as both a *who* and a *what*, but also that sovereignty resides ultimately not with the decision on the state of exception, but with the resolution of the question of the *who*. This each time concrete question remains foreign and 'spectral' (*gespenstlich*) with regard to the concept (*Begriff*) and abstract spirit (*Geist*) (117). Yet – here lies the epistemological thrust of Derrida's critique of Schmitt – the spirit will always, in its own turn, return to haunt the concrete *who* of the enemy. Schmitt will have to heed the Aristotelian lesson that a *who* devoid of a *what* cannot even fashion the husk of a spectre.

The Schmittian excursus is important here because it sets into relief Derrida's own commitments. While Derrida is palpably impatient with Schmitt's dangerously idiosyncratic privileging of the enemy over the friend as the ground of politics, he is even more impatient with the latter's naively polemic privilege of the *who* over the *what*. At the same time, he is fascinated by the pronouncement that Schmitt appropriates from Theodor Däubler: 'The enemy is our own question as a figure' (*Der Feind is unser eigene Frage als Gestalt*) (150). Derrida recognises that the *who* returns to query the *what* and that without it friendship and selfhood collapse. As such, the *who* is the supplement without which the *what* would be fulfilled – if only it could in the first place exist. Inversely, as long as the *what* exists, the *who* prevents its dissolution; in Schmitt's terms the *who* functions as the *what*'s *katechon*.

Beyond the *Politics of Friendship* the *who–what* differential (*tis*) shows its pervasive ubiquity and principal character. Discussing Kafka, Derrida exclaims: 'Here, we know neither *who* nor *what* is the law, *das Gesetz*. This, perhaps, is where literature begins.'[29] And then:

> In German it [*das Gesetz*] is capitalized, like a proper name. We do not know what it is, who it is, where it is. Is it a thing, a person, a discourse,

> a voice, a document, or simply a nothing that incessantly defers access to itself, thus forbidding *itself* in order thereby to become something or someone?[30]

Indeed, *différance* itself is a *tis*: 'But *what* defers or *who* defers? In other words, what is *différance?*'[31] Not least, *différance* is a *tis* in its affinity with the ontological difference, as the latter opens up a field between the *who* of *Dasein* and the *what* of *Sein*, and as the *Sein* locates itself in the heart of the *Da* summarising the ontological difference in a hyphen: *Da-Sein*. Heidegger and Derrida both think from within the field of this difference, which they understand ultimately as the field of philosophy. For Heidegger, the Heraclitean *philein to sophon* constitutes the originary accord from within which thought sets forth. And Derrida underwrites the gesture: 'The question "What is friendship?," but also "Who is the friend (both or either sex)?" is nothing but the question "What is philosophy?"' (240).

If the question at the heart of *tis* encompasses all of philosophy, across the history of its auto-deconstruction, Aristotle undoubtedly, if silently, trembles. Yet, at the same time the question seems unavoidable: why Aristotle, why friendship? For no other reason perhaps than the poignancy of the friend's figure in collecting the forces of the *who* – the friend who is always more than a figure, more than a trope, a thing, a place. Indeed, in the *who* of the friend one discovers that friendship is *atopos*: 'outside all place or placeless, without family or familiarity, outside of self, expatriate, extraordinary, extravagant, absurd or mad, weird, unsuitable, strange, but also "a stranger to"' (178). Even more disturbingly, the *who* is not only severed from all *what*, reducing it to *no-thing*, but also from itself, itself as a departure point: 'and in not knowing *who*, in not knowing the substantial identity of *who* is, prior to the declaration of love, at the origin of who gives and who receives, *who* is in possession or not of what happened to be offered or requested' (220). Up until the event of friendship the *who* is nobody, the *what* is nothing.

For Derrida, this event is always to come. This is the lesson of Nietzsche and Blanchot, who announce a friendship of distance, 'an infinite distance, the fundamental separation on the basis of which what separates becomes relation'.[32] This separation is both space and time: it is becoming. But if the tremor of friendship is always to come, its silent anticipation is all too eloquent. A rich history of the *who–what* differential tells of a past and a future, which include not only the hominisation of the human *who*, from the technological *what*, but also of all the non-human *whos*, that we are at long last learning to understand as actors.[33] Such an actor is friendship's proverbial bushel of salt, writing its own history, balancing in itself across the *who–what* differential, opening up another field as it prepares, facilitates, anticipates the unforeseeable event of friendship.[34]

Notes

1. Jacques Derrida, *Politics of Friendship*, trans. George Collins (London: Verso, 1997); Jacques Derrida, *Politiques de l'amitié: suivi de L'Oreille de Heidegger* (Paris: Galilée, 1994). Hereafter, page references to the English translation are given in parenthesis in the text (*PF*).
2. Derrida, 'Ousia et Grammē: Note on a Note from *Being and Time*', in Derrida, *Margins of Philosophy*, trans. Alan Bass (Brighton: Harvester Press, 1982), pp. 29–67.
3. Jacques Derrida, *Heidegger: The Question of Being and History*, trans. Geoffrey Bennington (London: University of Chicago Press, 2016), p. 4.
4. Derrida, *Heidegger*, p. 9.
5. Ibid.
6. Jacques Derrida, *Of Grammatology*, trans. Gayatri Chakravorty Spivak (London: Johns Hopkins University Press, 1997), p. 5.
7. Aristotle, *Eudemian Ethics*, 1237b11–14. All references to classical texts are to standard pagination, unless otherwise indicated. No single theme or question dominates the totality of the two works; there is no single vantage point from which their totality should be read. This is perhaps less surprising if their character as compilations is taken into account. At a minimum, however, in both works, the essays on friendship comprise the most extensive sections, in terms of length.
8. Ibid. 1234b18–20.
9. Plato, *Lysis*, 204b.
10. Hermias, *On Plato, Phaedrus 227a–245e*, trans. Dirk Baltzly and Michael Share (London: Bloomsbury Academic, 2018), p. 135.
11. The general issue of untranslatability is raised, but sidelined: reciprocity and symmetry are not made contingent upon the commensurability of *amitié* to *philia*. In fact, in the 2002 documentary *Derrida*, *amour* is also dissected along the *who–what* differential: 'the difference between the who and the what at the heart of love, separates the heart'.
12. Aristotle, *Eudemian Ethics*, 1235b29–30.
13. Plato, *Lysis*, 220b. The other three hypotheses cast friendship as (1) either being passively loved or actively loving, (2) of the similar being drawn to the similar or (3) of the dissimilar being drawn to the dissimilar.
14. Ibid. 218b–c and 219b.

15. Ibid. 221e.
16. The aporia is summed up in the impossible choice between, on the one hand, making the good congenial to everything and evil congenial to nothing, and on the other, making only the good congenial to the good and evil to evil, which results in the same structural problems faced by one of the two earlier hypotheses of the dialogue, of friendship as similarity.
17. Plato, *Lysis*, 212a.
18. Ibid. 223c.
19. Derrida reads the phrase countless times through the work, proposing a major second interpretation, on the basis of a divergent grammar. This 'recoil' version, which focuses not on the impossibility of friendship but on its law of scarcity, is separated from the canonical version, by an iota subscript, an 'almost nothing' (190). Here, a different recoil, a different 'almost nothing' is proposed, on the basis of the internal silence of the *what* in the *philos*.
20. Aristotle, *Eudemian Ethics*, 1238a3–4.
21. Ibid. 1236b2–4, 1236a23–27, 123b24–25. The relation of the *pollachōs legomenon* to J.-L. Nancy's singular plural must still be examined; however, the former may inform the latter, certain irreducible differences between the two remain, which friendship, no less than Being, makes apparent.
22. Derrida's attempt to show how the finitude of friendship carries within it the 'inexorable injunction of its infinitization, and hence also of its Christianization', begins here (233). At the same time, the injunction that the *who* be preserved in the *what* of God, in the guise of the personal character of the son, will always return finitude into infinity's heart.
23. The Schmittian nexus is explored in the following.
24. Aristotle, *Eudemian Ethics*, 1239a5–6, 1239a1–5, 1239a20–21.
25. Jan Patočka, *Plato and Europe*, trans. Petr Lom (Stanford: Stanford University Press, 2002), p. 209.
26. Plato, *Republic* X, 595b–c.
27. Plato, *Phaedo*, 91b–c.
28. Aristotle, *Nichomachean Ethics*, 1096a10–15.
29. Jacques Derrida, 'Before the Law', in Derrida, *Acts of Literature*, trans. Derek Attridge (London: Routledge, 1992), pp. 181–220 (p. 207).
30. Ibid. p. 208.
31. Jacques Derrida, 'Différance', in *Margins of Philosophy*, p. 14.
32. Maurice Blanchot, 'Friendship', in Blanchot, *Friendship*, trans. Elizabeth

Rottenberg (Stanford: Stanford University Press, 1997), pp. 289–92 (p. 291).

33. Bernard Stiegler, *Technics and Time 1*, trans. Richard Beardsworth and George Collins (Stanford: Stanford University Press, 1998), pp. 121–2; Bruno Latour, *Reassembling the Social: An Introduction to Actor-Network-Theory* (Oxford: Oxford University Press, 2005), p. 72.
34. Aristotle, *Eudemian Ethics*, 1238a2–3.

2

Derrida, Montaigne and the Time of Friendship

Jennifer Rushworth

This essay offers a literary reading of Jacques Derrida's *Politics of Friendship* – a reading, more precisely, that is literary in two distinct ways. First, in marked contrast to the many philosophers with whom Derrida is in dialogue in this work, I focus instead on one particular literary figure: the sixteenth-century author Michel de Montaigne.[1] Montaigne's many writings on friendship include his essay 'Of Friendship' which Derrida very explicitly cites and discusses throughout *Politics of Friendship*.[2] Indeed, the phrase 'O my friends, there is no friend', a phrase which opened each seminar and which is cited at the outset of chapter 1 and analysed throughout, comes from this essay by Montaigne, where it is in turn cited as a quotation attributed to Aristotle (*PF*, 1).[3] Montaigne adds a distinctively literary, autobiographical voice to the chorus of philosophers on friendship whom Derrida assembles.

Second, and as a result of this focus on Montaigne, my reading is literary because it privileges the specific over the general, and therefore interrogates Derrida's divergence from Montaigne's example in this respect, at least in *Politics of Friendship*. Constant throughout Montaigne's reflections on friendship is the focus on one specific friend, another sixteenth-century writer: Étienne de La Boétie, author, most notably, of the *Discourse on Voluntary Servitude*. As Ullrich Langer writes at the start of his entry on friendship in the *Dictionnaire de Michel de Montaigne* (2007), 'In Montaigne the discourse on the value of friendship can hardly be separated from the account that he gives of his actual friendship [*amitié réelle*] with Étienne de La Boétie and of the death of this friend, in 1563.'[4] In contrast, what we find in Derrida's *Politics of Friendship* is a discourse on friendship that has been divorced from specific friends; in other words, Derrida self-consciously follows the path of philosophy rather than that of autobiography, despite the inspiration he derives from Montaigne.

My essay is structured around two different times of friendship, past and future. In the first part, 'Spectres of Friendship Past', I consider the example of friendship afforded by Montaigne, his role in 'the history of a canonical sentence' (189) and the connection between friendship and mourning established in practice by Montaigne and discussed more theoretically by Derrida. In the second part, 'Spectres of Friendship Yet to Come', I consider Derrida's reasons for not writing about his own particular friendships in *Politics of Friendship*, including his commitment to openness and futurity and his interest in the role of the reader. In speaking of spectres, I am drawing on Derrida's argument, in this text, that 'All phenomena of friendship, all things and all beings to be loved, belong to spectrality' (288), where spectrality is understood not only in light of loss and mourning but also as inevitable anachronism and as various forms of undecidability (between presence and absence, for instance, or between spirit and flesh).[5] What Derrida demonstrates, more precisely, is that the spectres of friendship include not only spectres of the past – in Montaigne's case, La Boétie – but also unnamed, anticipated spectres of the future.

Spectres of Friendship Past

Montaigne's writings on friendship are rooted both in a particular friendship, which is declared to be unique and incomparable, and in a broader philosophical discourse on friendship, which is thereby polemically argued to be inadequate. In the essay 'Of Friendship', Montaigne describes his friendship with La Boétie as extremely rare and unparalleled in either life or art:

> so entire and so perfect that certainly you will hardly read of the like, and among men of today you see no trace of it in practice. So many coincidences are needed to build up such a friendship that it is a lot if fortune can do it once in three centuries.[6]

Later in the same essay, Montaigne reaffirms this uniqueness: 'Our friendship has no other model than itself, and can be compared only with itself.'[7] Consequently, experience is argued to exceed theory: 'the very *discourses* that antiquity has left us on this subject seem to me weak compared with the feelings I have. And in this particular the facts surpass even the precepts of philosophy'.[8] Similar claims are also reiterated elsewhere by Montaigne: 'no spoken or written statement in the schools of philosophy ever represented the rights and duties of sacred friendship as exactly as did the practice that my friend and I formed together'.[9]

Notwithstanding such statements, in Montaigne's writings on friendship we do still also find recourse to these belittled and maligned 'precepts of philosophy'. Most notably, 'Of Friendship' relies upon references to and citations from a range of philosophers and writers, including not only Aristotle but also Horace, Virgil, Terence, Catullus and others. It is, as already noted, in the essay 'Of Friendship' that we find the phrase that Derrida takes from Montaigne, or rather from (pseudo-?)Aristotle via Montaigne:

> Let not these other, common friendships be placed in this rank. I have as much knowledge of them as another, and of the most perfect of their type, but I advise you not to confuse the rules of the two; you would make a mistake. You must walk in those other friendships bridle in hand, with prudence and precaution; the knot is not so well tied that there is no cause to mistrust it. 'Love him,' Chilo used to say, 'as if you are to hate him some day; hate him as if you are to love him.' This precept, which is so abominable in this sovereign and masterful friendship, is healthy in the practice of ordinary and customary friendships, in regard to which we must use the remark that Aristotle often repeated: 'O my friends, there is no friend.'[10]

In his reading of this phrase, Derrida will repeatedly point out its polyvalency and ambiguity, a result not only of its cryptic brevity and apparent self-contradiction, but also of related issues of source and translation. That Montaigne describes this phrase as a 'remark that Aristotle often repeated' already suggests that the declaration does not have a single source (27). The source itself need not trouble us here, although the most frequent explanation given is that it is a citation, already secondhand, from Diogenes Laertius's *Life of Aristotle*.[11] More interesting, as Derrida shows, is a question of accentuation in the original Greek, which means that Montaigne's version – favoured by many others, and therefore noted by Derrida as 'the *canonical* version' (212) – is likely a mistranslation resulting from a mistranscription. The truer version, which Derrida dubs 'the *recoil* version', loses the vocative and concerns instead quantity, implying, in Derrida's gloss, that 'He who has friends – too many friends – has no friend' (212). Ultimately, however, Derrida is also keen to undermine the stark distinction between the two versions, suggesting that both are similar in that each implies a form of address (214).[12]

For Montaigne, the phrase is mobilised in support of a contrast between 'sovereign and masterful friendship' (in the singular) and 'ordinary and customary friendships' (in the plural). In this regard, the quantitative interpretation is highly pertinent. Yet the Aristotelian phrase in its vocative form also sounds in Montaigne's essay as a lament; 'there is no friend', because the one unique friend La Boétie has died. The remaining friends – 'O my friends' – are called upon to witness this unique grief, even as their status as friends is undercut by the statement that follows. Derrida takes from Montaigne not only explicitly the Aristotelian phrase, replete with its uncertain origins and problematic translation, but also, more especially, this connection between friendship and mourning. As Derrida writes, inspired by the example of Montaigne (though not solely), 'Our hypothesis here is that no great discourse on friendship will ever have eluded the major rhetoric of *epitáphios*, and hence of some form of transfixed celebration of spectrality' (94). The end of *Politics of Friendship* reiterates this point:

> the great canonical meditations on friendship (Cicero's *De Amicitia*, Montaigne's 'On Friendship', Blanchot's *L'amitié*, for example) belong to the experience of mourning, to the moment of loss – that of the friend or of friendship – [. . .] through the irreplaceable element of the named they always advance in testimonial order to confide and refuse the death of the unique to a universalizable discourse. (290)

Politics of Friendship is also, therefore, about the politics of grief. At stake in both is, as we have already seen for Montaigne, a desire to assert 'the unique' and consequently to resist 'universalizable discourse'. Derrida recognises this tension here, and yet on his own account, unlike Montaigne, he omits 'the irreplaceable element of the named', that is, the specific, unique friend, at least in *Politics of Friendship*. As we have seen, Montaigne rhetorically claimed the inadequacy of philosophical discourses on friendship, while also producing a discourse of his own that, as Derrida shows, has become a canonical text for subsequent philosophies of friendship. Yet in building his own discourse on friendship in dialogue with Montaigne, Derrida at the same time strikingly goes against Montaigne in excluding his own personal experience of friendship.

Where Derrida also diverges from Montaigne is in the connection forged between mourning and the time of friendship. For Montaigne, the connection between friendship and grief is rooted in the past and backwards-looking, because of the death of La Boétie. Derrida, instead, shifts the grounds for concern to the future, considering bereavement as an inevitable and anticipated future prospect:

> The anguished apprehension of mourning (without which the act of friendship would not spring forth in its very energy) insinuates itself

a priori and anticipates itself, it haunts and plunges the friend, before mourning, into mourning. This apprehension weeps before the lamentation, it weeps death before death, and this is the very respiration of friendship, the extreme of its possibility. Hence surviving is at once the essence, the origin and the possibility, the condition of possibility of friendship; it is the grieved act of loving. This time of surviving thus gives the time of friendship. (14)

In this passage, Derrida argues that the anticipation of death is the 'respiration', that is, the vital, living rhythm of friendship, recalling that 'convertibility of life and death' (3) that will later emerge in discussion of the convertibility of friend and enemy, two further concepts which 'consequently intersect and ceaselessly change places' (72). Montaigne's writings on friendship similarly stem from a 'time of surviving' the death of La Boétie. Yet Derrida shows here that the 'time of surviving' begins not with death but rather with friendship itself, and with the awareness that the friend *will have* died. The 'undeniable future anterior' is, therefore, 'the very movement and time of friendship' (249). As Derrida elaborates in a different text, anticipated mourning 'casts over each the pall of an implacable future anterior. One of us two *will have* had to remain alone. Both of us knew this in advance. And right from the start'.[13] In other words, for Derrida friendship is a concern for the future, rather than for the past, even as the future anterior irrevocably destabilises the boundaries between the two times.

Spectres of Friendship Yet to Come

The example of Montaigne's recording of his friendship with La Boétie ultimately raises the following question, by way of contrast or omission: who, or where, is (are) Derrida's friend(s)? In this question, the undecidability of the singular or plural is a necessary response to the extensive reflections on rarity and quantity in *Politics of Friendship*. But my concern is not with numbers but rather with examples – and indeed with another of Derrida's favourite concerns, that of proper names. In the final two chapters of *Politics of Friendship*, Derrida does anticipate this question at brief moments, revealing his awareness of the issue and offering various forms of justification for this absence. In chapter 9, Derrida already suggests a possible tension between what he calls '*taking a stand*' (*se déclarer*) and his 'theoretical or philosophical approach':

Who could ever answer for a discourse *on* friendship without *taking a stand* [sans *se déclarer*]? The urgency of this question is no way lessened

> by the fact that this discourse on friendship, this *de amicitia*, claims to be theoretical or philosophical. Who will answer for a treatise *perí philías* without taking a stand, hence without assuming the *responsibility* of this stand [. . .]? Can one speak of love without declaring one's love, without declaring war, beyond all possible neutrality? Without avowing, if only the unavowable? (228)[14]

Paraphrasing Derrida – and sidestepping issues of the difference between love and friendship, as between friend and enemy, also invoked in this passage and explored at length in *Politics of Friendship* – our question is: can one speak of *friendship* without declaring one's *friendship*?

As if troubled by his own question, Derrida does make a few fleeting allusions to his own friendships in the book's final chapter:

> Without seeking to conceal it, it will have been understood that I wish to speak here of those men and women to whom a bond of friendship unites me – that is, I also want to speak *to them*. If only through the rare friendship I am naming, which always occasions in me a surge of admiration and gratitude. (302)

This friendship is 'rare' both because of the law of scarcity evoked elsewhere (true friends are necessarily few in number) and because it goes against the general unspoken rule, in *Politics of Friendship*, of Derrida's silence about his particular friendships. Here, Derrida then uncharacteristically names explicitly Maurice Blanchot and Michel Deguy as friends and writers who have cited 'Aristotle's quasi-citation' (302), and a few pages later reiterates 'the admiring and grateful friendship which binds [him] to' the former (304).[15] These acknowledgements are welcome and even long overdue, but they are also incredibly brief. Instead, the overwhelming habit of *Politics of Friendship* is one of silence towards such friendships.

Derrida justifies this silence in a number of different ways. First, already in chapter 3, he cites the following interdiction from Nietzsche: '*Silentium*. One should not talk (*reden*) about one's friends: otherwise one will talk away the feeling of friendship.'[16] Second, in the final chapter Derrida returns to this question of silence parenthetically, this time in terms of a deliberate avoidance of concrete examples:

> (As you will have noticed, we have deliberately refrained from recourse to 'illustrations' to 'actualize' our analyses or in an attempt to demon-

> strate their necessity *today*, by delving into the most spectacular 'news' on political scenes: local, national, European or worldwide. We have done so through a concern with sobriety: first, we do not want to exploit that which, as it were, *screens out* reflection by projecting itself with the pathetic and 'sensational' violence of images on to a too easily mediatizable scene. Then again, these examples are in the mind, heart and imagination of anyone who would be interested in the problems we are dealing with here; such people, let us hope, will have found the path of these mediations by themselves. Lastly, the overabundance of such 'illustrations' would have swamped the least of our sentences. [. . .]) (272)

These comments relate to politics, but, given the book's focus, they are just as relevant to friendship. Particularly interesting is the suggestion that it is the task of the reader to provide examples.

A third explanation relates to this same question of silence and sobriety, considered afresh from the perspective of death. In Derrida's words:

> It is *thanks* to death that friendship can be declared. Never before, never otherwise. And never if not in recalling (while thanks to death, the friend recalls that there are no friends). And when friendship is declared during the lifetime of friends, it avows, fundamentally, the same thing: it avows the death thanks to which the chance to declare itself comes at last, never failing to come. (302)

As we have seen, as much is confirmed by the example of Montaigne's declaration of friendship for La Boétie, which follows his friend's death. The same also holds true for Derrida's collection of texts on the deaths of friends, published first in English under the title *The Work of Mourning* (2001).[17] *Politics of Friendship* is perhaps best read alongside *The Work of Mourning*, so that the universal and singular discourses can be mutually illuminating – and even mutually correcting. If, as Derrida notes, to declare friendship while one's friend is alive is to avow death, not declaring friendship represents, conversely, a futile attempt to eschew death.

The final and most important justification concerns, however, the relationship between friendship and futurity. Derrida once declared in an uncharacteristically pithy and didactic manner that 'It's better to let the future open [*L'ouverture de l'avenir vaut mieux*] – this is the axiom of deconstruction.'[18] A similar openness to the future is also crucial for friendship, according to Derrida, as he explains in his emphasis on the importance of 'peut-être' ('perhaps', or more literally 'maybe') in *Politics of Friendship*:

> Now, the thought of the 'perhaps' perhaps engages the only possible thought of the event – of friendship to come and friendship for the future. For to love friendship, it is not enough to know how to bear the other in mourning: one must love the future. And there is no more just category for the future than that of the 'perhaps'. Such a thought conjoins friendship, the future, and the *perhaps* to open on to the coming of what comes – that is to say, necessarily in the regime of a possible whose possibilization must prevail over the impossible. (29)

Perhaps, then, Derrida's omission of friends in *Politics of Friendship* ought to be understood not as a failure to follow Montaigne's example, but rather as a necessary consequence of this commitment to openness, futurity and possibility, seen elsewhere in Derrida's thought in relation to promises and the messianic. The same motivation also underpins Derrida's interest, in *Politics of Friendship*, in forms of address whose addressee is undecidable. As he writes, returning to the Aristotelian phrase:

> however it is read, in the canonical or recoil version, and whoever its author, such a sentence is addressed to someone. The fact that this is absolutely necessary does not prevent – on the contrary, it commands – that the task of determination or identification of this addressee remain unfulfilled and always exposed to some undecidability. (214–15)

The address of Derrida's own text stems, as we have seen, from a 'wish to speak here [*to*] those men and women to whom a bond of friendship unites me' (302). In the text on Paul de Man in *The Work of Mourning*, Derrida draws a contrast between speaking *of* instead of speaking *to* and *with* someone, the first being mortifying (in the etymological sense) and the second being full of life.[19] But speaking *to* also means allowing the addressee to remain uncertain and unpredictable; this, after all, is Derrida's definition of writing as something that functions in the absence of the addressee. Accordingly, where Montaigne's friend is spectral because deceased, Derrida's is spectral not only because of being unnamed and abstract (to evoke Derrida's reading of the spectral in Schmitt), but also because this friend is yet to come (117).

Spectres of Friendship Present?

In this essay I have considered two times of friendship: on the one hand, both the past of the literary and philosophical tradition of writing on friendship and the pastness of Montaigne's own particular friendship with La Boétie; on the other hand, the future of anticipated mourning that, for Derrida, haunts every friendship in advance of bereavement and, furthermore, the openness of the unpredictable future friend who is addressed and interpellated in these manifold discourses on friendship. This dual focus is appropriate to a book that begins by reading the phrase '"O my friends, there is no friend"' as 'two times [. . .] two theses – two *moments*, perhaps' (1). These 'two times [*deux temps*]' form what Derrida calls a '*contretemps*': a mishap, argument or dispute. I have staged a similar *contretemps* between Montaigne and Derrida over the role of the friend in their respective reflections on friendship.

What my analysis has overlooked, however, is the role of the present, especially the present time of the Aristotelian phrase and its renewed reiterations in different present times across the centuries. As Derrida notes at the outset, 'the two times [. . .] appear *together*, they are summoned to appear, in the present: they present themselves as in a single stroke, in a single breath, in the same present, in the present itself' (1). What, then, about a final spectre, the spectre of friendship present? In a moving passage of *Politics of Friendship*, we get a glimpse of a possible answer, an answer that calls on the reader to respond, and in so doing identifies the reader, too, as a spectral, present friend:

> I am saying nothing, then, that can be said or sayable.
>
> And yet my saying, the declaration of love or the call to the friend, the address to the other in the night, the writing that does not resign itself to this unsaid – who could swear that they are consigned to oblivion simply because no said can speak them exhaustively?
>
> The response no longer belongs to me – that is all I wanted to tell you, my friend the reader [*ami lecteur*]. (70)

Notes

1. I acknowledge not only that 'literature' is an anachronistic term in this context but also that both Montaigne and Derrida blur the category boundaries of literature and philosophy. Still, I find the distinction helpful here in combination with that between the specific and the general.
2. All quotations from Montaigne are taken from *The Complete Works of Montaigne*, trans. Donald M. Frame (Stanford: Stanford University Press, 1957). For the essay 'Of Friendship', see pp. 135–44 in that volume. For in-depth studies of friendship in Montaigne, see Gérard Defaux, *Montaigne et le travail de l'amitié* (Orléans: Paradigme, 2001)

and Marc D. Schachter, *Voluntary Servitude and the Erotics of Friendship: From Classical Antiquity to Early Modern France* (Aldershot: Ashgate, 2008). In terms of existing contemporary theoretical readings of Montaigne, see *Montaigne After Theory, Theory After Montaigne*, ed. Zahi Zalloua (Seattle: University of Washington Press, 2009). On Derrida and Montaigne especially, see Lawrence D. Kritzman, *The Fabulous Imagination: On Montaigne's Essays* (New York: Columbia University Press, 2000) and Katie Chenoweth, 'The Force of a Law: Derrida, Montaigne, and the Edict of Villers-Cotterêts (1539)', *The Comparatist*, 36 (2012), 67–85.

3. Jacques Derrida, *Politics of Friendship*, trans. George Collins (London: Verso, 1997); Jacques Derrida, *Politiques de l'amitié: suivi de L'Oreille de Heidegger* (Paris: Galilée, 1994). Hereafter, page references to the English translation are given in parenthesis in the text (*PF*). See also Montaigne, 'Of Friendship', p. 140.
4. Ullrich Langer, 'Amitié', in *Dictionnaire de Michel de Montaigne*, ed. Philippe Desan (Paris: Honoré Champion, 2007), pp. 34–7 (p. 34; translation my own).
5. On Derrida and spectrality, see also Jacques Derrida, *Specters of Marx: The State of the Debt, the Work of Mourning and the New International*, trans. Peggy Kamuf (New York: Routledge, 2006) and Colin Davis, 'Hauntology, Spectres and Phantoms', *French Studies*, 59.3 (2005), 373–9.
6. Montaigne, 'Of Friendship', p. 136.
7. Ibid. p. 139.
8. Ibid. p. 143.
9. 'To Michel de L'Hôpital: Dedicatory Epistle to La Boétie's Latin "Poems" [April 30, 1570]', in *The Complete Works of Montaigne*, pp. 1058–60 (p. 1060).
10. Montaigne, 'Of Friendship', p. 140.
11. For discussion of this 'nomad phrase', see Judith Still, *Derrida and Hospitality: Theory and Practice* (Edinburgh: Edinburgh University Press, 2010), pp. 95–6.
12. I return to this point at the end.
13. Jacques Derrida, *Sovereignties in Question: The Poetics of Paul Celan*, ed. Thomas Dutoit and Outi Pasanen (New York: Fordham University Press, 2005), p. 140.
14. See Derrida, *Politiques de l'amitié*, p. 255.
15. On Derrida and Deguy, see Christopher Elson and Garry Sherbert, *In the Name of Friendship: Deguy, Derrida and 'Salut'* (Leiden: Brill, 2017).

On Derrida's own friendships as implicit in *Politics of Friendship*, in particular the figures of Blanchot, Michel Foucault and Paul de Man, see Paul Allen Miller, 'Ghosts in the *Politics of Friendship*', in *Dead Theory: Derrida, Death, and the Afterlife of Theory*, ed. Jeffrey R. Di Leo (London: Bloomsbury Academic, 2015), pp. 111–32.

16. Friedrich Nietzsche, *Human, All Too Human: A Book for Free Spirits*, trans. R. J. Hollingdale (Cambridge: Cambridge University Press, 1986), 2, 252, cited in *Politics of Friendship*, p. 54.
17. Jacques Derrida, *The Work of Mourning*, ed. Pascale-Anne Brault and Michael Naas (Chicago: University of Chicago Press, 2001); *Chaque fois unique, la fin du monde*, ed. Pascale-Anne Brault and Michael Naas (Paris: Galilée, 2003).
18. Jacques Derrida and Bernard Stiegler, *Echographies of Television: Filmed Interviews*, trans. Jennifer Bajorek (Cambridge: Polity Press, 2002), p. 21; *Échographies de la télévision: entretiens filmés* (Paris: Galilée; Institut national de l'audiovisuel, 1996), p. 29.
19. Derrida, *The Work of Mourning*, p. 72.

3

Is There a Politics to Friendship? Derrida's Critique of the Couple in Montaigne, Kant and Levinas

Cillian Ó Fathaigh

> . . . (of the friendship of this legendary pair of friends of this century to which, Kant would add, a third reliable friend came to join them, already in fact being there from the very beginning, Levinas [. . .]) (*PF*, 293)[1]

Politics of Friendship is a significant critique of fraternity as a model of community. Yet what is perhaps of equal importance, though less acknowledged, is its major challenge to the couple as a model for friendship. For Derrida, as we will see, it is not only that the Western philosophical tradition understands friendship through brotherhood, but that it also does so through a paradigm of friendship between *two* brothers. In this chapter, I will show how this is a constant target in Derrida's reading of both Michel de Montaigne and Immanuel Kant. In so doing, I will also address an interconnected question posed implicitly in the epigraph of this text: where is Levinas in *Politics of Friendship*? This citation appears in the closing moments of the text and reminds us that Levinas has been entirely absent from Derrida's discussion of friendship and politics. Indeed, as we can see, it is not even Derrida who adds Levinas to this text, but rather Kant who 'would add (Levinas as) a third reliable friend'. This third friend, or even third wheel, is only introduced to shed light on – perhaps with candle in hand – this 'legendary pair of friends', Blanchot and Bataille.[2] Yet Levinas here is represented as a friend, just as reliable as the other two, and 'there from the very beginning'. What are we to make of this cryptic, intertextual passage and what does it say about the notable absence of any discussion of Levinas in *Politics of Friendship*?

By breaking down each part of this curious phrase, I will demonstrate that Levinas is far from absent in this text. Indeed, as we will see, his presence between Bataille and Blanchot here is tacit acknowledgement of the way the Levinasian framework structures Derrida's analysis of friendship. With this approach, Derrida points to a double bind in the *face-à-face* (face-to-face) of the couple and its relation to other friends and society in *le tiers* (the third party). This is presented as an irresolvable tension between a desire to deploy friendship as an apolitical relation between two individuals, as well as a ground and guide for politics. Yet, looking more closely at Derrida's approach, we come to see that Derrida subtly deploys Levinas's own system against Levinas himself, bringing out how Levinas may still neglect the primacy of the third party and the consequences of this for a thinking of friendship. As such, Derrida demonstrates the necessity to think of friendship as political all the way down, without any apolitical or pre-political moment. Through the figure of the couple of friends, this is a position that Derrida explicitly critiques in Montaigne and Kant, and silently challenges in Levinas.

This Legendary Pair of Friends

Beginning with the first part of our epigraph, we can follow the reference to this 'legendary pair of friends of this century'.[3] This leads us directly to Montaigne, who maintains – along with Cicero and Kant – that 'there are no friends', because friendship is a rare occurrence: 'a great friendship comes along every three or four centuries' (258). Blanchot and Bataille, then, have truly lucked out, conveniently landing in one of those rare centuries. This subtle reference to Montaigne, many chapters after his first appearance, consolidates Derrida's earlier reading of the couple in Montaigne. At that stage, we saw how Montaigne viewed friendship through a paradigm of the couple of (male) friends. This couple articulates the indivisibility and singularity of friendship, but a singularity which is divided between two bodies: 'the friend *qua* one soul (singularity) but in two bodies (duplicity)' (178). Montaigne maintains that his conception of friendship as 'one soul in two bodies' comes down to him from Aristotle.[4] Yet, in Montaigne we see even greater stress on the indivisibility of friendship. What is important is that while the body can be divided, the soul must remain indivisible, 'for the perfect friendship I speak of is indivisible'.[5] Such indivisibility is an essential part of the couple, as 'an *indivisible* community of the soul between two who love one another [*entre deux qui s'aiment*]' (179). From this perspective, it would hardly be accurate to describe friendship as *between* two different people, but rather as an engagement or commitment that connects one shared soul.

From here, Derrida brings forth how Montaigne's conception of friendship is based on the unity and singularity of each couple, 'not only the indivisibility or the uniqueness of the soul, but the singularity of the couple' (182). We see then that it is not only the model of brotherhood that structures community, but also the model of the couple as *two* brothers. Indeed, this is one of the motivations behind Montaigne's rejection of natural brotherhood in favour of a chosen or social 'brotherhood'. The former is an attribute, part of 'common, customary friendship', at least in part because we can have several brothers; whereas the latter is a perfect friendship as the couple is both singular and indivisible for Montaigne: 'the fraternity of alliance or election [. . .] is the indivisible essence of "perfect friendship"' (181). Derrida's analysis helps us see that it is not simply brotherhood, but the paradigm of *two* brothers that is at play here.

The singularity and unity of the couple is a fundamental part of Montaigne's thinking of friendship. Yet the couple also serves as the ground of politics, and it is here that Derrida pulls at the contradictory threads of Montaigne's reading. Montaigne wants this singular friendship to be withdrawn from society and politics, the couple of friends wholly united and complete within themselves, attaining 'a certain transcendence of friendship with respect to the public or civic realm'; and yet, he also presents this friendship as a ground for and guide to the political, whereby this couple is 'regularly engaged in an extremely politicized scene' (182). As Derrida stresses, this conception of friendship 'marks off the simultaneously political and apolitical, or a-civic, structure of a perfect friendship which accepts (*assume*) the impossibility of honouring multiple demands and doing one's duty beyond the couple of friends' (182). And yet, as Derrida also stresses in the term 'a-civic', the *civitas* is also at play, acknowledging that 'all the couples of friends which serve as examples for Cicero and Montaigne are citizen couples' (184).

The consequences of this citizenship cannot easily be dismissed, not least because it forms a structural part of how Montaigne believes these rare friendships are guided. They are guided by reason and virtue: 'this pair were guided by virtue and led by reason (*without which it is impossible to harness them together*)' (183–4). And for Montaigne, both virtue and reason are not private, but rather these concepts are 'brought to bear in advance on the space of the *res publica*' (184). Indeed, within this tradition it is not possible to think a conception of reason or virtue 'that would not be in essence homogeneous to the best reason of State' (184). As we will see when we turn to Kant, Montaigne is far from alone in tying the comportment of these two friends to the state.

What Derrida's analysis of Montaigne brings out is not only that the couple serves as an essential model for friendship, but that it is also caught between a desire to withdraw from the political – as a unique and singular relationship – as well a desire to found the political realm. The couple for Montaigne is this dream of an apolitical moment that can at the same time guide the political: 'Yet Montaigne seems to continue to dream of a fundamental apoliticism or transpoliticism [. . .] [which would] divide reason or virtue' (184). Importantly, Derrida's aim here is not to resolve this conflict, to find a framework where we can accommodate these demands, but rather to fully exhibit this conflict for what it is: a double bind. Indeed, 'this *double bind* does not happen to fraternity like an accident, but draws an interior and tragic structure out to its limit' (184). This aporia is precisely the tragic choice 'between the sovereign fraternity of secrecy between two, in the friendship of exception, and, on the other hand, the brotherhood or the conjunction of political secrecy, which begins with three' (184). In this conflict, therefore, we see that the couple plays a fundamental role as both sides of the same precious coin. One shares the secret uniquely between two, whereas the other involves the political and public connection, itself presented as another type of secret. The latter, importantly, begins with the third friend. And this leads us to the next part of our epigraph, the 'third reliable friend' which 'Kant would add' to Blanchot and Bataille.

Kant Would Add

In Montaigne, we have seen the importance of the couple as the model of friendship, but also the aporia that Derrida exposes; two singular and unique friends as removed from the political but caught by the desire to present this as a foundation of the political. Derrida's reading throughout *Politics of Friendship* confirms this but takes on a particularly interesting form in his reading of Kant. Indeed, as we will see, if Derrida selects Kant to be the one who would 'add Levinas' to the discussion, there is good reason for this.

As in Montaigne, for Kant it is the paradigm of the couple which determines the concept of friendship. And Kant ties this even more explicitly to the secret. Here, moral friendship is defined as 'absolute confidence, a confidence such that "*two people*" must share not only their impressions, but even their secret judgements' (257).[6] By this Kant means that the couple must be capable of sharing their whole opinions on politics, religion and a series of other topics, some of which might lead them to being pursued by the state. And it is this commitment to not share the secret which is the condition of friendship whereby friends commit 'to renounce all public profit, all political or institutional consequence, to the possession or circulation of this secret' (258). It is for this reason, like Montaigne and so many others in *Politics of Friendship*, that Kant insists that true friendship is a rare thing. The couple of friends is tied directly to an absolute secret, one shared only between two people.

Secrecy, for Kant, defines friendship. We should have no secrets between ourselves and the friend and should protect the secrets they share. Yet the problem emerges when another friend comes along, a third friend, with whom we should also have no secrets. As in Montaigne, we see that the couple is interrupted precisely at the moment that makes them perfect friends, at the arrival of that third friend:

> If there is a problem with the secret, on the other hand, it is in so far as there are two friends *plus one* ('another friend, believed equally reliable', notes Kant) and to the extent that this discourse on the secret supposes the couple's rupture. (259)

The third friend arrives to interrupt the unified relation between the two: the couple would secret itself away from the social, but this is resisted by the possibility of having more than one friend. Importantly, this problem of the third party and the secret carries political problems with it, and once again this same fractured desire of the political and the apolitical.

This split desire – one which we have seen already at work in Montaigne – is best captured in Kant's conception of the *friend of man*, one who loves all of humanity, not just one friend, but all friends. Importantly, this *friend of man* is defined by an Idea of equality between all human beings, but also a sense of obligation towards this idea: 'Equality is *necessary* [*il faut*]. [. . .] For it is *obligation* that the soundness [*la justesse*] or justice of this *consideration* adds to the representation' (260). This obligation is important because it moves us towards a political conception where the *friend of man* is obliged and indebted to men. Importantly, debt and obligation for Kant are wholly political and public concepts. As in Montaigne, it is the morality or virtue of friendship, and particularly reason, that moves friendship directly into the political realm, which 'intersect(s) in the ethics or virtue of friendship: responsible friendship *before* reason, when reason makes the Idea of equality an obligation' (276). It is this connection between these public values of reason and virtue, and particularly obligation, which disrupts the possibility of a purely apolitical, singular and undisrupted friendship. Indeed, this point is far from a secondary aspect in Kant's work, but tied to some of his most significant political concepts. Derrida states this clearly: 'It goes without saying that cosmopolitanism, universal democracy, perpetual peace, would not have the slightest chance of being announced or promised, if not realized, without the presupposition of such a friend' (261).

We can see, therefore, that this couple and the third friend structure Derrida's reading of Kant as much as Montaigne. Again, we have a singular, unified and fusional couple presented against political community, but at the same time presented as a foundation for the political. It is at this point in Derrida's reading of Kant that we see Levinas arrive on the scene. This crucial moment in his interpretation is couched in Levinas's vocabulary:

> In principle this double dimension maintains the absolute singularity of the other and that of 'my' relation to the other, as a relation of the other to the other I am myself, as its other for itself. [. . .] This discourse on universality can determine itself in the regions of morality, of law or of politics, but it always appeals to a third instance [*tiers*], beyond the face-to-face of singularities. (276)

Here, therefore, we see that this couple is presented precisely as a *face-à-face* and the third instance, party or friend as *le tiers*. This appeal to the Levinasian concepts is far from accidental. The face-to-face marks a moment of singular relation to alterity, the third party the moment of the interruption by society and politics; presented in this way, we can see that these categories have structured Derrida's reading of friendship from the outset. Indeed, though the idea in our epigraph that Kant would be the one to 'add' Levinas to the discussion may at first seem surprising, we can see that it is a quite direct allusion to the role Levinas played in Derrida's interpretation of Kant. And, as we have already shown in Montaigne, this is not an exception, but rather plays a key structural role in Derrida's reading throughout the text. In this sense, in spite of the lack of explicit reference to Levinas, an engagement with his work plays a major role in structuring Derrida's own readings of these canonical figures of friendship.

Already in Fact Being There from the Very Beginning

Yet, if Derrida's engagement with Levinas plays an important structural role throughout the text, that is not to suggest that this is a simple 'application' of a Levinasian framework to this tradition. Instead, there is good reason to understand this as a critical engagement with Levinas, one which suggests that Levinas himself is not immune to the conception of fraternity that Derrida targets so persistently.

It is difficult to summarise the complex dialogue between Emmanuel Levinas and Jacques Derrida, which extends far beyond *Politics of Friendship*, but one constant point at issue is the status of the third party. In 'Violence and Metaphysics', Derrida criticises Levinas for presenting the third party as a secondary instance in *Totality and Infinity*.[7] In many ways, Levinas's next great text, *Otherwise than Being*, serves as a response to Derrida, placing a great deal of further emphasis on the third party and proposing that this plays a fundamental role within his thinking. However, unlike 'Violence and Metaphysics' where the difference is reasonably clear, it is difficult to decipher to what degree Derrida found Levinas's response convincing, and particularly as to whether Levinas has resolved all of his concerns around the priority of the third party. As we have seen above, this question is of major significance in a thinking of friendship, fraternity and political community.

If Derrida does not explicitly address fraternity in Levinas in *Politics of Friendship*, we might look to his last significant engagement with Levinas, *Adieu*.[8] This work is at once both helpful and unhelpful for our purposes. It is helpful as Derrida proposes that alongside hospitality and humanity, fraternity is one of the three great themes of Levinas's *oeuvre*. Yet having maintained that it represents such an important position, Derrida then only offers us eight lines, stating, 'I will not pause here to discuss this further, since this is really not my theme.' In spite of this claim, this footnote does offer a range of citations of Levinas demonstrating the prominence of fraternity in his thought,[9] both in *Totality and Infinity*, 'fraternity is the very relation with the face', and *Otherwise than Being*, which describes 'the structure of the-one-for-the-other inscribed in human fraternity'.[10] There's good ground, then, to suggest that Levinas relies on fraternity and the couple as much as any of the thinkers referenced in *Politics of Friendship*.

Furthermore, the footnote in *Adieu* takes on an even more significant position as Kant is invoked yet again and serves as the prism through which Derrida understands fraternity in Levinas. In fact, Derrida suggests that Kant and Levinas share a similar position on fraternity, and he directs us to the pages on Kant in *Politics of Friendship* where he brings forward *le tiers*: 'Levinas here comes to, among many others, the Kant of the *The Doctrine of Virtue* [. . .] I analyse this [fraternal] relation at some length (*Politics of Friendship*, pp. 252–63)'.[11] In Kant, as we have seen, it is the arrival of the third party that disrupts the singular and unified couple which was represented as apolitical. And this should make us pay particular attention to the chronology of the third party. In citing Levinas in this footnote, Derrida suggests that though the third party is at times on equal footing with the face-to-face, this is not always the case, pointing out that first there is relation to fraternity in the face-to-face, and '*next* comes the deduction of the "third" and of the socio-political "We"' (145). This is a crucial and suggestive 'next', pointing to Derrida's earlier concerns about the primacy and chronology of the third party in Levinas. Indeed, given that this formed a core part of his reading of Kant, whom Derrida makes complicit with

Levinas, we can see that this engagement with a Levinasian framework is far from neutral.

In this respect, Derrida suggests that Levinas repeats the errors of Kant, Montaigne and others; he begins with the couple, the *face-to-face*, as a model of ethics, and then addresses the third party. Even if Levinas might take steps to evade this, there is still a suggestion of some mode of relation to the other outside of the political, which might later guide the political. Yet Derrida insists that this third friend or brother needs to be thought at the same time as this couple. In this, therefore, we can begin to see not only an engagement with Levinas's framework, but a critique of it. This recalls Derrida's previous critique of the lack of prominence of the *tiers* in *Totality and Infinity*. Importantly though, Derrida does not limit his argument around fraternity to that text alone, but includes citations also from *Otherwise than Being*, suggesting that there still remains a suggestion of the privilege of the face-to-face over the third party.

Indeed, this problem of the chronology of the third party or friend, relative to the face-to-face or couple, appears to be carefully and consistently stressed by Derrida throughout *Politics of Friendship*. In discussing the secret in Kant, he states: 'It supposes in any case that the third-party, *qua friend*, as reliable and as equal as the other two, is *already* around' (259);[12] or, similarly, returning to the epigraph of this chapter which speaks of Levinas as 'a third reliable friend [. . .] already in fact being there from the very beginning' (293).[13] This repetition of the 'already' is crucial in light of the importance of this chronology, not only in Derrida's previous readings of Levinas, but also in his overall reading of friendship and the couple. If Levinas's work is not a prominent reference in *Politics of Friendship*, therefore, this does not suggest that it is not implicitly engaged with throughout the text. Indeed, not only does this Levinasian framework structure much of Derrida's reading of the couple, but *Politics of Friendship* also marks a significant departure from it.

Derrida's approach, therefore, presents Levinas as one of several thinkers who prioritise the ethical or apolitical couple as the ground for friendship, but who also seek to later move this to a ground of the political. Yet, Derrida's objection then is to the assumption of a prior apolitical and pure engagement with singularity which the couple – but we can now see also the *face-à-face* – as a model of friendship assumes. While Levinas, Kant and others acknowledge that society or the third party comes to interrupt this moment, this is not without a nostalgia for a prior singular relation, like Montaigne who continues 'to dream of a fundamental apoliticism or transpoliticism' (184). This 'interruption', therefore, becomes an undesirable afterthought or secondary event, rather than, as Derrida insists, *already there*.

Yet where is 'there'? This captures the interruptive *topos* that Derrida seeks to expose in *Politics of Friendship*, this 'strange *atopia* of the friend', which never has 'a place of his own [*un lieu propre*]' (177/8). A truly interruptive friendship, one which takes account of the politics of *le tiers* and indeed the true alterity of the infinite number of other friends, would have to think about this separation as the site of friendship. Unlike Montaigne's couple, who took the site of friendship to be the unified and indivisible shared soul, the site of the friendship that Derrida seeks to elaborate looks instead to the interruptive *tiers*.[14] It is in this friendship that we find Derrida's answer to the question, 'How can a politics of separation be founded?' (55).

Politics in Friendship

Though Levinas may at first appear absent in *Politics of Friendship*, we can see that his work is engaged throughout this dense volume. This is taken as an implicit structure, one which Derrida uses to exhibit the *double bind* at work in thinkers like Montaigne and Kant, but in so doing also demonstrates the limits of this structure. This can help us see that what is at stake in Derrida's text is not simply brotherhood, but the model of the couple or pair of brothers. In Montaigne and Kant, but we can now also see in Levinas, this is taken as a form of singularity or unity to which the third friend only arrives late. This unity carries with it a form of relation to others that would transcend the political and allow for a pure engagement with singularity, on which a politics can *later* be built. Approaching *Politics of Friendship* through the perspective of the couple, we can see that Derrida's insistent aim is to reject this. His reading maintains that there is always an inescapable politics to friendship and our relation to singularity. It is that commitment to the irreducible and unavoidable politics which offers the potential for a new *politics* of friendship: one which acknowledges that there is no neutral site from which to conceive of politics, no anti-political moment to begin with, and no apolitical ways to care for and relate to others.

Notes

1. For my friend Connla Ó Dúláine – *ní bheidh a leithéid aríst ann.* I am grateful to Emily Fitzell for her generous and insightful comments on earlier stages of this work. This work was financially supported by The Bill & Melinda Gates Foundation via The Gates Cambridge Trust (Grant Number: OPP1144). Jacques Derrida, *Politics of Friendship*, trans. George Collins (London: Verso, 1997); Jacques Derrida, *Politiques de*

l'amitié: suivi de L'Oreille de Heidegger (Paris: Galilée, 1994). Hereafter, page references to the English translation are given in parenthesis in the text (*PF*). Translations modified.

2. The French for third wheel is *tenir la chandelle*, to hold the candle.
3. Throughout this chapter I have used the term 'couple' to describe what Derrida at times references as a 'pair' and at times a 'couple'. This is not to elide the different potential meanings around them, but to highlight the main focus of my attention here: the relationship between *two* (male) friends as between self and other. Of course, one important resonance of such a 'couple' that is only lightly explored in *Politics of Friendship* is a romantic homosexual couple. As we will see, this is tied closely to Montaigne's dismissal of marriage as having an 'imaginary resemblance' to the 'holy bond' of '[male] friendship' (180).
4. Michel de Montaigne, *The Complete Essays of Montaigne*, trans. Donald M. Frame (Stanford: Stanford University Press, 1958), p. 141.
5. Montaigne, *The Complete Essays of Montaigne*, p. 141.
6. My emphasis.
7. Jacques Derrida, 'Violence and Metaphysics', in *Writing and Difference*, trans. Alan Bass (Chicago: University of Chicago Press, 1978), pp. 79–153; Emmanuel Levinas, *Otherwise than Being or Beyond Essence*, trans. Alphonso Lingis (The Hague: Martinus Nijhoff, 1981); Emmanuel Levinas, *Totality and Infinity*, trans. Alphonso Lingis (Pittsburgh: Duquesne University Press, 1969).
8. Jacques Derrida, *Adieu to Emmanuel Levinas*, trans. Pascale-Anne Brault and Michael Naas (Stanford: Stanford University Press, 1999).
9. Derrida, *Adieu*, p. 67.
10. Levinas, *Totality and Infinity*, p. 278; Levinas, *Otherwise than Being*, p. 166.
11. Derrida, *Adieu*, p. 144.
12. My emphasis.
13. My emphasis.
14. I have considered the site of such a politics in relation to Derrida's own political engagements elsewhere. See Cillian Ó Fathaigh, 'Critical Institutions: Alternative Modes of Institutionalisation in Derrida's Engagements', *Derrida Today*, 14.2 (2021). This chapter forms part of the activities for the research projects: (1) "Differential Ontology and the Politics of Reason," funded by the Regional Government of Madrid; and (2) "The Politics of Reason" (PID2020-117386GA-I00).

4

Beyond Presence: Derrida's Fidelity to Husserl in *Politics of Friendship*

Giovanni Menegalle

Husserl occupies a unique place in the development of Derrida's thought. As commentators on Derrida's early writings have noted, this role is neither accidental nor accessory.[1] His position as it emerged in his mature publications of 1967 – in particular, his notions of trace and *différance* – was not just formulated within the medium of Husserlian phenomenology but presupposes many of its key principles. In *Of Grammatology*, for example, one finds him insisting that '*a thought of the trace can no more break with a transcendental phenomenology than be reduced to it*'.[2] In later interviews, he confirms this decisive albeit complicated role of phenomenology.[3] While marking Heidegger as an important influence, Derrida situates his formative works within a rationalist and epistemologically oriented form of phenomenology, which, starting in the 1950s, drew on Husserl's thinking on science and ideality in reaction to the humanist existentialism of figures such as Sartre. '[F]rom that point on,' he observes, 'I dedicated myself to the Husserlian discipline, to which I have always remained faithful' (*fidèle*).[4] He became, in his own words, its 'disciplined disciple' (*disciple discipliné*).[5]

This engagement began with his thesis of 1953–4, *The Problem of Genesis in Husserl's Philosophy*, informed by Husserl's later unpublished writings held at Louvain.[6] In 1956 he attended the International Colloquium on Phenomenology in Krefeld and in 1959, following his return from military service in Algeria, presented his first paper, '"Genesis and Structure" and Phenomenology', at Cerisy-la-Salle, later republished in *Writing and Difference* (1967). The year 1962 saw the publication of his translation and accompanying commentary of Husserl's *Origin of Geometry*, for which he was awarded the Prix Cavaillès. Before then he had also been working on a translation of Husserl's *The Crisis of the European Sciences* at Merleau-Ponty's behest until the latter's death brought the project and their correspondence to an end.[7] This engagement culminated in the late 1960s with two further articles on Husserl, in 1966 and 1967, and the publication of *Voice and Phenomenon* in 1967, drawing on courses and texts produced in the years 1965 and 1966 for the preparation of ENS students for the *agrégration* programme on Husserl's *Formal and Transcendental Logic*.[8] During this period, all of Derrida's book reviews published in philosophical journals are of phenomenological works. In the following decade, Derrida withdrew from this 'disciplined' engagement, but its continuing impact can be discerned into his later writings. What then is the nature of Derrida's 'fidelity' to Husserl in *Politics of Friendship* and what are its implications for a grasp of its political dimension?

In 1990, a year after Derrida's original seminar on *Politics of Friendship*, his thesis on the problem of genesis was finally published. In the 1953–4 preface, he asserts that to recognise the impossibility of securing an atemporal foundation for philosophy 'allows us [. . .] to remain faithful [*fidèles*] to Husserl in his reference to an originary absolute'.[9] As the thesis argues, Husserl himself affirms the temporally finite character of experience (consisting in passive synthesis or 'genesis') in a way that contradicts his tendency to hypostatise the intuition of ideal forms. In the 1990 preface, Derrida adds that – despite its totalising ambitions and use of terms such as 'dialectic' – this first text articulates 'an inaugural divergence that no analysis could *present, make present* in its phenomenon or reduce to the point like nature of the element, instantaneous and identical to itself'.[10] This is also the question at the heart of *Politics of Friendship*.

If in his early work Derrida had sought to show how exposure to the otherness of time undermines the identity of the present/presence, Derrida now emphasised the ethical and political consequences of this lack of atemporal or omnitemporal foundations. 'The question "What is friendship?",' he declares, 'is nothing but the question "What is philosophy?"' (*PF*, 240).[11] Throughout the Western tradition, friendship and philosophy are found to share in 'this value of *presence*' or 'the truth of *proximity*' (240). This is because the problem of how to identify the friend, as well as the enemy, emerges as an example of the question of the possibility of a knowledge of essence (*eidos*). Recalling a point made in the essay 'The Ends of Man' (1968) – later the theme of a conference on the political dimension of Derrida's thought organised by Jean-Luc Nancy and Philippe Lacoue-Labarthe in 1980 – the question of the foundations of philosophy as a universal discourse is co-essential with that of politics or the political conceived as an act of judgement or decision upon the essence of the other and time (146, 240).[12]

Derrida's aim in *Politics of Friendship* is thus to argue for the impossibility of this ideal of presence upon which both philosophy and the political would be founded. He calls for a 'principle of a possible resistance to the reduction of the political, even the ethical, to the ontophenomenological,' identifying Husserl's notion of the 'living present' as paradigmatic of this gesture of reduction (6, xi). To liberate politics from 'the *schematic* of filiation' – such as those of brotherhood, fraternity, kinship and race that seek to bind or institute individual and collective identities in essentialist or exclusive terms – it is necessary to think a form of finite relation that does not disavow temporal otherness or difference. The 'truth of friendship', as much as the 'truth of the political', must instead lie in what '*disjoins* the presence of the present' and in what marks 'the passage between two absolutely heterogenous orders' (14–16). Such a passage, which, as he says, is also a kind of disjuncture, applies both to the other and to time. The other vacillates between the appearance of its singularity (a who) and a knowledge of its essence (a what); while time – in a way that is perhaps more fundamental and which conditions our relation to an other in general – is torn between the finite time of experience and the omnitemporal mode of an ideal present (17). As Derrida states in *Voice and Phenomenon* (1967), 'what connects these two decisive moments [of the other and time] together' is the 'non-presence of the living present, a non-belonging of the living present to itself'.[13] This is the paradoxical '*contretemps*', invoked at the very start of *Politics of Friendship*, of the impossible address to the friend, in which 'two times' or 'two *moments*' would 'appear together,' be 'summoned to appear, in the present' (1).

The analysis of Aristotle that follows is underwritten by these themes. Aristotle's notion of 'primary friendship' (*prōtē philia*) – the idea of friendship based on virtue rather than mere pleasure or utility – is presented as an example of the problem of the possibility of a knowledge of essence (*eidos*), which 'is first accessible on the side of its subject' (10). The subject's epistemic primacy means that the essential feature of friendship turns out to be a kind of unilateral knowledge. One can be certain of one's own love for the other, but not of the other's in return. The former defines friendship in its essential form, while the latter can only be accidental to it. Yet, given this phenomenological closure, how can one secure confidence in the other as a true friend? The problem is that knowledge of the other, as much as of oneself in relation to the other, is at once conditioned and threatened by what challenges the subject's stability and identity from within, namely, otherness in its most radical and irreducible form: time. Aristotle's concept of mind (*psykhē*), Derrida claims, is a 'unifying feature' which 'binds together two times in the same time, a duration and an omnitemporality at the same time' (16). Without this unity in and of *psykhē*, the identities upon which our knowledge depends for its intelligibility and universality escape our finite grasp. What 'we have here,' Derrida suggests, is 'the whole story of *eidos* all the way up to the Husserlian interpretation of the idealization or production of ideal objects as the production of omnitemporality' (16–17).

The choice of Aristotle here is not coincidental. Husserl had developed his account of the subjective constitution of ideal objects upon a revision of Brentano's concept of intentionality or object-directed consciousness. Brentano had borrowed the term from scholastic philosophy and cited Aristotle's theory of perception as foreshadowing the idea of what he called the 'in-existence' of mental phenomena.[14] The notion that 'the sensed object, as such, is in the sensing subject' and not a material thing was adapted from Aristotle, who in *De Anima* claims that 'the stone is not in the soul, but its form'.[15] For Husserl, this irreality is redoubled on the side of the subject. Through the act of reduction or *epokhē*, the sense (*Sinn*) of phenomena as underpinned by their form (*noēma*) comes to constitute no longer a psychological but a transcendental condition of knowledge.[16] On this score, Derrida follows the phenomenologist Aron Gurwitsch, whose interpretation of Husserl was dominant in post-war France. This reading seems to have lent some support to the thesis of a metaphysics of presence by linking the objectivity of phenomena to the immanent contents of intuition. As distinct from both the real object and conscious acts, Gurwitsch identifies the *noēma* with an ideal totality or infinity of finite adumbrations of the same intentional object across time. It represents 'an irreal or ideal entity' conferring sense upon a manifold of intuition.[17] As Derrida puts it in his 'Introduction' to the *Origin of Geometry* (1962), the *noēma*'s irreality 'permits the repetition of "sense" and makes the idealization of identity in general possible'.[18]

Derrida's analysis of Schmitt echoes this language. Through his definition of the political, we are told, Schmitt constructs a concept of the enemy 'in synthetic a priori fashion' following 'some sort of phenomenological procedure' and 'what resembles at least an eidetic reduction,' whereby non-essential 'regional' determinations such as economic, psychological or moral factors are suspended to obtain 'the ideality of the political' (87, 114). Schmitt employs a vocabulary of presence, life, intensity and concreteness to suggest an immanent encounter or direct confrontation with the other, in which the enemy is identified in its 'real actuality/effectivity or real possibility' (*die reale Wirklichkeit oder Möglichkeit*) (113). However, in contrast to the Aristotelian distinction between possibility and actuality – which seems to guard against this quasi-positivistic political metaphysics – Schmitt's notion of a 'real possibility' of conflict acts to force an extreme virtuality into the present as 'a fact from which an essence can be read' (124, 131). 'We have just referred to phenomenology (and it is indeed a matter of a phenomenology of the friend as well as of the enemy),' Derrida notes, 'because at stake is indeed "the phenomenon of the political", as Schmitt himself says, and the sense of this phenomenon, the presentation of its presence after the eidetic reduction of everything it is not; but also what is at stake in the same stroke is indeed a phenomenalization as revelation, manifestation, unveiling' (131). This desire to grasp the identity of the other within an immanent presentation constitutes an example of what Derrida here denounces as the ontophenomenological 'subjection of the *who* to the *what*' (6).

Nevertheless, what makes any philosophical decision or judgement on the other inherently political (and vice versa) is that it entails an ungrounded positing within time of an essence (*eidos*) that is in some sense outside time. Derrida does not deny this necessity. The problem, he recognises, is that it 'takes time to reach a stability or a certainty which wrenches itself from time,' that it 'takes time to do without time' (17). On one reading, which I pursue here, Derrida goes along with the notion that the sense of phenomena is constituted (in a manner of speaking) outside time because it is not given directly within the present/presence of intuition. Rather, it rests on the irreal (*irreell*) horizon of the *noēma*, at once included in consciousness as part of the structure of intentionality and transcendent of the immanent contents of experience. Metaphysics – in the pejorative sense in which Derrida employs the term – erases this difference by recasting these conditions as real (*reell*) entities, either as positive properties of the world or as Platonic forms behind appearances. How a politics can emerge that acknowledges this phenomenological condition, while resisting, as Derrida also desires, a reduction of the political to a metaphysics of presence is a fundamental difficulty that remains to be specified.

To decide on or for the other, for others or on their behalf, on or for a possible future, is to go beyond or even against the immediacy of experience, outside the time of the present, without ever transcending the time of experience as such. A look back at Derrida's early phenomenological thought, however, suggests that a politics of friendship must exceed a mere affirmation of finitude and an ungrounding of philosophy in its metaphysical disposition to presence. Just as important is the way this critical orientation – which, it should be clear by now, is both philosophical and political – is structured by a certain demand for the infinite. As Derrida goes on to suggest, 'the philosophical horizon of *philía* [. . .] carries in its determination, in the very form of its finity *qua* horizon, the potential but inexorable injunction of its infinitization' (233). Such a statement can only be understood in the context of its implied Husserlian background, such as Derrida's observation, in the 'Introduction' to the *Origin of Geometry*, that phenomenology is always '*stretched* between the *finitist* consciousness of its *principle* and the *infinitist* consciousness of its final *foundation*'.[19]

At issue in Derrida's critique of phenomenological presence is not a straightforward rejection of intuition but a reversal of the metaphysical priority of presentation (*Gegenwärtigung*), associated with the plenitude of the living present (*lebendige Gegenwärt*), over re-presentation (*Vergegenwärtigung*). According to Derrida's analysis, whether it is a case of conceiving of an object or meaning as being the same across time, or the same as one intended by another subject, or of conceiving of oneself as the identical intending subject of the same object or meaning (thereby intending oneself as an object), these synthetic acts of correlation rest on discontinuous re-presentations that break with the supposed underlying unity of the living present. Derrida and Husserl agree that this discontinuity applies to re-presentations of the other's intentions and the reactivation of one's past intentions through recollection (secondary retention).[20] In *Cartesian Meditations*, for example, Husserl proposes that within phenomenological reflection the sense of the other's ego is revealed as transcendent and secondary to one's own. This in turn shows that, since there can be no immediate presentation of the other's consciousness, the latter is reconstructed via imaginary 'mirroring' procedures of 'analogical apperception', which serve to correlate particular contents (such as speech-sounds or gestures) to the idea of another ego founded on one's own sense of self.[21] The other, for Husserl, is precisely not experienced as an object but as an inaccessible other subject. Derrida reiterates this point in *Politics of Friendship*. He comments that, 'as the phenomenologist says, what is proper to the alter *ego* will never be accessible, *as such*, to an originary bestowing intuition, but only to an analogical appresentation,' and that 'the other appears as a being whose appearance appears without appearing, without being submitted to the phenomenological law of the originary and intuitive given that governs all other appearances, all other phenomenality *as such*' (54, 232).

Nevertheless, Derrida departs from Husserl by taking such discontinuity to apply to all synthetic acts, including notably the subject's own temporal self-apprehension. To grasp this difference, it is essential to return to Husserl's account of the temporal continuity of the living present. As in the example of hearing a melody or observing a physical movement, perception of duration presupposes an extension of the present moment between the (primary) retention of a just-been and the protention of an about-to-be.[22] For Husserl, only recollection proper (secondary retention) is temporally discontinuous because it involves the reactivation of a past memory. In

Voice and Phenomenon, however, Derrida proceeds to radicalise and finally overturn this distinction. He starts by affirming what Husserl himself recognises, namely, that the punctual now (primary impression) of duration is a formal limit-concept and that there are no immanent boundaries between the present and its retentive and protentive extensions.[23] Against Husserl, he then rejects the idea that primary retention constitutes a modification of the present, given the latter's purely formal identity. On this basis, he goes on to collapse the difference between primary and secondary retention. Though he acknowledges descriptive differences between these two modes, he denies that they are of ultimate epistemological value. As a result, the form of direct presentation in intuition privileged by phenomenology as its founding 'principle of principles' turns out to be a mode of re-presentation.[24]

In his writings on time-consciousness, Husserl concedes that the temporal character of perception must extend to all intentional acts and that consequently any attempt to secure an ideal atemporal foundation leads to an infinite regress.[25] But he attempts to stem this regress by appealing to a concept of pure temporality in which consciousness would apprehend itself in a moment of self-presentation (*Selbstgegenwärtigung*). More generally, Husserl appeals to a Kantian infinite Idea to regulate the process of idealisation. In fact, for Husserl, the ideal unity of temporal experience constitutes a special and privileged case of the infinite Idea. It is on this exception that Derrida's interpretation turns.[26] An infinite Idea – such as that of the world as infinite totality – can never be the object of a finite intuition. It may be a necessary horizon in constituting the objectivity of our perceptions, but it can never appear as such. As Gurwitsch argues, the *noēma* itself takes the form of an infinite Idea, 'the very idea of an infinite system or continuum of appearances all realised in actual sense-experience'.[27] In the case of temporal experience, the unity of time is also a vanishing limit that escapes direct presentation. Yet, according to Husserl, this infinity can be seized within the continuum of the living present according to an evidence 'completely different from the one that obtains for the being of experiences, i.e., those that come to be purely given in immanent perception'.[28] It is the Idea of infinity that is grasped, not infinity itself. Not given in an intuition, this Idea is contingently 'motivated' and freely assumed from the standpoint of a finite intentionality as the necessary horizon of the indefinite progression of differentiated temporal experience.[29]

There are times in his early works where Derrida aligns his own thinking to the horizon of a purely regulative un-intuitable Idea of indefinite determinability.[30] Declaring in the closing pages of *Voice and Phenomenon* that the 'appearing of infinite *différance* is itself finite,' Derrida appears to follow Husserl's account.[31] Derrida is deeply sceptical of the privileged status Husserl confers upon this concept through its association with the purported continuity of the living present. However, he embraces the notion that its grasp consists in an intention without presence. As he had already remarked in his thesis, '[t]his totality remains formal and the intuition that claims to aim at it cannot be "fulfilled" by an originary presence'.[32] It does not prescribe a rational principle of unity for experience; rather, in its very non-automaticity, it constitutes a form of ungrounded rationality that is both theoretical and practical. In his 'Introduction' to Husserl's *Origin of Geometry*, Derrida also refers to Husserl's later unpublished manuscripts where the Kantian infinite Idea is associated with the notion of God to designate an infinite principle of Reason. If conceived non-metaphysically, this infinite principle 'would be only the indefinite *openness* to truth and to phenomenality for a subjectivity that is always finite in its factual being'.[33] In 'Violence and Metaphysics', he makes a similar point, suggesting that 'the infinity of the Husserlian horizon has the form of an indefinite opening' which resists rather than asserts the totalising force of presence.[34]

In *Politics of Friendship*, Derrida highlights this relation between the finite and the infinite which 'implicitly organizes all reflection on the possibility of a politics of friendship' (19). It is embodied not only in the relative notion that true friendship, according to Aristotle, must be limited in quantity since a 'finite being could not possibly be present *in act* to too great a number,' but also in the more absolute 'proposition according to which there could never be (primary) friendship between God and man' (21, 19). Friendship with God is impossible because of the radical separation that this relation to an infinity would involve.[35] This distance is so absolute that no common measure could emerge by which the other could be recognised or made present in their essence (222–3). Although one may wish a friend to be like a god – to possess an infinity of that which makes them a true friend – this hyperbolic *telos* of friendship can only be realised at the cost of an absolute disproportion exceeding all relation. Nonetheless, it is this infinitising demand that constitutes the formal condition of true friendship as well as its phenomenological impossibility.

As mortal beings, this infinite or, better, indefinite openness constitutes the condition of our relation to an other in general (224). This relation is never given, but must be claimed, each time anew, beyond the immediacy of the present and without metaphysical guarantees. Friendship can never be a 'present given' or be 'satisfied with what is' (236). The problem of deciding upon the identity of the other – as friend or as enemy – lies in the fact that such an other must both refer to a singularity (a who) and constitute itself as an iterable essence (a what) (215–16). This is the aporia 'at the very heart of friendship' (277). In its singular otherness, the other resists automatic recognition under a universal law. Schemas of fraternity, filiality or community seek to circumvent this aporia by means of a sensible sign or quality, which serves to graft or bind the generality of an essence onto the presence of a singular instance (277). Here one can think of the marks of gender and race as purported expressions of an interior essence which determines membership of a particular category or group. The same can be found in our attitude to time, through whose traces, through memory and the imagination, we seek to make present a particular history or destiny. To think of friendship beyond fraternity requires an escape from this logic. Derrida defines an aporetic relation to a horizon of infinitisation as the 'heteronomic and dissymmetrical curving of a law of originary sociability' (213). This would constitute the fundamental condition of a 'democracy to come' in which a principle such as equality no longer requires the presence of a mark of identity (232). It would instead take the form of a 'motivated infinity' whose idea can already be found in his early reading of Husserl.

Notes

1. Edward Baring, *The Young Derrida and French Philosophy*, 1945–1968 (Cambridge: Cambridge University Press, 2011), p. 82; Martin Hägglund, *Radical Atheism: Derrida and the Time of Life* (Stanford: Stanford University Press, 2008), p. 52; Christina Howells, *Derrida: Deconstruction from Phenomenology to Ethics* (Cambridge: Polity, 1998), p. 6; Joshua Kates, *Essential History: Jacques Derrida and the Development of Deconstruction* (Evanston: Northwestern University Press, 2005), p. xvi; Leonard Lawlor, *Derrida and Husserl: The Basic Problem of Phenomenology* (Indianapolis: Indiana University Press, 2002), p. 3; Paola Marrati, *Genesis and Trace: Derrida Reading Husserl and Heidegger* (Stanford: Stanford University Press, 2005), p. xiv; Dermot Moran, *Introduction to Phenomenology* (London: Routledge, 2000), pp. 436–7.
2. Jacques Derrida, *Of Grammatology*, trans. Gayatri Chakravorty Spivak (Baltimore: Johns Hopkins University Press, 1997), p. 62, emphasis original.
3. Jacques Derrida, 'Punctuations: The Time of a Thesis', trans. Kathleen McLaughlin, in Derrida, *Eyes of the University: Right to Philosophy 2* (Stanford: Stanford University Press, 2004), pp. 113–28 (pp. 116–17); Dominique Janicaud, 'Jacques Derrida: Interviews of July 1 and November 22, 1999', in Janicaud, *Heidegger in France*, trans. François

Raffoul and David Pettigrew (Bloomington: Indiana University Press, 2015), pp. 337–63 (pp. 339–41).

4. Janicaud, 'Jacques Derrida', p. 341.
5. Ibid. p. 341.
6. Derrida Papers: Subseries 1.3. Work on Husserl, 1953–1957 2: 26–30, Notes de travail fait à Louvain, Husserl Archives.
7. Moran, *Introduction to Phenomenology*, pp. 438, 516n9. Typed drafts of the translation are held at the Derrida archives at UC Irvine.
8. Baring, *The Young Derrida*, pp. 239–43.
9. Jacques Derrida, *The Problem of Genesis in Husserl's Philosophy*, trans. Marian Hobson (Chicago: University of Chicago Press, 2003), p. xx.
10. Derrida, *The Problem of Genesis*, p. xv.
11. Jacques Derrida, *Politics of Friendship*, trans. George Collins (London: Verso, 1997); Jacques Derrida, *Politiques de l'amitié: suivi de L'Oreille de Heidegger* (Paris: Galilée, 1994). Hereafter, page references to the English translation are given in parenthesis in the text (*PF*).
12. Jacques Derrida, *Margins of Philosophy*, trans. Alan Bass (Brighton: Harvester Press, 1982), p. 111. Cf. Philippe Lacoue-Labarthe and Jean-Luc Nancy (eds), *Les Fins de l'homme: À partir du travail de Jacques Derrida* (Paris: Galilée, 1981).
13. Jacques Derrida, *Voice and Phenomenon: Introduction to the Problem of the Sign in Husserl's Phenomenology*, trans. Leonard Lawlor (Evanston: Northwestern University Press, 2011), p. 6.
14. Franz Brentano, *Psychology from an Empirical Standpoint*, trans. Antos C. Rancurello, D. B. Terrell and Linda L. McAlister (London: Routledge, 1995), p. 88n.
15. Ibid. p. 88; Aristotle, *De Anima*, trans. Christopher Shields (Oxford: Clarendon Press, 2016), 432a, p. 65.
16. Edmund Husserl, *Ideas for a Pure Phenomenology and Phenomenological Philosophy, First Book: General Introduction to Pure Phenomenology*, trans. Daniel O. Dahlstrom (Indianapolis: Hackett, 2014), § 85, pp. 167–8. See Burt C. Hopkins, *The Philosophy of Husserl* (Durham: Acumen, 2011), p. 84.
17. Aron Gurwitsch, 'On the Intentionality of Consciousness', in *The Collected Works of Aron Gurwitsch (1901–1973), Vol II: Studies in Phenomenology and Psychology*, ed. F. Kersten (Dordrecht: Springer, 2009), pp. 139–56 (p. 149).
18. Jacques Derrida, *Edmund Husserl's* Origin of Geometry: *An Introduction*, trans. John P. Leavey, Jr. (Lincoln: University of Nebraska Press, 1989), pp. 66–7n61. Cf. also *Specters of Marx*, trans. Peggy Kamuf (London:

Routledge, 2006), pp. 237–38n6, where Derrida associates the notion of spectrality with the 'intentional but *non-real* [*non-réelle*] component of the phenomenological lived experience, namely, the *noema*'.

19. Derrida, *Edmund Husserl's* Origin of Geometry, p. 138 [translation adapted].
20. Another example of this discontinuity would be the expectation of a future in phantasy as distinct from protention, which for Husserl remains an extension of the present. Derrida does not devote much space to this.
21. Edmund Husserl, *Cartesian Meditations: An Introduction to Phenomenology*, trans. Dorion Cairns (The Hague: Martinus Nijhoff, 1960), pp. 94, 108–11. See also Edmund Husserl, *Logical Investigations, Volume 1*, trans. J. N. Findlay (London: Routledge, 2008), Investigation I, § 7, pp. 189–90.
22. Dermot Moran, *Husserl: Founder of Phenomenology* (Cambridge: Polity, 2005), pp. 139–44.
23. Edmund Husserl, *On the Phenomenology of the Consciousness of Internal Time (1893–1917)*, trans. John Barnett Brough (Dordrecht: Kluwer, 1991), p. 42.
24. Derrida, *Voice and Phenomenon*, pp. 38–9n, 72n.
25. Husserl, *On the Phenomenology of the Consciousness of Internal Time*, p. 123.
26. Derrida, *Voice and Phenomenon*, pp. 8, 86–7.
27. Aron Gurwitsch, *The Field of Consciousness* (Pittsburgh: Duquesne University Press, 1964), p. 227.
28. Husserl, *Ideas*, § 83, p. 160.
29. Ibid. § 143, p. 285.
30. Derrida, *Edmund Husserl's* Origin of Geometry, pp. 138–40.
31. Derrida, *Voice and Phenomenon*, p. 87. On this question, cf. Marian Hobson, *Jacques Derrida: Opening Lines* (London: Routledge, 1998), pp. 49–50.
32. Derrida, *The Problem of Genesis*, p. 99.
33. Derrida, *Edmund Husserl's* Origin of Geometry, p. 148.
34. Derrida, *Writing and Difference*, trans. Alan Bass (Chicago: University of Chicago Press, 1978), p. 150.
35. Aristotle, *Nicomachean Ethics*, trans. Roger Crisp (Cambridge: Cambridge University Press, 2002), VIII, 7, 1159a, p. 152.

5

Hostility in Philosophy – Between Hegel and Heidegger

Susanna Lindberg

'The question "What is friendship?," but also "Who is the friend (both or either sex)?" is nothing but the question "What is philosophy?."'[1] Derrida associates the question of friendship to the question of philosophy itself at the outset of a reading of Heidegger's *Was ist das – die Philosophie?*, in which Derrida relates Heidegger's interpretation of Heraclitus's thinking of the love of wisdom, *philein* to *sophon*, to Heidegger's scarce remarks on friendship.[2] Heidegger would thus follow the ancient tradition which extends philosophy as love of wisdom to the entire community of those who love wisdom, bound together and bound to one another by the common cause, the most lovable thing, the truth of being.

But as Derrida shows more clearly in 'Heidegger's Ear: Philopolemology', published as part of the French edition of *Politics of Friendship*, Heidegger does not repeat such a tradition without attempting to deconstruct it profoundly.[3] Thus Heidegger wants to express a more originary loving, *philein*, that he translates by '*das Lieben*, loving, before any distinction between the loving of love and the loving of friendship, what in French, in a seminar I am devoting to these questions [*Politics of Friendship*], I call *aimance*'.[4] More originary than the *philia* and philosophy such as it was understood by Plato and Aristotle, *philein* is, according to Heidegger, first brought to words by Heraclitus, who strives to hear the *logos* of being itself, and to correspond to it in his speech, *legein*.[5] The love of wisdom thus depends on a more originary loving of being itself, which is not our love of being but being's love of us. To put it in modern terms, being is *loving* insofar as it *is*, rather than *not*; being is loving insofar as it is somehow *apparent*, if not downright *manifest* to us (but Heidegger would reject the Hegelian echo of the word *manifestation*).

As *logos* gathers the loving of being, the philosophers who love it are gathered together and brought to mutual love or friendship by their common love of the lovable. As Derrida also shows in his article,

> When Heidegger speaks of the saviours of '*phileîn*' that have taken responsibility for *lógos* and being, for the essential *Versammlung*, he says 'a few,' the small number of those that, as men or free subjects could make a choice about this, have taken on themselves such a responsibility, the responsibility of responsibility, the responsibility of corresponding in *Entsprechen* with being, *lógos*, and *phileîn*.[6]

No doubt these few are bound together by 'friendship for what is to be thought' even when it is to be won by hard struggle.[7] In *Introduction to Metaphysics*, Heidegger says that those who carry the responsibility of the *logos*, and who also endure the *polemos* for it, are the creators: 'The originary struggle is then carried on [*getragen*] by those that open (creators), poets, thinkers, statesmen' (in later texts, for obvious reasons, Heidegger will drop statesmen and only speak of the originary struggle of poets and thinkers).[8] So, a few exceptional persons are gathered together in a common combat through which they carry responsibility for the openness of being. It seems to me that Heidegger's interpretation of Hölderlin in 'Homecoming / To the Kindred Ones' actually suggests that these few might also give, if not the *logos* of being, at least the words of creation that answer to it, *legein*, to the entire *Dasein* of the people.[9] In any case, the common *logos* brings together those who have been touched by it. As Heidegger says in 'Hölderlin and the Essence of Poetry':

> We are a conversation [*Gespräch*], that always also signifies that we are *one* conversation. The unity of a conversation consists in the fact that in the essential word there is always manifest the one and the same on which we agree, on the basis of which we are united and so are authentically ourselves.[10]

The philosophical friends are brought together by the common cause, the loving of being. My question comes from the side: is Hegel such a friend of Heidegger's? Do they both love the one and the same although they disagree on it? Are they united by this love although they reject each other's ways of saying it?

Given that it is difficult to think that the truth of being would *not* be *fundamentally* one and the same, are friends of truth really friends with one another? It seems to me that the concord of philosophers in the fundamental tonality of being is not as evident as it may seem. As we shall see, it is not so for Heidegger, and Derrida's *Politics of Friendship* helps us see why it may not be so in philosophy in general. To put it in a nutshell, the loving of being as transcendental condition of philosophy might well be incompatible with the friendship of philosophers as existential and political condition of philosophising. The unfriendliness between philosophers would thus not be a mere empirical mishap due to contingent reasons. The discord and dispute between philosophers would be a necessary condition for approaching the violence of truth itself, an element of the 'absolute hostility [. . .] as the affair of philosophy, its very cause' (*PF*, 133). In this case, it may not be just anecdotic if even philosophers who seem to be close, like Foucault and Blanchot, or Derrida, Blanchot and Nancy, can only cultivate their friendship on the condition of a distance that must ultimately be analysed in terms of death, which marks the definitive separation. This is how, as Derrida points out, Blanchot says that, on the matter of friendship, he can declare his friendship to Foucault only after the death of the latter.[11] More gently, Derrida himself declares his admiration of Bataille's, Blanchot's and Nancy's works on 'friendship without friends' and on 'community of those without community' in *Politics of Friendship*, in which he declares his 'admiring friendship' to these friends at the same time as he proposes to turn against their 'brotherhood'.[12]

Let us now study the relation between love of truth and friendship of philosophers and see in a concrete case how these luminous forms of *philein* turn into the negativity of truth and hostility between philosophers. My example is the relation between two philosophers par excellence, Hegel and Heidegger. They do not exemplify the classical philosophical friendship first formulated in the city of Athens, because, although they seem to share a place, Germany, they do not share a time but are separated by history, and hence by death. But it seems to me that better than any friendship with contemporaneous colleagues, their conflictual 'friendship' over times exemplifies the particular kind of *aimance* and *aimantation*, loving and attraction, required by modern philosophy, such as its vocation is defined by them, as we shall see in a while. The particular philosophical relation between Hegel and Heidegger is not studied in *Politics of Friendship*, but in a general manner their debate and the necessity of thinking through both of them, although – and maybe *because* – they are *stricto sensu* incompatible, is primordial to Derrida who has made many readings of both. He studies their proximity and opposition explicitly in the brilliant lecture course from 1964 to 1965 published in 2013: *Heidegger: The Question of Being and History*.[13]

Politics of Friendship is above all a book about the *philia* that is constitutive of political communities.[14] For my part, I will now bracket the political *philia* and concentrate only on the *philia* that is constitutive of philosophy itself. 'Friendship *qua* philosophy, philosophy *qua* friendship, philosophical-friendship, friendship-philosophy, will always in the West have been a concept indissociable with itself: no friendship without some *philosophía*, no *philosophía* without *philía*.' (146).[15] Heidegger, Hegel and fundamentally all philosophers think that *philosophia* is love of wisdom and love of truth: interrogation of the highest truth of being, that Hegel thought to be ultimately intemporal and universal, and that Heidegger was maybe the first to think of as the gift of being tied to the gift of time. But none would think of philosophy as a projection of human desires, for example political agendas. The *philein* at the origin of philosophy is the supra-human or inhuman generosity of being itself.

Now unlike (presumably) the ancient philosophers, neither Hegel nor Heidegger think that this originary *philein* is simply given and present to the philosopher. *Philein* does not give itself without combat: being gives itself as nothingness, it manifests itself as negativity. As Derrida points out, Heidegger describes this negativity in many ways. On the one hand, it is the concealment or withdrawal (*kryptesthai*) of being expressed in Heraclitus's *physis kryptesthai philei*: the mode of being, *physis*, is concealment.[16] On the other hand, it is the struggle or the combat, *polemos*, that Heraclitus names the 'father of all things'.[17] *Polemos*, which Heidegger translates by *Auseinandersetzung*, *shows* beings and makes them *appear* as what they are:[18] this appearing takes place in *logos*, for '*polemos* and *logos* are the same'.[19]

Notwithstanding a very different conceptuality, Hegel is close to Heidegger in the comprehension of the manifestation of truth in terms of negativity. Surely Hegel wants to 'make philosophy lay aside the title of love of knowing and be actual knowing'.[20] In the language inherited from Christianity this means that the 'absolute is not jealous' but that it wants to manifest itself and 'be with us'. [21] This was already the originary Greek lesson of the mysteries of Eleusis: the true mystery of Eleusis was that there is no mystery, God was present and manifest. 'The mystical is neither the concealment of a secret, nor is it ignorance. Rather, it consists in the self-knowing itself to be at one with the essence and the essence therefore being revealed.'[22] Heidegger thinks that *physis* gives itself in *philein*; similarly, Hegel thinks that the absolute loves us because it manifests itself. In the same way, Hegel encourages us moderns to consider ourselves worthy of the highest truth. However, our situation is more complicated. We are still and more than ever worthy of the absolute, which is manifest to whoever is ready to encounter it, not by means of art and religion, but by means of philosophy, which is our destination. But our relation to the absolute is mediated by discursive negativity: first, of the history of philosophy, for we can only win our access to philosophy by a long stay at the 'shady realm of death' (*Schattenreich*) of concepts inherited from history, and second, of philosophy itself, whose truth is not present to intellectual intuition but only to discursive, dialectical *logos* that reveals truth only through negativity and contradiction.[23] Like Heidegger's *physis*, Hegel's absolute shows itself through a *polemos*.

As we already saw, Heidegger connects the truth of being to a few 'guardians' of this truth – poets and thinkers who can bear the polemo-logos of physis. Hegel, too, takes for granted that the philosopher does not work alone. No doubt, he is a teacher, but the school of philosophy in the Athenian style ties the students by love only to a master, not yet to truth itself. Philosophy rather progresses towards truth in dialogues with mature peers, such as the one between Fichte and Schelling that Hegel staged in *The Difference Between Fichte's and Schelling's Systems of Philosophy*, and such as the one between himself and Schelling implied in the introduction to *Phenomenology of Spirit*, even if the price of the dialogue was the definite breakup between former friends, like in the latter case. However, Hegel hardly thematises these philosophical encounters between friends; he left the theme of intellectual community to the Jena Romantics.[24] Instead, Hegel thematised the necessity of philosophical encounters in the history of philosophy. As Derrida underlines in *Heidegger: The Question of Being and History*, Hegel was the first to raise history of philosophy into an indispensable element of philosophy as such, as long as history of philosophy was not understood as a part of history but as a part of philosophy, that encounters past philosophers in debates and refutations (*Widerlegungen*).[25] Thus, the community of all philosophers of history, marked by the negativity of time, replaces the positivity of the present philosophical community described by Plato and Aristotle. History is marked by negativity, firstly of death: Hegel's repeated metaphor for the history of philosophy is the realm of shadows, the realm of Hades into which the Ulysses of philosophy descends in order to speak with the shadows of the dead. These dialogues are also occasions of a relative resurrection of past spirits, who are not entirely dead insofar as they still speak to us. But they are still not our contemporaries: a dead spirit, the spirit of a bygone time, speaks in their works, a spirit that we today need to contradict, refute and overcome. This is the process of the *Erinnerung* of the past (translated by Terry Pinkard as 'inwardizing recollection'): both an intense work with the *Gestalten* of past philosophy and the return to actuality enriched by past wisdom but no more burdened by it.[26] Only such labour with history will enable the 'birth of a new figure of spirit'.[27]

Heidegger, too, believes that the truth of being must be won by the *Destruktion* of the history of philosophy, which is, as Derrida tells us too, as close as possible to Hegelian refutations, and yet there is a displacement between the Hegelian refutation and the Heideggerian destruction.[28] Heidegger, too, practises his 'deconstruction' through polemical dialogues with past thinkers, such as Hegel, with whom he dialogues with an exceptional acrimony precisely because Hegel is probably the closest to his own philosophy, and therefore the greatest threat to his own identity as philosopher.[29] Underlining his respect for the 'greatness' of Hegel, Heidegger has made many different readings of Hegel, but the most characteristic of them are 'confrontations', *Auseinandersetzungen*, in which he actively distantiates himself from his rival. Like Hegel, Heidegger thus replaces *philia* with contemporaries by *polemos* with past philosophers; of course, such a *polemos* is a form of *philia*, but it is turned into its negative by the force of death and disagreement. This is how, in Hegel and in Heidegger, the antique luminous *philia* turns into a shadowy modern theory of *polemos*: *polemos* of being that refuses to show itself or that gives itself only by hard struggle; and *polemos* of the philosophical communities where philosophers are no more contemporaneous and present to one another, but separated by death and by length of history. As I have shown elsewhere, the 'friendship' between Hegel and Heidegger is an exemplary example of this situation: a historical dialogue on the sense of historical dialogue.[30]

Derrida has shown that the classical theory of friendship inherited from Aristotle relies on the values of presence and of proximity (240). In a vast deconstructive reading, he has shown how this presence is actually marked by death:

> One cannot love without living and without knowing that one loves, but one can still love the deceased or the inanimate who then know nothing of it. It is indeed through the possibility of loving the deceased that the decision in favour of a certain lovence (*aimance*) comes into being. (10)

What remains present in spite of death is survival, hence, '*philía* begins with the possibility of survival' (13). For me, the philosophical history of philosophy, here exemplified by the strange attraction and repulsion between Hegel and Heidegger, friendship over death turning into fundamental hostility, is an important illustration of this complicated structure.

I playfully called my earlier reading of Hegel and Heidegger a 'double deconstruction'. By this I meant that my aim was not only to present Heidegger's de(con)structive readings of Hegel but also, in return, a projection of what Hegel's deconstructive reading (rather than refutation) of Heidegger could be. With this aim I made Hegel answer to the Heideggerian question of finitude and Heidegger answer to the Hegelian question of recognition (*Anerkennung*). Now, could the deconstructive reading of Hegel and Heidegger, inspired by Derrida, bounce back upon Derrida? If the Derridean question 'of the *philopolemos*' helps to bring forth ignored features of the debate between Hegel and Heidegger (for instance, the role of affects like love and hate in philosophy), what kind of a question would these master philosophers address in return to Derrida, as if beyond death? After all, Derrida should not be surprised to see spectres of the dead return to him with insistent questions. Could Hegel's and Heidegger's spectral questions reveal abandoned margins and blind spots in Derrida's own work, in front of *our* eyes? What if precisely the question of philosophy as philopolemology, such as it *returns* from the debate between Hegel and Heidegger, turned out to be such a question? Derrida's best friends may find this question impertinent; but then again, Derrida himself has always liked the posture of a playfully insolent *voyou*, hasn't he?

I cannot really investigate such a file here: it is a question of deconstruction, and such questions require a lot of space to do the necessary textual work. But I can outline the abstract of such a possible investigation in view of a later work.

We saw that the theme of philopolemology that Derrida brought to light has two dimensions: the love of truth and the friendship of philosophers. The latter is easier. In the context of Hegel's and Heidegger's works, the friendship of philosophers took the form of history of philosophy. Now, history of philosophy is of course very important to Derrida, too: after all, his thinking develops through deconstructive readings of past (and present) philosophical (and other) texts, such as Hegel and Heidegger. *Heidegger: The Question of Being and History* testifies particularly well to his proximity to the debate between Hegel and Heidegger on the history of philosophy; one symptom of this proximity is Derrida's use of the word 'deconstruction', sometimes replaced by 'solicitation' and 'shaking', to translate Heidegger's '*Destruktion*'.[31] Only later Derrida will appropriate and redefine the word 'deconstruction' to his own use.

Of course, Derrida's 'deconstruction' is not the *same* as Hegel's 'inwardising recollection' (*Erinnerung*) and Heidegger's 'remembering' (*Andenken*) of past philosophers. Like Hegel and Heidegger, Derrida works by debating with past (and present mortal) thinkers. Like them, he refuses to write philosophy as simple history that reduces past thinkers to objects of study, and summons past masters as speaking, writing subjects of their own works. Like theirs, his readings are not consensual presentations of the most evident theses of the past masters but provocative debates that bring forth unnoticed fatal prejudices in their works. But Derrida's readings are neither refutations (*Widerlegungen*), nor conversations (*Gespräche*), nor confrontations (*Auseinandersetzungen*); they rather resemble the psychoanalytic way of driving out the unsaid, the unintentional, the unexpected. Also, while Hegel and Heidegger organise past thinkers into a singular history (unified by teleology of reason or by epochality of being), Derrida is looking for a community of philosophers without a gathering centre:

> The central question of this essay [*Politics of Friendship*] – and we have already seen why this 'question' comes 'before' the question – indeed, 'before' the affirmation that precedes it, from the moment of the *perhaps* that they both presuppose – would be that of a friendship without hearth, of a *philía* without *oikeiótes*. (154–5; cf. 296–9)

Derrida rather summons both historical and contemporaneous thinkers and writers around singular words and themes (writing, friendship) that need not arouse unanimity, even less cover all of history. Rather than a history or a genealogy, these thinkers form a virtual transhistorical community of spectrally present friends, or enemies (Derrida shows that one never goes without the other). Developing the thematics of *Specters of Marx* we could indeed say that Derrida encounters the other thinker or writer as a *spectre*: he (rarely she) is present only in his distance and absence; he may speak but he also emits massive silences that call to speak, to respond and to bear responsibility of the other's silence.[32] This is how many of Derrida's texts can be read as strong and provocative responses to, say, Heidegger's utterances and silences – rather than as direct affirmations of Derrida himself. It is rare that he would say: 'I, Jacques Derrida, affirm this . . .,' and much more common that he says: 'Aristotle says, but doesn't he also imply . . .' or 'Heidegger says, but doesn't he thereby end by saying also . . .'. This is not philosophy as commentary, this is responsive, responsible philosophy, that is also responsible for the possibility of a future, the dimension of which may be, in the Nietzschean manner, 'the Messiah, the thinker of the dangerous "perhaps"' (174), or more generally the messianicity without messianism explained in *Specters of Marx*.

It is more difficult to say how Derrida would respond to the first dimension of Hegel's and Heidegger's philopolemological provocation. Each in his own manner, Hegel and Heidegger aim at the *philopolemos* of the sense or the truth of being. In principle, this is what Derrida rejects most firmly, for the question of being is the very question that opens and lays ground to what from early on he has rejected as phallo-logo-centrism: the fixation of a master-logos. But isn't the question of being nonetheless much more than a fallen god, a question that deserves an answer or at least a responsible reading? Hasn't the apparent lack of such an answer exposed Derrida to endless hostile accusations of relativism, nihilism, mere literary scribbling? It seems to me that Derrida can very well block such accusations, only he does it with such a complex series of blows that many adversaries cannot really follow them (and friends cannot follow them in a small space). However, it is clear that, like Hegel and Heidegger, but more obviously than them, Derrida approaches the question of the *philopolemos* of being by elaborating on its *logos*. But his theory of *logos* is very different from Hegel's and Heidegger's. In *Politics of Friendship* he once suggests, actually like Heidegger in certain texts, that its *logos* would be that of the translation of the untranslatable (166).

But in most earlier works one can see Derrida principally *read* the *logos* of philosophy as *writing*, of which he underlines the absence of any originary *logos*. As trace, writing is not a name of the truth of being but of its impossibility; and this frustrates the commentator who can never fix the truth of being but only show the impossibility of such a definite truth. Derrida hardly uses the word 'truth'; it has a ring of impossibility, but at the same time, truth is for him in the order of impossibility, like the future which is not possible but which remains, precisely for this reason, still *to come*. Not the possibility that comes, but the maintaining-oneself-in-the-impossibility – or in the 'aporia of the *perhaps*' (67). This is not another name of the truth of being. But this is another way of bearing responsibility for the question of the truth of being even when it turns into disaster, a way that the philopolemological question may make audible.

Notes

1. Jacques Derrida, 'Heidegger's Ear: Philopolemologies', in *Reading Heidegger: Commemorations*, ed. John Sallis and trans. John P. Leavey Jr. (Bloomington: Indiana University Press, 1993), pp. 163–218 (p. 240).
2. 'The voice of the friend which every Dasein carries with it': Martin Heidegger, *Being and Time*, trans. John Macquarrie and Edward Robinson (Oxford: Basil Blackwell, 1985), § 34. On the reading of Hölderlin's 'But where are the friends?', see Martin Heidegger, *Elucidations of Hölderlin's Poetry*, trans. Keith Hoeller (London: Humanities Press, 2000), p. 108ff.; the reading of Trakl's 'Soul's Spring', in Martin Heidegger, *On the Way to Language*, trans. Peter D. Hertz (New York and San Francisco: Harper & Row, 1971), especially p. 191.
3. Jacques Derrida, *Politics of Friendship*, trans. George Collins (London: Verso, 1997); Jacques Derrida, *Politiques de l'amitié: suivi de L'Oreille*

de Heidegger (Paris: Galilée, 1994). Hereafter, page references to the English translation are given in parenthesis in the text (*PF*).

4. Derrida, 'Heidegger's Ear', p. 180.
5. Ibid. p. 181.
6. Ibid. p. 190.
7. Ibid. p. 386.
8. Ibid. p. 211.
9. Heidegger, *Elucidations of Hölderlin's Poetry*, pp. 47–9.
10. Ibid. p. 57.
11. Derrida, 'Heidegger's Ear', pp. 299–302.
12. Ibid. pp. 46–8n15.
13. Jacques Derrida, *Heidegger: The Question of Being and History*, trans. Geoffrey Bennington (Chicago and London: University of Chicago Press, 2016). The relation between Hegel and Heidegger was the subject of my doctoral dissertation on the 'double deconstruction' of Hegel by Heidegger and of Heidegger by Hegel. An abridged version has been published as Susanna Lindberg, *Heidegger contre Hegel: Les irréconciliables*, (Paris: L'Harmattan, 2010) and Susanna Lindberg, *Entre Heidegger et Hegel: L'éclosion et vie de l'être* (Paris: L'Harmattan, 2010), and a complete version is available at https://uta-fi.academia.edu/SusannaLindberg. Some elements of this work have been published in English in Susanna Lindberg, 'From Finite Thinking to Infinite Spirit: Hegel after Heidegger's Translation', in *Translating Hegel. The Phenomenology of Spirit and Modern Philosophy*, ed. Brian Maning Delaney and Sven-Olov Wallerstein (Huddinge: Södertörn University College Press, 2012), pp. 87–102; Susanna Lindberg, 'Reading against Hegel', in *Die Stile Martin Heideggers*, ed. Patrick Baur, Bernd Bösel and Dieter Mersch (Freiburg and Munich: Verlag Karl Alber / Alber Philosophie, 2013), pp. 96–111. That work was originally motivated by the desire to better understand Derrida, and Derrida's question of friendship was a great formal inspiration for it. Today, I am pleased to find this occasion for pointing at Derrida's role in that work, and for paying him homage by rereading *Politics of Friendship* in the light of questions originally inspired by it.
14. *Politics of Friendship* is a contribution to an important discussion on community that had first taken place between Nancy and Blanchot, the aim of which was to think existence as being-with (*être-avec*, which is Nancy's critical reformulation of Heidegger's *Mitsein*): Jean-Luc Nancy, *Being Singular Plural*, trans. Robert D. Richardson and Anne E. O'Byrne (Stanford: Stanford University Press, 2000), p. 26. Political theories

made by Hegel, but especially those formulated by Schmitt and implied by Heidegger – see also Jacques Derrida, *Of Spirit*, trans. Geoffrey Bennington and Rachel Bowlby (Chicago and London: Chicago University Press, 1989) – exemplify the totalitarian theories rejected by Nancy and Blanchot. Derrida salutes their work but he also introduces a critical angle to the discussion by showing how the interpretation of the originary 'with' as 'friendship' both reveals important aspects of its history as the history of *philia*, and deconstructs it, for friendship is in many ways rebellious to politics. By showing how friendship has generally been thought as fraternity, Derrida also points at the ambiguous exclusions hidden in *philia*, which overlooks women, and also other interpretations of *Geschlecht* (the other race, people, clan, tribe . . .).

15. Of course, this may suggest that philosophy is political and politicised – this doubt or conviction animates especially the debates concerning Heidegger, to which Derrida's texts are also a contribution. But this necessary interrogation should not hide the real motivation of philosophy.
16. Derrida, 'Heidegger's Ear', p. 193.
17. Ibid. pp. 196–7.
18. Martin Heidegger, 'Aletheia', in Heidegger, *Early Greek Thinking: The Dawn of Western Philosophy*, trans. David Farrell Krell and Frank Capuzzi (New York: HarperCollins, 1984), p. 119.
19. Derrida, 'Heidegger's Ear', p. 198.
20. Georg Wilhelm Friedrich Hegel, *The Phenomenology of Spirit*, trans. Terry Pinkard (Cambridge: Cambridge University Press, 2018), p. 6.
21. Robert R. Williams, *Tragedy, Recognition, and the Death of God: Studies in Hegel and Nietzsche* (Oxford: Oxford University Press, 2012), p. 377; as underlined in Martin Heidegger, *Off the Beaten Track*, trans. Julian Young and Kenneth Haynes (Cambridge: Cambridge University Press, 2002), p. 153.
22. Hegel, *The Phenomenology of Spirit*, p. 415.
23. Georg Wilhelm Friedrich Hegel, *The Science of Logic*, trans. George di Giovanni (Cambridge: Cambridge University Press, 2010), p. 37.
24. See the introduction of Philippe Lacoue-Labarthe and Jean-Luc Nancy, *The Literary Absolute: The Theory of Literature in German Romanticism*, trans. Philip Barnard and Cheryl Lester (Albany: SUNY Press, 1988).
25. Derrida, *Heidegger: The Question of Being and History*, p. 2ff.
26. Hegel, *The Phenomenology of Spirit*, p. 467.
27. Ibid. p. 9.
28. Derrida, *Heidegger: The Question of Being and History*, p. 9.
29. This is the 'stratagem of obliteration' by distancing the rival who

comes too close, described by Philippe Lacoue-Labarthe in a reading of Heidegger's readings of Nietzsche: 'Obliteration', in *The Subject of Philosophy*, trans. Thomas Trezise et al. (Minneapolis and London: University of Minnesota Press, 1993).

30. Lindberg, *Heidegger contre Hegel.*
31. Derrida, *Heidegger: The Question of Being and History*, pp. xviii–xix, 158.
32. Jacques Derrida, *Specters of Marx: The State of the Debt, the Work of Mourning and the New International*, trans. Peggy Kamuf (London: Routledge, 1994).

6

Responding Justly to 'the Friend'

Joseph Cohen and Raphael Zagury-Orly

Our reading will focus on a text absent from the English edition of *Politics of Friendship* (1997), which however appeared in the French *Politiques de l'amitié* (1994).[1] 'Heidegger's Ear: Philopolemology (*Geschlecht* IV)' appeared independently in an English translation as a book chapter in the edited volume entitled *Reading Heidegger: Commemorations*, published in 1993 – therefore, *before* the French edition, where it appears as the last chapter of *Politiques de l'amitié*, as well as *before* the English translation, where it was not reproduced.[2] As the title of Derrida's text indicates, it belongs to the series of *Geschlecht* essays and, in this sense, represents a further supplement to the French philosopher's long and rich, profound as well as critical, dialogue with Heidegger's philosophy.[3] Simple editorial reasons are most certainly the reason for the non-publication of 'Heidegger's Ear' in the English edition of *Politics of Friendship*. However, we find it necessary here to offer a reading and interpretation of this text and to show why Derrida returns yet again to Heidegger's philosophy in the context of the *politics of friendship*. Furthermore, we will demonstrate how and why Derrida radicalises in an unprecedented manner the deconstruction of the history of Being, and thus of the central motif at work in this 'historicity' (*Geschichtlichkeit*), which Heidegger marks and determines as 're-collection' (*Versammlung*).

Through the 'voice of the friend' – which, according to *Being and Time*, is carried within and by every *Dasein* – Derrida meticulously examines and undermines the major trait of the meaning of Being, namely *Versammlung*: that gathering and re-collecting essence which originally unifies and conciliates, assigns and engages in the truth of Being.[4] He does so by conducting nothing less than a deconstruction of the signifier of the gift and the *logos* of giving prevalent and primary in Heidegger's philosophy. In this sense, Derrida's reappraisal of Heidegger's thought deploys a unique critique which dismantles the foundational determination of this ontology and which affects all the domains it structures and signifies: the question of truth, of history, of justice, of politics.

Why speak of a unique critique? For Derrida refrains from asserting a counter-position or passing judgement against Heidegger. Rather, through a patient, rigorous and attentive reading of Heidegger's writing, he shows how and why it ultimately reveals its own confines and limitations, and therefore where and according to what trajectory it exhausts its own concepts, voids out the very distinctions it claims to present, and uses up the ideas it seeks to develop and rethink. Indeed, in 'Heidegger's Ear' Derrida exposes the entire breadth of the thought of Being whereby all is always brought back to one unique, determined essence and presence, the gift of an appropriating *Versammlung* from which the totality of what is present, the entirety of what is manifest in history and which calls upon our responsibility, always and already remains the *same*: the truth of Being.

The Derridean reading is *at least* double: as it exhibits the acuity, complexity, elasticity of Heidegger's philosophy to the point where it resolutely explicates the very question it seeks to develop – the truth of Being – it also shows how this explication always entails and involves unbeknownst perplexities and incessantly supposes insurmountable *aporias*. For Derrida, it is as though Heidegger's breakthrough in philosophical thinking foreclosed the very possibility of a *just* way of thinking about friendship, but also – and at the same time – of truth, history, justice and politics.[5] Indeed, Derrida demonstrates how the determination at work in Heidegger's ontology, its philosophical suppositions and effects, whereby a unique Greco-German structure can or may signify the meaning of thinking, leaves untouched the possibility of *responding justly to 'the friend'*. What remains of friendship in the already determined 'dispositive' of ontological thinking?[6] That is, what is left of the *singularity* of friendship – both its returning past and its future to come – if it is always brought back and appropriated in one, unified and comprehensive ontological gift emanating from an already signified and determined origin, language or event?

Derrida begins by firstly showing how and why the 'friend', for Heidegger, remains irreducible to any anthropological or psychological determination as such. The 'friend' is rather another *Dasein* which every *Dasein* carries 'with itself (*bei sich*)'. Without resorting to an autonomous decision or initiative, each *Dasein* carries 'the voice of the friend', which is not recognisable as a specific and definite gender, subject, figure, person, face or name.[7] In this ontological analysis, therefore, the 'voice of the friend' is irreducible to a present appearance or representation; rather, as a voice which every *Dasein* carries with itself, it is always the voice of *another Dasein* and ultimately voices Being itself, which already speaks and is heard in *all Daseins*. Following Heidegger's elliptical phrase in § 34 of *Being and Time* – a chapter where the 'existential analytic' deploys the first lineaments of the relation between *Dasein* and other *Daseins*, *Mitsein* and *Mitenandersein*, through the ontological analysis of 'hearing' and 'speaking' – Derrida shows how the 'voice of the friend' symbolises nothing less than the ground and context for Heidegger's formulation of the ontological determination of alterity, and thus of community and furthermore of the political. And indeed, Derrida's effort is not only to enquire as to what is meant by 'friend' and what is signified by the 'voice of the friend', but – at a deeper level – to investigate from what standpoint the 'friend' is determined and according to what law his or her 'voice' can be carried and is to be heard. Derrida explicates how and why, as the 'voice of the friend' remains indeterminate as far as its embodiment or form are concerned, it is always in tune and in accordance with the topology and the tone of Being and thus, in this sense, already determined by the truth and meaning of Being. The 'voice of the friend' always requires a unique mode of *hearing* for each *Dasein*, one entirely other than listening to a physical sound. It requires a hearing capable of remaining assigned to the opening of the meaning of Being. The 'voice of the friend' is that which only a *Dasein* can carry and hear, as only a *Dasein* can remain assigned to its own-most potentiality towards the meaning of Being. That is, only a *Dasein* can remain determined, engaged and compelled by its openness to the originary essence of the truth of Being.

This ontological explication and consequently determination of *Dasein*'s own-most disposition towards the originary essence of Being – a disposition which entails that only a *Dasein* can carry or hear the 'voice of the friend' for that voice is always the voice of a *Dasein* – sets the stage for Heidegger's focal point: the possibility through which all *Daseins* are kept and safekept in the call of Being. Derrida's reading, remarkably, brings out this focal point and shows how it constitutes and structures Heidegger's philosophy as a whole around the idea of an appropriating *Versammlung*, where the relation between *Dasein* and the essence of the truth of Being is gathered and assembled, collected and brought together. Naturally, Derrida here remarks how Heidegger remains curiously close to Aristotle, while incessantly questioning both his account of *logos* and his definition of man as rational animal. Indeed, for Derrida, this

> double reservation regarding Aristotle does not prevent Heidegger from defining the voice of the friend in such a way that only the opening of a *Dasein* is up to it. *Dasein* being the essence of man then is not contradictory to the Aristotelian proposal according to which there is friendship par

> excellence only between men: not between gods and men, not between animal and man, not between gods, not between animals. On this point, Heidegger would remain Aristotelian: *Dasein* alone has a friend, *Dasein* alone can carry it *bei sich*, man alone as *Dasein* pricks up, opens, or lends an ear to the voice of the friend, since this voice is what permits *Dasein* to open itself to its own potentiality-for-being. The animal has no friend, man has no friendship properly so called for the animal. The animal that is 'world poor', that has neither language nor experience of death, etc., the animal that has no hand, the animal that has no friend, has no ear either, the ear capable of hearing and carrying the friend that is also the ear that opens *Dasein* to its own potentiality-for-being and that [. . .] is the ear of being, the ear for being.[8]

Despite Heidegger's critical appraisal of Aristotle's metaphysics and his philosophical gesture of thinking the question pertaining to the meaning of Being *before* Aristotle, and hence through an essential alliance between pre-Platonic Greek thought and the German language, this analysis demonstrates how, for Derrida, Heidegger is caught up in the same structures as the onto-theology he pretends to dismantle or destroy. It also indicates why the hearing and carrying of the 'voice of the friend' for all *Daseins* is only possible and effective if it is always Being which hears itself, its own calling and voice, through all *Daseins*. Ultimately, it is always Being, its essential truth and history, which deploys itself in the 'voice of the friend' which all *Daseins* carry and hear as such and as their own potentiality-for-being. Hence, the 'voice of the friend' is always and already that voice which gathers and assembles all in the deployment of the meaning, the truth, and the history of Being. The 'ear of Being' as the 'ear *for* Being' is what defines and constitutes the possibility and effectivity of the 'voice of the friend' carried and heard by all *Daseins*. In a way then, the friend is possible for the *Dasein* – is carried and heard by the *Dasein* – if and only if it is engaged with a voice that is always in tune with Being. This essential gathering through the deployment of Being marks an accord, a harmony, a non-dialectical conciliation and reciprocity which furnishes the 'for-the-other *Dasein*' (*fureinander Dasein*) its ultimate ontological signification. As Derrida shows, beyond *Being and Time*, and especially in Heidegger's readings of Heraclitus (GA 55) and Anaximander (in *On the Way to Language*): the meaning of friendship (*philia*), and thus of hearing and carrying the friend, is determined in its full essence through the opening of the grace and the favour, the gift to the other.

Heidegger does indeed return to the idea of friendship in his reading of Heraclitus. First, he remarks – repeating yet again his emblematic philosophical gesture and turn – that friendship, in that it is authentically thought, is 'friendship for what is to be thought', that is: for what is yet to come to thinking and which is nothing other than the possibility to turn and return to the originary source of the truth of Being as conciliation in the unison of an appropriating *Versammlung*.[9] But, as Derrida very clearly demonstrates by following the letter of Heidegger's text, this friendship – through a hearing that remains irreducible to the simple heeding of sounds, noises or audible phenomena – is 'to accord a grace or a favour'.[10] However, according grace or favour does not mean showing *clemency* towards such and such an act or *favouring* something over something else. This according of grace and favour signifies an *originary offering*. Indeed, Heidegger remarks: 'Offering in an originary way is to accord to the other what comes back to it [what is due it] because that belongs to its being [or essence] insofar as that carries [supports, bears, carries with it, includes, *trägt*] its essence.'[11]

This grace, favour and originary offering as a gift to the other is the gift not of an object or a thing, nor of one's self in a sacrificial substitution for the other; rather, it is the gift of that which always originally belongs to the other: that through which the other finds itself – and itself only – in the unfolding of Being.[12] In this sense, the originary offering to the other, in and through friendship, signifies the gift of *what the other already has and what the other already is*. It is the gift of a certain *letting the other be* its being in its own-most propriety, potentiality and resolution for Being; the gift of what the other always has *bei sich* by appropriating and being appropriated by and for Being. To give that which the other always has by and for itself alone is to offer the other his/her/their own-most gathering in the history of Being and furthermore that it always and already *is* in the call of the truth of Being.

Derrida furthers this analysis of the authentic friendship by which all *Daseins* are gathered in the call of Being, all *Daseins* listen to the truth of Being and remain resolutely turned and tuned to the history of Being, by indicating how the gift to the other in friendship always emerges from that which one does not have, and indeed cannot have, to give. The gift of friendship is giving what one does not possess for oneself to another who already and always has it. For giving to the other means, in truth and authentically, letting its being be in Being. In this sense, it means giving to the other what it is already opened to, and therefore that which it always *has* and *is*: its own-most and un-substitutable resolution towards Being.

The underlying assumption of this ontological analysis of the authenticity of friendship, from *Being and Time* to the interpretation of Heraclitus, remains Being itself, Being alone. It is through Being that authentic friendship occurs between *Daseins* and, conversely, it is through the originary gift of friendship that the opening and resolution of each *Dasein* in the gathering of Being is revealed. Authentic friendship is friendship with Being and it always finds its source in Being. Consequently, authentic friendship is not only an access to Being: it is Being which offers a place where the grace of this friendship can disclose itself in all *Daseins*. Through this analysis of *philia*, Derrida will show how and why, for Heidegger, the gift of Being in authentic friendship also constitutes the essence of justice, that is of *dike* as *Fuge*, accord and accordance, adjoining concordance. One notices that the idea of justice here emerges yet again in Derrida's *Politics of Friendship*. Certainly, for Heidegger, as Derrida demonstrates, the idea of justice does not constitute a central signifier in the ontological dispositive. Justice is always thought, defined and determined, for Heidegger, as occurring within the horizon of the meaning, truth and history of Being; therefore, it is already signified by the anteriority of an essential accordance and conciliation.

Why does Derrida bring up the problematic idea of justice when discussing Heidegger's ontological dispositive and the determined relation between authentic friendship and the truth of Being? We will be further examining this breakthrough. However, suffice it to say for now that, after presenting the reduction of the idea of justice to the priority of Being and the context of the truth of Being in Heidegger's philosophy, Derrida seeks to envisage a different idea of justice, and hence a different approach to friendship – one removed from the ontological grasp of Heidegger's dispositive and wholly other than the one entrapped within the structure of the gift of presence.

This entire movement whereby authentic friendship, the structure of the gift and the essence of justice are seized and grasped within the unifying and attuning truth of Being succinctly manifests the signification of a specific kind of politics and education. It is a politics and an education of the *Volk* – and Derrida deploys it here by closely reading this ontological analysis to the point where one can see the sacrificial and apocalyptic logic at work in Heidegger's philosophical construction, and therefore understand the limits and limitations of this very dispositive. The *Volk* involved here already gathers itself by remaining tuned, always joins up and is brought into the resolution of the unitary essence of the history of Being.[13]

The Heideggerian dispositive, as Derrida presents it, culminates in a structure of the gift of the gathering essence of the truth of Being. However operative this ontological dispositive may be in determining friendship and justice within the parameters of presence, Derrida engages in a deconstruction of its central signifier. Indeed, Derrida's deconstructive questioning of Heidegger's thought and politics primarily sees its structure of gift – where all is always and already gathered in a determined essence of the event of Being

– not only as a reduction of friendship and justice, but also – and especially – as their *foreclosure* in a predetermined and enclosing signification. The Derridean deconstructive questioning and dismantling of Heidegger's dispositive involves a *wholly other* orientation to rethink friendship and justice outside the sphere of the essential deployment of the gift of Being. It entails a rethinking of friendship and justice where no identifying or identified gathering, no ontological meaning or source, no truth or history, no defining structure of the gift of their possibilities and effectivity through – and as – the gift of Being can subsist or endure. In the light of this, we can pose two types of questions, both of which – without any priority of one over the other – lead to a deconstruction of the ontological structure of gift, of the gathering essence of Being, confining friendship and justice within its ownmost appropriation.

First: why dissociate the ideas of friendship and justice from their determinations and definitions within the truth of Being, and isolate these from the ontological structure of the gift of presence? And second: why does Derrida approach an idea of friendship and justice outside the scope of the ontological structure of gift and donation and the essential gathering and unifying dispositive of the history of Being? These questions, on the one hand, point to a certain failure within the Heideggerian dispositive to confront the *singularity* of justice and friendship – perhaps also a certain failure to face *singularity* itself (for example, the singularity of historical events as these are always and already brought back to the determined ontological dispositive of the truth and meaning of Being).[14] On the other hand, they entail a profound reformulation of the very significations of the ideas of justice and friendship. In this sense, Derrida's deconstruction always deploys, at least, a dual form of questioning. It shows and displays the limits and indeed failures of a given philosophical system in both its pretentions and its constitution. And in this sense, Derrida's deconstruction also expects philosophical thinking to confront – beyond the clutch and grasp of used-up signifiers – the *singularity* of an idea or a concept, situation or event, to the point where it requires their incessant reinvention.

In interrupting, through deconstructive questioning, the all too perfectly tuned and efficient ontological alliance of friendship and justice, Derrida reiterates both these ideas *otherwise* than according to their ontological context, thus impelling each *singularly* towards an unforeseeable and unpredictable future. This is a friendship and justice *yet to come*, and which would be awoken by that which (him/her/that, or some other entirely different who) returns *and* arrives: *returning* as that which arrives each time singularly, and *arriving* as that which never slips into an appeased past; resisting, in the name of a rebellious and irreducible idea of friendship and justice, their fixation and contentment, their assurance and guarantee in the gift of presence as the truth of Being. Derrida engages with nothing less than the idea of a friendship and justice extracted from the predominant ontological signifier of presence and its inherent logic of gift, offering, in order to rethink at once a friendship and a justice, a justice for friendship as well as a friendship for justice, perpetually dislocating the temporality of presence, disrupting the presence of representation, disarticulating the present dichotomies between past and future, between what has passed and what is to come, between the repetition of the past and the predictability of the future. In this sense, this friendship and this justice command a responsibility towards 'him/her/that, or some other entirely different who' is *yet to come* – as both *returning* from the past as arriving each time singularly from the future and as coming unpredictably from a future which never integrates a temporal narrative.

This call to a responsibility requires us to rethink friendship by understanding it as no longer subservient to the ontological structure of presence, but as awoken in and by an idea of justice irreducible to the truth of Being. What could resemble friendship in the wake of an idea of justice heterogeneous from the essence of a gathering opened only by the determined gift of presence? What could be justice for the friend? What and how can one respond justly to the friend?

Perhaps justice for the friend and responding justly to the friend would require responsibility towards *spectres* both past and future, the '*revenants*' and the '*arrivants*' each time haunting the friend. Derrida recalls the idea of *spectre* throughout *Politics of Friendship* and does so where this idea is inseparable from that of a *justice to come*, that is from justice towards the singular *spectres*, past and future, returning and occurring, haunting each singularity, and where no possibility to give oneself the 'good conscience' of a resolved and pacified relation to both past and future can be determined. In this sense, the idea of *spectre* and of justice towards *spectres* calls for an enduring kind of responsibility urgently responding more than what it could settle for – an *incessant supplement of responsibility*. This kind of responsibility, then, would not be a function of the gift, but a certain type of *attention* towards that which the friend never possesses for itself and which yet incessantly traverses it, its presence, its identity, its own-most propriety and possibility. That is, a responsibility towards the returns and occurrences of the multiplicities of *spectres* haunting the friend: *spectres* neither absent nor present and yet both present and absent, both and at the same time within and outside the friend. Responding where responsibility means listening to that which remains without voice in the friend, that which is unspeakable and unsayable, or even unthinkable, and yet speaks wholly otherwise than the presence of a voice or the voice of presence in the friend.

Notes

1. Jacques Derrida, *Politics of Friendship*, trans. George Collins (London: Verso, 1997); Jacques Derrida, *Politiques de l'amitié: suivi de L'Oreille de Heidegger* (Paris: Galilée, 1994). Hereafter, page references to the English translation are given in parenthesis in the text (*PF*).
2. Jacques Derrida, 'Heidegger's Ear: Philopolemology (*Geschlecht IV*)', trans. John P. Leavey Jr, in *Reading Heidegger: Commemorations*, ed. John Sallis (Bloomington: Indiana University Press, 1993), pp. 163–217.
3. Derrida's *Geschlecht* essays – *Geschlecht* I. 'Sexual Difference, Ontological Difference', *Research in Phenomenology*, 13 (1983), 65–83; *Geschlecht* II. 'Heidegger's Hand', in *Martin Heidegger*, ed. Stephen Mulhall (London: Routledge, 2017); *Geschlecht* III. *Sex, Race Nation, Humanity*, ed. Geoffrey Bennington, trans. Katie Chenoweth and Rodrigo Therezo (Chicago: University of Chicago Press, 2020); *Geschlecht* IV. 'L'oreille de Heidegger. Philopolémologie' – all focus on Heidegger's philosophy. The German word is untranslatable into either French or English. It refers at once to sex, race, nation and humanity.
4. 'Listening to [. . .] is *Dasein*'s existential way of Being-open as Being-with for Others. Indeed, hearing constitutes the primary and authentic way in which *Dasein* is open for its own-most potentiality-for-Being as in hearing the voice of the friend whom every *Dasein* carries with it.' Martin Heidegger, *Being and Time*, § 34, trans. John Macquarrie and Edward Robinson (London: Blackwell, 1962), p. 206.
5. Derrida, 'Heidegger's Ear', p. 170.
6. The use of the term 'dispositive' could seem surprising to describe the inherent movement of the history of the truth of Being. As we know, Heidegger describes the 'essence of technology' as a 'dispositive' (*Gestell*) through which occurs the 'enframing' of entities and the 'abandonment' of the meaning of Being. Consequently, the thought of Being decides for a turning out of the planetary devastation of technology and thereby 'sojourns' in the gift of the truth of Being which remains irreducible to the technological order. We, however, have recourse to this term in our reading to suggest how and why Heidegger's philosophy is 'caught up', in spite of its own intention and pretention, by what we have called a *hypertechnicity* which always and already pivots binarily between, on the one hand, the thought of Being and, on the other, the 'abandonment'

of the meaning of Being. In other words, we suspect the very dynamic of the thought of Being to reproduce, against itself, a technological structure, which incessantly reiterates the same binarism between, on the one hand the 'danger', the 'peril', and, on the other, 'that which saves' (amongst many such occurrences of this determined logic and structure, cf. Martin Heidegger, 'The Question Concerning Technology', trans. David F. Krell in *Basic Writings* (London: Routledge, 2010), pp. 311–41). A complete critical appraisal of this binarism and its overcoming in an essential and originary *Versammlung* in Heidegger's philosophy can be found in Joseph Cohen and Raphael Zagury-Orly, *L'adversaire privilégié* (Paris: Galilée, 2021).

7. Derrida, 'Heidegger's Ear', p. 165.
8. Ibid. p. 172.
9. Ibid. p. 193.
10. See Derrida's explication in 'Heidegger's Ear', pp. 187–8: 'the ear is not for Heidegger an organ of the auditory sense *with* which we hear. Hearing (*das Hören*), in the authentic sense, is a gathering, a self-recollection (*Sichsammlen*) toward the word [*parole*] that is addressed to us (*Anspruch, Zuspruch*). The gathering of hearing is done starting from the address and not from the organ of hearing. We hear when we forget the ears and auditory sensation in order to carry ourselves, through them, toward what is said and of which we are part (*gehören*). In other words, Heidegger unceasingly reminds us that *Hören* (*entendre*, hearing, understanding) must be thought of starting from listening or lending an ear (*Horchen*), not the reverse. Everything is played out in the difference between *hören* and *horchen*. In order to hear (*hören*) what *hören* means, it is necessary to listen, to hearken (*horchen*) and not only hear. "Hearing is first a gathered hearkening. The heard has its being in hearkening. We hear when we are all ears." This gathering in "all ears" [literally in the "all ear"] is why we do not hear *with* one or two auditory organs. As he will repeat in *Der Satz vom Grund*, Heidegger underscores that we do not hear because we have ears, but we have ears because we hear'; Derrida, 'Heidegger's Ear', p. 194.
11. Heidegger, *Heraklit*, 1. *Der Anfang des abendländischen Denkens* / 2. *Logik. Heraklits Lehre vom Logos*, GA 55, ed. Manfred S. Frings (Frankfurt: Klostermann, 1979). Quoted by Derrida, 'Heidegger's Ear', p. 194. This passage is translated by Derrida and the square brackets are his own.
12. Indeed, in § 47 of *Being and Time*, Heidegger strongly undermines the sacrifice for the other as substitution in order to focus his whole existential analytic on the mineness of *Dasein*'s own-most potentiality for being

in its un-substitutable and inexpressible 'being-towards-death'. The gift to the other is therefore *not* a sacrifice for the other, that is, a substitution of one's own death for the other's life. And Heidegger always stresses the same law: '*No one can take the Other's dying away from him.* Of course someone can go to his death for another. But that always means to sacrifice oneself for the other "in some definite affair". Such "dying for" can never signify that the Other has thus had his death taken away in even the slightest degree. Dying is something that every *Dasein* itself must take upon itself at the time. By its very essence, death is in every case mine, in so far as it "is" at all. And indeed death signifies a peculiar possibility-of-Being in which the very Being of one's own *Dasein* is an issue. In dying, it is shown that mineness and existence are ontologically constitutive for death' (Heidegger, *Being and Time*, § 47, p. 284.) For a complete reading of the question of sacrifice in *Being and Time*, see Joseph Cohen, 'On the Possibility of Sacrifice', *International Journal of Philosophical Studies*, 22.4 (2014), 552–68. It may be worth adding here – given the numerous interpretative misunderstandings both within Levinas scholarship and among critics of Levinas – that the ethical commandment of infinite responsibility towards the other is not assimilable to a self-sacrifice for the other. Quite on the contrary, Levinas engages a response to the other always interrupting and suspending the *economy* and *resolution* of sacrifice: that is, an infinite responsibility towards the other persistently extirpating the other from its death by incessantly renewing, reformulating and reiterating its singular response to the other's call and commandment. For Levinas, the resolved economy of sacrifice never encompasses or grasps the ethical response and responsibility for the other. We are recalling this also to claim that Derrida's reflection, most notably in *The Gift of Death*, is much closer to Levinas's ethical responsibility, which undermines the logic of sacrifice, than it is to Heidegger's critique of sacrifice as a substitution which opens itself up to a resolved economy of ontological sacrifice.

13. The politics of the *Volk* is associated by Heidegger to the 'camaraderie of the front', where soldiers are unified in their 'proximity to death' as primordial access to the history and truth of Being, in his reading of Hölderlin's hymn 'Germania'. See Heidegger, *Hölderlins Hymnen: 'Germanien' und 'Der Rhein'*, GA 39, ed. Susanne Ziegler (Frankfurt: Klostermann, 1980), pp. 72–3. This association clearly marks how and why, for Heidegger, the gift of Being gathers and brings together *Daseins* within the presence of an originary community rooted in the deployment of a history, where it is always and already the unfolding of Being

which orders and assigns, deploys itself and determines itself through sacrifice and the freedom of a sacrificial gift in the name of Being. In this sense, this authentic community of historical beings is essentially determined as assigned and therefore as responding to the givenness of the unicity and unity of Being alone: 'With soldiers, the camaraderie of the front does not come from the need to assemble because other persons who are afar have left us, nor from an accord to be enthusiastic together; its most profound, its unique reason is that the proximity of death as sacrifice has firstly brought each one to identical annulations (*Nichtigkeit*) which has become the source of an absolute belonging to each other. It is precisely the death that each man must die for himself alone and which isolates to the extreme each individual, it is death and the acceptance of the sacrifice it obliges, which creates the space of the community from where surges camaraderie. If we do not integrate in our *Dasein* forces which bond and isolate as absolutely as death as sacrifice freely consented, that is that do not take hold of the very roots of the *Dasein* of each individual and which reside as profoundly in an authentic understanding, there will never be a camaraderie: at most a particular form of society.' We owe the translation quoted here to James Phillips, in *Heidegger's Volk: Between National Socialism and Poetry* (Stanford, A: Stanford University Press, 2005), pp. 69–70.

14. Joseph Cohen and Raphael Zagury-Orly, 'History Supposes Justice', *Das Questoes*, 9.1 (2020), 43– 67.

7

Another Friendship

Pheng Cheah

Politics of Friendship was the earliest introduction of Derrida's thought to mainstream Anglo-American moral and political philosophy. Discussion has understandably focused on his interpretation of canonical figures such as Aristotle, Kant, Nietzsche, Michelet, Montaigne, Cicero, and especially his deconstruction of Schmitt's enemy/friend distinction, because their writings are concerned with friendship as an existential relation among subjects. What then are we to make of Derrida's startling claim in chapter 9 that one of his main aims is to 'follow the discreet lead of an unceasing meditation on friendship in Heidegger's path of thinking' in order to take Heidegger's ontological understanding of friendship, which rejects 'the "subjective", "psychological", "metaphysical" interpretation of *philia* and its "politics"' beyond its limits, 'in another direction'? (*PF*, 245, 246).[1]

In this chapter, I argue that Derrida's allusive and cryptic engagement with Heidegger in *Politics of Friendship* is the key to understanding his thought on friendship. I first discuss Heidegger's account of ontological friendship in his interpretation of *physis* as *philia* by focusing on his 1943–4 seminar on Heraclitus. Derrida's critique of Heidegger's restrictive limitation of *philia* to a fraternal-familial schema leads him to the thought of friendship as an auto-immune relation to the inhuman other that results in a radical regrounding of being-with others (*Mitsein*). This, I argue, is an implicit response to the shortcomings of Hannah Arendt's anthropologisation of *Mitsein* as *human* plurality.

Ontological Friendship

Derrida suggests that we need to understand friendship ontologically because the question of 'what is', the question of essence or truth that is fundamental to philosophy, has always arisen '*from out of a certain experience of* *phileîn* and *philia*' (240). This requires a more thorough consideration of Heidegger's account of philosophy's original connection to friendship. Broadly speaking, *philia*, one of the etymological components of *philosophia*, refers to the deep emotional connection between kin, where *philoi* (nominative plural) are those with whom one has the closest (quasi-)familial connections. *Philia* and *philos* are usually translated as 'love' and 'friend'. Hence, *philosophia*, which joins *sophia* with *philein*, is conventionally translated as the love of wisdom. Heidegger rejects this psychologistic and anthropologistic interpretation of *philosophia* as sentimental and stuffy (*großväterlich*).[2] In early Greek thinking, he argues, *sophia* is not a hypostatised substance (wisdom). Instead, it is derived from an adjective, *sophos*, meaning 'the correct taste, "a nose", an instinct for the essential'. *Sophia* was originally used by Homer and Hesiod to describe a craft such as carpentry or seafaring, that is, practical know-how.[3] Hence, philosophising is a relation to things in which one seeks to comprehend or understand their essence in the practical sense of *how* they are as opposed to *what* they are. This relation is *philia*, which Heidegger describes as 'an original inclination towards things', an 'inner friendship with things'.

> The process of understanding [*Das Verstehen*] requires a peculiar and persistent effort, which must in advance be subjected by an original inclination [*einer ursprünglich Neigung*] towards things. This inclination, this inner friendship with things, is what *philía* designates, a friendship that, like all genuine friendship, fights in accordance with its essence that which it loves [*um das, was sie liebt, kämpft*].[4]

Ontological friendship thus grounds the intentionality of consciousness in understanding's complex love for things. True friendship simultaneously involves accord and battle, unity and strife. *Philia*, Heidegger stresses, is 'the voluntary, fighting, genuine inclination [*die freiwillege, kämpfende, echte Neigung*]' towards things.[5] On the one hand, this friendship is a process of accord and harmony, the reciprocal joining of understanding with things, whereby understanding is openness to things even as things make themselves accessible for understanding, a reciprocal openness.

> *Philein*, to love, signifies here in the Heraclitean sense, *homolegein*, to speak [. . .] in correspondence with the Logos. This correspondence is in accord [*Einklang*] with the *sophon*. Accordance is *harmonia*. That one being reciprocally joins itself with another, that both are originally joined to each other because they are at each other's disposal [*Dies, daß ein Wesen dem anderen wechselweise sich fügt, daß sich beide ursprünglich einander fügen, weil*

> *zueinander verfügt sind*] – this *harmonia* is the distinctive feature of *philein*, of 'loving' in the Heraclitean sense.[6]

On the other hand, in joining with things, understanding, as genuine friendship, must also maintain a reciprocal openness by not extinguishing their independence. Not showing things as they are is detrimental to understanding them. Hence, truly friendly understanding is an embattled process that seeks to maintain a harmony whereby a mutual fitting of one with the other can continue.

But how are things made accessible to understanding so that it can join them in the first place? In his 1943–4 seminar on Heraclitus, Heidegger argues that *physis* itself is *philia*, which he translates as the giving of favour (*Gunst*) and friendship (*Freundschaft*). *Physis* is conventionally translated as 'nature' because of its interpretation in Roman thought as *natura* (birth or origin) on the basis that the coming into being of beings is like the generation and course of natural phenomena such as the genesis and growth of plants from seed to flower and fruit or the rising of the sun. Heidegger argues that this interpretation obscures the true character of *physis* by generalising the naive experience of natural phenomena to describe the fundamental ground of such experience: the coming-forth into presence such that there is something instead of nothing.[7] This coming-forth is the condition of there being anything like nature:

> *phúsis* names that prior emerging within which earth and sky, sea and mountain, tree and animal, human and god emerge and thereby show themselves as what emerge, so that they, in light of this emerging are known as 'beings'. What we call 'natural processes' first became visible to the Greeks in the way of their emerging within the light of *phúsis*.[8]

The translation of *physis* as *natura* metaleptically substitutes a dynamic process of giving with a pre-given substance (nature) that the giving generates.

Accordingly, Heidegger rejects the conventional translation of Heraclitus's Fragment 123, *physis kruptesthai philei*, as 'nature likes to hide itself'. First, *physis* is an emerging that in its essence is simultaneously a submerging. Second, the characterisation of *philei* as the predilection of nature in the sense of 'children like to snack' turns *physis* into a metaphysical subject. Heidegger argues that we should understand *philei* as the affordance of a favour in that something is brought into being where there was previously nothing. He translates the fragment as 'emerging to self-concealing gives favor [*das Aufgehen dem Sichverbergen schenkt's die Gunst*]'.[9]

What is the manner of this giving, which brings into the phenomenality of light, such that the emerging is also necessarily a self-concealing? Why is this friendship? Because *physis* brings into being something where there was nothing before, the process of emergence is necessarily also a self-concealing. A process of emergence only deserves that name if the things to which it gives being are released and left to be by the withdrawal of being. More importantly, since we cannot take for granted that any being will come into and remain in being because of the radical finitude of all beings, once a being has come into being, it is, by its essence as a finite being, released by the process of emergence and left on its own to develop freely. For Heidegger, this relation of generation and withdrawal between *physis* and all beings, where *physis* distances and withholds influence, is best characterised by friendship:

> We now translate the *philein* in Heraclitus's saying as 'to give favour [*die Gunst schenken*]'. In doing so, we understand favour in the sense of the originary granting and bestowal, and therefore not in the secondary meaning of 'benefit' and 'patronage'. This originary granting is the bestowing of what is owed to the other because it belongs to the other's essence, insofar as it bears that essence. Accordingly, friendship, *philía*, is the favour that grants to the other the essence that the other already has [*die Gunst, die dem anderen das Wesen gönnt, das er hat*], and in such a way that through this granting the granted essence blossoms into its proper freedom. In 'friendship' the essence that is reciprocally granted is freed to itself. Neither excessive solicitude nor even 'jumping in' to help in emergencies and dangerous situations is the defining characteristic of friendship: rather it consists in being-there for another [*sondern das füreinander Dasein*], which does not require any kind of event or proof, and which works by abstaining from exerting influence.
>
> It would be a mistake to believe that such bestowal of essence comes about all by itself, as though 'being-there [*Dasein*]' were here nothing other than something present-to-hand [*Vorhandensein*]. The bestowing of essence requires knowledge and patience, and granting is the ability to wait until the other finds itself in the unfolding of its essence and for its part does not make a big fuss about this discovery of essence. *Philía* is the granting of favor that gives something that does not at bottom belong to it; this favor, however, must give a guarantee of the other being so that it can remain in its own essence [*was ihr im Grunde nicht gehört und die doch Gewähr geben muß, damit des anderen Wesen im eigenen verbleiben kann*].[10]

Ontological friendship is the support of *physis* for all beings in the sense that *physis* enables their being-there. Being-there, being something as opposed to nothing or, better yet, being as opposed to not being, should not be taken for granted the way we take the mere presence of objects for granted. Although *physis* gives every being essence insofar as every being has its own essence, *physis* does not dictate that essence because as a process of emergence that immediately withdraws, it releases every being. Put another way, the essence of the beings that *physis* grants is not originally found in *physis* and does not belong to it and they are left alone to develop their own essence. Accordingly, ontological friendship is the steady support of being-there for the other and not an intrusive over-caring or intervention that hastens to influence, direct or prescribe the other's essence. It is characterised by a patient waiting, a withholding of influence or even abstention that allows the other's essence to unfold autonomously, thereby allowing the other to remain in its own essence. Such abstention is not irresponsible negligence towards the other but a knowing 'force' that lets the other be other. In Heidegger's words, 'in *phúsis*, favor prevails [*waltet*] [. . .] in the sense of the granting that grants nothing other than the allotting, the bestowing, and keeping safe [*das Vergönnen, die Gewährung und Wahrung*] of that which unfolds as emerging'.[11]

Ontological friendship is not the anthropomorphic imposition of a human subject's personal lived experiences of friendship onto *physis*. Heidegger rejects the suggestion that Heraclitus attributed a subjective human attitude to objective nature by noting that this argument not only dogmatically assumes that favour and bestowal are the special right and property of the subject but also anachronistically projects the modern ontological determination of the human as 'subject' onto early Greek thought. Friendship in the Heraclitean sense is important precisely because it points to an original ground that precedes and exceeds the subject. To the extent that lived experiences and life itself originate from *physis*, ontological friendship points to the fundamental foreignness or alterity of human experience. Heidegger observes that because every aspect of experience originates from the favour of another, the lived experiences we take for granted as *proper* to us and *our very own* 'could in their essence perhaps not belong to us [*nicht unser Eigentum sein*]'.[12]

The Radically Other Friend

Derrida's account of friendship departs from Heidegger's characterisation of *physis* as ontological friendship. He affirms Heidegger's rejection of anthropologising, psychologising and subjectifying determinations of friendship and emphasises that 'when Heidegger evokes the friend or friendship, he does so in a space which is not – or no longer, or not yet – the space of the person or the subject, nor that of *ánthropos*, the object of anthropology, nor that of the *psychē* of psychologists. Nor, therefore, that of an attendant politics' (243). Ontological friendship comes from 'a region [. . .] withdrawn from metaphysical subjectivity' (244). The unmooring of friendship from a metaphysics of subjectivity has radical implications. Because friendship is the matrix for understanding not only the political but also all master concepts of the modern ontic social sciences such as 'the social' and 'the anthropos' on which sociology and anthropology are founded, we would need to rethink these concepts and their corresponding disciplines from the ground up (243).

Derrida finds ontological friendship attractive for two reasons. First, it is 'a minimal "community"', a community prior to all positive community, that is, prior to all positive relations with those we conventionally call friends and enemies (244). Indeed, this pre-positive community is so original that it is more fundamental than *Mitsein*, the existential being-with other beings that characterises *Dasein*. Being-with others already presupposes the favour of *physis* by which we come into being. Second, Heidegger's emphasis on the friend's strangeness provocatively suggests that being comes from a radical alterity that cannot be thought within the order of being even as this otherness opens up all being (241).

In Derrida's view, however, the alterity of ontological friendship is not radical enough. Although Heidegger notes the friend's foreignness and emphasises that the favour of *physis* is an opening that is also simultaneously a hiding, he minimises the original ambivalent tension of the favour through the motif of accord, which he characterises as a gathering-together.

> *Qua philía, phúsis* accords. It is the accord, the accord in itself of harmony and given accord, but its solicitude for revelation is also accorded to the dissimulation of self. [. . .] And, as always for Heidegger, under the law of a *lógos* that assembles and gathers up. The gathering (*Versammlung*) always prevails, even if it accords the tensions of a false note. *Phúsis* and *philía*, *phúsis qua philía*: one, like the other, guards this at once generous and jealous relation to itself, as it were, it lives (in) hiding. [. . .] [I]t bestows the gift of what thus couples in order to accord them, *phúsis* and *philía*, and *phúein* to *phileîn*, with one another. (242)

But if being is only given by that which must withdraw and guard itself, then the favour comes from somewhere that cannot be in *accord* with being in two senses. First, it is that which cannot be *together with* being. Second, this withdrawal also disrupts and breaks (with) being because it marks the possibility of not being. There is no guarantee that the favour that gives being will continually be given. Hence, being comes from that which is so radically other that it cannot be *of* the order of being. Yet, there is being only by this favour that simultaneously opens up even as it renders being impossible. For Derrida, this requires 'a thought of friendship which could never thrive in that "gathering" [*Versammlung*] which prevails over everything and originarily accords *philía* to *phúsis* and *lógos*' (244). Such friendship comes out of and from the absolutely other. The affirmation of the radically other friend 'does not allow itself to be simply incorporated and, above all, to be presented as a present-being (substance, subject, essence or existence) in the space of an ontology, *precisely because it opens this space up*' (249). Because its favour cannot be foreseen or anticipated in advance, the radically other friend replaces the certitude of an accord or harmony at the very heart of being with the radical undecidability of a 'perhaps' that contaminates and overflows being. Perhaps there will or will not be being, perhaps we will or will not be. Being's constitutive openness to the coming of the entirely other is a vulnerability without defence to whoever or whatever may come and, in this sheer defencelessness, it is impossible to distinguish the friend from an enemy.

The radically other friend is the key to understanding Derrida's explorations of the aporias of friendship. His extended riff on the apocryphal remark, 'O my friends, there is no friend', attributed to Aristotle and quoted by Montaigne, Kant and Nietzsche, he notes, 'means initially and finally this overrunning of the present by the undeniable future anterior which would be the very movement and time of friendship. Does not the sentence avow an undeniable future anterior, the absolute of an *unpresentable* past as well as future – that is, traces that can be disavowed only in convoking them into the daylight of phenomenal presence?' (249–50). This obsession with an absolute alterity that constitutes presence and is its condition of (im)possibility is the principal animation of Derrida's entire *oeuvre*.

In *Politics of Friendship*, Derrida argues that the concept of the political, with its emphasis on the sovereignty and autonomy of collective human existence, entails the effacement of being's fundamental heteronomy. We regard the political sphere as being based on a familial schema – that of 'stock, genus, species, sex [*Geschlecht*], blood, birth, nature, nation' – because we have conventionally connected the family to birth, natality and the origin of life. The family has become the figure for recognising life, giving it significance as the target of cultivation and, subsequently, as the bearer of social and political value. But this substitutes an anthropologistic interpretation of *philia* for the ontological friendship at the origin of life. 'This is once again,' Derrida notes, 'the abyssal question of the *phúsis*, the question of being, the question of what appears in birth, in opening up, in nurturing or growing, in producing by being produced' (viii).

The usurpation of *physis* effaces the radical alterity of its favour. Following the separation of the political sphere from the family, we commonly regard fraternity as the privileged political figure of *philia* because the political is defined as a relation or tie with others whom I recognise to be the same as me, because we appear to be alike or to share similar interests and so forth. Hence, democracy is inevitably determined through the figure of confraternity or brotherhood. Its underlying principle of sameness, Derrida argues, epitomises the effacement of being's constitutive indebtedness to alterity: '*At the centre of the principle, always, the One does violence to itself, and guards itself against the other*' (ix). Two consequences follow from this. First, this familial and fratrocentric schema determines that the political is always founded on exclusion. Second, because all being is constituted by radical alterity, the protection of the political self against the other is also a violence to the self. Derrida argues that despite his critique of anthropologism, Heidegger's obscuring of the friend's radical alterity in the motif of a harmonising accord with *physis* leads to a tacit genealogical determination of *philia* that is continuous with its political figures such as autochthonism and fratrocentrism (242–43). This continuity, he implies, makes Heidegger's thought susceptible to National Socialism.

Regrounding *Mitsein*: The Politics of Autoimmunity

I have argued that Derrida takes ontological friendship to its limit and rethinks the political on the basis of a radically other friendship that is prior to being. We can better understand what is at stake by contrasting his approach with that of another of Heidegger's readers, Hannah Arendt. Arendt criticised Heidegger for displaying the philosopher's traditional contempt for political affairs, which led him to privilege contemplative thought over political action, and for his solipsistic account of human existence, which led him to disregard the plurality of human life.[13] Because political life is premised on human plurality, Heidegger was unable to elaborate on authentic political forms of being with others.[14] Arendt proceeded to 'de-ontologise' Heidegger's thought by suturing it to a Kantian metaphysics of the subject. She anthropologised the process of emergence as the force of natality from which she derived the human subject's capacity for freedom and action. The birth of human beings, she argues, introduces newness into the world. Free human action, which spontaneously initiates a new causal chain, originates from this power of beginning: 'action as beginning corresponds to the fact of birth, [. . .] it is the actualisation of the human condition of natality'.[15] Accordingly, she reformulates *Mitsein*, the being-with that follows from the fact that every being is amidst other beings, as human plurality: 'we are all the same, that is, human, in such a way that nobody is ever the same as anyone else who ever lived, lives, or will live'.[16] In response to this plurality, we act to distinguish ourselves and achieve a unique individuality.

Arendt's anthropologising of the self-withdrawing friendship of *physis* effaces the constitutive role of alterity in two respects. First, she installs the quasi-theological principle of sovereign autonomy in human existence. Second, she limits being with others to intersubjective human relations. The sameness and equality that characterises political community, she argues, are the defining features of the human condition because only human beings are capable of transcending merely biological life (*zōē*) and living a meaningful life (*bios*) constituted by words and deeds.[17] The political realm shelters us from the corrosive finitude of our being because we achieve a degree of permanence when we express our uniqueness and attain meaningful distinction in the public gaze of others. Such meaningful distinction is humanity's privilege. We share 'the curious quality of *alteritas*' with all beings because each being is different from other beings. But alterity is only the meaningless proliferation of beings in the world. Living beings are distinguished by their complex variability: 'Otherness in its most abstract form is found only in the sheer multiplication of inorganic objects, whereas all organic life already shows variations and distinctions.'[18] *Human* life, however, is distinct in a special manner. 'Only man,' Arendt suggests, 'can express this distinction and distinguish himself [. . .]. In man, otherness, which he shares with everything that is, and distinction, which he shares with everything alive, become uniqueness, and human plurality is the paradoxical plurality of unique beings.'[19] We have the power of appropriating or taking ownership of the otherness of our being so that it becomes *our* uniqueness, something we express as *our own* to distinguish ourselves from other subjects.

Instead of reducing *Mitsein* to intersubjective relations that enable us to transcend human finitude, Derrida regrounds it in the radical alterity of finite being. Because we are together with others by virtue of our openness to the absolutely other, being-with is marked by sheer chance. We are unsure of the continuation of our own being and that of others and, hence, of how long we can be with others. The radical undecidability of this 'perhaps' structures all our practical relations.

Derrida elaborates on the implications of this sheer vulnerability to the other for the free subject of action in his idea of the passive decision. Action presupposes the decision of a subject exercising free will. We decide to act and determine how we will act according to principles or to achieve certain effects. Every action thus presupposes the subject's presence to himself in the moment of decision. But all presence is constituted by the 'perhaps' of a radical alterity that withdraws from the realm of presence. For the subject of action, this takes the form of the event. An event is by definition unforeseeable. If we could predict or anticipate it, it would be predetermined by a causal chain that we could calculate in advance and would not be an event. Hence, an event is such only if it comes from the radically other. As Derrida puts it, an event 'must surprise both the freedom and the will of every subject – surprise, in a word, the very subjectivity of the subject, affecting it wherever the subject is exposed, sensitive, receptive, vulnerable and fundamentally passive, before and beyond any decision – indeed, before any subjectivation or objectivation' (68). Whenever we make decisions and act to regulate the event's unexpectedness, we suspend its undecidability and efface its alterity by drawing it into the realm of presence.

However, because a decision arises in response to the event's otherness, it is never originally that of the subject or owned by it. It comes upon the subject and surprises him before any of his *own* decisions. The event is the decision of the other in me and it makes every subjective decision to act originally passive:

> The passive decision, condition of the event, is always in me, structurally, another event, a rending decision as the decision of the other. Of the absolute other in me, the other as the absolute who decides on me in me. [. . .] I decide, I make up my mind in all sovereignty – this would mean: the other than myself, the me as other and other than myself, he makes or I make an exception of the same. (68)

Elsewhere, Derrida describes this as 'a freedom that would no longer be the power of a subject, a freedom without autonomy, a heteronomy without servitude'.[20] But the passive decision, which precedes the freedom of the subject, is not inimical to it. Our original opening to the other is also the origin of the ethical and political imperative to act. We become free subjects by acting in response to the other.

Grounding our being-with determinate others on absolute alterity has important implications for all levels of ethical and political relations. Derrida distinguishes between three modalities of responsibility: as a subject, I answer for myself, to a determinate other and before a collective other that takes the part of the determinate other (252). Conventionally, we act responsibly on the basis of likeness and similarity. I determine that I have a responsibility to another because I am in self-present knowledge of who I am and know that I have something in common with another because he is like me. When I answer for myself, I claim that I have fulfilled my responsibilities through my actions and affirm my identity as a moral or political subject by discharging these responsibilities. The adjudicator of whether or not I have met my responsibilities is a collective other who confirms my identity in judging me.

Accordingly, a political decision determines how our actions accord with the interests of our political community. This presupposes a prior decision about what this community is, for example, a determination of who our friends and enemies are, that enables us to distinguish our collective self from determinate others or identify with them based on *seeing* and *recognising* who are the same as us, that is, the *presence* of a friend. Even when our responsibility goes beyond the exclusionary borders of territorial or ethnic belonging, it is still based on the presence of beings like us. For example, our responsibility to all members of humanity extends friendship to all beings we recognise as human. The determination of our duties to our fellows or compeers and whether we have fulfilled them is carried out by a third party according to the social, legal, political or moral norms of the community. These norms express the community's identity and what is good for developing and nurturing it. The third party is usually a social, legal, political, religious institution, but it may also be internalised in the subject, for example, the *Ideal-Ich* of psychoanalysis, the Kantian moral law or the proverbial voice of conscience.

Derrida's emphasis on the friend's radical alterity intensifies the ambivalent embattled nature of ontological friendship such that the logic of fraternal sameness is disrupted at every level. Because my being is a response to the other's coming, the modality of responding to the other becomes radicalised such that it renders my presence problematic. In order to be at home with myself, I must already have invited the radically other in, however disruptive this guest is to my continued being. The friend/enemy determination is suspended in this zone of absolute hospitality. Consequently, the collective other's adjudication of whether a member has fulfilled his responsibility becomes contaminated by undecidability. One of the forms this undecidability takes is a structural aporia where the other's singularity is effaced by the general norms meant to protect it. Because these norms are based on presence, their application necessarily violates the other's alterity, which cannot be presented. Yet, in implicit response to Arendt's emphasis on the importance of action, Derrida breaks with Heidegger's characterisation of friendship as the withholding of action and the patient waiting for the other to find its essence. Because our continued being with others can never be guaranteed, we must respond by recognising the other through norms of presence and by acting in the present. At the same time, the aporia makes it impossible to arrive at a conclusive point where we have fulfilled our responsibilities to the other and can be complacently satisfied in our good conscience. Our responsibility becomes interminable because we must continually attend to the violation-in-protection of the singular other.

Derrida evokes the radically other friend by replacing fraternity with an epidemiological figure: autoimmunity. *Politics of Friendship* marks the term's first occurrence in his thought:

> The modality of the possible, the quenchable *perhaps*, would, implacably, destroy everything, by means of a sort of auto-immunity from which no region of being, *phúsis* or history would be exempt. We could, then, imagine a time [that would] [. . .] resemble nothing, nor would it gather itself up in anything [. . .]. [I]t *would not be* – in other words, it would not be *present* – either *with* the other or *with* itself [. . .]. One would then have the time of a world without friends, the time of a world without enemies. The imminence of a self-destruction by the infinite development of a madness of auto-immunity. (75–6)

Autoimmunity is an apposite figure for radical alterity as the constitutive (im)possibility of being-with others. In the process of immunity, a body protects itself by producing antibodies to combat foreign antigens. However, autoimmunity is the perversion of immunity such that the organism protects 'itself against its self-protection by destroying its own immune system'.[21] Autoimmunity is a hyperbolical form of suicide where the sense of self (*sui*) itself is destroyed because the organism immunises itself against its own immunity.[22] All being is structurally autoimmune. A being that protects itself by immunising itself against absolute alterity does violence to itself because it closes itself off from the condition of possibility of its being, the other that is at the same time itself. However, surrendering to the other is also the loss of being. A politics of the radically other friend attends to the political exigencies of our autoimmune being-with others.

Notes

1. Jacques Derrida, *Politics of Friendship*, trans. George Collins (London: Verso, 1997); Jacques Derrida, *Politiques de l'amitié: suivi de L'Oreille de Heidegger* (Paris: Galilée, 1994). Hereafter references to the English translation are given in parenthesis in the text (*PF*).
2. Martin Heidegger, *Einleitung in Die Philosophie, Freiburger Vorlesung Wintersemester 1928–29, Gesamtausgabe, II. Abteilung: Vorlesungen 1919–1944*, ed. Otto Saame and Ina Saame-Speidel, 2nd edn, 101 vols (Frankfurt am Main: Vittorio Klostermann, 2001), vol. 27, p. 20. All translations of this text are mine.
3. Ibid. p. 21.
4. Ibid. p. 22. Heidegger repeatedly distinguishes *Verstehen*, the process of understanding, from *Verstand*, the understanding as a cognitive faculty of a subject, to emphasise the process's dynamic character and its openness to things. Understanding precedes the constitution of subjects and objects.
5. Ibid. pp. 23–4.
6. Martin Heidegger, *What is Philosophy?* (1955), trans. Jean T. Wilde and William Kluback (Lanham, MD: Rowman & Littlefield, 2003), p. 47, translation modified.
7. See Martin Heidegger, *Heraclitus. The Inception of Occidental Thinking and Logic: Heraclitus's Doctrine of the Logos*, trans. Julia Goesser Assaiante and S. Montgomery Ewegen (London: Bloomsbury, 2018), p. 68; Martin Heidegger, *Heraklit. Der Anfang des abendländischen Denkens Logik. Heraklits Lehre vom Logos, Freiburger Vorlesungen Sommersemester 1943 und Sommersemester 1944, Gesamtausgabe, II. Abteilung: Vorlesungen 1923–1944, Heraklit*, ed. Manfred S. Frings, 101 vols (Frankfurt am Main: Vittorio Klostermann, 1979), vol. 55, p. 90. Hereafter the English and then German page numbers are both given in notes. For a fuller discussion of Heidegger's understanding of *physis*, see Daniel O. Dahlstrom, 'Begin at the Beginning: Heidegger's Interpretation of Heraclitus', in *Interpreting Heidegger: Critical Essays*, ed. Daniel O. Dahlstrom (Cambridge: Cambridge University Press, 2011), pp. 135–55; and Susan Schoenbohm, 'Heidegger's Interpretation of Phusis in *Introduction to Metaphysics*', in *A Companion to Heidegger's Introduction to Metaphysics*, ed. Richard F. H. Polt and Gregory Fried (New Haven, CT: Yale University Press, 2001), pp. 143–60.
8. Heidegger, *Heraclitus*, p. 67; *Heraklit*, p. 88.
9. Heidegger, *Heraclitus*, p. 92; *Heraklit*, p. 123.

10. Heidegger, *Heraclitus*, p. 98; *Heraklit*, pp. 128–9. Translation modified.
11. Heidegger, *Heraclitus*, p. 100; *Heraklit*, p. 132.
12. Heidegger, *Heraclitus*, p. 99; *Heraklit*, p. 130.
13. Hannah Arendt, 'Concern with Politics in Recent European Philosophical Thought', in Arendt, *Essays in Understanding 1930–1954: Formation, Exile, and Totalitarianism*, ed. Jerome Kohn (New York: Schocken, 1994), pp. 428–47 (pp. 446n5, 432–3, 443).
14. Hannah Arendt, 'What is Existential Philosophy?', in Arendt, *Essays in Understanding 1930–1954*, pp. 163–87 (p. 176).
15. Hannah Arendt, *The Human Condition* (Chicago: University of Chicago Press, 1958), p. 178.
16. Arendt, *The Human Condition*, p. 8. This difference-in-sameness is the basis of the two defining characteristics of political community: equality and distinctness. See Hannah Arendt, 'The Tradition of Political Thought', in Arendt, *The Promise of Politics*, ed. Jerome Kohn (New York: Schocken, 2005), pp. 40–62 (pp. 61–2).
17. Arendt, *The Human Condition*, p. 97.
18. Ibid. p. 176.
19. Ibid. p. 176.
20. Jacques Derrida, *Rogues: Two Essays on Reason*, trans. Pascale-Anne Brault and Michael Naas (Palo Alto: Stanford University Press, 2005), p. 152.
21. Jacques Derrida, 'Faith and Knowledge: The Two Sources of "Religion" at the Limits of Reason Alone', in *Religion*, ed. Jacques Derrida and Gianni Vattimo (Palo Alto: Stanford University Press, 1998), pp. 1–78 (p. 73n27).
22. Jacques Derrida, 'Autoimmunity: Real and Symbolic Suicides: A Dialogue with Jacques Derrida', in *Philosophy in a Time of Terror: Dialogues with Jürgen Habermas and Jacques Derrida*, ed. Giovanna Borradori (Chicago: University of Chicago Press, 2003), pp. 85–136 (p. 94).

Part II
Echoes

8

The Time of Friendship: Mourning, Survival, Spectrality

Rozemund Uljée

Introduction

'O my friends, there is no friend.' Many chapters in *Politics of Friendship* commence with this paradoxical phrase that has been attributed to Aristotle by different thinkers within the philosophical tradition. According to Derrida, the two elements are the 'two disjoined members of the same sentence' (*PF*, 1).[1] Disjoined, indeed, because we find a reference to two different times; hence, we are not dealing with a straightforward contradiction. While the first element calls on the friends who were, or the friends who will be (the performative part summons them or remembers them – this is the time of the future and of the past), the following element is tied to the present in the sense that at this very moment, there is no friend. It is the aim of this short essay to trace this double temporality of friendship as articulated in the first chapter, 'Oligarchies: Naming, Enumerating, Counting', of *Politics of Friendship*. I seek to demonstrate how the temporality of interruption and disjunction indicates that friendship always already involves a type of mourning, and, thereby, survival. The second aim consists in showing how the notion of survival and its corresponding temporality might raise the suspicion that Derrida offers an interpretation of time as a transcendental condition of being, but must rather be read as an anachronous thinking of history.

The first two steps of my argument address the first aim: I begin by clarifying how Derrida's *survie* and the 'grieved act of loving' function as the condition of possibility of friendship, which means that the time of surviving *gives* the time of friendship. In this manner, Derrida offers a temporality of withdrawing, which takes place through a constant self-effacing. It implies that the present presents itself from within a light that comes from neither presence nor the self, and thus manifests itself as a mode of spectrality. Second,

I elaborate on the notion of spectrality and clarify how this enigmatic term shows that any determination is haunted by what it excludes. The final step addresses the second aim of this essay and consists in showing how spectrality reveals that Derrida must not be understood as a transcendentalist, but as offering a novel way of thinking about the movement of history.

Friendship as Loss and Mourning

'O my friends, there is no friend.' In this phrase, two different times, gathered to appear in one sentence in the present, in presence, call for a meditation on the notion of the *contretemps*. This term, poorly translated into English as 'accident', signifies the counter-logic to what can be repeated, iterated or programmed, insofar as the possibilities of repetition or representation are anticipated to secure both time and space into the present and the future.[2] In other words: the *contretemps* refers to a temporal dislocation that conditions all temporality. In so doing, it disturbs and interrupts the foundation of temporal linearisation and teleology and introduces a certain untimeliness into friendship, breaking it open and making it possible. More precisely, the *contretemps*, as the interruption of a single and organised temporality, 'delivers up the truth of friendship', because it disjoins the presence of the present; here, 'the present presents itself there only from within a source of phenomenal light' (14). Friendship is always torn between these two different temporal orders: it can never be fully and completely present, since it is haunted by both the temporality of stability and order, as well as by the future.

But how precisely? According to Derrida, friendship must stand the test of time; there is no friend without time, because it is only through and with time that confidence can be tested. Friendship implies duration, stability and a permanence, that always 'survives the living present' (15).[3] Yet, since the act of friendship is not an automatic movement, it also amounts to a gesture of faith, decision and responsibility as response, of which there is no friendship without. In this way, faith inscribes a temporal diachrony into the essence of friendship, by pointing towards a future that refers to terms put forward by Derrida such as the 'messianic' and the 'to come' of the *avenir*. This future to come is, for Derrida, always already the future of she who survives the friend. He writes: 'I do not survive the friend, I cannot and must not survive him, except to the extent which he already bears my death and inherits it as the last survivor' (13). This 'testamentary wisdom' means that my friend bears my death, and as such, in a certain way, the 'ownness' of my death has been 'expropriated in advance' (13). Therefore, the future to come is always already the future of the survivor.

Derrida notes that, in this way, friendship is always already bound up with loss and mourning, because it is impossible to survive without mourning. The very element in which friendship is constituted and can grow is mourning itself. Derrida will later write in one of the essays in *The Work of Mourning*: 'To have a friend, to look at him, to follow him with your eyes, to admire him in friendship, is to know in a more intense way, already injured, always insistent, and more and more unforgettable, that one of the two of you will inevitably see the other die.'[4] Mourning for a friend will be continued and repeated long after her death, and it has already begun long before it. As Derrida notes elsewhere: 'the melancholic certainty of which I am speaking begins, as always, in the friends' lifetime'.[5] This paradoxical suggestion makes us wonder what exactly we are mourning before mourning. As well as the future death of the friend, it seems that time is what mourning is about; not in the sense that we grieve about the passing of time, but in the sense that we always already mourn the future, because it is the future that brings loss, grief and death, thereby opening the question of survival.

In 'Living On/Borderlines', Derrida investigates the different meanings and interpretations of the term 'survival'. Referring to Shelley, Blanchot and Benjamin, he discusses survival as a certain 'seeing beyond: if we appeal [. . .] from *vie* to *vision*, we can speak here of *sur-vie*, of living on in a life-after-death, as survision, "seeing on" in a vision beyond vision' and in this sense, a seeing that is more than living.[6] But further on in the text, in his discussion of the term *arrêt*, Derrida also indicates that survival is an adjournment of death and dying. The discussion of the term *survivance* in the last seminar, titled *The Beast and the Sovereign*, is illuminating in clarifying the double meaning of the term. Here, Derrida investigates death, dying and survival by referring to Robinson Crusoe. It is noted that Crusoe kept a journal and might have wished that this journal would survive him. This survival, Derrida remarks, belongs to the 'living dead', because a book, as a trace, is both alive and dead. He writes, 'it begins with survival'. Derrida elaborates on an originary survival, as *survivance*, that dislocates each and every origin, order, foundation, identity and ground. Note that Derrida prefers the middle voice here. As Kas Saghafi remarks in his article 'Dying Alive', since the 'Différance' essay, Derrida has shown a preference for the -ance ending (like *différance*, *revenance*, *restance*), which remains suspended between the active and the passive voice.[7] In this way, '*survivance*' captures the fact that to survive does not mean to escape from death, or to continue living after life, but rather to die alive. As such, *survivance* is different from life, or death; a certain abyssal foundation from which we are opposed to what we think we can determine in the name of life and death. By noting that 'it' begins with survival, Derrida not only problematises common ideas regarding life and death; he also calls into question the stable and linear temporality these conceptions presuppose. Furthermore, he questions any identity of that which is supposed to possess a 'beginning' and 'end'. In other words: stating that 'it begins with survival' reveals that *survivance* is not something that happens at the end of life, or at the end of friendship, commencing only after the passing of the other, but instead renders life and death inextricably intertwined, conditioning each other in an aporia in which each identity always remains at the mercy of a difference that cannot be reduced to this very identity.

As such, the end is always and already there from the beginning: mourning is inextricably intertwined with any friendship at and in the present and thus, curiously, the notion of survival implies that the event of friendship can only take place when its temporalisation is haunted by a future that is still to come. It must be noted that this 'haunting' is a modality of mourning that reminds us of Levinas, because it was Levinas who remarked that we mourn the death of the other before the actual death; he stated, famously, that the death of the other is always the first. However, it is Derrida, and not Levinas, who discusses not only friendship, but any relation to alterity in terms of an 'originary mourning'. Derrida himself comments on this fact; in *Aporias*, he notes that neither Heidegger, nor Freud, nor Levinas speaks of mourning in this way, which, he adds, is his first and foremost concern.[8] As Derrida notes, survival, the 'grieved act of loving', is simultaneously the essence, origin and the condition of possibility of friendship; what is mourned is the interruption of time, meaning that friendship is never fully given, but must be re-performed and reiterated. As such, the temporality of friendship implies that friendship only succeeds in effacing itself, according to the different modalities of the *contretemps*.

Contretemps as Transcendentalism?

Deconstruction can be traced back to Heidegger's *Destruktion* of the history of philosophy as a metaphysics of presence. (According to Derrida, all the names that have been used for fundamental principles within this tradition refer to presence, namely: 'eidos, arché, telos, energeia, ousia, aletheia, transcendentality, consciousness or conscience, God, man, and so forth'.[9]) Nevertheless, Derrida, in 'Ousia and Grammē' and in *Of Spirit*, will call into question Heidegger's distinction between the 'vulgar', metaphysical and 'authentic' accounts of time. Yet, while he proposes that it is impossible to think a notion of time different from this one, he describes the *contretemps* as interrupting the time of the present. There are moments in Derrida's writing, where we, as readers, are left wondering whether, and if so, how, this interpretation of time as interruption serves as a ground or condition from which to think our present. Derrida's account of the *contretemps* and mourning in 'Oligarchies: Naming, Enumerating, Counting' is one such instant, since here he remarks that '*philia* begins with the possibility of survival' (13). This phrase seems to indicate that the aporia of time establishes an ontological necessity that would problematise any philosophy of mediation, recall or recovery. Or, in other words, the phrase '*philia* begins with the possibility of survival' might raise the suspicion that the aporia of the time of friendship constitutes a transcendental paradigm from out of which to think friendship. The question whether this is a correct suspicion amounts to asking whether Derrida, despite renouncing Heidegger's distinction between vulgar and authentic temporality, falls prey to the same logic.[10]

The text 'Ethics and Politics Today' is helpful in this regard. Here, Derrida comments on the strategy of deconstruction; he finds that deconstruction is 'pre-ethical-political' in that it does have a 'pre' as a preliminary prescription.[11] However, he adds that it is, precisely in this sense, 'perhaps' ethical-political, since the preliminary 'pre' that has to go together with each responsible decision (or determination) that could be called responsible, is emphasised. The problem, then, revolves around the question whether we see ourselves confronted with a normativity which, in a paradoxical manner, grants a privilege to a transcendentalism that would condition and structure presence itself, or whether this prescription is tied to a condition of possibility *as* condition of impossibility. If it is the former option, as suggested by Charles Deakin in his paper 'Derrida, Friendship and the Transcendental Priority of the Untimely', he can, as Deakin notes, be classified as having fallen prey to a 'Husserlian pathology'.[12] This means that Derrida would find himself in the same crisis that Husserl had diagnosed in the *Crisis of the European Sciences*. Here, Husserl writes that Europe is sick, in the sense that within its history it has engaged in the kind of thinking that had admitted a *telos* into the *eidos* beforehand. Derrida, in his writings on Husserl, calls this a 'transcendental pathology'. If it is the case that the *contretemps* referring to a temporality that is not present serves as the transcendental condition for the event of friendship, Derrida would have fallen prey to the same logic that Husserl had identified in Europe.[13] The alternative would be a different schema, in which the contretemps interrupts the present time while simultaneously holding on to it. This question warrants a closer look at the signification of the spectre and spectrality in Derrida's work.

Spectre and Spectrality

In *Specters of Marx*, Derrida remarks that the French *hantise* is similar to the English *haunting*, but with the added difference that the French also expresses the *return* of spectres, ghosts, spirits (or, in French, the *revenants*).[14] As a noun, *hantise* designates the place that is inhabited by the spirits, spectres, ghosts that keep coming back, and also points to a fear or obsession, or continuous and repetitive acts.[15] *Hantise* furthermore refers to movement, and unfixed passages between time and space, that do not lead to comfort or complacency, but to 'disadjustment of the contemporary' instead.[16] Derrida uses Hamlet's famous phrase 'the time is out of joint' to further clarify how different temporalities remain perpetually dislocated and haunted by each other: past events returning to our present as belonging to the future, and future events arriving into our present that cannot be relegated to the past, and thus do not cease to interrupt the present. All these connotations are combined into the mercurial and ephemeral notion of spectrality, which fragments all totalising aspects of ontology, history, metaphysics and presence. Thus, spectrality does not refer to the idea that the past is alive and working within the living present. Rather, as Fredric Jameson notes in *Ghostly Demarcations*, the 'living present is scarcely as self-sufficient as it claims to be', implying that we should not count on its 'density and solidity, which might under exceptional circumstances betray us'.[17]

In tandem with spectrality, Derrida introduces the portmanteau and neologism of 'hauntology' to call into question the limits of what exists: the living and the dead, past and present, and those not yet born. Because the 'h' is silent in French, hauntology and ontology are homophones. In tandem with *différance*, hauntology can be read as another gesture in the deconstruction of the metaphysics of presence, because Derrida emphasises with this neologism that any ontology is always already hauntology, trembling at the limits of ontological signification, linearity and certainty. Spectrality and hauntology reveal that what has taken place can never be simply relegated to the past, nor can the future be thought in terms of a present. The perspective of the spectre reveals that survival is always exposed to the returns of past deaths and lives to come. Here, we find an experience that is an exposure to the reiteration the aporia of time and thus history, and it is therefore impossible to commit to any transcendental foundation, whether in terms of presence or non-presence, from which a temporal horizon could be determined. To think otherwise, and to commit to an interpretation of the aporia as a condition for presence, would be a gesture of projecting a *telos* onto the undecidable, double movement of survival and, thus, spectrality.

Instead, spectrality reveals how the contretemps is tied to the double movement of condition of possibility as condition of impossibility in the sense that the present can only be thought in terms of its continuous interruption, which means that we are and remain confronted with what Derrida elsewhere calls the 'plural logic of the aporia', since hauntology, and its corresponding spectrality, open an interpretation of time and history that can only be understood in terms of its self-difference to itself.[18] As a consequence, it is impossible to commit to a presence, identity and telos wherein this difference remains gathered. In other words: time cannot be saturated, and therefore cannot be totalised.

Notes

1. Jacques Derrida, *Politics of Friendship*, trans. George Collins (London: Verso, 1997); Jacques Derrida, *Politiques de l'amitié: suivi de L'Oreille de Heidegger* (Paris: Galilée, 1994). Hereafter, page references to the English translation are given in the text (*PF*).
2. Jacques Derrida, 'Aphorism Countertime', trans. Derek Attridge, in Derrida, *Acts of Literature* (London: Routledge, 1992), pp. 137–42.
3. Just before, Derrida notes that 'there is no friendship without confidence (pístis), and no confidence which does not measure up to some chronology, to the trial of a sensible duration of time'.
4. Jacques Derrida, *The Work of Mourning*, trans. Pascale Brault and Michael Naas (Chicago: University of Chicago Press, 2017), p. 106.
5. Jacques Derrida, *Sovereignties in Question: The Poetics of Paul Celan*, trans. Thomas Dutoit (New York: Fordham University Press, 2005), p. 140.
6. Jacques Derrida, 'Living On/Borderlines', in Derrida, *Parages* (Stanford: Stanford University Press, 2011), pp. 103–91 (p. 91).
7. Kas Saghafi, 'Dying Alive', *Mosaic*, 48.3 (2015), 15–26 (p. 21).
8. Jacques Derrida, *Aporias*, trans. Thomas Dutoit (Stanford: Stanford University Press, 1993), p. 39.
9. Jacques Derrida, 'Structure, Sign and Play in Human Sciences', in *The Languages of Criticism and The Sciences of Man: The Structuralist Controversy*, ed. Richard Macksey and Eugenio Donato (Baltimore: Johns Hopkins University Press), pp. 247–64 (p. 249).
10. A point made by Charles Deakin, 'Derrida, Friendship and the Transcendental Priority of the Untimely', *Philosophy and Social Criticism*, 36.6 (2010), 663–76 (p. 664); but also by Jack Reynolds, in 'Time out of Joint: Between Phenomenology and Poststructuralism', *Parrhesia*, 9

(2010), 55–64 (p. 57). Reynolds is concerned that, too often, a transcendental critique of vulgar time, and 'other such "chronopathologies"', negotiate on 'claims of necessity that are either speculative' in the sense that such a claim is put forward as necessary, but is, in reality, a weak substitute for a better explanation; or, alternatively, such a critique depends on a 'moral and political tenor' that is associated with it – a situation that Reynolds also characterises as 'an empirico-romanticism' with dogmatist tendencies.

11. Jacques Derrida, 'Ethics and Politics Today', trans. Elisabeth Rottenberg, in Derrida, *Negotiations: Interventions and Interviews* (Stanford: Stanford University Press, 2002), pp. 295–314 (p. 300).
12. Deakin, 'Derrida, Friendship and the Transcendental Priority of the Untimely', p. 366.
13. See Jacques Derrida, *Edmund Husserl's Origin of Geometry: An Introduction*, trans. John P. Leavey (London: University of Nebraska Press, 1989), p. 80. Later, in *Rogues*, Derrida will refer to Husserl's statement that even before the Greek explosion of 'infinite telos of scientific and philosophical rationality', and even before the infinite idea in the Kantian sense, and the corresponding universal scientific reason that produces objectivity, there was a form of speculative knowing that had to make people immune to sickness, distress and death. See Jacques Derrida, *Rogues: Two Essays on Reason*, trans. Pascale Brault and Michael Naas (Stanford: Stanford University Press, 2005), p. 125.
14. Jacques Derrida, *Specters of Marx*, trans. Peggy Kamuf (New York: Routledge, 2006), p. 11.
15. Derrida, *Specters of Marx*, p. 177.
16. Ibid. pp. 99, 101.
17. Fredric Jameson, *Ghostly Demarcations: A Symposium on Jacques Derrida's Spectres of Marx*, ed. Michael Sprinker (New York: Verso, 1999), p. 39.
18. Derrida, *Aporias*, p. 20.

9

Friendship and Fission: Personal Identity in Derrida and Parfit

Kit Barton

The philosophy of Jacques Derrida generally comes under heavy criticism from analytic philosophers. His work is sometimes judged to be purely exegetical, a comment on the history of philosophy, and insufficiently focused on relevant, pressing problems. It is accused of lacking clarity and rigour, especially presenting arguments that appear to contain contradictions. These criticisms may be true some of the time but they are not true all of the time. There are certainly occasions where Derrida's philosophy does focus on a problem that analytic philosophers deem to be pressing and there are occasions where the apparent contradictions are a reasonable attempt at expressing a particularly complex philosophical difficulty or conundrum. It would be inconsistent with a philosophical principle of charity for an analytic philosopher to assume that Derrida's work makes no contribution to academically rigorous philosophy. Indeed, it is possible to see in *Politics of Friendship* where Derrida draws philosophical conclusions about personal identity that bring his work into parallel with one of the most widely respected analytic philosophers on this topic, Derek Parfit. Notwithstanding the supposed gap between continental and analytical philosophy, both of these philosophers share a similar critical argument directed at the Cartesian conception of the subject or self. For Derrida, this argument is contained within the 'Recoils' chapter and, for Parfit, the argument is in his 1984 book *Reasons and Persons*, both arguing that the Cartesian conception is needlessly constraining, and both suggesting that an advance in philosophical thinking is possible. To this end, Parfit offers one of his most famous thought experiments, Fission, and Derrida concludes his chapter with his own thought-provoking reply to Descartes, claiming 'I think, therefore I am the other' (*PF*, 224).[1] Derrida, alongside Parfit, succeeds in presenting reasons to consider personal identity beyond Cartesian limitations of singularity and indivisibility.

The central task of *Politics of Friendship* is to conduct a deconstructive examination of the Aristotelian text 'O my friends, there is no friend', with various chapters focusing on later interpretations of this phrase, especially those by Montaigne, Nietzsche and Blanchot. In 'Recoils', the eighth chapter of the book, Derrida concentrates on demonstrating that the phrase should be properly understood as a paradox. The addressee of the vocative phrase 'O my friends' seems to be undermined by the assertion that 'there is no friend'. Put another way, if there are no friends, then who are meant to be the recipients of the anterior, vocative phrase 'O my friends'? This conundrum attracts Derrida's attention and he proceeds with his usual deconstructive technique.

Of course, his objective might seem somewhat elusive to an analytic philosopher but it is consistent with Derrida's general deconstructive phenomenological approach. Derrida is true to his regular methodology, applying deconstruction to the particular subject of friendship. The deconstructive consideration of concepts requires an awareness of the margin of ideas that form the conditions of possibility of these ideas. They act as a boundary that both demarcates what is contained within the idea and indicates what is excluded from it. Derrida's deconstructive analysis concentrates on these margins, supplements, prosthetics and so on, in order to gain a more comprehensive philosophical understanding. Deconstruction typically reveals what any particular concept or idea is actually lacking, what is absent in the present, the speech excluded by the writing, the signified that is deferred by the signifier, the *pharmakon* that is chosen by the community and then expelled to the outside. For Derrida, philosophical analysis of a concept involves identifying the liminal boundaries of that concept. The margin will be both an extension of the idea, and therefore consistent with it in some way, and yet also external to the idea and therefore inconsistent with it. A fulsome consideration of a particular concept therefore will lead to some kind of inconsistency, contradiction or *aporia*. Derrida's deconstructive analysis usually contains some abyssal, contradictory concept, *différance* being the most famous. In sum, the philosophical consideration of an idea usually reveals the contradictory, marginal framework that conditions it and yet is also excluded by it. Derrida's analysis of the text 'O my friends, there is no friend' claims that friendship operates in this way, where the implied addressees, 'friends', are excluded by the assertion that follows, 'there is no friend'. The ten chapters that comprise *Politics of Friendship* approach this friendship conundrum in various ways, from the political, the ethical, and so on. The 'Recoils' chapter focuses on how the subject or self operates within this analysis.

Derrida argues that friendship necessarily requires a relationship between two people. Friendship is not possible alone; it needs another person. Moreover, it requires trust in the other person. For friendship to exist, Derrida argues, a subject must recognise the existence of another autonomous human being who is recognisably like oneself, insofar as the other person possesses freedom and autonomy, and yet who exercises this freedom separately from oneself. He writes that 'the knowledge we have of each other may be symmetrical and reflective [. . .]; it is nevertheless autonomous on both sides' (195). The experience of friendship is therefore capable of revealing a fundamental aspect of human existence: recognition of the existence of the other, the existence of another subject or self who is like us and yet fundamentally separate from us. He goes on to write:

> It is on the subject of my very self 'deep down' in myself; it is regarding myself in the inner recess of my 'regarding myself' that I entrust myself, without measure, to the other. I entrust myself to him more than to myself, he is in me before me and more than me. (195)

What Derrida is claiming here is that through an act of trust, which by definition surrenders freedom and autonomy, the self gives up an aspect of its fundamental constitution in order to gain an awareness of the autonomy of the other person. Without this act of trust, the knowledge of the self alone would be deficient, the self could not know friendship. He writes: 'Heteronomic trust exceeds the reflexive forms of knowledge and consciousness of a subject, all the certitudes of an *ego cogito*' (195). Here Derrida introduces the idea of a Cartesian subject, the *ego cogito* (on the next line referring to the Evil Genius of Descartes's first meditation). The Cartesian references continue throughout the chapter and culminate on the final page with Derrida's claim about a subject understood through his deconstruction, 'Translated into the language of a human and finite *cogito*, this gives the following formula: I think, therefore I am the other' (224). This is a clear transformation of the original Cartesian statement 'I think therefore I am' and it appears to be an obvious contradiction. It does not seem possible that a subject's thought could lead to their existence as another person. Here, it seems that Derrida is quite vulnerable to the criticisms about clarity and rigour often aimed at him by analytic philosophers. This Derridean-style *cogito*, 'I think, therefore I am the other', does not seem to make sense.

Perhaps this alternative *cogito* can be analysed with an alternative philosophical approach, in which case it might be interpreted without the contradiction. A dialectical, Hegelian interpretation, where the other is necessarily conceived in a fundamental, antithetical relationship with the subject, could avoid the contradiction. Further in that direction, it is certainly possible to interpret Derrida's claim that the other is 'in me more than me' in a Lacanian or Žižekian psychoanalytic mode as an assertion of an unconscious or repressed element that is nevertheless fundamental to human subjectivity. It might also be possible to interpret this Derridean *cogito* along Heideggerian or Levinasian lines, reading the other as a fundamental aspect of a human being who must ontologically be with others, *Mitsein*, or in an ethical relationship with the other as 'first philosophy'. Finally, perhaps this treatment of Cartesian philosophy could be regarded as an extension of Derrida's use of the *cogito* to reveal the limitations of Foucault's contention that civilised history is grounded in a claim about madness, contained in Derrida's early essay 'Cogito and the History of Madness'. These are all viable ways of making sense of this apparently contradictory assertion but they are all from within the continental philosophical tradition. As suggested earlier, and perhaps surprisingly, analytic philosophy can also be applied and demonstrate that this apparent contradiction is a viable way of considering personal identity, where the subject is considered to be an internal, thinking and solitary self and, simultaneously, another person or self.

A philosophical analysis of personal identity is one of the central objectives of Derek Parfit's *Reasons and Persons*. The book has been hugely influential in various fields of analytic philosophy, including epistemology, ethics and philosophy of mind, and it still remains very challenging, being cited frequently in contemporary work on population ethics, artificial intelligence and existential risk. Towards the conclusion of the section on personal identity, Parfit reveals his overall purpose, entitling the section 'Liberation from the Self'. He writes that the Cartesian understanding of the self can be a kind of prison:

> My life seemed like a glass tunnel, through which I was moving faster every year, and at the end of which there was darkness. When I changed my view, the wall of my glass tunnel disappeared. I now live in the open air. There is still a difference between my life and the lives of other people. But the difference is less. Other people are closer. I am less concerned about the rest of my own life, and more concerned about the lives of others.[2]

This first-hand account of the effect Parfit felt from believing something other than the Cartesian understanding of the self reveals the stakes in the game, as it were. It is possible to see why Parfit recommends this liberation from the Cartesian prison. The traditional *cogito* demands a separation of the individual subject or self from 'the lives of others', needless isolation, life in a glass tunnel. Parfit argues that this is not necessary and, like Derrida (although not achieved through deconstruction), he concludes that it is possible to conceive of the self without this strong sense of confinement. This alters the general idea of personal identity, what constitutes the notion of an individual subject or self, different and separate from other subjects or selves. By expanding the notion of personal identity, both Parfit and Derrida are able to espouse an alternative to the Cartesian *cogito* without falling into contradiction.

For Parfit, the Cartesian *cogito* implies what he calls the 'non-reductionist view', which is opposed to the 'reductionist view'.[3] Both of these views hold that personal identity relies on facts about psychological continuity and also about physical continuity. A person most often feels that they are the same self, day after day, as long as they feel either psychologically or physically connected to themselves over time. For example, a person makes plans for next week, continues to feel those plans as pressing over the passing days and then eventually enacts those plans when the time comes. It is the same self or person who makes the plans and then enacts those plans. The self is psychologically connected in this way. Further, a person has memories of themselves being in previous situations, such as where they were last month or last year, believing that they are the same self both then and now. This is what is meant by psychological continuity and it helps ground the conclusion that they are the same self or person. Similarly, physical continuity relies on a person believing that they have mostly the same body over time. Notwithstanding the hair and skin they shed in the shower, a person feels that the hands and feet that they have now are those that they have had before and expect to have in the future. Parfit notes that in most daily interactions and thoughts, these two beliefs, in both psychological and physical continuity, are sufficient to allow us to generally believe that we remain the same person, a continuous and consistent self over time. This is the reductionist view of personal identity; for Parfit, all claims about personal identity should be reducible to just these two types of beliefs: psychological and physical continuity.

However, most philosophical reflections of the self, including Descartes's, demand something more than just psychological and physical beliefs. For these, the self is not simply reducible to beliefs about continuity. Facts about psychological and physical connectedness are not sufficient to provide reasonable and satisfying philosophical conclusions about personal identity. This is the non-reductionist view where 'a further fact' is required in addition to just these two kinds of beliefs.[4] There must be some additional fact about personal identity, some proof of a continuous, purely mental entity, or perhaps spiritual substance or soul, in order to have warranted beliefs in a stable identity or self. A non-reductionist is not able to reduce the self to just psychological and physical facts, but rather requires something more, some further fact about the self, whereas a reductionist, like Parfit, is satisfied with a reductive account.

Parfit argues that the establishment of sufficient psychological and physical connectedness, which he refers to as adequate 'Relation R', is what fundamentally matters. He argues that 'personal identity is not what matters', if personal identity requires something more than Relation R.[5] ('What matters' is a particularly important phrase and subject for Parfit – his only other book is titled *On What Matters*.) The Cartesian, non-reductionist error is to insist on some further fact beyond Relation R to be what matters to personal identity and unfortunately this has become the prevalent view, both in philosophical writing and in general life. Parfit notes, 'Most of us have a false view of ourselves, and about our actual lives'.[6] But further, more hopefully, he writes, 'If we come to see that this view is false, this may make a difference to our lives.'[7] Given the deconstructive critique of the Cartesian ego self in 'Recoils', Derrida seems to have already made this advance in his thinking. Parfit and Derrida share the same critical perspective on the Cartesian self, both noting how it confines and isolates the self from others unnecessarily.

Returning to Derrida's alternative *cogito*, 'I think, therefore I am the other', it is possible to see how Derrida is also denying the non-reductionist view. It is a non-reductionist belief in a further kind of stable identity that causes Derrida's alternative *cogito* to appear to be a contradiction. If I believe that a person must have something beyond Parfit's Relation R connectedness, something like a kind of stable mental entity, perhaps a soul, then I would also be likely to believe that that there is no possible link between one person's internal thinking and that person simultaneously being another person. It would make sense, from a Cartesian perspective, to believe that a person's thinking is linked in a necessary and sufficient way to their own being, but it does not make sense that it might be linked to another person's being. This is the limitation imposed by the non-reductionist view. The self, deep down, is isolated from any other self. It is seemingly impossible to link one's personal identity with another; one cannot be two people. This is the grounds for the contradiction claim against Derrida. A person, as a person, cannot think internally, within themselves, and then be another person. An analytic philosopher, or anyone else, who insists that Derrida is contradicting himself relies on the Cartesian, non-reductionist view. Both Derrida and Parfit offer a way of moving beyond this limited understanding.

A feature of the non-reductionist view is that a person must remain numerically consistent to be regarded as the same person. So, a person cannot be themselves and, simultaneously, be another person. Derrida challenges this assertion of an indivisible singularity of personhood repeatedly in 'Recoils', showing how the single soul is linked to others. He examines how Aristotle justifies the possibility of friendship between a person and a slave. Aristotle's conception of a slave would be as an inhuman tool, but a slave is altered by the additional property of having a soul. If a slave did not have a soul, it could not be a friend. It is the soul that creates the possibility of friendship, 'What finally justifies friendship, is the soul [. . .] of the slave' (197). And yet this addition of a soul creates a shared characteristic between slaves and other humans, indeed creating the possibility of a category of 'all humans' and therefore the 'destiny' of a politics of 'all humans', such as a democracy with universal suffrage (197). Derrida demonstrates that the recognition of one soul in a slave ultimately leads to the possibility of recognising a multiplicity of souls in political discourse. He makes this point again when analysing the vocative 'O my friends . . .', claiming 'There is never a sole friend. Not that there would be none, but that there never is one. And one is already more than one' (215). Here, again, Derrida is breaking loose from a confining singularity in the conception of personhood and entering into philosophical territory that allows for what he calls 'singular multiplicity' (215). He sympathises with Montaigne's desire to meet the demands of friendship by being more than one person, by being 'twofold, threefold or fourfold' and having 'several souls' (215). While friendship seems to place a demand on an indivisible single person, Derrida claims 'indivisibility harbours the finite and the infinite in itself simultaneously' (216). The Cartesian non-reductionist view cannot accommodate this level of ambiguity. Derrida's deconstruction of friendship reveals these limitations and presents a way of thinking beyond them, moving beyond the singular, indivisible Cartesian person or soul.

Parfit does something similar through thought experiments, which act like Derrida's deconstructive analysis, introducing ambiguity that the Cartesian view cannot accommodate. Amongst the most widely known is the 'My Division' (or 'Fission') case study and this particular experiment, perhaps as a surprise to some of Derrida's critics, completely allows for his alternative *cogito*.[8] To paraphrase Parfit: I imagine I am one of a set of three triplets and that we are all involved in a terrible car accident. My body is destroyed as are the brains of my two siblings. My brain is divided (supposing this were technically possible) and a half is successfully put into the body of each sibling.[9] Each of the resulting two people believes that they are me, has my personality, my memories and intentions, and is therefore psychologically continuous with me. And each also has a body very similar to mine. The challenging question that this scenario raises for the Cartesian non-reductionist view is: what has happened to my personal identity? If personal identity is what matters then there must be an answer to this question. Possible answers are: I am dead (and therefore I am neither sibling); I am one sibling and not the other; I am the other sibling; and finally, I am both siblings. Each of these answers seems dissatisfying. The first answer, that I am dead, appears implausible insofar as there is at least one person who has psychological and physical connectedness with me (Relation R). The two middle answers, that I am one sibling and not the other, are implausible because there is no greater reason to choose one over the other. The final answer, that I am both siblings, seems wrong because I would then be two people. This offends the principle of numerical consistency – a person can only be one person. The Cartesian, non-reductionist is left frustrated, looking for a further fact that could allow for an acceptable philosophical answer to this thought experiment. The reductionist, on the other hand, does not need a further fact. Parfit writes:

> There will be two future people, each of who will have the body of one of my brothers, and will be fully psychologically continuous with me, because he has half my brain. Knowing this, we know everything. I may ask, 'But shall I be one of these two people, or the other or neither?' But I should regard this as an empty question.[10]

This allows for Derrida's assertion that a self, perhaps one of the siblings, can recognise that their thought might be linked to the other person in a fundamental way that the Cartesian *cogito* excludes with its insistence on numerical consistency.

It should also be noted how Parfit's thought experiment is meant to reveal an 'empty question'. It is not about providing an answer; it is about denying the necessity of the Cartesian conclusion. Similarly, Derrida structures 'Recoils' to avoid the necessity of a particular conclusion. This is characteristic of his general deconstructive method but it is particularly apparent in this chapter of *Politics of Friendship*. He warns against arguments that proceed from 'philological fundamentalism', that proceed in 'a straight line', and that lead to a more 'normalizing procedure' (206–8). Derrida recommends an alternative approach, which like Parfit's opens up a new, liberating perspective outside of his glass tunnel. Instead of the 'straight line', Derrida recommends the 'recoil version', which amongst other effects, 'reopens the question of multiplicity' (209). Like the teacher he describes, there is a part of him that 'is also striving *not* to be understood, approved, accepted in consensus – not immediately, not fully' (218). Instead, his alternative approach, his recoil manoeuvres, are meant to provoke 'new adventures in thought' that deviate from the 'canonical version' (208). Just as Parfit leaves us wondering about the four possible answers to his Fission case, despite our Cartesian demand for a clear resolution, Derrida leaves us with the 'undecideable that persists and repeats itself through the decision', despite the temptation to avoid it, which he says is the temptation of 'the book that you are reading' (218). One may wonder how Derrida's *cogito* might function? How can a person think and yet also be another person simultaneously? What Derrida is revealing is that the difficulty we may now have in deciding this matter does not mean that the 'undecideability' is unproductive. The possibility of 'more than one' answer or destination leads to a productive 'destinerrancy' that reveals further possibilities for thinking about personal identity (219). Parfit's thought experiment and Derrida's deconstructive method do not provide a clear, definitive answer about personal identity but they certainly argue that the Cartesian response leads to unnecessary constraint.

Both philosophers show how it is possible for a person to be a thinking person and also linked to another person. It is possible for a person to claim, 'I think, therefore I am the other' and not be in violation of some basic philosophical principle that demands a singular personal identity. *Politics of Friendship* generally, and the 'Recoils' chapter specifically, demonstrate that the traditional Cartesian subject, while in many ways useful for philosophical reflection, also confines and isolates the subject within its limitations and borders, crucially separating the self from others. Derrida offers his alternative *cogito* as a demonstration of a way of thinking without the Cartesian limitations, where friendship is not so easily reduced to a relationship between two separate and distinct people, where the strong distinction between self and other is purposely challenged.

Notes

1. Jacques Derrida, *Politics of Friendship*, trans. George Collins (London: Verso, 1997); Jacques Derrida, *Politiques de l'amitié: suivi de L'Oreille de Heidegger* (Paris: Galilée, 1994). Hereafter, page references to the English translation are given in parenthesis in the text (*PF*).
2. Derek Parfit, *Reasons and Persons* (Oxford: Oxford University Press, 1986), p. 281.

3. Parfit, *Reasons and Persons*, p. 210.
4. Ibid. p. 210.
5. Ibid. pp. 215–17.
6. Ibid. p. 215.
7. Ibid.
8. Ibid. pp. 254–8.
9. It should be acknowledged that Parfit's original Fission thought experiment states that the siblings would be his brothers. However, taking his reductive view one step further and noting how Derrida critically examines simple, binary sex/gender difference in *Politics of Friendship*, it is possible to suppose that a brother might identify as his own sister, and vice versa, if they felt there was sufficient psychological and physical (Relation R) connectedness. Arguments against this possibility rely on the non-reductionist 'additional' entity being integrally sexed or gendered. If there is no additional entity, on the other hand, which is both Derrida's and Parfit's reductionist view, then there is nothing to prevent the dead sibling from being his brother and/or his sister. Put simply, with no entity like a soul, there is no need to be concerned with whether it is possibly, and exclusively, male or female.
10. Parfit, *Reasons and Persons*, p. 260.

10

Two Structures of Friendship: On the Specular and the Spectral

Cathrine Bjørnholt Michaelsen

Towards the end of *Politics of Friendship*, Derrida ponders the possibility that there might be at least 'two different, even antagonistic or incompatible, structures' of friendship (*PF*, 277).[1] The first of these differing structures would refer to what Derrida calls the 'fraternal friendship'. He traces its trajectory back through the inherited apostrophe, 'O my friends, there is no friend', by way of 'Montaigne listening to Diogenes listening to Aristotle', and follows it forward 'from Plato to Montaigne, Aristotle to Kant, Cicero to Hegel', all the way up to Carl Schmitt's political writings (234, 277). This first structure would be canonical for the Western conception of friendship modelled on the discourse of the Greek *philia* and its Christianisation into the love of neighbour.

The second structure would refer to a different tradition, or, rather, to a community without community of thinkers – Nietzsche, Bataille, Blanchot and, to a certain extent, Levinas – who disrupt the very notion of tradition as well as the canonical notions of friendship 'which no longer mean what they were always thought to mean' (297). The word 'friendship' may be maintained by this community that shares nothing, but only by way of the 'profound and rigorous necessity to say things as contradictory, insane, absurd, impossible, undecidable as "X without X"' (42). This second structure thus convenes a certain 'friendship without friendship' consisting, or rather *de-sisting*, in a friendship of *solitaires* who are separate and unbound 'beyond all common appurtenance (familial, neighbourhood, national, political, linguistic and finally generic appurtenance), beyond the social bond itself' (298).[2] This other structure of friendship is reminiscent of Nietzsche's *Sternen-Freundschaft* – a disastrous relation without relation to the other that does not accompany me.

These two structures of friendship, each repeatedly marked by the subjunctive mood of the 'perhaps', would not belong to two separate domains in either historical time or thematic space. Rather, the structure of the other friendship, outside of all structure, already announces itself in the first structure in the shapeless form of an internal contradiction. As Derrida writes of Nietzsche's upheaval of the history of friendship, the disastrously starry friendship 'would inscribe in that history the scansion of an unprecedented event; but – hence the upsetting structure of the event – it would interrupt less than recall (and call again for) a rupture already inscribed in the speech it interrupts' (27).

For reasons of space, this essay will focus mainly on the first structure of friendship and attend only briefly to the other by way of closure. I will do so under the headings of the 'specular' and the 'spectral' as two modes of relating (without relation) to a f(r)iend and look at these modes through the lens of narcissism, which requires an initial detour through psychoanalysis.

The Specular Friendship: Derrida with Lacan

If there were one thing that Lacan and Derrida might agree on, perhaps it would be the circumstance that, as the latter writes, 'the other is the condition of my immanence' (42). In fact, one could argue that for both thinkers the term 'narcissism', as well as self-relation in general, denotes but ways of relating to this condition of originary alterity or alienation. To substantiate this suggestion, let us take a closer look at both Lacan's renowned theory of the 'mirror stage' and Derrida's remarks on narcissism in and beyond the *Politics of Friendship*.

According to Derrida, the structure of the fraternal friendship is inherently narcissistic because it holds to the ideals of, on the one hand, equality and symmetry – to love the friend as 'another self who must have the feeling of his own existence' – and, on the other hand, of altitude and hierarchy – to love the friend as a better version of myself, that is, as the 'projection of the ideal image' (3). On a first reading, it would therefore seem that the fraternal friendship is narcissistic because it envisions the friend both as a portrait (*exemplar*) and as a reflection or copy (*exemplum*) of oneself. In this sense, it would consist precisely in the dual relationship between a self and 'his ideal double, his other self, the same as self but improved' (4). Accordingly, it would appear that within the tradition of fraternal friendship the friend is cast according to the 'logic of the same' (4). As always, however, things are more complicated than they appear. For in tracing the fraternal friendship, with its inherent political connotations, not only of equality, liberty and democracy, but also of androcentrism and phallogocentrism, Derrida discerns in this tradition an internal contradiction between 'a respect for irreducible singularity or alterity' and 'the calculation of majorities [. . .] identifiable, stabilizable, representable subjects, all equal' (22). According to Derrida, 'political desire is forever borne by the disjunction of these two laws', that is, the brother-friend as the other and the brother-friend as the same, laws that are '[t]ragically irreconcilable and forever wounding' (229). As we will see, this wounding disjunction has something to do with narcissism. To help us further dissect this wound let us therefore turn to Lacan and his theory of the mirror stage.

The mirror stage is Lacan's psychoanalytic exposition of the formation of the ego. During the mirror stage, the human infant proceeds from uncoordinated sensations of a 'fragmented body' (*corps morcelé*) towards an image of itself that orthopaedically organises this body-in-pieces into a more or less coherent whole.[3] Although this unifying image may be fictional, its premature organisation of the body is decisive for the formation of the ego insofar as it provides the support by which the subject will be able to stand erect in 'an armor of an alienating identity that will mark with its rigid structure the subject's entire mental development'.[4] However, even if the mirror stage provides the subject with a certain sense of identity, unity and mastery, it does so only on the basis of a 'primordial discord' between the unified surface-whole of the mirror, which anticipates an ideal future to come, and the disorganisation, fragmentation and motor insufficiency of its current bodily state.[5] This discord precipitates the split between the *ideal ego* and the *ego*, brought on by the imaginary identification. Thus the premature formation of the ego in the mirror stage is correlated to what Freud in 1914 termed 'primary narcissism'.

In his essay 'On Narcissism' (1914), Freud argues that in proceeding from auto-eroticism '[t]he charm of a child lies to a great extent in his narcissism, his self-contentment and inaccessibility'.[6] In contrast, Lacan asserts that primary narcissism has nothing to do with an originally self-sufficient being who must gradually emerge from an involuted mode of self-love towards the uncoiled world of object love. Rather, primary narcissism has to do with the fact that the ego is originally ecstatic, always already outside itself. This is so, Lacan writes, because 'the total form of his body, by which the subject anticipates the maturation of his power in a mirage, is given to him only as a gestalt, that is, in an exteriority'.[7] In the mirror stage, the subject identifies itself as one and the same ego only by identifying with the coherent surface of the specular other, which means that the subject must retrieve its self-identity outside itself in order to obtain a delimited inside in the first place. Thus, in 'The Instance of the Letter in the Unconscious', Lacan's declared objective is to expose the 'radical heteronomy that Freud's discovery shows gaping within man' and to engage explicitly with 'the self's radical eccentricity with respect to itself'.[8] This original eccentricity and heteronomy is covered over, however, by the 'misrecognition' (*méconnaissance*) that is inscribed in recognising oneself fictionalising the oneness of the subject as something intrinsic in its own being. In 'The Subversion of the Subject and the Dialectic of Desire', Lacan writes:

> The ego is thus a function of mastery, a game of bearing, and constituted rivalry. In the capture it undergoes due to its imaginary nature, the ego masks its duplicity; that is, consciousness, in which the ego assures itself an indisputable existence [. . .], is in no way immanent in the ego, but rather transcendent.[9]

Here Lacan, like Derrida, echoes the young Descartes's *larvatus prodeo*, 'I come forward, masked', although Lacan would probably add to this statement that 'I didn't know which mask I was wearing' (cf. 160).[10]

According to Julien, Lacan's mirror stage thus effectively subverts Freud's account of primary narcissism in that '[t]he ego is not formed by means of *its* exteriorization, by a movement from interior to exterior, that is, by projection. Rather, the reverse occurs: the ego is from the start exteroceptive or there is no ego'.[11] Hence, for Lacan narcissism does not connote the sense of a self-contained being that must transcend its primary enclosed wholeness in order to encounter the exterior world of others only in a second move. Rather, the trials of narcissism originate from the fact that there is an 'outside constitutive of an inside, an original alienation'.[12] Because of the fundamental misrecognition of the mirror stage, however, this originary alienation retrospectively appears to the subject as a loss, or even as a theft, of its own original being one with itself. This is part of the duplicity of the mirror stage and its imaginary identification. On the one hand, the specular other is what presents the not-yet-formed ego with a fascinating image of its own oneness and 'future-perfect mastery' that it will seek to comply with unendingly.[13] On the other hand, however, this specular identification functions only on the basis of a doubling and thus of a splitting that alienates the ego from itself from its very inception. Phrasing it in a more Derridean manner, the specular other is both the condition of possibility and impossibility of the being one with myself. According to Lacan, this essential ambiguity of primary narcissism as self-recognition and self-alienation inscribes the ego into a tension of aggressiveness with regard to the specular other that corresponds to 'the rending of the subject from himself'.[14]

This brings us to a later emendation that Freud makes to the discussion of narcissism. In 'Group Psychology and the Analysis of the Ego' (1921), he suggests that instead of the infant being inaccessibly self-contained in its primary narcissism, it is already by being born that 'we have made the step from an absolutely self-sufficient narcissism to the perception of a changing external world and the beginnings of the discovery of objects'.[15] Furthermore, the transition from intra-uterine serenity to the agitation of extra-uterine existence is so difficult to endure 'that we periodically revert from it, in our sleep, to our former condition of absence of stimulation and avoidance of objects'.[16] In other words, rather than a propensity to boost and assert one's ego as independent and unique, which would require a separation from other egos and objects, narcissism has to do with a longing for the 'oceanic feeling' that Ferenczi comes to refer to as the 'thalassal regressive trend'.[17] As such, narcissism harbors an abyssal attraction to an oceanic gorge in which there are neither egos nor objects, nor others but only an undifferentiated and indifferent oneness. This thalassal trend of narcissism brings it into close contact with the death drive, which Freud describes precisely as a tending 'to restore an earlier state of things which the living entity has been obliged to abandon under the pressure of external disturbing forces'.[18] This earlier state of things towards which the death drive longs is the state of being unborn.

As Blanchot discerns it, there is a point at which the thalassal pull of Thanatos merges with the epitome of narcissism in such a way that 'the rigors of spiritual purification, even the absolute withdrawal into the void can be seen as narcissistic modes: relatively undemanding ways for a disappointed subject, or one uncertain of his identity, to affirm by annulling himself'.[19] In the failing oneness of oneself the self longs for a oneness with all, which entails the annihilation of self. There is a destructive tendency in narcissism understood as a drive towards a pure and undivided oneness, at which point it becomes difficult to distinguish life drives from death drives and the life drives may appear to be nothing but the 'myrmidons of death'.[20] As Derrida articulates the doubly destructive force of unification, '*At the centre of the principle, always, the One does violence to itself, and guards itself against the other*' (ix).

Returning to Lacan, this (self-)destructive tendency of narcissism latent in the imaginary identification of the mirror stage is directed as much 'outward' as 'inward', if these terms make sense any longer, that is, as much towards the specular other as the reflected subject, since the subject is nothing other than the other that nevertheless remains other. The tension by which I both am and am not identical to the other is the source of not only aggressiveness, hate, jealousy and rivalry, but also love and friendship, as long as these are contained within the oppositional relation of the imaginary. The specular friendship would thus be a friendship of the mirror in which I never see anything but my friend seeing me and therefore never see my friend as other than 'an*other* me'. The specular friendship would be engrossed in the imaginary dyad of the ego and the ideal ego, which is also a friendship in which the friend at any given moment may transmute into the enemy or the evil double. Since the specular other is the condition of my imaginary coherence, it also exposes my innate dehiscence and thus wields the unconditional power to destroy that coherence. Thus, in the aftermath of the mirror stage, the human subject continues to be haunted by 'images of castration, emasculation, mutilation, dismemberment, dislocation, evisceration, devouring, and bursting open of the body – in short, the *imagos* that I personally have grouped together under the heading "imagos of the fragmented body," a heading that certainly seems to be structural'.[21]

Derrida's initial question in the *Politics of Friendship*, whether the friend is 'the same or the other', now appears evermore difficult to answer (4). I suggest that a shift or a sliding, similar to the subversion that Lacan conducts on Freud's primary narcissism, occurs in Derrida's account of fraternal friendship. Lacan subverts the mechanism of primary narcissism from a projection of the same unto the other to not so much an introjection, which would require an anterior interior, but rather an 'exteroception' of the other, by which the same is first invented. In a similar manner, the wounding 'conflict' or 'disjunction' that Derrida traces in the relation of fraternal friendship, that is, between casting the friend as other or as same, is retraceable in the relation of the self in such way that 'one would find the other in oneself already: the same dissymmetry and tension of surviving in self, in the "oneself" thus out of joint with its own existence' (24). The tragic wounding of the disjunctive laws of politics are reflected in what Derrida elsewhere calls the 'narcissistic wound', which inflicts upon the self the same disjunction as that of the brother-friend.[22] Accordingly, the '*philía* most devoted to the other, the most heterotopical or heterophilial, is no other, finally, than the friendship of self, philautia, if not narcissism' (178). The catch, however, is that the wound gaping within both fraternal friendship and friendship of self 'would break all ipseity apart in advance, it would ruin in advance that which it makes possible: narcissism and self-exemplarity' (24). To get a better sense of why this is so, we must return to our initial shibboleth that 'the other is the condition of my immanence'.

Narcissism shares with the death drive a longing for pure oneness. Yet this very longing tells us that we have lost unity already at or even before our conception, or rather, that what we are longing for is, in the words of Blanchot, an originally 'lost loss' (*perte perdue*) disclosing the unsettling circumstance that there never was anything to lose in the first place.[23] Nevertheless, as narcissists we keep searching for an imaginary restoration of the oneness with ourselves that was enticingly presented to us in the mirror stage as an ideal future to come, and we continue to look for it in the specular other. Thus, as Derrida writes, we watch the fraternal friend 'looking at us, thus watching ourselves, because we see him keeping our image in his eyes – in truth in ours – survival is then hoped for, illuminated in advance, if not assured, for this Narcissus who dreams of immortality' (4). Within the bounds of fraternal friendship, we are looking for unbounded survival, an everlasting prolongation of ourselves, a friend to bestow on us the consistency that we lack in ourselves.

This no longer depicts a narcissism of self-containment or self-sufficiency but rather a Narcissus who, as Derrida writes elsewhere, 'gazes at himself only from the gaze of the other'.[24] This shadow side of Narcissus is what Derrida in *Memoirs of the Blind* refers to as the '*punctum caecum*' or the 'blind point' of narcissism, which is what 'cannot be "thought" in the specular or speculative mode – and thus is blinded because of this, blinded at this point of "narcissism," at that very point where it sees itself looking'.[25] Here we find the famous (s)tain of the mirror. Narcissus cannot see himself seeing. He therefore needs the gaze of the other to catch hold of the existence that is constantly eluding him. Yet in fraternal friendship the friend not only serves as the projection of ourselves as an ideal double staring back at us with a gaze of recognition; rather, the gaze of the other, on which my imaginary identity depends, essentially escapes our control and cannot be determinately deciphered. This uncertainty of the constitutive gaze of the other causes an anxiety of annihilation that may, in psychosis, turn into full-blown persecutory anxiety.

In this way, what Derrida calls 'narcissistic or fraternal violence' is at least double (13). On the one hand, the frater-narcissistic friendship is violent because it works according to a 'logic of the same', which reduces the otherness of the other to a projection of ourselves. On the other hand, however, this specular relationship is violent because the 'same' only ever arises from the gaze of the other in whose 'ocular globe' there is a (s)tain that threatens to dislocate the image that holds my bodily scraps together.[26] Within the fraternal friendship of the specular the friend may therefore suddenly and without warning mutate into an enemy, albeit an enemy on whom I depend as much as on the friend. Derrida writes:

> This enemy was a companion, a brother, he was like myself, the figure of my own projection; but an exemplarity more real and more resistant than my own shadow. My truth in painting. The enemy did not rise up; he did not come after the friend to oppose or negate him. He was already there, this fellow creature, this double or this twin. (172)

Here it becomes clear how aggressiveness is structurally embedded in the specular relation between the ego and its counterpart from its very inception and thus constitutive not only of the fraternal friendship but also of subjectivity. Lacan articulates the ambivalence thus: 'Only to man does this image reveal its mortal signification and, at the same time, that he exists. But this image is only given to him as an image of the other, that is to say, it is ravished from him.'[27] The fact that the narcissism as well as the fraternal friendship immediately try to cover over this threat of imaginary dismemberment, dissipation and deliverance to the specular other does not preclude the fact that it is there at its heterogeneous origin. To Derrida, this originary alterity entails that

> I must trust the other more than myself, and this sliver of mirror is indeed the sign that my friendship reaches towards, and is sustained in, the other. It depends more on the other than on myself [. . .] it is on the subject of my very self, 'deep down' in myself; it is regarding myself, in the inner recess of my 'regarding myself,' that I entrust myself, without measure, to the other. (195)

Yet, despite the idealisation of the other in fraternal friendship, the spectral other is also *another me*, meaning that the other, like the mirror according to Lacan, 'does not extend to infinity'.[28] The other is not only potentially fatal to my own self-image, but also mortal, and the mortality of the other inflicts a 'narcissistic wound' on the ego, which at the instance of the other's death 'enlarges infinitely for want of being able to be narcissistic any longer'.[29] Or rather, it becomes 'a narcissism which is never related to itself except in the mourning of the other' (187). Accordingly, as Derrida writes elsewhere, 'it is only starting from the other, from a kind of self-renunciation, that narcissism grows, and grows always in losing itself, and this contradiction is at once its limit and condition'.[30]

Approaching Spectral Friendship: The Excessive Measure of the Third

Both aspects of narcissistic violence – the longing to reduce the other to the same and the threat of the same being engulfed in the other – are immersed in the specular relation that defines both Derrida's fraternal friendship and Lacan's imaginary dyad; both consist in a dual relation, yet both long for unity. As Nietzsche has the solitary hermit complain:

> 'One is always one too many around me' [. . .] I and Me are always too earnestly in conversation with one another: how could it be endured, if there were not a friend? For the hermit that friend is always the third person: the third person is the cork that prevents the conversation of the other two from sinking to the depths. (277)

Even though neither Lacan nor Derrida believe in 'overcoming' narcissism, both hope that a partial interruption of the specular by a 'third' is possible. Lacan discerns this possibility in analysis, where the analyst, in order to break the spell of specular fascination and interrupt the imaginary transference that makes out the 'inaugural knot of the analytic drama', must 'efface' and 'depersonalise' her- or himself and offer the analysand only 'the pure mirror of a smooth surface'.[31] This smooth-surfaced mirror is one that reflects nothing, least of all the analysand her- or himself, for, as Lacan continues, '[i]f we imagine it, in the extreme case, experienced in the uncanny form characteristic of the apprehensions of one's double, the situation would trigger uncontrollable anxiety'.[32] Thus the analytic session establishes a sort of alternative mirror phase, in which the analyst makes her- or himself 'invisible to the subject', thus allowing 'the narcissistic image to be produced all the more purely and the regressive proteanism of its seductions to have freer range'.[33] But this only in order to inaugurate a symbolic transference, in the form of the discourse of the Other, capable of interrupting the entrancing entrapment of imaginary resemblances. This other Other, or this third Other, as Lacan writes in 'The Instance of the Letter in the Unconscious', is 'an alterity raised to the second power, which already situates him in a mediating position in relation to my own splitting from myself, as if from a semblable'.[34]

In *Politics of Friendship*, Derrida sets his sights not on an analytic interruption but on a second-order interruption of the 'rupture' or 'scansion' already marking the narcissistic structure of fraternal friendship. Instead of an oppositional space of rupture between the same and the other, this interruption of rupture would install a 'dissymmetrical curving' and an 'infinite heterogeneity' not only in relation to ourselves but also to the other, thus opening the possibility of another friendship, which would no longer be a specular quest for synchronicity but an affirmation of a spectral *contretemps*. Derrida writes:

> Now what is coming is still spectral, and it must be loved as such. As if there were never anything but spectres, on both sides of all opposition, on both sides of the present, in the past and in the future. All phenomena of friendship, all things and all beings to be loved, belong to spectrality. (288)

What Derrida hopes for is a new form of desire, which would no longer desire seeing oneself recognised in the other, but rather a desire 'to interrupt the jealous narcissism of the dual relation, which always remains imprisoned between "me" and "me," "I" and "me;" to do everything possible to keep it from sliding into the abyss of specular jealousy. Is there a worse jealousy than jealousy of self? In truth, is there any other?' (276). Moreover, Derrida dreams of a law that would command not a love of the neighbor, the congenial, the close by, but that would rather 'command me to recognize the transcendent alterity of the other who can never be anything but heterogenous and singular, hence resistant to the very generality of the law' (277).

Yet for both Derrida and Lacan a certain self-folding of narcissism remains irreducible even in the most loving of friendships. In fact, as Derrida puts it, 'the ruse of narcissism never comes to an end', precisely because the alterity of the other remains inappropriable.[35] As Derrida further explains in an interview,

> [t]here is not narcissism and non-narcissism; there are narcissisms that are more or less comprehensive, generous, open, extended. What is called non-narcissism is in general but the economy of a much more welcoming, hospitable narcissism, one that is much more open to the experience of the other as other [. . .]. The relation to the other – even if it remains asymmetrical, open, without possible reappropriation – must trace a movement of reappropriation in the image of oneself for love to be possible, for example. Love is narcissistic.[36]

So, love might be narcissistic in its very structure, but all things that are loved belong to a spectrality that repeatedly dislocates the ideal symmetry of the specular. Loving the spectral friend would thus also be a way of affirming 'an *absolute* excess and dissymmetry in the space of what relates us to ourselves'.[37]

This kind of love requires an 'active forgetfulness' of the primordial oneness or wholeness that never existed, in that ex-sistence, as Lacan emphasises, is nothing but 'the dehiscence from natural harmony [. . .] in which man, distinguishing himself from his essence, discovers his existence'.[38] This kind of love would be the active forgetting of the imaginary completeness that the specular other is both expected to provide me and accused of taking from me. Lacan thus calls for a relation beyond semblance when he evokes the vicissitudes of a modern society whose imaginary coherence is falling apart. To the human being living in modern society, 'this fracturing reveals that his formidable crack goes right to the very depths of his being'.The purpose and invention of analysis would be to take in this 'touching victim' of modern society whose imaginary being has become nothing but a 'being of nothingness', and to help this being broach another kind of relation. In analysis, Lacan writes, 'we clear anew the path to his meaning in a discreet fraternity – a fraternity to which we never measure up'.[39] Similarly yet differently, Derrida urges us to 'dream of a friendship which goes beyond this proximity of the congeneric double', that is, a friendship that would go 'beyond the home-fraternal and phallogocentric schema' and 'would at last be just, just beyond the law, and measured up against its measurelessness' (viii, 306).

Notes

1. Jacques Derrida, *Politics of Friendship*, trans. George Collins (London: Verso, 1997); Jacques Derrida, *Politiques de l'amitié: suivi de L'Oreille de Heidegger* (Paris: Galilée, 1994). Hereafter, page references to the English translation are given in parenthesis in the text.
2. See Derrida's essay 'Desistance' on the writing of Philippe Lacoue-Labarthe in Derrida, *Psyche: Inventions of the Other, Vol. II* (Stanford: Stanford University Press, 2008), pp. 196–230.
3. Jacques Lacan, 'The Mirror Stage as Formative of the *I* Function', in Lacan, *Écrits* (New York: W. W. Norton, 2006), pp. 75–81 (p. 78). Hereafter *Écrits*.
4. Lacan, *Écrits*, p. 78.
5. Ibid. p. 78.
6. Sigmund Freud, 'On Narcissism: An Introduction', in Freud, *The Standard Edition of the Complete Psychological Works of Sigmund Freud*, Vol. XIV (London: Hogarth Press, 1981), pp. 67–102 (p. 89). Hereafter SE.

7. Lacan, *Écrits*, p. 76.
8. Ibid. pp. 435–6.
9. Ibid. p. 685.
10. Jacques Lacan, *Anxiety. The Seminar of Jacques Lacan. Book X* (Cambridge: Polity, 2014), p. 5.
11. Philippe Julien, *Jacques Lacan's Return to Freud* (New York: New York University Press, 1994), p. 30.
12. Julien, *Jacques Lacan's Return*, p. 30.
13. Richard Feldstein, 'The Mirror of Manufactured Cultural Relations', in Feldstein, *Reading Seminars I and II: Lacan's Return to Freud* (New York: SUNY Press, 1996), p. 135.
14. 'Variations on the Standard Treatment' (1955), in Lacan, *Écrits*, p. 286. Hereafter 'Variations'.
15. Freud, SE XVIII, p. 130.
16. Ibid. p. 130.
17. Sándor Ferenczi, *Thalassa: A Theory of Genitality* (London and New York: Karnac, 2005), p. 52ff.
18. Freud, 'Beyond the Pleasure Principle,' SE XVIII, p. 36.
19. Maurice Blanchot, *The Writing of the Disaster* (Lincoln: University of Nebraska Press, 1995), p. 125.
20. Freud, SE XVIII, p. 39.
21. 'Aggressiveness in Psychoanalysis', in Lacan, *Écrits*, p. 85. Hereafter 'Aggressiveness'.
22. Jacques Derrida, *Psyche: Inventions of the Other*, Vol. I (Stanford: Stanford University Press, 2007), p. 9.
23. Blanchot, *The Writing of the Disaster*, 41.
24. Jacques Derrida, *The Work of Mourning* (Chicago: University of Chicago Press, 2001), p. 164.
25. Jacques Derrida, *Memoirs of the Blind: The Self-Portrait and Other Ruins* (Chicago: University of Chicago Press, 1993), p. 53.
26. Lacan, *Anxiety*, p. 6.
27. Lacan, 'Variations', *Écrits*, p. 287.
28. Lacan, *Anxiety*, p. 72.
29. Derrida, *Psyche*, p. 9.
30. Jacques Derrida, 'Portrait d'un philosophe: Jacques Derrida', in *Philosophie, Philosophie* (Saint-Denis: Université de Paris VIII-Vincennes 1997), p. 17. trans. Pleshette DeArmitt, in DeArmitt, *The Right to Narcissism: A Case for an Im-Possible Self-Love* (New York: Fordham University Press 2014), p. 118.
31. Lacan, 'Aggressiveness', *Écrits*, pp. 87, 89.

32. Ibid. p. 89.
33. Lacan, 'Variations', *Écrits*, p. 287.
34. Lacan, *Écrits*, p. 436.
35. Derrida, *Memoirs of the Blind*, p. 70.
36. Jacques Derrida, *Points . . . Interviews, 1974–1994* (Stanford: Stanford University Press, 1995), p. 199.
37. Derrida, *Work of Mourning*, p. 161.
38. Lacan, 'Variations', *Écrits*, p. 286.
39. Lacan, 'Aggressiveness', Écrits, p. 101.

11

Dividing the Ear

Isabelle Alfandary

In the chapter titled 'Ranges of Voice. Rhetoric of Friendship' (*Portées de voix. Rhétorique de l'amitié*), Jacques Derrida comments at length on the enigmatic wording of a phrase taken from Heidegger:

> In its strict grammaticality, the phrase says that *Dasein* carries with it the friend itself, and not only its voice: 'als Hören der Stimme des Freundes, den jedes *Dasein* bei sigh trägt' (*Sein und Zeit* §34). Through its voice that I hear, I hear the friend itself, beyond its voice but in that voice. I hear and carry the friend with me in hearing its voice.[1]

In this 'little phrase' of Heidegger's, Derrida finds an occasion to tacitly revisit a foundational *topos* of his own works, *Of Grammatology* and *Voice and Phenomenon*.[2] 'The voice of the friend is not reduced to the phoneme or to the acoustic phenomenon, does not merge with the noise perceived by an animal ear or auditory organ. This voice is an essentially understandable voice, the possibility of speech or discourse.'[3] If the *voice of the friend* is not synonymous with *phonē*, it cannot be assimilated into *logos* either: 'In any case, what matters here is not what the friend's voice says, not its said, not even the saying of its said. Hardly its voice. Rather what matters is the hearing [*das Hören*] of its voice.'[4] And yet, under Derrida's pen, the expression 'hardly its voice' catches us by surprise. Here, I wish to address the ambiguity concealed within this expression, and by extension, the rereading it invites of one of the foundational theses of Derrida's thought.

In reference to the psychoanalyst Theodor Reik, who conceived the psychoanalytic notion of the 'third ear',[5] Philippe Lacoue-Labarthe writes:

> In both cases, not only does everything happen at the level of audition or listening, but what is heard and begins to make sense (to 'signify,' not in

> the mode of signification but, if one may rely on a convenient distinction, in that of *significance*) is not, strictly speaking, of the order of language. Rather, it affects a language, and affects in the use of a language (although this cannot be understood in relation to the Saussurian *parole*, or in relation to linguistic 'performance') its *musical* part, prosodic or melodic. Reik is interested, as we see, in the *voice*: intonation, elocution, tone, inflections, melisma, rhythm, even timber (or what Barthes calls 'grain'). Or color. These are all things which are dealt with by ancient rhetoric (that of enunciation and diction, of *lexis*) and which might sustain up to a certain point the attention of a musical theory, as was the case in the long history of the development of the operatic recitative, or even a stylistics. But they do not fall under the jurisdiction of linguistic distinctions in the proper sense (of the type semiotic/semantic, for example) because, more fundamentally, they escape the metaphysical (theoretical) distinctions that always underlie them (sensible/intelligible, matter/form, body/spirit, thing/idea, and so on). A phenomenon of this sort is, finally, untheorizable.[6]

The voice in the *voice of the friend* is not primordial: it is caught in what Lacoue-Labarthe calls the 'register of hearing or listening'. Indeed, the register of listening as it integrates – though only partly – that of hearing contains within it a number of surprises.

In *Of Grammatology*, 'logocentric metaphysics' was interpreted by Derrida as a 'philosophy of presence', the exclusion of writing becoming, through the assumption of *phonē*, an experience of pure presence.[7] Full speech actualises pure presence, the fullness of the subject to itself through the intervention of a medium that is not one – voice. The voice is, according to Derrida, the subject's own, since metaphysics conceived and invented it, founded it. The voice does not belong to the subject, rather it is consubstantial with it. More than a faculty, it is its own manifestation, its most intimate quality, its own-most emanation. Unlike (*A la difference de*) writing, 'the exteriority of space' is *hardly* felt there.[8] In accordance with the powerful fiction invested in speech by metaphysics – a fiction which Derrida calls 'myth' – it becomes immune from any state of otherness. By its very definition, full speech excludes any exposure to the world as spacing, differently from with the self. Speech is said to be full precisely in the sense that it immediately grasps itself within a space which has the limited dimensions of a closed circuit. Speech is full of itself – this is the meaning of the metaphysical myth, wherein an experience is supposedly removed from the common conditions of experience. It is for this reason that full speech coincides with the live voice or living speech (*la vive voix*):

> One must understand speech in terms of this diagram. Its system requires that it be heard and understood immediately by whoever emits it. It produces a signifier which seems not to fall into the world, outside the ideality of the signified, but to remain sheltered – even at the moment that it attains the audiophonic system of the other – within the pure interiority of auto-affection. It does not fall into the exteriority of space, into what one calls the world, which is nothing but the outside of speech. Within so-called 'living' speech, the spatial exteriority of the signifier seems absolutely reduced.[9]

According to Derrida, full speech seeks to assert the metaphysical fantasy of meaning generated without the fall – 'It does not fall [*Elle ne tombe pas*]': without the outside, without the other.

And yet, the *voice of the friend* is carried by *Dasein*. While this *tragen* is hardly a meditation, it implies a difference between self and self which could be resolved by spelling this *difference* with an *a*, even if Derrida himself did not, in this case, venture to do so. For unlike the voice, the ear is capable of splitting in two (*dédoublement*). The *voice of the friend* is valued not only – not so much – as a voice, but as a voice carried by *Dasein*, a voice subject to a regime of listening. In his attempt to approach the sense of Heidegger's remark, Derrida comes to consider (in the following chapter, *Having, Being and Other* [*L'avoir, l'être et l'autre*]) the possibility of sharing listening – of listening as division:

> Heidegger accuses then the deafness of our modern and common ear before the extraordinary thing that he nevertheless just understood, heard [*hören*], and gave to be understood. Heidegger's ear then divides itself. More precisely, it is divided in two. There is a deaf ear like that of everyone today (Heidegger speaks in that case of what sounds 'for our ear,' ['*für unser Ohr*']), and this ear perceives as 'trivial' what has just been heard or said. The other ear over-hears the unheard through the deafness.[10]

Such a process of division implicitly echoes the work of the *mark* as described and analysed by Derrida from *Of Grammatology* to *Dissemination*. Without referring to his earlier texts explicitly, implicit yet obvious conclusions are drawn from them. Here, we are asked to read between the lines. The ear called upon to listen to the *voice of the friend* is not caught in the ideal logic governing the sense of hearing (as it is set out in Hegel's *Encyclopédie*).[11] Derrida takes care to distinguish this striking instance of *Dasein* 'that carries the friend in its voice or rather in hearing this voice' from psychic writing of Platonic inspiration.[12] The allusion Derrida makes to Plato is indirect yet unmistakable to anyone who has studied his theses on psychic writing, specifically the chapter he devotes to the parallel reading of Mallarmé and Plato in 'The Double Session'.[13] In *Philebus*, Derrida observes an inadvertent possibility which Plato envisages arising from *logos*:

> But from the instant this *logos* can have been formed, when the possibility of dialogue has come into being, it might happen, through an accident of circumstance, that I wouldn't have a partner handy: alone, then, I address this discourse to myself, I converse with myself in a sort of inward commerce. What I then hold is still a discourse but it is soundless, aphonic, private – which also means deprived: of its mouthpiece, its voice. Now, it is in connection with this deficient *logos*, this blank voice, this amputated dialogue – amputated of its vocal organ as well as of its other – that Socrates resorts to the 'metaphor' of the book. Our soul then resembles a book not only for the obvious reason that it is a kind of *logos* and dialogue (and the book is thus only a species within the genus 'dialogue'), but particularly because this reduced or mumbled conversation remains a false dialogue, a minor interchange, equivalent to a loss of voice.[14]

Dasein's position as it carries the *voice of the friend* is poles apart from that of Plato's false inner dialogue: far from 'hearing itself speak [*s'entendre parler*]', *Dasein* registers (*entend*) the voice of the other echoing within it. This voice, anything but *voiceless*, is marked with the seal of the other, intimate but no less foreign: 'The friend's voice, the friend in its voice is not in itself [*en soi*], but in me.'[15] The *voice of the friend* carrying *Dasein* within it, Derrida concludes,

> supposes a critique or rather a 'destruction' of the Aristotelian interpretation of *logos* [. . .] Among other things, this means that everything in the future that will articulate, in an essential way, in Heidegger's thought *legeîn* or *logos* and *phileîn* will claim to come back to a pre-Aristotelian, in truth, a pre-Platonic, hearing of *logos*.[16]

The author of *Politics of Friendship* professes to hear the *voice of the friend* in both senses of this term (*entendre*), listening and understanding – to hear this voice as it manifests outside of the sphere of speculative activity whose ancient identification is noted by Lacoue-Labarthe: 'An old secret heritage of Platonism: the voice, diction, the audible in general (and music) are attainable only by speculation.'[17] This relation to *phonē* is one rejected by the Heideggerian analysis of *Sprache* and *logos*. For the voice in question, Derrida specifies, is not an inner voice, the superego voice of consciousness ('that eye of conscience that accompanies, keeps watch over, and oversees'), nor is it 'the inner voice of conscience'.[18] The *voice of the friend* evoked by Heidegger's 'little phrase' is another voice: 'Here there is no phenomenon of ideal self-presence in the inner voice. It is really a matter of the voice of the other.'[19] It is as if, for Derrida, the possible relation to the voice as other opened up by Heidegger's evocation of the *voice of the friend* extends an opportunity for him to examine afresh – albeit locally and silently – his deconstruction of metaphysics from Plato to Husserl, as well as the terms of his relation to Heidegger's philosophy.

As Derrida recalls in *Voice and Phenomenon*, 'interior monologue' was, for Husserl, the paradigmatic linguistic situation of the original conditions of expression. In the case of the *voice of the friend*, the situation is one of hetero-affection – it being irreducible to the process of 'hearing-oneself-speak' as analysed by Derrida in relation to Husserl in 1967.[20] For the phenomenologist, the silence of interiority is the most satisfactory representation of the relation of speech to signification. It is only through interior monologue – where the subject speaks to themselves without emitting a sound, presenting the effective possibility of the reduction of natural speech – that the conditions for the production of signification as intentionality are revealed. What follows is the act of utterance, which *hardly* registers.[21] Here, the ideality of the *voice of the friend* is not in question – Derrida reiterates that this is not the voice of a person, much less the voice of a friendly person. And yet, the resulting affection involves a certain experience of otherness, even if this is not synonymous with 'the agency of exteriority, of the world, or of the non-proper in general'.[22] The *voice of the other*, insofar as it is carried by *Dasein*, can, in this regard, be considered *unheimlich*. Recalling Freud's observation of the particular way in which this term encompasses its opposite meaning, *heimlich*, we can say that the *voice of the friend* is strangely familiar.[23]

The *voice of the friend* establishes the dimension of listening, a pillar of existential analysis which is constitutive of 'this opening of *Dasein* to its ownmost, its most authentic potentiality-for-being'.[24] This listening, Derrida specifies, is not 'an acoustic phenomenon of the physiopsychological order'.[25] Then what kind of listening is it? Drawing on the Reikian notion of the 'third ear' cited above, Lacoue-Labarthe examines psychoanalytic listening in terms of a Gothean resonance, of 'repeated reflections': 'This is precisely the situation of listening with the third ear: what one might call a listening by echo, or catacoustic interpretation.'[26] The *voice of the friend*, Derrida restates, is not the voice of a particular friend, rather a human voice which he describes as 'figureless [*le sans-figure*]'.[27] This term could be translated into Lacanian vocabulary through the notion of the 'little other [*petit autre*]':

> Everything happens as if the friend were not one figure among others, and therefore could play an exemplary role for being the figureless [*le sans-figure*], or as is said in French *le figurant* or similarly in English, the figurehead, that individual being no one can be anyone, the exemplary, then at once singular and general, configuration of every possible other, of every possible figure, or rather of every possible voice of the other.[28]

Except that, for Lacan, this little *a*, this *little other*, is not a voice but an image:

> The little *a* is the little other, the other insofar as he is our semblable, insofar as his image grabs, captivates and supports us, and insofar as we constitute around him this first order of identifications which I have defined for you as narcissistic identification, which is the small *e*, the ego.[29]

The *voice of the friend*, as a metonymic representation of an other with suspended determinations, is to *Dasein* the condition of its own being.

This voice says nothing in particular, hardly speaking, and yet it accompanies *Dasein*, it is there by its side. The condition of *being there* expressed by *Dasein* seems in places to coincide with the condition of the subject in psychoanalysis. As we hear Lacoue-Labarthe observing: 'Because the very hypothesis of the unconscious, as Reik says ingenuously, places us before an "antinomy" (access "to the deepest and most vital region" of the Ego is forbidden to consciousness), any understanding of the Ego "needs to be reflected in another".'[30] If an echo is analogous to a reflection, then the *voice of the friend* enables *Dasein*, if not to know itself, to at least catch sight of itself in the mirror.

Alongside melody, this voice maintains a certain resemblance which merits further exploration: 'For a person with a musical memory [*le mélomane*]', Lacoue-Labarthe writes, 'it is not necessary for the melody to be played all through for him to recognize it. After only a few bars, the reminiscence of the whole melody, or at least of its essence, will occur spontaneously to the listener.'[31] In a way, the *voice of the friend* has the form of a melody which *Dasein* carries within it, without even needing to hear it, understand it, or formally summon it. The dimension of accompaniment (*bei sich*), commented on by Derrida at length, is a way of being with the other, a unique *Mitsein*, midway between presence and absence:

> *Dasein* has an ear and can hear then only insofar as *Dasein* carries 'bel sich' the friend, the voice of the friend. No ear without friend. No friend without ear. *Dasein*'s opening to its *ownmost* potentiality-for-being, as hearing the *voice of the other as friend*, is absolutely originary. This opening does not come under a psychology, a sociology, an anthropology, an ethics, or a politics, etc. The voice of the other friend, of the other as friend the ear that I prick up to it, is the condition of the own-proper-being. But this voice nevertheless defines the figure of an originary sharing [*partage*] and an originary belonging, of a *Mitteilen* or of everything that is, as Heidegger says in this passage, 'shared' (*geteilt* [. . .]) with the other in the *Mitsein* of discourse, of address and response.[32]

What exactly should be heard and understood here by the word 'friend'? This question is not without importance, since it is *Dasein*'s capacity to assume the role of listening to the *voice of the friend*, to the voice 'of the other as friend', to the *voice of the friend* as other. Even if Derrida only circles such a formula without explicitly proposing it, we might venture to suggest that *who founds it in its being, calls it into being*. The friend is a figure of otherness: its voice is designated explicitly as the voice of the other. This is what distinguishes it from Platonic psychic writing, as well as from its phenomenological avatar, where the encounter with the voice of the other is only ever conceived according to the model of splitting in two (*dédoublement*) as staged in the self-address of *phonē*:

> One would not be able to pose on this subject questions of a critical or deconstructive type that recourse to the monologue or to the purely inner voice of the *ego* in Husserl's *Logical Investigations* could call for. Here there is no phenomenon of ideal self-presence in the inner voice. It is really a matter of the voice of the other.[33]

We could also consider this in terms of what Lacan calls, in his seminar on *The Ethics of Psychoanalysis*, 'the desire of the analyst', on which he predicates the capacity of the analyst to take up the role of listening to the other. The condition of what the analyst has to 'give' to the other is based on an openness to listening to the voice of the other, to the voice as well as the other, which is primordial – establishing the analyst as desire and psychoanalysis as ethics.[34] In his commentary on Heidegger, Derrida specifies:

> The friend has no face, no figure [*figure*]. No sex. No name. The friend is not a man, nor a woman; it is not I, nor a 'self,' not a subject, nor a person. It is another *Dasein* that each *Dasein carries*, through the voice it hears, with itself [*bei sich trägt*], neither within itself, in the ear, in the 'inner ear,' inside a subjective interiority, nor far away, too far from the ear, for one can also hear from afar, in an exterior space or in some transcendence, but in its vicinity [*parages*].[35]

In this regard, and contrary to the Claudelian metaphor, if the eye of *Dasein* is not listening, it could be that its ear is writing. This 'auditory writing [*écriture auditive*]', this all but physiological capacity of the ear to 'divide itself [*se partager*]', implicates a return to and questioning of the modality of psychoanalytic listening: 'There is a deaf ear like that of everyone today (Heidegger speaks in that case of what sounds "for our ear," ("für unser Ohr")), and this ear perceives as "trivial" what has just been heard or said. The other ear over-hears the unheard through the deafness.'[36] This Heideggerian definition of the ear recalls the Reikian notion of the 'third ear':

> It can be demonstrated that the analyst, like his patient, knows things without knowing them. The voice that speaks in him, speaks low, but he who listens with a third ear hears also what is expressed almost noiselessly, what is said *pianissimo*. There are instances in which things a person has said in psychoanalysis are consciously not even heard by the analyst, but none the less understood or interpreted.[37]

This third ear, an ear that *reads*, emerges from a process of splitting in two (*dédoublement*) – one in which Lacan explicitly engages the analyst in *The Situation of Psychoanalysis and the Training of Psychoanalysts* in 1956 through a call to suspend stereophony:

> May one of your ears become as deaf as the other one must be acute. And that is one that you should lend to listen for sounds and phonemes, words, locutions, and sentences, not forgetting pauses, scansions, cuts, periods, and parallelisms, for it is in these that the word-for-word transcription can be prepared, without which analytic intuition has no basis or object.[38]

In his 1934–5 seminar series on Hölderlinn's *The Rhine*, Heidegger refers to this 'inner ear [*oreille du dedans*]' as 'poetic'. Here is the commentary Derrida offers in response:

> This ear is poetic [*dichtende*] because it hears *in advance* just what it causes to burst forth. It *gives* itself to hear what it hears [*Elle* donne *elle-même à entendre ce qu'elle entend*]. It is *dichtende* because it speaks, says, poetizes itself. It is interior in that it produces in some way of itself what it hears: it hears it in advance, is in advance of what it hears and gives to be heard, as if the ear were speaking or were speaking itself, hearing itself speak in advance, fore-telling itself, outside of all conscious or speculative reflectivity, outside of all absolute identity, indeed all proximity, with itself.[39]

This poetic ear is ahead of time and has, so to speak, a kind of knowing in advance – a knowing which does not know itself. Its poetic listening is a listening to *logos*, to a Heideggerian *logos* which Derrida judges his is not – neither is it Platonic, nor Aristotelian. Rather, his listening is to a *logos* which the author of *Sein und Zeit* seeks to deconstruct below the metaphysical threshold. Nonetheless, this listening is posed – earmarked – as thought: 'And when we speak of thinking as hearing or hearkening, this is not a metaphor.'[40] As proof of an impregnable metaphysical insistence, Derrida takes the Heideggerian argument that not hearing or not hearing well is 'an essential possibility of hearing'.[41] If, having maintained a certain philosophical suspense by following Heidegger along the path of such an ear, he is ultimately reluctant to go any further, this hesitation draws attention to the foundational state of mourning (*deuil*) that such a homological model of listening conceals: [42]

> This nostalgia is the origin of philosophy. It is a reaction to the loss of the originary *phileîn*, of the l'*homolégeîn*, of the correspondence with *logos*. One could even say that every *philosophical*, for example Aristotelian, determination of the *proté philia* or of the *teleia philia* inhabits the space of mourning, but also of reactive nostalgia, sometimes triumphant as mourning can be, the space of semi-deafness that still hears [*entend*] without hearing any longer the *homolegeîn* of the originary *phileîn*.[43]

With almost clinical analysis, Derrida presents philosophy as the mourning of a form of listening conceived according to the model of *entendre* (hearing and/as understanding), in a way that seems to inscribe itself into the Freudian line of thinking formulated in 'Mourning and Melancholia' (1917). This Derridean interpretation of philosophy as 'reactional nostaliga' contains a critique of the metaphysical imprint that places emphasis on listening to *Dasein*, as well as on analytical listening, which is distantly aligned with the tradition of lost understanding (*l'entente perdue*).

Undoubtedly, Lacan was interested, fascinated even, by Heidegger's account of listening. We know he went so far as to translate the article 'Logos'– the very one referred to by Derrida.[44] In this article, Heidegger presents a commentary on Heraclitus' 50th fragment, through which he distinguishes the physiological act of listening from that of hearing, which is brought under another type of relation to the other:

> So long as we are only listening to verbal articulation as the mode of expression of the speaking person, we are not yet listening. We do not actually get to hear anything. But when then? We have heard only when we *are in agreement* [*sommes en entente*] with that which is addressed to us.[45]

This Heideggerian 'being-in-agreement' (*être-en-entente*), as Lacan translates it, surely orientated Derrida's conception of analytical listening. For Lacan, hearing implies the opening of oneself to the dimension of otherness – a word he does not hesitate to capitalise as concept, at the risk of countersigning the German text: 'It is not towards me that you must extend your ear (as one fixes their gaze). What it is to hear for the mortal must be orientated towards something Other [*quelque chose d'Autre*].'[46]

In turn, Derrida attaches great importance to the unique 'evocation' of the friend in Heidegger, as well as to the occasion through which its voice is evoked. Without aligning his own thought with Heidegger's, Derrida explores, piece by piece, the various facets of his 'little phrase', taking it as an opportunity to revisit his critique of the metaphysics of voice, in which he perceives, however furtively, the muffled persistence of the *topos* of the *voice of the friend*: 'That perhaps is what one can be authorized to say, in order to begin, about the friend such as it is apparently named, only once named, in a brief parenthetical clause of *Sein und Zeit*.'[47]

Translated by Emily Fitzell

Notes

1. Jacques Derrida, 'Heidegger's Ear: Philopolemology (*Geschlect* IV)', in *Commemorations: Reading Heidegger*, ed. John Sallis, trans. John P. Leavy Jr (Bloomington and Indianapolis: Indiana University Press, 1993), pp. 163–218 (p. 164).
2. Derrida, 'Heidegger's Ear, p. 173; Jacques Derrida, *Of Grammatology* (Baltimore and London: Johns Hopkins University Press, 1976); Jacques Derrida, *Voice and Phenomenon* (Evanston: Northwestern University Press, 2011).

3. Derrida, 'Heidegger's Ear', pp. 174–5.
4. Ibid. p. 164
5. 'To capture the messages that emanate from it [from the deep secret layers of the soul], the psychoanalyst calls on his own unconscious. He has to sense them, divine them, while waiting to be able to finally decipher them; know how to listen with the "third ear" to what his patients say to him and what they hide from him; practice detecting the *infrasounds* [*infrasons*] of the unconscious process.' Theodor Reik, *Fragment d'une grande confession*, trans. Jacqueline Bernard (Paris: Denoël, 1973), pp. 280–1. TR – my translation from French edition.
6. Philippe Lacoue-Labarthe, 'The Echo of the Subject', in Lacoue-Labarthe, *Typography: Mimesis, Philosophy, Politics* (Cambridge, MA and London: Harvard University Press, 1989), pp. 139–207 (p. 159).
7. Derrida, *Of Grammatology*, p. 106.
8. Ibid. p. 165.
9. Ibid. p. 166.
10. Derrida, 'Heidegger's Ear', p. 184.
11. 'Sight is imperfectly theoretical and ideal (it lets the objectivity of the object be, but cannot interiorize its sensuous and spatial opaqueness). According to a metaphor well coordinated with the entire system of metaphysics, only hearing, which preserves both objectivity *and* interiority, can be called fully ideal and theoretical.' Jacques Derrida, *Margins of Philosophy* (Brighton: Harvester Press, 1982), p. 93.
12. Derrida, 'Heidegger's Ear', p. 172; 'It is *Dasein* and not *psukhé*, man, self, nor subject, conscious or unconscious, that carries he friend in its voice or rather in hearing this voice.' (Ibid.).
13. Please see my analysis of this concept in my text, *Derrida – Lacan, l'écriture entre psychanalyse et deconstruction* (Paris: Hermann, 2016), pp. 175–80; Jacques Derrida, *Dissemination* (London: Athlone Press, 1981), p. 173.
14. Derrida, *Dissemination*, p. 184.
15. Derrida, 'Heidegger's Ear', p. 166.
16. Ibid. p. 172.
17. Lacoue-Labarthe, 'The Echo of the Subject', pp. 163–4.
18. Ibid.
19. Ibid.
20. Derrida, *Voice and Phenomenon*, p. 67.
21. 'Thus all of what constitutes the actuality of what is uttered, the physical incarnation of the *Bedeutung*, the body of speech, which in its ideality belongs to an empirically determinate language, is, if not out-

side of discourse, at least foreign to expressivity as such, to this pure intention without which no discourse would be possible.' Derrida, *Voice and Phenomenon*, pp. 28–9.

22. Ibid. p. 67.
23. 'For us the most interesting fact to emerge from this long excerpt is that among the various shades of meaning that are recorded for the word *heimlich* there is one in which it merges with its formal antonym, *unheimlich*', Sigmund Freud, *The Uncanny*, trans. David McLintock (New York: Penguin Books, 2003), p. 134.
24. Derrida, 'Heidegger's Ear', p. 173.
25. Ibid.
26. Lacoue-Labarthe, 'The Echo of the Subject', p. 164.
27. Derrida, 'Heidegger's Ear', p. 175.
28. Ibid.
29. Jacques Lacan, *The Seminar of Jacques Lacan: Book V, Formations of the Unconscious, 1957–1958*, trans. Russell Crigg (Cambridge: Polity, 2017), p. 293.
30. Theodor Reik, cited by Lacoue-Labarthe in 'The Echo of the Subject', p. 165.
31. Ibid.
32. Derrida, 'Heidegger's Ear', p. 174.
33. Ibid. p. 175.
34. 'What the analyst has to give, unlike the partner in the act of love, is something that even the most beautiful bridge in the world cannot outmatch, that is to say, what he has. And what he has is nothing other than his desire, like that of the analysand, with the difference that it is an experienced desire [*un désir averti*]', Jacques Lacan, *The Seminar of Jacques Lacan: Book VII, The Ethics of Psychoanalysis 1959–1960*, trans. Dennis Porter (New York and London: W. W. Norton, 1992).
35. Derrida, 'Heidegger's Ear', p. 165.
36. 'Hearing is constitutive of discourse, but does not consist in an acoustic phenomenon of the physiopsychological order' (ibid. p. 173); ibid. p. 184.
37. Theodor Reik, *Listening with the Third Ear* (New York: Farrar, Straus and Giroux, 1948), p. 145.
38. Jacques Lacan, *Écrits*, trans. Bruce Fink (New York and London: W. W. Norton, 2002), p. 394.
39. Derrida, 'Heidegger's Ear', p. 186.
40. 'This gathering in "all ears" [literally in the "all ear"] is why we do not hear *with one* or *two* auditory organs. As he will repeat in *der Satz vom*

Grund, Heidegger underscores that we do not hear because we have ears, but we have ears because we hear. And when we speaking of thinking as hearing or hearkening, this is not a metaphor [*Übertragung*] transferring a "properly so-called" or allegedly authentic hearing [*audition*] onto the spiritual plane [*auf das Geistige*]' (ibid. p. 188).

41. Ibid.
42. 'Heidegger writes *what I have just given you without conviction* but as the premise of what is going to follow: "When we hear a Greek word with a Greek ear [*Wenn wir ein grieschisches Wort grieschisch horen*], then we are docilely following its *légein*, its immediate exposition [*seinem unmittelabren Darlegen*]. What it exposes is there before us"' (ibid. p. 181). My emphasis.
43. Ibid. p. 190.
44. Martin Heidegger, 'Logos', trans. Jacques Lacan, in *La psychanalyse*, vol. 1 (1956), pp. 59–79.
45. Ibid. p. 67.
46. Ibid, p. 69.
47. Derrida, 'Heidegger's Ear', p. 165.

12

Narcissus as an Anti-Narcissus

Timothy Secret

> We are speaking about anything but narcissism as it is commonly understood. (*PF*, 24)[1]

Derrida stated in *Specters of Marx* that the twentieth century was, among other things, the century 'of the *ego cogito* – and of the very concept of narcissism whose aporias are, let us say in order to go too quickly and save ourselves a lot of references, the explicit theme of deconstruction'.[2] Although one can make too much of such rare, bombastic moments that seem to offer a 'master-concept' around which we might understand Derrida's *oeuvre* as a unified whole, it is not difficult to imagine some of the references he could have offered to demonstrate that narcissism has indeed been his theme, albeit not always terribly explicitly. For example, although *Voice and Phenomenon* never uses the word 'narcissism', its deconstruction of the 'ideal or absolute solitude of "proper" subjectivity' in its supposedly '*pure auto-affection*' – performed via exposing the constitutive role of the indicative sign in 'hearing-oneself-speak'– can be understood as an engagement with narcissism in at least two senses.[3] Not only does it dispute the tenability of the phenomenological philosopher's narcissistic dream of achieving the view from nowhere of a pure and objective scientific knowledge, it does this through showing that the closed-in-on-itself, world-constituting, self-constituting and self-sufficient transcendental subject or *ego cogito* is an illusion, in at least the Freudian sense. Husserl's 'absolute subjectivity' would have 'to be erased as soon as we think the present on the basis of *différance*', since there is 'no constituting subjectivity', only '*a priori and in general*' a constituted subjectivity – the supposed origin of meaning is no origin.[4] Indeed, psychoanalysis already argued that this illusion of an original, hermetically sealed monadological ego is formed as a defensive reaction against an original risky exposure to the other, or, shifted to a Levinasian vocabulary, that even the language within which the subject might declare '*ego cogito*', along with its splendid narcissistic self-sufficiency, is a gift premised on the enigmatic trace of the other as a past that has never been present. However, it is also clear that Derrida's engagement with narcissism encompasses something more and other than the mere exposure and humbling of a phallogocentric philosophical tradition that founds itself in the modern period on the transparency of self-consciousness as an unmediated self-relation. After all, Derrida famously demanded that the 'right to narcissism must be rehabilitated'.[5]

Nevertheless, a reader might anticipate that raising the theme of mankind's inescapable narcissism in a text dedicated to friendship constitutes a bluntly critical move. Surely such a narcissism places limits on the possibility of friendship, if not suggesting its outright impossibility. After all, few figures seem more opposed to the various models of friendship that populate the Western mythological and literary imaginary than Ovid's Narcissus. We picture him squatting motionless by the water – having rejected the advances of Echo and various youths with the declaration 'May I die before I give you power o'er me!' – cursed by Nemesis for refusing love, he is abandoned in a self-absorbed rapture that stretches even beyond death.[6]

However, as is often the case in Derrida's works, 'the disconcerting logic of what is blithely called narcissism' or the 'infinite paradoxes of what is so calmly called narcissism' will lead us down less easily anticipated paths.[7] Although a familiar quasi-transcendental structure emerges, one in which narcissism is not only a condition of the impossibility of friendship but also a condition of its possibility, quite how it emerges and what follows from it remains rather obscure. In this chapter, we will show how a part of this obscurity comes from the movement at stake being almost the opposite of the one found in texts such as *Voice and Phenomenon*. The implicit dynamic is not one where exposure to the other plays a constitutive role in the construction of the narcissistic illusion of the closed subject, but rather one where narcissism is a condition for any relationship to the other. If such apparently countervailing movements can be thought together, which is certainly not a given in Derrida's works, it must be because Derrida is indeed speaking here of something quite different from 'narcissism as it is commonly understood' – perhaps different even to how it is understood in many of Derrida's other texts (24).

Archi-Narcissism

A series of references to narcissism marks *Politics of Friendship*, forming a recurrent leitmotif. First, we have the direct references to 'narcissism' and the 'narcissistic'. Added to these are occasional engagements with the figures of Narcissus and Echo. Then, there is a wider semantic field of terms, each with its own complex genealogical development across Western philosophy. These include *philautia, autou eneka, amour de soi* (translated as self-love), *amitié de soi* (friendship of self), *amour propre* and *égoïsme* (translated both as egoism or egotism) – a list that could easily be continued. Even putting aside this extended field, references to 'narcissism' and 'Narcissus' appear in more than half the book's chapters.

This leitmotif is nevertheless easy to dismiss or ignore. The most notable book-length study of *Politics of Friendship*, Alex Thomson's *Deconstruction and Democracy*, makes no direct reference to narcissism, Narcissus or any of the other terms listed above.[8] Equally, what is arguably the most important study of narcissism across Derrida's *oeuvre*, Pleshette DeArmitt's *The Right to Narcissism*, makes no reference to *Politics of Friendship*.[9] While other scholars have picked up on Derrida's references to narcissism in this text, it certainly seems that one can take narcissism to be inessential to *Politics of Friendship* and *Politics of Friendship* to be inessential to Derrida's deconstruction – and perhaps rehabilitation – of narcissism.

As DeArmitt has pointed out, direct references to narcissism, and particularly to the figure of Narcissus, appear most frequently in texts by Derrida on one of two themes: those on 'the image or the (self-)portrait' and his 'texts on and of mourning'.[10] This distinction is neatly captured in her section titles 'Blind Narcissus' and 'Black Narcissus', both offering paradoxical transformations of the traditional figure of Narcissus.[11] In the first, the figure of Narcissus transfixed by the beauty of his own image cannot readily be made sense of if he is blind. However, the association with mourning is perhaps even more surprising. Surely the fully narcissistic subject – cathecting their entire libido to their own self in psychoanalytic terms – is impervious to loss and incapable of any work of mourning, such work being understood as the painful withdrawal of libido invested in a lost love object. Nevertheless, the multiple references to narcissism in Freud's classic account show matters to be more complex. While it is precisely the 'sum of narcissistic satisfactions' that the mourner 'derives from being alive' that motivates the severing of attachment to the lost object in so-called healthy mourning, it is also a 'narcissistic object-choice' and possibly a 'narcissistic identification' with the love object that leads to melancholia, whose alternating mania is a consequence of the secondary narcissistic reinvestment of the self that follows in 'the process of regression from narcissistic object-choice to narcissism'.[12] As we will see, narcissistic object-choice and identification form a major theme in Derrida's engagement with the theory of friendship found in figures such as Aristotle, Cicero and Montaigne.

This dense thicket of technical uses of 'narcissism' and its compounds only grows more labyrinthine in the psychoanalytic tradition beyond Freud. As Peter Gay points out, the word rapidly enlarged its sphere of signification, 'first at Freud's hands and then far more irresponsibly in general usage, much to its damage as a diagnostic term', with the word entering general educated discourse as a label for a sexual perversion, a normal developmental stage, a symptom in psychosis, and a term of abuse that can be aimed at individuals, cultures or epochs.[13] Within Freud's works, we encounter primary narcissism, secondary narcissism, pathological narcissism, natural narcissism, the narcissistic neuroses, narcissistic object-choice, narcissistic personality types and many other assemblages – while Freud's joke about a narcissistic cat shows he was far from careful about protecting it as a diagnostic term.[14] Some later developments include André Green's distinction of positive and negative narcissism, the rethinking of narcissism in Lacan's mirror stage, and the rather different evaluation of narcissism in the tradition following Heinz Kohut or, even earlier, in the work of Lou Andreas-Salomé. Indeed, prior to Freud's publication of 'On Narcissism', the 5 March 1913 entry in Andreas-Solomé's *Freud Journal* shows the analytic community already involved in vigorous debate about the term, including her reflection that 'the concept is employed in two ways which could surely lead to extraordinarily disturbing misunderstandings, especially in enemy hands'.[15] This sense of multiplicity and conflict, if not conceptual imprecision and weakness, inhabits even apparently more precise technical compounds. For example, in Jean Laplanche's study of primary narcissism – 'one of Freud's most deceptive notions' – we learn that there are 'two manifest trends', both present from the outset yet often confused in Freud's text. These are an originary cathexis of the biological individual (which becomes dominant in Freud's later thought) and a cathexis of a particular psychical formation, the ego (which, since the ego is a relatively late psychic construction, shows that both the ego and the narcissism attached to it only 'pass themselves off to us, mythically, as "primal"').[16]

In the face of such multiplicity, it seems legitimate to ask *which* narcissism must be rehabilitated? Derrida himself offered the justification that he had often tried 'to put the concept of narcissism into question' on the basis that 'it is a very important question that has been poorly defined'.[17] However, it seems his attempts to improve that definition have little methodological relation to the subtle marking of distinctions and ambiguities found in Laplanche's 'interpretations' of Freud's text. Indeed, even the rather minimal assistance of specifying whether a particular claim is about primary or secondary narcissism, pathological or natural narcissism, is almost always absent in Derrida's references to narcissism, including those in *Politics of Friendship*.

How then are we to begin with these scattered references to narcissism across the text? Perhaps Nicolas Abraham's notion of the archi-psychoanalytic – itself appropriating Derrida's archi-writing and that 'sheaf' without 'taxonomical closure' including gram, reserve, incision, trace, supplement, pharmakon, and so on, that serve as 'points of economic condensation' or 'sites of passage' – suggests a manner to approach these references to narcissism that would be foundational for both psychoanalytic and philosophical conceptuality.[18] If we are to ambitiously reinscribe into Derrida's use of narcissism an archi-narcissism, one that encompasses both the auto-affection of narcissism and the relation to the other, it would be in a sense parallel to that archi-writing that is at stake in both traditional writing and speech. Perhaps, just as there is no speech that is pure of writing, there are 'not narcissism and non-narcissism; there are narcissisms that are more or less comprehensive, generous, open, extended'.[19]

I'll Be Your Mirror

At the culmination of the first chapter of *Politics of Friendship*, Derrida summarises his opening discussion in terms of having drawn out a conflict in the 'philosophy of *philein*', particularly 'the Aristotelian philosophy of friendship' (24). This conflict is difficult to capture naturally in French and English, where the language of friendship assumes by default the symmetrical bond of mutual friendship rather than distinguishing between subject and object, active and passive (in the way erotic language recognises lover and beloved, desirer and desired). For Plato and Aristotle, classical Greek readily distinguished between the role of the loving friend, *philein*, from that of the loved friend, *phileisthai*, leading to a question of which role better captures the essence of friendship that might not occur to us.

The conflict Derrida points to is between a model of *philein* based on unilateral dissymmetry and one based in bilateral symmetry. In passages where Aristotle's claims seem to be based on the former structure, true friendship is connected to the manner of being of the lover rather than the loved. This privilege is already found in Plato's *Lysis* and Diotima's speech in the

Symposium, both of which shift from interrogating the dissymmetrical roles involved in actual relationships towards sketching the role of the philosopher who lacks but loves wisdom, virtue and the good, as opposed to the God who already possesses them. In other passages, however, Aristotle advanced claims based on a structure of bilateral symmetry, where true friendship is a bond between two people equal in virtue. This 'logic of the same' will be carried forward in figures including Cicero and Montaigne, forming the basis of Derrida's earliest references to narcissism in the text. For Cicero, 'his *exemplar* is projected or recognized in the true friend, it is his ideal double', which as such is nothing other than a 'narcissistic projection' of the self. The greatest benefit of such friendship is that it delivers to the projector the 'unequalled hope' that through such friendship, as Cicero's puts it, friends 'live on after they have died', or, in a simpler translation of *mortui vivunt*, 'the dead live' (vi, 3–5).

At first glance this appears to be a standard, pejorative use of the label 'narcissism'. Is Cicero not slightly ridiculous when pitched by Derrida as 'this Narcissus who dreams of immortality' – one who hopes that through 'narcissistic identification', which for Freud so often results in melancholia, he can produce an 'absolute future' for himself beyond death. Surely such a fantasised beyond 'appears only from within this narcissism and according to this logic of the same' (4). If we were to pursue friendship driven by such a dream of personal immortality, we would violate a central ethical pillar of the Aristotelian account of friendship: that a friend 'wants good things – or what he thinks to be good things – for someone, not on his own account but for the sake of that person'.[20] Rather than sitting within the context of the rehabilitation of narcissism that DeArmitt tracks in other texts by Derrida, we seem to have a narcissism here that only contaminates and compromises friendship by rendering it useful. For Aristotle, this would push us from the primary friendship 'grounded in virtue', in which friends are a good 'not because they are useful but in another way', towards those friendships based on use-value that for Aristotle must be based on difference, 'for the like is useless to the like', even if this difference is reduced to one of the two specular doubles being dead.[21] Indeed, if one takes the provocation of Derrida's text as the challenge to 'dream of an unusable friendship' and a politics 'at last grounded in this friendship, this one and no other', and so breaking 'with the entire history of the political, this old, tiring and tired, exhausted history', then it seems to be precisely the narcissistic dimension of Cicero's friendship (itself a paradigm of the tradition) that compromises it (217–18).

Of course, first glances can be deceptive. We might wonder whether Derrida would really begin *Politics of Friendship*, coming before even its foreword, with the quotation from Cicero that through friendship '*mortui vivunt*', 'the dead live', if he was so bluntly opposed to this dream (vi). Indeed, Derrida it far less condemnatory of this model of the ideal double than it seems. The friend as mirror image certainly 'makes friendship proceed from self-love [*l'amour de soi*], from *philautia*', yet this 'is not always egoism or *amour-propre*' (24). Despite the vocabulary, this does not seem to be quite the Rousseauian distinction of a broadly good *self-love* and broadly bad *amour-propre*, a distinction that often finds modern expression in the opposition of empowering self-esteem and reprehensible narcissism. However, at this point in the text Derrida rapidly moves on to an even more provocative possibility and leaves the above statement hanging. Perhaps we can understand this abandoned first step if we jump ahead to the digression on Montaigne's reading of Aristotle (or rather Diogenes Laertius's Aristotle) in chapter 7. Here, Derrida engages with the '*doubly singular*' definition of the friend as 'one soul (singularity) but in two bodies (duplicity)' (178). This mirroring model of the friend will not be dismissed as an egoism closed to alterity since it opens a far more hyperbolic and uncanny set of possibilities in which standard ethical schemas break down. The friend narcissistically projected as one's own soul in another body produces 'the ruin of the ordinary meaning of words', since, in Montaigne's words, when everything 'is genuinely common to them both: their wills, goods, wives, children, honour and lives', this means that just as 'I feel no gratitude for any good turn I do to myself' I will similarly feel no gratitude to the perfect friend – 'they can neither lend nor give anything to each other' (Montaigne in citation 178–9).

The utopian communism found in those perfect friendships that lie beyond brotherhood, in which each of two male-specified subjects might say 'he is me', are described by Montaigne as 'the rarest thing to find in the world' (185). He also explicitly blocks that this could form the basis of a politics as it cannot be turned 'into a plural, into a confraternity' – in Derrida's words, this 'political and apolitical communism which does not count – no further than to "one"' (185). Nevertheless, it would be wrong to see Derrida as simply dismissing the model either for its incapacity to form the basis of a politics or for the clear problems of its fraternalism and logic of the same – that is, to its closure to the other who is absolutely other. For, despite those problems, this self-love or *philautia* opens onto those introjections and incorporations that we normally find addressed in Derrida's eulogies, but that are here engaged with in a political register where:

> The body of the friend, his body proper, could always become the body of the other. This other body could live in his body proper like a guest, a

> visitor, a traveller, a temporary occupant. Friendship would be *unheimlich*. How would *unheimlich*, *uncanny*, translate into Greek? Why not translate it by *atópos*: outside all place or placeless, without family or familiarity, outside of self, expatriate, extraordinary, extravagant, absurd or mad, weird, unsuitable, strange, but also 'a stranger to'? (177–8)

It is within this context that 'the friendship of self, *philautia*, if not narcissism' could be the '*philia* most devoted to the other, the most heterotopical or heterophilial' (178). It is also in this context that the dream of immortality, of that friendship that delivers on Cicero's promise that through it 'the dead live', cannot be dismissed as merely the logic of the same. Is it not rather a logic that, when traced, flips like a Möbius strip into a logic of alterity? Turning back to the first chapter, there too we find Derrida pushing beyond the apparent dead end of the other as double towards a strange possibility hedged in a language of 'perhaps' and 'unless' – that is, the chance that one would find the other 'in oneself, already', producing 'the same dissymmetry and tension of *surviving* in the self, in the "oneself" thus out of joint with its own existence' (24).

The practical consequences of these dizzying logics of the same and the other, in what we are terming 'archi-narcissism', emerge most directly in Derrida's texts of mourning. Using the example of Derrida's memorial text for Gadamer, 'Rams', the one who survives, apparently left without the other, finds that 'the dialogue continues, following its course in the survivor' who 'believes he is keeping the other in himself', allowing the other to 'speak inside himself'.[22] Yet, this is not only an account of mourning following the death of a friend, but an engagement with the structure of friendship itself. Derrida states that from the first encounter, 'interruption anticipates death . . . One of us two *will have* had to remain alone. [. . .] One of the two *will have* been doomed, from the beginning, to carry alone, in himself, both the dialogue [. . .] and the memory of the first interruption'.[23] The survivor characterised as alone, beyond or before the world, in the world outside the world and deprived of the world, *atopos*, is handed the responsibility 'to carry both the other and *his* world, the other and *the* world that have disappeared'.[24]

In the domain of a terrible, melancholic yet also possibly joyful responsibility, Cicero's dream of survival has found its uncanny realisation. However, what pushes these reflections from 'Rams' back into the domain of the political is that we also find around this interruption a possibility of friendship that counts beyond one. The interruption of dialogue between these friends does not only continue in Derrida, but 'in a very studious and eloquent, often fecund, fashion, through a large number of philosophers the world over [. . .] who attempted to take charge of and reconstitute this still virtual or suspended exchange, to prolong it or to interpret its strange caesura'.[25] What we have here is a model of a particular political community and its activity, that of the academy, emerging from a reflection on friendship. Rather than being characterised directly by the common love and pursuit of wisdom, as emerges in Plato's *Lysis* or Diotima's speech in the *Symposium*, it is forged in the responsibility of survivors to carry the dead and through this to give life. While this is far from being all that is at stake in the richness of *Politics of Friendship*, we have seen that the sketch of these *atopic* beyonds must begin from a narcissism that is, indeed, anything but how it is commonly understood.

Notes

1. Jacques Derrida, *Politics of Friendship*, trans. George Collins (London: Verso, 1997); Jacques Derrida, *Politiques de l'amitié: suivi de L'Oreille de Heidegger* (Paris: Galilée, 1994). Hereafter, page references to the English translation are given in parenthesis in the text (*PF*). Translations modified.
2. Jacques Derrida, *Specters of Marx* (London: Routledge, 1994), p. 122.
3. Jacques Derrida, *Voice and Phenomenon* (Evanston: Northwestern University Press, 2011), pp. 36, 68, 74.
4. Ibid. p. 72n.
5. Jacques Derrida and Marie-Françoise Plissart, *Right of Inspection* (New York: Monacelli Press, 1998), p. 28.
6. Publius Ovidius Naso, George P. Goold and Frank Justus Miller, *Ovid: vol. 3: Metamorphoses 1. Books I–VIII*, Loeb Classical Library, 42, 3rd edn (Cambridge, MA: Harvard University Press, 1977), pp. 151–9.
7. Jacques Derrida, *Psyche: Inventions of the Other, Vol. 1* (Stanford: Stanford University Press, 2007), p. xiii; Jacques Derrida, *On the Name* (Stanford: Stanford University Press, 1995), p. 12.
8. Alex Thomson, *Deconstruction and Democracy* (London: Continuum, 2005).
9. Pleshette DeArmitt, *The Right to Narcissism* (New York: Fordham University Press, 2014).
10. DeArmitt, *The Right to Narcissism*, p. 97.
11. Ibid. pp. 104, 106.
12. Sigmund Freud, *Complete Psychological Works of Sigmund Freud, Vol 14: 'On the History of the Post Psychoanalytic Movement', 'Papers on*

Metapsychology' and Other Works (London: Vintage Classics, 2001), pp. 255, 258, 251, 265, 250.
13. Peter Gay, *Freud: A Life for Our Time* (New York: W. W. Norton, 1988), p. 340.
14. Lou Andreas-Salomé, *The Freud Journal* (New York: Basic Books, 1964), p. 89.
15. Andreas-Salomé, *The Freud Journal*, p. 110.
16. Jean Laplanche, *Life and Death in Psychoanalysis* (Baltimore: Johns Hopkins University Press, 1976), pp. 70–2.
17. Jacques Derrida, *A Taste for the Secret* (Cambridge: Polity, 2001), p. 23.
18. Jacques Derrida, *Positions* (Chicago: University of Chicago Press, 1998), p. 40.
19. Jacques Derrida, *Points* (Stanford: Stanford University Press, 1995), p. 199.
20. Aristotle, *Aristotle's Ethics* (Princeton: Princeton University Press, 2014), 1240a 20–30.
21. Aristotle, 1237a 10–2, 1235b4.
22. Jacques Derrida, *Sovereignties in Question: The Poetics of Paul Celan* (New York: Fordham University Press, 2005), p. 139.
23. Derrida, *Sovereignties in Question*, p. 140.
24. Ibid. p. 140.
25. Ibid. p. 136.

13

The Apparition of Feminine Alterity in Derrida's *Politics of Friendship*

David Ventura

In *Politics of Friendship*, Derrida seeks to critically call into question the Western philosophical tradition's insistent valorisation of fraternity as the essential model of friendship. As a way of resisting the exclusion of feminine[1] alterity that this valorisation has traditionally entailed, Derrida's text also intends to signal the possibility of an *alternative* politics of friendship that operates 'beyond the principle of fraternity' (*PF*, viii).[2] But if these objectives are discernible enough, *Politics of Friendship* remains perplexing on a number of other fronts. One cannot help but notice, and this issue is my central focus in this chapter, that where in other texts Derrida both cites and devotes at least some attention to actual feminine voices, *Politics of Friendship* – despite criticising thinkers like Carl Schmitt for perpetuating an 'absolute silence' on feminine figures of friendship – is itself marked by an absence of engagement with such voices (156).[3] Indeed, as the text's Foreword explicitly states: 'having done so too often elsewhere, we will here avoid convoking Antigone, here again *all the Antigones of history*, docile or not, to this history of brothers that has been told to us for thousands of years' (ix).[4] But why has Derrida decided *not* to include these feminine voices – or indeed, any actual experiences or examples of friendships involving women and other others – in the very text where he also attempts to signal a new politics of friendship that is less bound to the tradition's valorisation of fraternity? Moreover, how justified is this move on Derrida's part?

My argument is that Derrida avoids engaging actual feminine voices and experiences in this way because he wants to performatively position an irreducible feminine alterity as the *spectral other* of the Western tradition's hegemonic, fraternal conception of friendship. In other words, Derrida's refusal to include the 'Antigones of history' in *Politics of Friendship* attempts to highlight the haunting presence of certain feminine *ghosts* or *spectres* within a tradition which has sought mostly to exclude experiences of friendship involving women from within itself. With this strategy, I suggest, Derrida also attempts to signal the possibility of an alternative, more just and democratic, politics of friendship that is less bound to the tradition's violent exclusions.[5]

Yet, while this attempt is admirable, it also faces certain problems. Specifically, while the decision not to include the 'Antigones of history' perhaps allows Derrida to successfully highlight a feminine spectrality at the heart of traditional thought on friendship, *Politics of Friendship* is not wholly justified in excluding an actuality of feminine voices and experiences from its treatment of friendship *either*. Indeed, as I argue by drawing on feminist thinkers who have similarly dealt with questions of spectrality, while appealing to past ghosts can certainly help us announce the possibility of a different future, it remains equally important that we continually relate those ghosts to the *actuality of our present* – that is, to those practices and experiences by which friendship is reconfigured *today*. For only in that way can we hear something determinate of what those ghosts want us to remember. But this *Politics of Friendship* does not do. And it is here, I suggest, that the text could have benefited from a greater attention to actual experiences of friendship involving, among others, women.

The Exclusion of Feminine Alterity in the Western Tradition of Friendship

Politics of Friendship directs itself to the relation that the Western philosophical tradition has maintained between the ideas of politics and friendship. According to Derrida, while friendship is certainly no more than a marginal concept in many classical political theories, in others it 'plays an organising role in the definition of justice, of democracy even'.[6] Similarly, while the canon has regularly dissociated friendship from the political, it remains the case that 'the figure of the friend [. . .] seems to spontaneously belong to a *familial, fraternalist* and thus *androcentric* configuration of politics' (xvii). When the Western philosophical tradition thinks the friend, it invariably invokes the figure of the brother, and the brotherhood between men: '*the great philosophical and canonical discourses on friendship* will have explicitly tied the friend-brother to virtue and justice, to moral reason and political reason' (277). But we almost never hear of the sister, or the woman. Indeed, such is the hegemony of this tendency to think friends as male, that the canonical concept of friendship can itself be described as 'phallocentric or phallogocentric'.[7]

On Derrida's reading, this hegemonic philosophical paradigm involves a 'double exclusion of the feminine' (279). On the one hand, we are here faced with the exclusion of the friendship between a man *and* a woman.[8] As Derrida shows, when thinkers like Cicero and Montaigne reflect on the ideal or exemplar model of friendship, what they cannot admit is the idea that such a friendship might be heterosexual: 'friendship between a man and a woman cannot be, in Montaigne's view, "sovereign"'. On the other hand, the tradition also omits any serious consideration of the friendship *between* women themselves: 'The bond between female companions or between a woman-friend and her companion could never be equal to its model: the bond of two male companions' (180). In both cases, women are excluded in favour of entirely male bonds and relations, and phallogocentrism presents itself as the tradition's most indispensable schema (262).

This double exclusion of the feminine means that 'there is inequality and repression in the traditional concept of friendship such as we inherit it'.[9] Indeed, as Derrida stresses, although the tradition has frequently related the friend to the political ideals of justice and democracy, it has historically been far from just and democratic to the singularity of feminine experiences. By thinking friendship in phallogocentric terms, the Western tradition has given 'less chance to the woman, to the daughter, to the sister' (293).[10] Specifically, it has given them less chance of being counted as friends whose irreducible alterity makes them worthy of democratic respect and equality (22).[11] As such, the tradition of friendship has not only violently supported the historical exclusion of women from the institutions of democracy, but it has even justified their exclusion from the sites of the political itself: the state, the city and the country (200).

Nevertheless, for Derrida, it remains possible to think *another*, more democratic, politics of friendship that does less violence to the singular alterity of women, daughters and sisters. However, for that possibility (or promise) to become meaningful, politics itself has to be 'articulated with another concept of friendship, another experience of friendship which wouldn't simply be dependent on or subordinate to [. . .] the prevalent canonical concept of friendship (phallogocentric, male, and so on . . .)'.[12] Put differently, to think the promise of a more just and democratic politics of friendship, we need to find ways of *experiencing* friendship without subordinating it to the tradition's phallogocentric principle. We must experience a form of friendship that not only respects the singularity of feminine alterity, but also distances itself from those presuppositions – like 'presence' and 'proximity' – by which that alterity has violently been excluded from the canon (238–40).[13] But how can we arrive at this alternative experience of friendship without simultaneously finding ourselves recaptured by the traditional hegemony of phallogocentrism? Derrida states that an answer to this question is precisely what he is 'trying to elaborate in the *Politics of Friendship*'.[14] And I suggest that it is by keeping this question in mind that we can begin to understand his decision not to appeal to the 'Antigones of history' in the text.

The Apparition of Feminine Alterity in *Politics of Friendship*

If the canon has evidently privileged a fraternal politics of friendship, it is equally clear that *Politics of Friendship* wants to 'break with the entire history of politics, this old, tiring and tired, exhausting history' (218). Yet, and while Derrida frequently reflects on how thought might begin to 'resist', 'interrupt' or 'distance' itself from the tradition's phallogocentrism, he never unequivocally argues in favour of *including* actual feminine voices and experiences as a way of concretising this rupture. Indeed, as Derrida suggests in a passage on Schmitt, while we might object that the latter's theory of the partisan – with its focus on 'men, men, and more men' – unduly excludes an account of the historical involvement of women in wars and resistance movements, this strategy is not particularly effective in displacing the phallogocentrism that constitutively imbues Schmitt's definition of politics. For even Schmitt could concede that the inclusion of feminine experiences into a theory of the partisan is 'legitimate, even urgent', whilst nonetheless continuing to hold that such inclusion 'has no political pertinence as such', that 'the subject of the political is genderless' (156–8).

This passage illustrates one of Derrida's earliest warnings in *Politics of Friendship*: 'The fratriarchy may *include* brothers and sisters but [. . .] including may also come to mean neutralising' (viii). Said differently, while we cannot doubt the legitimacy of the strategic attempt to include into thought on friendship those feminine voices and experiences that the canon has so regularly excluded, we should likewise remain mindful that this cannot, by itself, guarantee an alternative politics of friendship which functions 'with an altogether different mobilising force' (158). For phallogocentrism, as Derrida points out, is well accustomed to incorporating those voices and forces that purport to oppose and exceed it.[15] This incorporation is even how phallogocentrism *maintains* itself, since by incorporating and including, phallogocentrism can also reappropriate, assimilate and neutralise what is other than itself. For this reason, Derrida insists, a transformation of the political requires *more* than the inclusion of what the latter has traditionally excluded. This is particularly true if that transformation also seeks to be *democratic*, that is, if it attempts to 'free a certain interpretation of *equality* [. . .] from the phallogocentric schema of *fraternity*' (232). For democracy, as Derrida continually reminds us, 'has seldom represented itself without the possibility of at least that which resembles [. . .] the possibility of a *fraternisation*' (viii).

Faced with these issues, Derrida argues, we cannot hope to move beyond a traditional politics of friendship without *also* seeking, in some way, to involve ourselves *with* it, 'without ceasing to intervene therein to transform it' (159). Indeed, if friendship and democracy have always been held back by the possibility of phallogocentrism, then to create a politics of friendship that effectively revokes that possibility, we must also 'keep the "old name" [of politics], and analyse the logic and the topic of the concept differently' (158).[16] We must continue to engage the tradition not only so that we can explain how its phallogocentric schema has come to define the political itself, but also, and significantly, so that we can show that the stability of this schema already contains within itself other, divergent possibilities for friendship. As Derrida writes in *Glas*, 'the system of phallogocentrism [. . .] is always precarious and neutralises itself, *contains* what contradicts it'.[17] As such, while the canon has systematically excluded experiences of friendship involving women, those experiences, and the feminine friends they involve, are nonetheless never entirely *absent* from the canon. In a certain sense, they are still there, 'giving off signs or symptoms of a stance of survival [*survivance*] through all the old and tired features' (104). And this is why, according to Derrida, engaging the canon remains so strategically vital: so that we can glean what heterogeneous possibilities for friendship continue to *survive* or *live-on* (*sur-vie*) within the tradition in spite of all its repression and exclusion.

Crucially, however, these surviving possibilities are never quite reducible to the canon's explicit or declarative statements (46n5). Instead, for Derrida, this survival is best understood as a sort of 'trace' or 'remainder' which subsists in the tradition as its *other* side.[18] What survives is an *unspoken* heterogeneity which distinguishes itself both from the tradition's self-identity with itself, and from the temporality of the living present in general. In other words, what lives-on are a number of *ghosts* or *spectres*, that is, 'certain *others* who are not present, nor presently living', but who nonetheless remain, and regularly present themselves in the paradoxical modality of a non-present being-there – or in what Derrida calls the modality of *apparition*.[19] Now, though they live-on in the history of friendship, these ghosts are not strictly reducible to the past; they are not figures merely representing a past-present. Rather, ghosts are *revenants*: they are beings who ceaselessly *return*, and who, in so doing, continually mark both the past and the present with an untimely disjunction (288).[20] In this sense, what survives in the tradition is not simply the trace of an excluded past-present which was never lived. What survives is a past spectral alterity which, by returning or making an apparition, also provides 'the unknowing anticipation of a future appearance, indeed of a future still to appear'.[21] And in effect, it is the apparition of such untimely spectres that *Politics of Friendship* attempts to *conjure*, or *make come*, through its extended deconstruction of the tradition of friendship.[22]

It is, moreover, against the backdrop of this spectral evocation that Derrida's decision not to convoke the 'Antigones of history' must be understood. Indeed, when at the outset of his work Derrida states that he will not convoke a long line of actual feminine figures against the phallogocentric history of friendship, he is already operating under the presumption that this history remains haunted by a number of spectres: 'there is the spectre, lodged within the political itself' (138). Now, because spectres haunt the political in this way, the latter is never entirely a site of sheer exclusion. When the tradition is approached through its ghosts, it can also become the occasion for the return 'of that which should not return' or appear within it, that is, for the apparition of 'the very thing it is not or which it excludes from within itself' (292–3, 300). From within the tradition, *and even without evoking them in their actuality or former presence*, one can already bear witness to the untimely survival of those friends that the tradition has always sought to exclude from itself: the woman, the daughter, the sister. One can sense the paradoxical presence of these feminine friends that are 'returned as the phantoms of our past [. . .] [and which] can speak, and speak to us in an icy voice, "as if we were hearing ourselves"' (292–3). And in short, it is these icy spectral voices – these *untimely feminine voices* that remain irreducible to any history or actuality that might be cited against the Western history of friends qua brothers – that Derrida's text seeks to convoke and expose.

This attempt to evoke a number of feminine voices as the tradition's spectral others permeates the entirety of *Politics of Friendship*, but it perhaps achieves its clearest expression in Derrida's reading of Schmitt. As Derrida himself admits, the deconstruction of Schmitt's ceaseless appeal to the concrete is intended above all to make us 'attuned to a certain effect of haunting' (177). Put differently, it serves to highlight the repeated apparition of the spectre in precisely that site which is said by Schmitt to most radically expunge it: the concrete. Now, when we come to explore Schmitt's theory of the partisan with this effect of haunting in mind, we can also begin to sense just *who* the spectre(s) of this philosophy – and its tradition – might be. Considering that this theory traditionally frames the partisan as that absolute enemy who is also a brother, and considering, moreover, that Schmitt has nothing to say on what distinguishes this brother from a sister ('Not a woman in sight [. . .] [not] the slightest allusion to sexual difference'), it is an irreducible feminine alterity that can be felt as haunting this theory's most assured categories:

> If the woman does not even appear in the theory of the partisan – that is, in the theory of the absolute enemy – if she never leaves a forced clandestinity, such an invisibility, such a blindness, gives food for thought: what if the woman were the absolute partisan? And what if she were the absolute enemy of this theory of the absolute enemy, the *spectre* of hostility to be conjured up for the sake of the sworn brothers, or the other of the absolute enemy who has become the absolute enemy that would not even be recognised in a regular way? (156–7, emphasis added)

Otherwise said, if the woman here impresses herself as the absolute enemy of Schmitt's thought, this is because that philosophy, despite its explicit attempts to expunge both the abstraction of the spectral and the relevance of gender for politics, nonetheless remains haunted by the paradoxical presence of what it attempts to exorcise: the feminine spectre. And it is the coming of this spectre, and of the other feminine spectres that haunt the tradition, that *Politics of Friendship* attempts to conjure through its deconstruction of the latter's foreclusionary structures.

But what does Derrida hope to achieve in conjuring feminine alterity as the canon's spectral other in this way? In *Specters of Marx*, Derrida clarifies that his obsession with ghosts cannot be separated from the question of justice: 'If I am ready to speak at length about ghosts [. . .] it is in the name of *justice*.'[23] In *Politics of Friendship*, likewise, it is justice that drives the appeal to the tradition's feminine spectres. More accurately, this convocation is how Derrida hopes to signal another, more just and more democratic, politics of friendship (cf. 104). As previously noted, Derrida stipulates that for the promise of this alternative politics to be thought, thought itself must undergo an experience of friendship that does not simply subordinate alterity to the tradition's phallogocentric schema, or indeed, to the valuation of presence which has traditionally underlaid it. Put differently, to think this promise, we must undergo a certain experience of the *impossible*: one where that feminine alterity which cannot possibly figure within the tradition of friendship manifests itself, or arrives, as 'altogether other [*tout autre*]' and without the possible reappropriation of any principle or present in general (232). For without this experience, which consists of 'letting the other come', we can never quite effectuate the rupture with phallogocentrism that is required by justice and democracy (46). Indeed, as Derrida says, 'without this experience of the impossible we might as well give up on both justice and the event' (Cf. 36).[24]

In this context, the evocation of the tradition's feminine spectres assumes a strategic importance in *Politics of Friendship*. For as we have seen, Derrida considers ghosts to precisely distinguish themselves from both the tradition's self-identity with itself and the temporality of the living present. When Derrida evokes the feminine ghosts that survive in the canon of friendship, he is therefore not simply extending the endless monologue of that canon with itself. He is instead attempting to engender that alternative experience of friendship – perhaps still 'unthinkable today' – which consists of 'a non-appropriative relation to the other that occurs without [the] violence' of phallogocentrism and its associated temporal modalities.[25] Ultimately, as mentioned, it is this impossible experience that Derrida does not quite believe a strategy of inclusion can deliver for thought on friendship. Yet, it is just this experience, and the politics that might be suggested by it, that he hopes to make possible by means of a deconstruction that does not appeal to (or include) an actuality of feminine voices and experiences: 'the "come" of a certain democracy which is no longer an insult to [a] friendship [. . .] beyond the homo-fraternal and phallogocentric schema' (306).

Relating the Spectral to the Actual

What are we to make of Derrida's effort to go beyond phallogocentrism in *Politics of Friendship*? It cannot be denied that the text's deconstructive strategy, despite not referring to a lineage of feminine practices and experiences of friendship, does not straightforwardly replicate the violent and exclusionary mistakes of the tradition it engages. In appealing to the survival of certain feminine *revenants* within the canon, the text not only works to fissure and unsettle that history from within, but also attempts to make us hear the untimely call of '*another justice*', one where friendship and democracy are no longer thought in terms of the tradition's indispensable phallogocentric axioms (64).

And yet, while this attempt is laudable, there are still questions to be asked of Derrida's decision not to include an actuality of feminine voices, practices and experiences of friendship within the text. For as feminist thinkers who have similarly dealt with questions of spectrality show, the move to cast feminine experiences into a shadowy or vaporous domain of spectrality has *also* historically functioned as phallogocentrism's way of *denying* and *exorcising* the singularity of such experiences. Indeed, as Terry Castle argues, the gesture to 'wave off' these experiences into a phantasmic domain (which presumably bears no relation to reality) has often been used to regulate the 'threat' that intra-feminine relations present to patriarchal culture.[26]

Of course, this is not to suggest that even in such classic phallogocentric manoeuvres feminine ghosts entirely lose their 'powerful and perverse' ability to disjoin the present from itself.[27] Crucially, however, Castle insists that we can begin to sense this disruptive power only by calling feminine spectral figures 'back to passionate, imbricated life'.[28] Said differently, it is only by connecting our past ghosts to *actual, embodied or performed practices and experiences* that we can convoke those ghosts not simply as negative figures at the margins of our tradition, but rather as figures who hold the potential to radically subvert the current conditions of patriarchal culture. For without tracing such connections between the spectral and the actual, it remains difficult to hear something determinate of what those ghosts want us to remember in the present.[29] It remains difficult to hear in the spectre's voice anything more than a vague and empty call for another future.

Now, as is well known, Derrida's thought by no means denies a constitutive connection between the spectral and the actual.[30] Indeed, as *Politics of Friendship* explicitly states, its deconstruction of the tradition is directly connected to a number of '"present-day" examples' – like current political interventions on borders, immigration and citizenship – which express, to varying degrees, both the tradition's dogmatism and its possible upheaval (272). However, and while Derrida does elsewhere engage in lengthy discussions on how such actualities relate themselves to the call of certain spectres, *Politics of Friendship* decidedly avoids such reflection: 'we have deliberately refrained from recourse to "illustrations" to "actualise" our analyses or in an attempt to demonstrate their necessity *today*' (272).[31] Particularly, the text never stops to consider the extent to which the feminine spectre's call for another justice might *already resonate* with actual forms of friendship involving women and other others – be they the 'Antigones of history' or those of the present. But to what extent, for instance, do the 'romantic friendships' between women in the nineteenth and early twentieth centuries already *incarnate* or *embody* the feminine spectre's appeal to a friendship that operates beyond the homo-fraternal and phallogocentric schema?[32] Alternatively, to what extent do the current friendships between women and other others in male-oriented urban spaces already *resonate* with the feminine spectre's call for a break with that doxa of friendship which 'binds the state (the city, the polís) to the phatry (family, generations, fraternity in general)'?[33]

While Derrida does not confront such questions, it is clear that they might have provided him with interesting examples for the alternative politics of friendship he wants to signal. More importantly, perhaps, addressing such questions might also have allowed Derrida to demonstrate that the feminine spectrality that survives in the tradition is not simply an abstract promise indifferent to all social determinations, but rather one which specifically responds to the present, actual emergency where women and other others *still* struggle to experience and speak of friendship without the mediation of violent patriarchal schemas.[34] However, without establishing this linkage between the actual and the spectral, it remains unclear why the feminine ghosts that inhabit the tradition of friendship are relevant for us *today*. What kind of practical lessons or maxims for a more democratic friendship can we derive from our exposure to the spectral call that echoes within the tradition? Unfortunately, Derrida's decision not to relate the tradition's spectres to an actuality of practices of friendship renders *Politics of Friendship* incapable of answering this question. But this question *must* be answered if the democracy that Derrida seeks is to become possible or even thinkable. For, as Ernesto Laclau says, 'We can move to a more democratic society only through a plurality of acts of democratisation.'[35]

Now, certainly, these considerations do not entirely discount the value of Derrida's deconstruction of the tradition. Neither do they undermine the strength of his warning that the rupture of phallogocentrism demands more than a strategy of inclusion.[36] But what such considerations do show, *pace* Derrida, is that to successfully overcome phallogocentrism, we cannot exclusively devote our attention to the tradition's spectres either. Indeed, if, as feminist thinkers show, we can hear the radical content of spectral calls only by relating their trace to concrete forms of actuality, then for the promise of another politics of friendship to *truly* become thinkable, we must also continue to devote our attention to those practices and experiences by which feminine friendship continues to be redefined today. Indeed, and particularly if the gesture to speak of feminine spectres in isolation from any reality also belongs to the phallogocentric tradition, thinking and talking about how our spectres relate themselves to actual practices of feminine friendship remains 'an absolute insurgency'.[37]

In this sense, while *Politics of Friendship* certainly provides a vital initiation into an impossible form of friendship that does greater justice to feminine friends, it by no means effectively delivers the possibility of that impossibility either. For this impossibility to truly become possible, or thinkable, we must also go beyond the confines of Derrida's text and ceaselessly confront a number of practical questions that more directly respond to the urgency of the actual situation where women and other others still experience friendship through a phallogocentric prism that strips friendship of its radical potential. In sum, the overcoming of phallogocentrism also demands a greater strategic attention to actual experiences of friendship involving (among others) women than *Politics of Friendship* presently offers. It also involves ceaselessly asking the question, recently posed by Erin Wunker: 'What would [or does] female friendship as a way of life look like?'[38]

Notes

1. My use of the term 'feminine' in this chapter must be understood in light of Derrida's own philosophical usage of that term and some key developments in twentieth-century French feminist philosophy. Specifically, when I speak of 'feminine alterity' or 'feminine voices' in relation to Derrida's work, this usage is meant in a resolutely non-essentialist and non-binary manner. The 'feminine' in these phrases does not contain an essential reference to the 'being' or qualities of women and/or female sexed bodies, just as it does not derive its sense from a strict binary opposition to other gendered terms like 'male' and 'masculine'. Instead, what gives the term 'feminine' its sense in this context is the work that it performs, as a textual force, in deconstructing normative, phallogocentric and androcentric conceptions of gender identity and sexual difference. This is precisely how Derrida defines the term in *Spurs*, where 'feminine' is not a determinable entity that can be 'hastily mistaken for a woman's femininity, for female sexuality, or for any other of those essentializing fetishes', but is rather the textual divergence or non-identity of phallogocentrism with itself; Jacques Derrida, *Spurs: Styles of Nietzsche*, trans. Barbara Harlow (London: University of Chicago Press, 1979), esp. pp. 47–62. It seems to me that it is also this kind of deconstructive textual force that Derrida has in mind when he speaks of feminine figures in *Politics of Friendship*, and specifically, as we shall see, when he speaks of the haunting apparitions that are engendered by what he calls 'the double exclusion of the feminine' in the Western tradition of friendship. Crucially, this sense of the term also resonates with the notion of *écriture féminine* that emerges in the work of the French feminist thinkers Luce Irigaray, Julia Kristeva and, more significantly for Derrida, Hélène Cixous (with whom he shared a long personal friendship). Indeed, when Cixous articulates what is meant by a 'feminine practice of writing', she insists that what gives this writing its feminine sense is not the fact that it is penned or performed *by* a woman or female sexed body, but rather that it works to 'always surpass the discourse that regulates the phallocentric system'; Hélène Cixous, 'The Laugh of the Medusa', *Signs*, 1.4 (1976), 883. Accordingly, when elsewhere in this chapter I refer to actual practices or experiences of 'feminine' friendship, this is also not to be understood literally as referring exclusively to the friendships

between women and/or female sexed bodies, but more generally to those friendships involving *any* subjects (including women, certainly, but also a multiplicity of other others) whose performances, practices and lived experiences subvert and exceed normative, phallogocentric and androcentric conceptions of gender identity and sexual difference. For further discussions of this distinctly philosophical sense of the term 'feminine', see also Catherine Malabou, 'Le Sens du "Féminin"', *Revue du Mauss*, 39.1 (2012), esp. 236–7; Stella Sandford, 'Feminism against "the Feminine"', *Radical Philosophy*, 105 (2001), 6–14.

2. Jacques Derrida, *Politics of Friendship*, trans. George Collins (London: Verso, 1997); Jacques Derrida, *Politiques de l'amitié: suivi de L'Oreille de Heidegger* (Paris: Galilée, 1994). Hereafter, page references to the English translation are given in parenthesis in the text (*PF*).
3. This approach finds a notable contrast in the first few pages of Jacques Derrida, *Given Time: I. Counterfeit Money*, trans. Peggy Kamuf (London: University of Chicago Press, 1992), pp. 1–5.
4. Translation modified and emphasis added. The mention of Antigone refers to the analysis of Hegel in *Glas*, where, alongside focusing on the organising role that Antigone plays in the *Phenomenology of Spirit*, Derrida also extensively reflects on Hegel's relationship with his sister Christiane (or 'Nanette') Hegel. See Jacques Derrida, *Glas*, trans. John Leavey and Richard Rand (London: University of Nebraska Press, 1986).
5. Jacques Derrida, *Specters of Marx: The State of the Debt, the Work of Mourning and the New International*, trans. Peggy Kamuf (New York: Routledge, 2006), p. viii.
6. Jacques Derrida and Geoffrey Bennington, 'Politics and Friendship: A Conversation with Jacques Derrida', Centre for Modern French Thought: University of Sussex (1 December 1997), n.p. Published online at: http://hydra.humanities.uci.edu/Derrida/pol+fr.html.
7. Following Derrida, I here understand phallogocentrism 'as the complicity of Western metaphysics with a notion of male firstness'. Jacques Derrida and Christie McDonald, 'Choreographies', *Diacritics*, 12.2 (1982), 66–76 (p. 69).
8. This exclusion is not *absolute*: 'It doesn't mean that a woman couldn't have the experience of friendship with a man or with another woman. It means simply that within this culture [. . .] there was no voice, no discourse, no possibility of acknowledging these excluded possibilities.' Derrida and Bennington, 'Politics and Friendship', n.p.
9. Derrida and Bennington, 'Politics and Friendship', n.p.

10. In speaking of *less* rather than of *no* chance, Derrida here suggests the *possible return* of that figure which has traditionally been excluded from philosophies of friendship: the feminine friend.
11. 'There is no democracy without respect for irreducible singularity or alterity' (*PF*, 22).
12. Derrida and Bennington, 'Politics and Friendship', n.p.
13. As Derrida repeatedly argues, the idea that 'the friend is the near one and [that] friendship grows with presence' has been one of the means by which traditional thought has excluded women from friendship, as the case of Michelet so well illustrates.
14. Derrida and Bennington, 'Politics and Friendship', n.p.
15. Derrida, 'Choreographies', p. 72.
16. See also Judith Still, *Derrida and Hospitality: Theory and Practice* (Edinburgh: Edinburgh University Press, 2010), pp. 104–5.
17. Derrida, *Glas*, p. 129L; cf. *PF*, pp. 290, ix.
18. Geoffrey Bennington, 'Derridabase', in Jacques Derrida and Geoffrey Bennington, *Jacques Derrida* (London: University of Chicago Press, 1993), pp. 75–6.
19. Derrida, *Specters of Marx*, p. xviii.
20. cf. Derrida, *Specters of Marx*, p. 245n39.
21. Simon Wortham, *The Derrida Dictionary* (London: Continuum, 2010), p. 194.
22. Conjuration, for Derrida, has a dual sense: it signifies both the attempt to expel or exorcise spectres, and the attempt to '*evoke*', '*convoke*' or 'make come', some ghost. Derrida, *Specters of Marx*, p. 50.
23. Derrida, *Specters of Marx*, p. xviii.
24. Ibid. p. 82.
25. Jacques Derrida, 'Remarks on Deconstruction and Pragmatism', in *Deconstruction and Pragmatism*, ed. Chantal Mouffe (London: Routledge, 1996), p. 85.
26. Terry Castle, *The Apparitional Lesbian: Female Homosexuality and Modern Culture* (New York: Columbia University Press, 1993), p. 34. Importantly, Castle makes this argument with reference to the lesbian ghosts of Western literary culture. By appealing to her work, I do not mean to equate lesbian relations with practices and experiences of friendship. However, I do believe that Castle's focus on specifically feminine ghosts who challenge and haunt the norms of patriarchal culture is still instructive for assessing the merits of *Politics of Friendship*.
27. Castle, *The Apparitional Lesbian*, pp. 46–7.
28. Ibid. p. 65.

29. Victoria Hesford, 'Feminism and Its Ghosts: The Spectre of Feminist-as-lesbian', *Feminist Theory*, 6.3 (2005), 227–20 (p. 229).
30. Derrida, *Specters of Marx*, p. 48. To this extent, Derrida clearly avoids what Castle calls the 'classically homophobic distinction between the "phantasmatic" and the "real"'. Castle, *The Apparitional Lesbian*, p. 56.
31. Cf. Derrida, *Specters of Marx*, pp. 96–117.
32. These friendships are extensively documented by Lillian Faderman, *Surpassing the Love of Men: Romantic Friendships and the Love Between Women from Renaissance to Present* (New York: William Morrow, 1981).
33. For a timely analysis of such friendships, see Leslie Kern, *Feminist City: Claiming Space in a Man-made World* (London: Verso, 2020), pp. 55–86.
34. On this emergency, see Erin Wunker, *Notes from a Feminist Killjoy: Essays on Everyday Life* (Toronto: BookThug, 2016), pp. 111–52.
35. Ernesto Laclau, 'The Time is Out of Joint', *Diacritics*, 25.2 (1995), 85–96 (p. 94).
36. This warning continues to be echoed by feminist thinkers engaging with friendship today: 'How quickly we are recapitulated into the same systems that we try to dismantle.' Wunker, *Notes*, p. 132.
37. Wunker, *Notes*, p. 139.
38. Ibid. p. 117.

14

The Possible Echo

Peggy Kamuf

Politics of Friendship points out over and over again the long-standing exclusion of women from the idea of friendship first iterated by the Greeks and reiterated ever since: what is excluded is friendship between men and women no less than friendship between women. This double exclusion is sometimes explicit, as in Nietzsche ('Woman is not yet capable of friendship') or Michelet ('She can spell the sacred word of the new age, *Brotherhood*, but cannot yet read it'), but more consistently it is implied through the absence of all reference to women and sexual difference in the corpus the book is sifting through (*PF*, 283/314, 238/266).[1] Derrida is relentless in tracking signs, whether explicit or implicit, that the fraternal model of friendship bequeaths a politics which would leave out women while pretending to ignore sexual difference, as if the human species regenerated itself only as brothers.

Far less apparent than the persistence with which Derrida remarks this distortion or contortion in the thinking of friendship is the figure of Echo, whose proper name is threaded through the text. Indeed, hers is one of the very few feminine proper names that call out, in all these pages spent among the band of friend-brothers. You could say that her name literally echoes there. This Echo seems to emanate from deep within Derrida's extensive reading of Carl Schmitt, which traverses nearly the whole book. When he turns to the concluding pages of *Ex captivitate salus*, the collection of short texts Schmitt wrote while in an American prison camp after the war, Derrida highlights right away a certain echo that resounds at the end of the last prose piece in the collection, before a sort of epilogue written in rhymed verse: 'just before the epilogue, a *double echo* resounds' (165/190). It is the echo of the name Echo, whom Schmitt twice names in the conclusion of this piece, 'Wisdom of the Cell', before quoting lines by his friend the poet Konrad Weiss that also name Echo. Or rather, since we are talking about an antonomasia, that is, the figure that generalises a proper name, it would seem that only the last of these occurrences, the poetic one, properly names Echo, the lover of Narcissus. But before quoting this line, Schmitt reflects on the nature of rhyme, particularly on the genius of German rhyme (*Raum, Rom, Reim, Heimat*) and then exclaims: 'The German rhyme is not the fireworks of the rhymes of Victor Hugo. It is echo, clothing, and ornament and at the same time a divining rod for the location of meaning.'[2] As for Derrida, however, he does name Echo without antonomasia, Ovid's Echo, when he turns to the three lines quoted from Weiss's poem with which Schmitt closes the piece:

> The last words are those of a poem. As untranslatable as its rhymes. It names Echo, it calls out to her as, naturally, she is born, grows or matures [*wächst*], like *phúsis*, in front of each word, before all speech, and she in fact comes first, she is also the first word of the poem.
>
> *Echo wächst vor jedem Worte.*
>
> Everything begins with Echo. But only in one language, for one people, and for one nation. (166/192)

Derrida will go on to call Schmitt's rhyming figure a 'particular Germanic Echo', for she seals the belonging of a language, *Wort*, to place, *Ort*, opens the door, *Pforte*, on which this echoing message hammers and thunders (167/193). The play of the rhymes, within only one language, recalls – echoes – Derrida says, the most sombre, an echo of German speech with 'the power to make tremble'. Here are the three lines of Weiss's poem, *Der Christliche Epimetheus*, with which Schmitt ends this text and that also conclude chapter 6 of *Politics of Friendship*:

> *Echo wächst vor jedem Worte;*
> *wie ein Sturm vom offnen Orte*
> *hämmert es durch unsre Pforte.*

Although Derrida refrains from offering a translation of these lines, the English version of Schmitt's essay gives only a translation, as if his reflection on untranslatable German rhyme were without consequence:

> Echo grows before each word;
> like a storm from the open place
> it hammers through our gate. (167/193)

'Word', 'place' and 'gate' hammer their echo home only in one language as *Worte, Orte, Pforte*. And that is Schmitt's point. Derrida had already encountered and responded to a very similar gesture, an echo, in Heidegger's '*Erörterung*' of Georg Trakl's poetry, where it is not rhyme but sense, *Sinn*, and, for example, the sense of *Fremd*, foreigner, that are reserved for the German language alone.[3]

Everything begins with Echo. Echo is the first word – or name – in the lines from the poem, which is in German. But 'Echo' is not German or in German, strictly speaking, any more than it is in English or French or Italian or Spanish or Russian or even the Latin and Greek into which it was born. Rather, Echo echoes among these and other languages without belonging, no more than any other proper name, to one or the other of them. It is this effect, this echo effect, that, on my reading, Derrida wants to retrieve from appropriation, whether in Schmitt or Heidegger, by one language, one people, or one nation.

He wants, that is, to listen for another Echo. This intent or desire is signalled very close to the end of the book's first chapter, albeit elliptically:

> We are speaking about anything but narcissism as it is commonly understood: Echo, the possible Echo, she who takes speech from the other's words, she who takes the other at his word, her very freedom preceding the first syllables of Narcissus, his mourning or his complaint. (24/42)

I read an ellipsis here in the punctuation of the colon ('. . . narcissism as it is commonly understood: Echo, the possible echo . . .'). Derrida does not fill in, he elides the parallel construction of the implicit, logical syntax, which would be: we are not speaking of narcissism (rather, we are speaking of) Echo. By means of the ellipsis, as I'm calling it, Echo is not named as an object of 'our' discourse but rather as 'she who takes up speaking from others' words', she who 'takes the other at his word'. Not an object, then, but a subject, albeit a subject of repetition. But this Echo who learns to speak, like everyone else, from others' words, who iterates what she hears, like everyone else – for every speaker of a language echoes words that necessarily precede their own speech – she also speaks from out of a freedom or liberty that precedes what she hears from Narcissus, the syllables of his mourning and his complaint. And it is to this Echo, who is free despite, before or beyond the constraints of the repetition to which she (like everyone else) is condemned, that Derrida would give an ear.

This attunement to Echo's free speech is marked once again as Derrida approaches his reading of Schmitt's Germanic Echo, which we've just reviewed. A few pages before that, he comments on an earlier disparaging allusion that Schmitt makes to Echo:

> [Schmitt] takes up the theme of deceit or imposture – more precisely, of self-delusion, of 'deceiving oneself' (*Selbstbetrug*), of this Narcissus victim of the 'dupery of self proper to solitude', of this 'poor Self who can marry only his own Echo' (as if Echo was unable to speak as well, and Schmitt quickly forgets his *Metamorphoses*; yes, as if Echo had not invented the ruse necessary in order to speak in her own name, to reclaim speech, to call the other while feigning to repeat the ends of sentences. (160/184–5)

Once again, Derrida insists on Echo as speaking up again or taking back speech ('*reprendre la parole*') by means of an invention, a ruse, whereby she speaks in her own name even as she repeats the other's words. Echo signs her invention, but Schmitt appropriates it and her when he dismisses the poor Narcissus-ego 'who can marry only *his own* Echo'. In other words, Echo is an after-effect, an after-thought and secondary, whereas Derrida wants to reserve the place of 'Echo, the possible Echo' whose freedom of invention precedes and makes possible what it seems to repeat.

There is one last mention of Echo in *Politics of Friendship*. It comes as Derrida is taking leave of 'Wisdom of the Cell' and, for the moment, of Schmitt. It has the ring of a promise to make good on these several elliptical, tantalising hints as to what has been called 'the possible Echo'. Right before signing off on this chapter, Derrida defers to another time this explication: 'Another time, we will say something else in honor of Echo – the Echo of the *Metamorphoses* in any case. This is not the place' (167/193).

Eight years later, in 2002, Echo returns at the beginning of *Rogues*, in the preface titled 'Veni'. She can be heard on its first page inaugurating the book, for it is once again her inaugurating word to which Derrida remains attuned here, as in *Politics of Friendship*. Right away, in a paragraph devoted to her and to the *Metamorphoses*, an echo is set off in her name: first echo, then Echo. 'Two lectures here seem to echo one another. They perhaps answer one another, just as Echo [. . .].'[4] With this 'just as Echo', Derrida puts *Rogues* under the sign of Echo, of her 'Veni!' that responds to the other's call to come. Echo responds, she does not just repeat or reiterate, and her response has the nature of an event, of a coming that is a coming about. The paragraph continues:

> They perhaps answer one another, just as Echo might have feigned to repeat the last syllable of Narcissus in order to say something else or, really, in order to sign at that very instant in her own name, and so take back the initiative of answering or responding in a responsible way, thus

> disobeying a sovereign injunction and outsmarting the tyranny of a jealous goddess.[5]

This echoing difference between repetition and response is what allows her feint to pass censure. Elsewhere, in *The Animal That Therefore I Am*, Derrida aligns the human/animal distinction with a similar one between reaction and response. 'A reaction is not a response', affirms Lacan, and animals (only) react, they do not respond.[6] A reaction can be something like a mechanical repetition, a response in the sense that nerve endings respond to stimulus. Such an alignment of the animal/human divide with the scene of Echo points up the only barely human place of women on this spectrum. It is the same place consigned to them as described in *Politics of Friendship*: only barely human. Recall Zarathustra's saying quoted close to the conclusion of that book: 'Woman is not yet capable of friendship: women are still cats and birds. Or, at best, cows' (qtd. 282/314). To be sure, and as always with Nietzsche, things are not so simple, for Zarathustra goes on to ask: 'Woman is not yet capable of friendship. But tell me, you men, which of you is yet capable of friendship?' (qtd. 283/315).

Nietzsche might have cited Echo as illustration of another of Zarathustra's maxims: 'In woman, a slave and a tyrant have all too long been concealed. For that reason, woman is not yet capable friendship: she knows only love' (qtd. 282/314). Here is how Derrida comments on this dictum:

> This thesis thus concerns not only woman, but the hierarchy between love and friendship. Love is *below* friendship because it is an above/below relation, of inferiority and superiority, slavery and tyranny. It is implied, then, that friendship is freedom plus equality. The only thing missing is fraternity. (282/314)

Disrupting this hierarchy between love and friendship is one of the stakes of *Politics of Friendship*. As Derrida writes early in the first chapter: 'Beyond all ulterior frontiers between love and friendship, but also between the passive and active voices between loving and being-loved, what is at stake is *aimance*', forging this word in what would be the middle voice, neither active nor passive, of the verb *aimer*, to love (7/23). Like *différance*, like 'a nonoppositional and infinitely differentiated, qualitative and intensive difference', *aimance* disarms the hierarchy and with it one of the principal alibis that has rationalised the double exclusion of women from the higher realm of friendship and thus from the political arena, at least for the longest part of the history of the West.[7]

These *renvois* to the set of nested distinctions – human/animal, response/reaction, love/friendship – will aid us as we return to 'Veni' and to the interpretation of Echo we had begun to read there. We pick it up where we left off above:

> Echo thus lets be heard by whoever wants to hear it, by whoever might love hearing it, something other than what she seems to be saying. Although she repeats, without simulacrum, what she has just heard, another simulacrum slips in to make her response something more than a mere reiteration. She says in an inaugural fashion, she declares her love, and calls for the first time, all the while repeating the 'Come!' of Narcissus, all the while echoing narcissistic words. She overflows [*déborde*] with love; her love overflows the calls of Narcissus, whose ending or send-off [*la chute ou l'envoi*] she seems simply to reproduce.[8]

Echo's ruse is to invent a simulacrum of 'mere reiteration', while responding and still calling for the first time (to) her beloved such that her call of love 'overflows the calls of Narcissus'. This figure of overflowing love, of *amour débordant*, can be heard here not just exceeding borders, like a river over its banks, but undoing them, *dé-bordant*, dismantling or disordering them. Echo's overflowing love would thus engage the *aimance* that, as we read above, carries beyond 'any ulterior frontier between love and friendship, but also between the active voice and the passive voice, between loving or being loved' and dislocates all these distinctions.

Echo's overflow, excess or *démesure*, however, also remarks the dissymmetry and inequality that lead Derrida to link more explicitly her scene with Narcissus to the concern with democracy to come, which is the principal concern of *Rogues*. He does so as the paragraph continues by way of two sentence fragments, without any verb, that leave one to draw out the link between them. 'A dissymmetrical, unequal correspondence, unequal, as always, to the equality of the one to the other: the origin of politics, the question of democracy.'[9] Echo and Narcissus do not correspond symmetrically, the one is not a reproduction or repetition of the other. Instead there is asymmetry introduced, inaugurated by Echo's *débordante*, unequalled response. Her call of 'Come!' asymmetrically responds to, without repeating, Narcissus. It also disrupts the symmetry of his reflection in the pond. This is the sense in which the dissymmetry of their correspondence is 'inégale', uneven, like the mirror's broken glass. She is not in his own image, but another being. They do not equal each other, and this inequality 'is unequal to the equality of the one to the other'. Derrida switches registers here from one inequality to another, from the register of the inequality of sheer dissymmetrical difference to that of a political (in)equality. To be sure, this switch allows him to link up with the 'question of democracy', which is, as I've said, the principal concern of, especially, the first part of *Rogues*, 'The Reason of the Strongest'. But it also situates 'the origin of politics' – no less – in this unequal, dissymmetrical correspondence of *aimance*. The politics of *aimance* succeeds the politics of friendship once the latter or *if* the latter has been deconstructed in its structuring hierarchy of love/friendship.

The rest of the paragraph we're reading is in parentheses, or not quite, because these open but do not close. (After editing a few of Derrida's seminars, I've learned to watch for unclosed parentheses.) It addresses more pointedly, less elliptically, the question of what Ovid's Echo has to tell us about the to-come of democracy, which is, as Derrida says, 'the most insistent theme of this book'.[10]

> (If I seem to be insisting a bit too much on these *Metamorphoses*, it is because everything in this famous scene turns around a call to come [*à venir*]. And because, at the intersection of repetition and the unforeseeable, in this place where, each time anew, by turns [*tour à tour*] and each time once and for all, one does not see *coming* what remains *to come*, which is the most insistent theme of this book. 'Veni!' says Narcissus; 'Come!' 'Come!' responds Echo. Of herself and on her own account. You can reread what follows.[11]

I implied that this excursus on Echo at the beginning of *Rogues* fulfilled in a sense the promise made in *Politics of Friendship* to say something else, elsewhere, 'in honor of Echo'. But another text, written during the decade between these other two works responds no less to that promise. It is not, as one might have thought, *Echographies* (1996) where, despite its title, Echo's name is never pronounced in these 'filmed interviews' between Derrida and his interlocutor, Bernard Stiegler. No, I mean the text titled 'Pregnances' that was first published in 1993, accompanying or accompanied by four washes (*lavis*) by the contemporary French painter Colette Deblé. It has been collected in the 2013 volume *Penser à ne pas voir*, which gathers this and many other hard-to-find texts by Derrida on the visual arts.

At several points in this ten-page essay, Derrida turns to Echo's invention so as to draw out what he sees in the works of Deblé, which feign to quote or copy representations of women in the masterworks of Western art history. Before he invokes Echo's figure, however, Derrida aligns this tradition of Western representation with (male) narcissism. 'Narcissus,' he writes, 'is the

Painter', meaning the recognised, authorised, canonised painter(s) whom Deblé quotes. Her quotations, however, are not repetitions or copies or reproductions: like Echo, she ruses with her models so as to bring forth something new, 'at the intersection of repetition and the unforeseeable', as he will put it in 'Veni'. It is comparable to 'the ruse of the sublime Echo' in *Metamorphoses*, which Derrida calls 'perhaps the most consonant work' with Deblé's own.[12]

This assertion introduces a brief, but densely suggestive passage that draws on Book III of Ovid's poem, lines 453–659, which recount the stories of the ill-fated pair. Derrida first sketches in the profile of Narcissus who is brought by his ordeal to utter the vainest of wishes (and Derrida quotes this line): '*O utinam a nostro secedere corpore possem!*', 'Oh, would that I were able to secede from my own body'.[13] It is significant, perhaps, that he recalls this complaint of Narcissus before turning to 'sublime Echo' and her invention of a response. Significant because it reverses the order in Ovid of the stories of how each of them died for love: first Echo falls in love with Narcissus, who cruelly spurns her, and only then do we learn how Narcissus finds his reflection in the pond and falls mortally in love it. By reversing the episodes, Derrida has Echo respond in effect to the most desperate pleas of her beloved after she has already been chased from the scene. In Ovid's poem, Echo is silent throughout Narcissus's ordeal, until the end: 'As often as the wretched / boy cried "Alas!" she answered with "*Alas!*"' and then right before he dies, when Narcissus directs his final words to the youth in the pond 'whom I have vainly cherished': 'and when he cried "Farewell!" "*Farewell!*" cried Echo back'.[14]

Thus, Derrida places Echo's rusing, poetic responses in counterpoint to the insoluble dilemma of the other's desperate passion. 'Oh, would that I were able to secede from my own body,' he quotes, and then continues:

> So what did Echo do? What had she *already* attempted, condemned by the jealous Juno never to speak first and merely to repeat, a little, just the end of the other's sentence, thus to quote a fragment, or even only the final word [*la chute*]? She played on the language, irreproachably, as a docile and ingenious interpreter. She pretended to quote, following Narcissus, where a repeated fragment became again a sentence that was whole, invented, original and spoken, for who could hear and understand it, in her own name signed Echo, without the proof of her seal ever being liable to expose her to divine vengeance. For example, Narcissus: 'Anyone here?' '*Here!!*' answered Echo ('"*ecquis adest*" *et* "*adest*" *responderat Echo*'). Or else: 'Here let us come together!' . . . Echo gave her heart with her reply, '*Come! Together!*' ('"*huc coeamus*" *ait* . . . "*coeamus*", *retullit Echo*').[15]

As in the passage quoted above from 'Veni', Derrida remarks on the chance that Echo's invention might not be heard and understood, that it fall on ears like those of Narcissus stopped up by his own voice even as he yearns for a response from the other. To the boy in the pond he muses that 'the movement / of your bow-shaped lips suggests that you respond with words to mine – although I never hear them!' ('*et, quantum motu formosi suspicor oris, / verba refers aures non pervenientia nostras!*').[16] It is this inaudible response that finally (finally!) tips him off that he has fallen for his own image '*iste ego sum: sensi, nec me mea fallit imago; / uror amore mei: flammas moveoque feroque*', translated by Charles Martin as: 'But *now* I get it! *I* am that other one! / I've finally seen through my own image! / I burn with love for – *me*! The spark I kindle / is the torch I carry.' Rather than saving him from his madness, this recognition sends him towards his death.[17]

I am reviewing these moments in *Metamorphoses* in order to read the final reference to Echo in the essay. It comes in the last paragraph, where Derrida figures Narcissus not only hearing Echo's call – too late – but also understanding what is called its 'lesson'. Once again, it is a dense passage with a number of ellipses, like the incomplete complete sentences that Echo invents out of fragments. The paragraph indeed begins with this very kind of invention, this Echo effect, as if it is quoting Echo quoting the other. To hear this effect, one has to back up to the end of the previous sentence, which is a quotation from Colette Deblé: '*Soliloque intérieur, je me parle* à travers *moi, tu te parles* à travers *toi et moi* (Interior soliloquy, I speak to myself *through* me, you speak to yourself *through* you and me).' Derrida's new paragraph will begin by repeating the last four syllables of this sentence in a fragment that becomes part of a different, original and elliptical sentence: '*Vers toi et moi*', it echoes, followed by another fragment that attributes this invention to Echo: '*Prononce Écho en son nom*', 'Pronounce(s) Echo in her own name'. That is, one may also hear there an imperative, an injunction to pronounce Echo's name, in her own name. Here is the whole paragraph:

> *Vers toi et moi. Prononce Écho en son nom.* Narcissus (too late but there is no more irreversible time for this history or this myth), at the moment of saying 'Farewell' (*Vale*) and of sinking into the waters of the Styx where he was still contemplating himself, it's a little as if he had not only heard Echo's declaration but understood its lesson. The lesson would have come back to him, after the farewell. Beyond the voice, like a lesson in painting, beyond the farewell that she reflects or quotes again ('. . . *dictoque vale "vale" inquit et Echo*').[18]

What is the lesson of Echo's declaration? And how is it 'like a lesson in painting'? The lesson came back to Narcissus, he understood it too late, after the farewell, with a delay like an echo, which is not, however, the echo or repetition of his own voice. That is perhaps the lesson, pronounced by Echo in her own name: to hear and understand another's call to come, '*coeamus!*', come together, '*vers toi et moi*'. As for being a lesson in painting, is that because it is signed '*fecit Echo*'? Or because it carries 'beyond the voice' to a different order of the sensible, not audible but visible, not spoken but painted, not language but figuration or taking form? But no doubt it is also because we are to hear, understand and above all see it as the lesson of a painter, Colette Deblé, alias Echo.

It is, we read, 'as if' Narcissus had heard and understood it. And it is *as if*, with this figure of invention, Derrida opened a story and a history to a *different* repetition, an iteration that is not a reiteration of the same. Hearing it, Narcissus can never be the same thereafter.[19]

Notes

1. Jacques Derrida, *Politics of Friendship*, trans. George Collins (London: Verso, 1997); Jacques Derrida, *Politiques de l'amitié: suivi de L'Oreille de Heidegger* (Paris: Galilée, 1994). Hereafter, page references to the English/French translation are given in parenthesis in the text (*PF*). English translations are occasionally modifed.
2. Carl Schmitt, *Ex captivitate salus: Experiences, 1945–47*, ed. Andreas Kalyvas and Federico Finchelstein, trans. Matthew Hannah (Cambridge: Polity, 2017), p. 72, emphasis added and translation modified. Curiously, the French translation from which Derrida quotes puts a capital letter on 'Écho', returning it to the proper name. Of course, in German the capital initial does not distinguish proper from common nouns, but Schmitt had more plausibly written a series of common nouns: 'Er ist Echo, Kleid und Schmuck [. . .]'.
3. See Jacques Derrida, *Geschlecht III: Sex, Race, Nation, Humanity*, ed. Geoffrey Bennington, Katie Chenoweth and Rodrigo Therezo, trans. Katie Chenoweth and Rodrigo Therezo (Chicago: University of Chicago Press, 2020).
4. Jacques Derrida, *Rogues: Two Essays on Reason*, trans. Pascale-Anne Brault and Michael Naas (Stanford: Stanford University Press, 2005), p. xi.
5. Derrida, *Rogues*, pp. xi–xii.
6. Jacques Derrida, *The Animal That Therefore I Am*, ed. Marie-Louise Mallet, trans. David Wills (New York: Fordham University Press), p. 124.

7. Derrida, *The Animal*, p. 126.
8. Derrida, *Rogues*, p. xii. Translation modified.
9. Ibid. p. xii.
10. Ibid. p. xii.
11. Ibid. p. xii.
12. Jacques Derrida, *Penser à ne pas voir. Écrits sur les arts du visible, 1979–2004*, ed. Ginette Michaud, Joana Masó and Javier Bassas (Paris: La Différence, 2013), p. 172.
13. Ovid, *Metamorphoses*, trans. and ed. Charles Martin (New York and London: W. W. Norton, 2010), p. 79 (ll. 607–8).
14. Ibid. ll. 639–40, ll. 644–6.
15. Derrida, *Penser à ne pas voir*, p. 173. My translation. In a remarkably fine essay on Ovid's myth, Claire Nouvet is interested above all in the echo that affects speech at the origin: 'What Ovid's text suggests is much more radical: the echo does not affect an original utterance "afterward", it constitutes it from the very beginning. Although presented as coming "after" the sentence, the audible echo points in fact to the inaudible echo which affects the sentence in the present of its enunciation. As soon as it appears, language "echoes", that is, diffracts into a potentiality of alternative meanings . . .' Claire Nouvet, 'An Impossible Response: The Disaster of Narcissus', *Yale French Studies*, 79 (1991), 103–34 (p. 107).
16. Ovid, *Metamorphoses*, ll. 597–8.
17. Ibid. ll. 599–602. This self-recognition fulfils the prophecy of Tiresias, as recounted in a passage just before the myth of Echo and Narcissus unfolds. Asked by his mother if her son, Narcissus, 'would live to ripe old age, / Tiresias responded with these words: / "If he knows himself – not"'. Ibid. ll. 447–9.
18. Derrida, *Penser à ne pas voir*, p. 178. My translation.
19. This essay gratefully acknowledges the interpretive insight with which my friend Pleshette DeArmitt approached Derrida's reference to the myth of Echo as a figure or allegory for a non- or post-narcissistic subject. DeArmitt surveys this reference or response to Echo's call in a number of other texts by Derrida that I was not able to discuss here. See Pleshette DeArmitt, 'Resonances of Echo: A Derridean Allegory', *Mosaic*, 42.2 (June 2009), 89–100.

Part III

Polemics

15

Political Friendships to Come? Futurity, Democracy and Citizenship

Rosine Kelz

Introduction

This chapter explores how Derrida's *Politics of Friendship* can help investigate the relationship between two central questions in contemporary social and political thought: how transformations towards a more democratic and just future can be conceptualised; and how the political sphere can be opened to 'others' who are excluded from current political communities. The notion of 'democracy to come', briefly discussed in *Politics of Friendship* and elaborated further in *Rogues* and other texts, reminds us of the temporal character of the political sphere, where democracy is related to a radically open future. However, even though Derrida insists 'democracy to come' cannot be prefigured, in *Politics of Friendship* this notion of democracy emerges from a deconstructive reading of Western political thought. Therefore, this possible future democracy appears to be at risk of remaining tethered to Western tradition. Derrida's deconstructive engagement does not just raise the question of the openness of the future, however. With the theme of political friendship as fraternity, the question of openness to others emerges as an issue long inscribed into European thought. In Derrida's reading, fraternity links conceptions of political community and citizenship to notions of autochthony where a connection is drawn between 'blood', land and nation. A 'democracy to come', however, would need to go against this logic, in order to give room to an ethics of alterity, where political friendship could build on an appreciation of difference.

After first outlining some of the core points of Derrida's critique of political friendship in the Western tradition, this chapter briefly discusses the notion of 'democracy to come' as an idea that introduces a different temporality of the political. Not only is the political oriented towards the future, a democratic future in Derrida's terms has to be understood as the possibility of the radically new. In closing, I want to show how Derrida's engagement with the notion of democracy can contribute to recent debates about the concept of citizenship in literature about social movements for refugee and migrant rights.

(Political) Friendship and Exclusiveness of Political Community

Politics of Friendship is a book about the tensions and (im)possibilities of (political) friendship in the European (and, despite the inordinate amount of space dedicated to Schmitt, Derrida insists, particularly French) tradition. In Derrida's engagement, a temporal rhythm emerges that marks the European canon of political philosophy as a cohesive body of thought, which is held together by returns and repetitions – by quotations of quotations. When friendship descends from the ideal of an extraordinary, exclusive, unique bond between two ('one soul in two bodies') to a bond that unites many into a political community, it collapses into the 'sameness' of kinship, the familial, and – most markedly – fraternal (*PF*, viii, 92).[1] This political discourse appealing 'to birth, to nature or to the nation', this 'familialism', Derrida points out, consists in a renaturalisation of the 'legal fiction' of kinship and brotherhood (93). Even though invoking fraternity is meant to ground political community in ineluctable nature, the brother, Derrida insists, is never 'natural'. Instead, '[f]raternity requires a law and names, symbols, a language, engagements, oaths, speech' (149). As the relations between brothers depend on convention and contract – '[t]he brother is never a fact' – this also means that fraternal political community always runs the risk of brotherly betrayal (158–9).[2] The grounding of political community, then, involves a mystification that covers over the fragility of prior bonds and the need for unending negotiations – the familial political order seeks to hide that political community can never be set on firm, non-contingent foundations.

As a grounding move for a modern democratic republic, the notion of fraternity is problematic, because it retains the homogenising and exclusive implications of the blood-bond. This tendency remains active even where fraternity becomes linked to universalism. Commenting on Michelet, Derrida argues that the 'alleged universalism' of this discourse on fraternity is formulated 'by way of the exemplarist logic in which we have recognized the profound strategy of all nationalisms, patriotisms, or ethnocentrisms' (237). The universalism of fraternity relies on the exclusion (and production) of an Other. This (internal) Other of friendship and the political, Derrida points out repeatedly, is 'Woman'. Women cannot – or cannot yet – be friends. They cannot be part of the political community. As Derrida writes, 'a political phallogocentrism has, *up to this point*, determined *its* cosmopolitical democracy, *a* democracy, *qua* cosmo-phratrocentrism' (263). The 'virility' of political friendship at times needed to be explicitly stated – in particular when a move towards universalism seemed to open the door to the political arena to excluded others. More often, however, this exclusion functions through the 'natural' absence of women, of female friends and sisters in the famous texts of the Western tradition (149, 202, 239, 253). While the 'fratriarchy may [at times] include cousins and sisters,' Derrida writes, 'including may also come to mean neutralising. Including may dictate forgetting, for example, with "the best of all intentions", that the sister will never provide a docile example for the concept of fraternity' (viii). Thus, in discussing Schmitt, Derrida asks 'what if the woman were the absolute partisan? And what if she were the absolute enemy of this theory of the absolute enemy, the spectre of hostility to be conjured up for the sake of the sworn brothers' (157).

While European women, as Derrida rightly stresses, are an internal other of the European political tradition, the modern European nation-state system can only be properly understood as an outcome of its colonial history. The boundaries of modern Europe have, paradoxically, come into existence through the expansive politics of colonialism and imperialism. The European Enlightenment and the rise of modern European nations depended on the exploitation of other continents which became properties of European states, without being included within them – a territorial logic only possible through the production of racialised others. The people the colonisers encountered, while being treated as enemies and worse, as commodities and resources, mostly remain unmentioned in the canonical European political writings. Or, like women, they are represented as those who shall be educated in the virtues of modern universalism – who are not ready 'yet' for the bond of political fraternity. The tendency to overlook the importance of colonialism for Western modern political thought is also perceptible in Derrida's text. By concentrating on the European canon he is able to analyse its internal exclusionary logic, but misses the opportunity to bring the role of colonialism – and the voices of non-Europeans – more forcefully to the fore. When Derrida addresses Schmitt's worries about imperialist globalism as undermining the political, for example, it would be important to include a more explicit reminder of how, from the outset, modern European nations were built on a colonial and imperial history of 'global' genocide and slavery. In addition, we might ask how we can still speak about the

French Revolution, as Derrida does in *Politics of Friendship*, without discussing why the Haitian Revolution was largely ignored in European political writing. Pointing towards a Eurocentric tendency in the scope of sources Derrida engages with in *Politics of Friendship*, however, does not diminish the importance of Derrida's approach. Derrida's work enables us to explore the silences, instabilities and exclusions of the European tradition. His understanding of language, his critique of universalism and notion of the singular have been core reference points for postcolonial thought.[3] Derrida's work reminds us that it is only via a careful re-engagement with the past, where the actively forgotten is brought to the fore, that we can address how the exclusionary logic of the European political and intellectual project structures our present. Nevertheless, futural or 'open' political thought will also mean going beyond the traditional European canon of voices and ideas. A critique of the exclusionary logic of the European tradition then also needs to involve rediscovering marginalised non-European perspectives *within* European political thought, and engaging with non-European historical accounts of colonialism and non-European traditions of political thought.

A Different Friendship: The Futural Other and Democracy to Come

Politics of Friendship is concerned with the persistence of tradition, where difference lies in reiteration. Nevertheless, the '*problematic* scansion' which appears in Derrida's reading of the history of friendship, 'a scansion which would have introduced dissymmetry, separation and infinite distance in a Greek *philia* which did not tolerate them *but nevertheless called for them*', signals the *possibility* of another idea of friendship (232).[4] He even declares this possibility the 'central question' or 'single thesis' of the text (154–5, 158). This other friendship would enable inventing 'other names and other concepts' – the possibility of another politics that moves 'out beyond this [current] politics without ceasing to intervene therein to transform it' (159). Engaging with a deconstructive reading of the tradition of friendship then aims towards this possibility of another political future, a 'democracy to come' that would '*be a matter of thinking an alterity without hierarchical difference at the root of democracy*' (232).[5]

This desire for another democracy is thus linked to the tensions that arise in the interlaced history of the concept of democracy and the discourses on friendship. In the discussion of friendship the question of numbers is never far away. While for Aristotle, Derrida argues, there is a clear restriction against having 'too many friends', friendship also 'resists enumeration, counting-off, or even pure and simple quantification' (21). This problem becomes central to the concepts of democracy and citizenship. As Derrida writes,

> [a]mong all the questions of number that should attract an essay on the politics of friendship, let us never give short shrift to what is called demography. It has always been a sensitive and classic stake of the democratic tradition. How far beyond a certain number of citizens can a republic still claim to be a democracy? If this becomes problematic well before the canonical examples of Athens, Corsica, Geneva or Poland, if this begins with number itself, with the supplement of 'one more [*plus un*, also 'no more']', what will be said, beyond the billions, of a universal democratic model which, if it does not regulate a world State or super-State, would still command an international law of European origin? (101)

The problem, however, is not only about the possible size of a democratic political community. As Derrida writes,

> There is no democracy without respect for irreducible singularity or alterity, but there is no democracy without the 'community of friends' (*koina ta philōn*), without the calculation of majorities, without identifiable, stabilizable, representable subjects, all equal. These two laws are irreducible one to the other. Tragically irreconcilable and forever wounding. (22)

From this irreconcilability, however, 'political desire is forever borne by the distinction of these two laws' (22). These contradictory demands add to the 'futural' character of democracy as a concept and practice. As Derrida's earlier work already makes clear, futurity is inherent in language and politics as such. Any concept carries within itself the structure of a promise, which makes it open to the future. With the notion of iterability, Derrida stresses that all meaning remains in a process of becoming – a promise for change is prior to identity.[6] Even if futurity is inherent in language and in politics, however, this openness to change, to a future that differs from the present, can be undermined when it is not acknowledged. Modern democratic theory argues, therefore, that non-democratic politics seeks to stifle futurity by striving towards stabilisation and closure. Modern democracy, by contrast, would understand itself as a project that aims to involve 'everyone' in a constant process of perfectibility.[7] With the phrase 'democracy to come', Derrida wants to go beyond this modern futural understanding of democracy. In the former, a futural orientation expresses the need for the possibility of renegotiation, but the future can still be understood as prefigurable in principle. Moreover, the possibility of a perfectly just democracy in the future is often assumed. In contrast, 'democracy to come' points to an understanding of the future as Other – as what arrives unexpectedly, and cannot be known. What is 'to come' would therefore be radically different, a break with tradition. This future does not follow necessarily from the present because of the linear progression of time; the future 'to come' is not guaranteed. Moreover, because of the tensions inherent in its conceptual history, Derrida understands democracy as an *unfulfillable* promise. A democratic process of perfectibility cannot only always fail; the actual arrival of a perfect democracy also needs to remain impossible. Derrida's perfectionist understanding of democracy thus remains close to (Kantian) teleology, but avoids a strong understanding of teleology by insisting on the radical openness of the future – always to come. Because a 'real' future remains incalculable, democracy as a regulative ideal also needs to remain underdetermined. By retaining the name 'democracy' for a new, yet unfathomable politics, for the open political future, Derrida hopes to go 'beyond a certain determination of law and calculation (measurement, "metrics"), but not of law or or [*sic*] justice in general, this democracy would free a certain interpretation of equality by removing it from the phallogocentric schema of *fraternity*' (232).

For thinking non-fraternal friendship as the basis of a 'democracy to come' Derrida finds one possible beginning in Kant, who introduces distance 'into the continuum of a tradition, which is none the less confirmed by him'. Distance here is 'a principle of rupture or interruption that can no longer be easily reconciled with the values of proximity, presence, gathering together, and communal familiarity which dominate the traditional culture of friendship' (254–5). This idea of friendship with the Other to whom a respectful distance is kept, who cannot become fully known, no part of a homogeneous 'we', is then the 'central question' of the essay on a politics of friendship that remains only in outlines: 'a friendship without hearth, of a *philia* without *oikeiotēs*. Ultimately, that is, a friendship without presence, without resemblance, without affinity, without analogy. Along with presence, truth itself would start to tremble. [. . .] Is an aneconomic friendship possible?' By leaving the answer open, by saying the only answer for it can be 'perhaps', Derrida points towards an opening of the future, beyond European tradition (154–5; see also 25, 50, 55).

A Politics of Solidarity Beyond Nation and Community?

With *Politics of Friendship*, Derrida does not make a direct intervention into concrete political debates. Nevertheless, his discussion of how the idea of friendship is linked to the notion of a clearly bounded political community is highly relevant for current debates about migration regimes and access to citizenship in Europe. Moreover, in his remarks about 'democracy to come' he points towards the possible tensions between the desire for a radically different politics and the need to remain able to intervene in concrete political issues in the present. This possible friction has been a recurrent topic in debates about transformative politics, and is also taken up again in academic discussions about the strategies of social movements for migrant rights.[8]

The question of migrant rights can be approached in terms of broadening access to citizenship. As Derrida argues, 'questions of number' seem to be at the heart of European democracy, where the boundaries of political community ultimately remain linked to notions of kinship, sameness and autochthony. By broadening eligibility for, or the definition of, citizenship, some hope, however, that the modern 'nationalist' conception of citizenship can be gradually altered. This understanding is closely related to the notion of modern democracy as a process of perfectibility outlined above. For Engin Isin and Greg Nielsen, for example, the social movements for refugee rights engage in 'acts of citizenship', which can bring forth new forms of political subjectivity through political struggle.[9] The category of citizenship, it is argued, has always been in motion and is incapable of closure, because the very notion is bound up with struggles for participatory rights of those excluded from the political realm.

We might argue, however, that this approach too easily moves over the intrinsically exclusionary logic that is also retained in the concept of citizenship. Moreover, broadening the category of citizenship while holding on to a commitment to the nation-state system would not lend itself to building a more fundamental normative argument about universal freedom of movement. Therefore, some have argued for the need to develop other forms of political subjectivity, which do not primarily direct themselves towards the state.[10] Informal forms of solidarity are developed, which do not presuppose pre-existing communalities. What binds people together, instead, are the acts of solidarity themselves – these can be understood as acts of friendship, where friendship does not presuppose previous mutual knowledge or closeness, but develops from socio-political interactions. A political identity of friendship is thus understood as formed via shared political engagement. Such politics of friendship involve organising networks of support, which fill in or replace absent or restrictive institutional avenues for receiving basic forms of protection and political representation. Migrant groups and support groups within European countries have organised protests and basic social services and private sea rescue organisations have played an important role where European states have failed to fulfil basic ethical commitments. These practices might not be precisely the 'aneconomic' friendship Derrida gestures towards. Nevertheless, they are based on an understanding of political responsibility that does not build on a previously shared political identity, but instead often explicitly acknowledges that ethical and political responsibility is connected to different levels and forms of precarity and insecurity between migrants and non-migrants.[11] However, there is also political danger in overemphasising or romanticising mobility and networks of solidarity and rejecting demands for citizenship.[12] In the current European system, it is still only citizenship that ultimately offers legal protection and social and political rights. While solidarity networks can hope to somewhat lessen the worst impacts of European migration policies and raise popular awareness, they currently cannot replace the forms of protection and political participation citizenship offers. Therefore, as Imogen Tyler and Katarzyna Marciniak write, while 'immigrant protests might be understood as "acts" against the exclusionary technologies of citizenship', activists are still often 'compelled to make their demands in the idiom of the regime of citizenship they are contesting'.[13]

In political activism, as in political thought, then, multilayered approaches are called for. Derrida's work shows how important it is to appreciate the ambiguities and aporias within the conceptual history of European political thought. From this awareness, we can find political voices, which, at the same time, are able to appeal with the normative promise inherent in traditional European notions of democracy, justice and citizenship, and try to further develop political practices and ideas that go beyond the necessary limitations of current mainstream political thought and institutions. This double move, however, also needs to involve engaging with historical and current non-European (or Euro-American) perspectives and political practices that have been largely ignored by Eurocentric scholarship. However, as Derrida reminds us, 'including may also come to mean neutralizing', if the aim is to integrate 'the Other' into one 'universal' narrative (viii). Instead, the task remains to develop an ethics of alterity, where it is precisely the multiple differences of perspectives that are highlighted in approaches that seek to overcome Eurocentric positions. An understanding of alterity and difference is thus at the heart of any democratic project to come.

Notes

1. Jacques Derrida, *Politics of Friendship*, trans. George Collins (London: Verso, 1997); Jacques Derrida, *Politiques de l'amitié: suivi de L'Oreille de Heidegger* (Paris: Galilée, 1994). Hereafter, page references to the English translation are given in parenthesis in the text (*PF*).
2. Fraternal unity, Derrida seems to argue, can never be trusted. By organising the text around quotations and re-quotations of 'O my friends, there is no friend' (highlighting the undecidability of translation and repetition), a mistrust of friendship is revealed as a central theme of the Western tradition. This mistrust is deeply ingrained in Greek thought and also in the Judeo-Christian tradition, where the narrative of brotherly betrayal repeatedly emerges. For a book on friendship, then, hostility plays a significant role. The brother-friend can also always be revealed to be the brother-enemy, and the homogeneous community ends up being held together not by bonds of 'natural' love but by the identification of the shared enemy – which ultimately may lie hidden 'within'. As Derrida tries to bring to the fore in his prolonged engagement with Schmitt, the idea of friendship or community in the discourse of nation disappears into a politics that can only exist in its relation to war, to hostility. It is against this understanding of politics as antagonism that Derrida seeks to formulate a different notion of a 'democracy to come' (see e.g. pp. 172, 253).
3. See e.g. Jane Hiddleston, 'Jacques Derrida: Colonialism, Philosophy and Autobiography', in *Postcolonial Thought in the French Speaking World*, ed. Charles Forsdick and David Murphy (Liverpool: Liverpool University Press, 2009), pp. 53–64. It has been argued that post-structuralism as a philosophical movement was a response not to May 1968, but to the Algerian War of Independence. See e.g. Robert Young, *White Mythologies: Writing History and the West*. (London: Routledge, 1990). In his book *Monolingualism of the Other*, Derrida addresses more directly his experiences of growing up in Algeria. For Hédi Abdel-Jaouad, these experiences explain Derrida's 'unquenchable desire *de donner à lire l'interruption*, in an ever-proliferating lexicon of interruption, of which the term "deconstruction" has become the most legible signature, synonymous with Derrida himself. Indeed, what is deconstruction if not absolute outsideness, non-belonging, and étrangeté in the Camusian sense?' Hedi Abdel-Jaouad, 'Derrida's Algerian Anamnesis; or Autobiography in the Language of the Other', in *Remembering Africa*, ed. Elizabeth Mudimbe-Boyi (Portsmouth, NH: Heinemann, 2002) (pp. 266, 260).

However, Derrida has also been criticised for his ahistorical engagement with colonialism. When he writes that 'all culture is originally colonial', for example, this can also be read as insensitivity to the differences in experiences of colonial violence.

4. Italics in original.
5. Italics in original.
6. Luzia Sievi, *Demokratie ohne Grund – kein Grund für Demokratie?* (Bielefeld: transcript Verlag, 2017), pp. 377–8.
7. See e.g. Hubertus Buchstein and Dirk Jörke, 'Das Unbehagen an der Demokratietheorie', *Leviathan*, 31 (2003), 470–95 (p. 473).
8. Ilker Ataç, Kim Rygiel and Maurice Stierl, 'Introduction: The Contentious Politics of Refugee and Migrant Protest and Solidarity Movements: Remaking Citizenship from the Margins', *Citizenship Studies*, 20.5 (2016), 527–44.
9. Engin Isin and Greg Nielsen, *Acts of Citizenship* (London: Zed Books, 2008).
10. Dimitris Papadopoulos and Vassilis Tsianos, 'After Citizenship: Autonomy of Migration, Organisational Ontology and Mobile Commons', *Citizenship Studies*, 17.2 (2013), 178–96 (p. 179).
11. Rosine Kelz, *The Non-Sovereign Self, Responsibility, and Otherness: Hannah Arendt, Judith Butler, and Stanley Cavell on Moral Philosophy and Political Agency* (London and New York: Palgrave Macmillan, 2016), pp. 148–56.
12. Ataç, Rygiel and Stierl, 'Introduction', p. 534.
13. Imogen Tyler and Katarzyna Marciniak, 'Immigrant Protest: An Introduction', *Citizenship Studies*, 17.2 (2013), 143–56 (p. 146).

16

The Rhythm of Democracy, the Pulse of Deconstruction

Naomi Waltham-Smith

> Two or three minutes later, her pulse became irregular, it beat violently, stopped, then began to beat again, heavily, only to stop again, this happened many times, finally it became extremely rapid and light, and 'scattered like sand'.
>
> Maurice Blanchot, *L'arrêt de mort*

The concept of democracy rarely announces itself, Derrida declares in the preface to *Politiques de l'amitié*, without the possibility of fraternisation (*PF*, 11/viii).[1] That is to say, democracy does not present itself without reference to nation, birth, species, *Geschlecht* – without reference, in short, to blood. And later the epigraph to chapter 6, which is taken from Carl Schmitt's *Der Begriff des Politischen*, reads:

> Following its meaning in German (as in so many other languages), 'friend' is originally only the person to whom a genealogical bond unites. Originally the friend is but the friend of blood, the consanguine parent or again the 'parent by alliance' through marriage, oath of fraternity, adoption or other corresponding institutions.[2]

In the epilogue to the chapter, Derrida sets his sights on the 'fraternal resonance [*den geschwisterlichen Klang*]' of the 'obscure friendship of rhyme' whose kinship forges an alliance between speech and the place of the motherland, between the poem and belonging. Echo, with her auto-affection, means that rhyme always risks serving the law of the worst – of nationalism, of racism. And yet, glossing Schmitt's reading of Konrad Weiß's poem, 'the stamp of the rhyme, like the hammer of a storm', also syncopates the sibling sonority, deconstructing the unifying tone of *Geschlecht*. Echo is a name for the testamentary structure of *survivre* that Derrida discerns in friendship and which prises *la démocratie à venir* away from democracy's attachment to filiation and fraternity. Not an ideal double but a friend of oneself, Echo takes the words of the other and carries them away after their death, exposing democracy's irreducible temporal dislocation.

As Derrida argues in *Geschlecht III*, the type, as the strike or hammer blow of inscription, produces 'the generality of the genus', gathering together a series of singularities that 'fall under the *same type*'.[3] In the unifying *Schlag* (blow) of Heidegger's fundamental tone, however, there is also a *Verschlagen*, a shattering, breaking into multiple shards, iterability, prostheticity, and with it the rupture of the fraternal homeland. Instead of rhyme's ipseity, there is rhythm, the punctuating rhythm of dissemination that Derrida characterises in 'La double séance' as working towards a textual 'decapitation'.[4] It is this knot between rhythm and democracy that interests me, but this cannot be grasped without looking at other passages in Derrida's published writings and seminars that illuminate the intimate connection between rhythm and the pulsation of blood, and specifically the bloody incision of a death sentence.

To give some sense of context, the entanglement of rhythm and fraternity plays an important role in *Geschlecht III*, a text extracted from the end of the seventh up to the thirteenth and final session of the seminar that Derrida gave at the École des Hautes Études en Sciences Sociales in 1984–5. This first year of a four-year seminar devoted to 'Nationalité et nationalisme philosophiques' marks the beginning of an arc that passes through the 1988–9 seminar on 'Politiques de l'amitié'. While the concept of *Geschlecht* would appear to be the prevailing preoccupation of this period – *Geschlecht II* stems from the sixth and the remainder of the seventh session, while *Geschlecht IV* is printed as an epilogue in the French edition of *Politiques de l'amitié* – rhythm can also be seen to operate as a clandestine governing concept across these texts that links the issues of nationalism to that of democracy. In *Geschlecht III*, an irregular rhythm of reading disrupts the strike that gathers difference under a single type or family.[5] Unlike the rhythm that flows from the unicity of this unique *Grundton*, Derrida's *dissémination* breaks with Heidegger's rhythm precisely in keeping step with it – which is to say, redoubling it, re-marking it, re-typing, typing over, or overprinting,[6] and thus double striking in a syncopation of its beat.

As Geoffrey Bennington elucidates, *dissémination* is not a proliferation of meaning – such as the manifold meaning that is held together, as it were, by the term *Geschlecht* – but is at an altogether incommensurable level added to or subtracted from the series of meanings at which a differential spacing or articulation of textuality makes any semantics possible – that is, *Geschlecht* not as signifier but simply as a *Schlag* that re-marks or a type that is an example of what it names.[7] Or more precisely, as Derrida argues in 'La double séance', it names the generative opening of that opposition between semantics and syntactics.[8] This complication that disrupts the very destination of meaning – a re-mark that cuts across, intersects, *incises* the text – and not simply an excess of meanings, is what makes dissemination unmasterable. In short, what is at stake in deconstruction is a rhythmic punctuation. This rhythm, though, might more accurately be described, following Derrida's preface to Philippe Lacoue-Labarthe's *Typography: Mimesis, Philosophy, Politics*, as an 'arrhythmic' rhythm that interrupts the alternation between the two and oppositionality in general.[9] The transcendental, in other words, is rhythmed, syncopated, dislocated, and thus ruined from the outset because it beats, strikes against itself.

Elsewhere, Geoffrey Bennington suggests that a 'differential rhythm' without self-contained indivisible elements would be a way to think about Derrida's *démocratie à venir* and might just present an answer of sorts to democracy's 'tragically irreconcilable' laws of equality of all and singularity of each (40/22) by pointing to a mix of association and dissociation or 'the relative gathering of a scatter'.[10] The two disjunct laws are not simply tragically irreconcilable but moreover 'forever wounding [*blessantes*]':

> This wound [*blessure*] opens with the necessity of having to count one's friends, to *count* the others, in the economy of one's own, there where every other is altogether other [*tout autre est tout autre*]. But where every other is *equally* [*également*] altogether other. (40/22)

The challenge of democracy, as Derrida later elaborates in a discussion of Nietzsche's views on friendship, is therefore to think an equality beyond this economy of calculation and of appropriation:

> What would an equality then be, what would an equity be, which would no longer calculate this equivalence? Which would, quite simply, no longer calculate at all? And would carry itself beyond proportion, beyond appropriation, thereby exceeding all reappropriation of the proper? (83/64)

Unlike the desire for possession that characterises love in Nietzsche's estimation, democracy demands a certain dissymmetry or disproportionality that breaks with reciprocity for which friendship might be the '*just name*' (86/66). Specifically, it entails an experience of the new that is distinguishable from the drive to appropriation (*pulsion d'appropriation*) or accumulation of new property (84/65).

This observation allows Derrida to figure the incision or wound that divides democracy's two laws expressly as a rhythmic pulsation (*pulsion rythmée*). The path by which the first *pulsion* is transformed – or, we might say more accurately, is dislocated, syncopated, rhythmed – into the second is worth tracking closely. In the first instance, the new kind of non-appropriative 'lovence', insofar as it is beyond any calculation or knowledge, can only be experienced '*just once*, perhaps, for the first time (another perhaps), once and only once, therefore for the first and last time (perhaps, perhaps)' (88/66). This new form of lovence only arrives with the chanciness of the perhaps beyond the scope of any sovereign calculation as to what will come. It will always be necessary that it may or may not happen – per*haps*. Like *la démocratie à venir*, it thus has the character of an impossible event or what Derrida will go on to describe as a 'passive decision [*décision passive*]' (87/68).

Whilst the decision makes the event, it is also what interrupts and neutralises that which

> must surprise both the freedom and the will of every subject – surprise, in a word, the very subjectivity of the subject, affecting it wherever the subject is exposed, sensitive, receptive, vulnerable and fundamentally passive, before and beyond any decision – indeed, before any subjectivation or objectivation. (87/68)

Whence the aporia of the traditional understanding of a free, voluntarist subject and his sovereign decision according to which nothing would ever *happen* to a subject who remains self-identical, unaffected by and indifferent to even the very decision that he wills. This suggests that 'before' any sovereign decision there is another decision that makes possible the event, a passive decision, the rending (*déchirante*) as the decision of the other that is always already in me, the decision of the me as other who thereby makes an exception for/of me (87/68–9). Not simply responsible for myself before the other, I am in the first instance '*responsible for the other before the other*' (88/69).

It is at this point that Derrida introduces the metaphor of rhythm through the figure of the *heartbeat* (*battement du cœur*) – the heartbeat of sovereign autonomy by which it opens onto itself and thus onto heteronomy. A few sentences later comes a more detailed elucidation of this figure that is worth reading at length since it explains why Derrida refers not simply to the heart but to its *beat*:

> *In sum, a decision is unconscious* – insane as that may seem, it involves the unconscious and nevertheless remains responsible. And we are hereby unfolding the classic concept of decision. It is this act of the act that we are attempting here to think: 'passive,' delivered over to the other, suspended over the other's heartbeat [*suspendu au battement du cœur de l'autre*]. For a few sentences earlier on, 'its heartbeat' had to be necessarily accorded thus: as the heartbeat of the other. Where I am helpless, where I decide what I cannot fail to decide, freely, necessarily, receiving my very life from the heartbeat of the other [*recevant jusqu'à ma vie du battement de cœur de l'autre*]. We say not only heart but heartbeat [*Nous ne disons pas seulement le cœur mais le battement de cœur*]: that which, *from one instant to another*, having come again from an other of the other to whom it is delivered up (and this can be me), this heart receives, it will *perhaps* receive in a rhythmic pulsation [*pulsion rythmée*] what is called blood [*sang*], which in turn will receive the force needed to arrive [*la force d'arriver*]. (88/69)

'My' decision and 'my' life come from the heart of the other and more specifically from its *beat*. This *perhaps* arrives as a rhythmic pulsation – which can be the beat of my own heart as the other of me in me. And this would also be a definition of democracy that would interrupt the homophilial, autochthonous equality of fraternity and birth (116/95). But what dislocates this aristo-democracy of brothers that tends irrevocably towards oligarchy – and this perhaps comes as a surprise – is nothing other than *blood*, even when it is blood that Derrida so fervently wants to escape. What, though, would divide this giving and receiving of blood from the heartbeat of the other from the consanguinity of filiation and fatherland?

One answer would be to pursue the idea of the gift of friendship, of friendship as gift, which, by definition exceeds any obligation to return the favour and thus redirects friendship away from equivalence and exchange towards dissymmetry, disproportionality, non-reciprocity and the *pré-venance* of the other (82/63). It is impossible to gain a full understanding of the reference to the heartbeat in *Politiques de l'amitié* without closely reading passages in the first year of *La peine de mort* where the same metaphor of the heartbeat is used and its relation to the aneconomic is articulated via a discussion of *interest*, understood in all its polysemia. Derrida observes the interest, or investment, on both sides of the debate – among supporters of the death penalty and abolitionists – in disinterestedness: that is, in a value beyond any price or economy. On the one hand, a Kantian affirmation of the *jus talionis* as the categorical imperative of penal justice puts this principle beyond any worldly interests, insisting on an equivalence between crime and moral compensation or indemnification that transcends empirical calculation. On the other, abolitionists assert the dignity and value of life above any market value.

Some rather suspect that the abolitionists' disinterest in the inviolability of life in general conceals a hypocritical interest in wanting to save their own necks. This is where the issue of fraternity at stake in *Politiques de l'amitié* comes into view as Derrida tracks Marx on abolition of the political death penalty amidst a fraternalist fervour in the Revolution of February 1848. This merely served the interests of a hegemonic bourgeoisie which could temporally coincide with those of the proletariat before the hollowness of universal brotherhood was exposed as a passing moment in the class antagonism between capital and labour. Derrida, though, owns his interest: 'Yes, I am against the death penalty because I want to save my neck, to save the life I love, what I love to live, what I love living.'[11] He adds a crucial qualification, however, arguing that the abolitionist cause is driven by another figure of interest as yet undefined but which consists in a certain displacing substitutability: 'And when I say "I," of course, I mean "I," me, but also the "I," the "me," whoever says "I" in its place or in mine'.[12]

It is at this point in the tenth session that Derrida links this interest to the theme of *pulsion*, the pulse of my life and the heart of the other in terms strongly reminiscent of *Politiques de l'amitié*:

> What is an interest here? I can believe in and affirm what is called life, what I call, what an 'I' calls, life only by setting out from and within a 'my life' even if this belief in 'my life,' the sense of 'my life,' originarily passes by way of the heart of the other. Even if my life drive [*pulsion*], my life pulse [*pouls*], is first of all confided to the heart of the other and would not survive the heart of the other [*ne survivrait pas au cœur de l'autre*]. Consequently, in general, even before the question of the death penalty, I can put the living before the dead only on the basis of the affirmation and preference of my life, of my living present, right there where it receives its life from the heart of the other [*Je ne peux faire passer le vivant avant le mort que depuis l'affirmation et la préférence de ma vie, de mon présent vivant, là même où il reçoit sa vie du cœur de l'autre*].[13]

It is in this interest – this preference and affirmation – that one can begin to discern a definition of the friendship that is to underscore democracy in *Politiques de l'amitié* where Derrida speaks in similar terms of how the 'singular preference destabilizes and renders dissymmetrical the equilibrium of all difference' (23–4/7). Both abolitionists and supporters of the death penalty each claim to put life before death and to that end invoke a life beyond life and above its calculating interests. From the abolitionist standpoint, to be *for life* is to be invested in 'survival, in the priceless interest of life, to save what is left of life'.[14] Here, though, Derrida argues that I can only put the interests of life before those of death, only put (one kind of) survival first and affirm my life, at the moment when I am survived by the other, by a life that exceeds and extends beyond mine, which is to say by another kind of survival that is not mine, the survival of the other or the other in me that comes before me and my life – what Derrida elsewhere calls *la vie la mort*, or life-death.

For this reason, however, the impulse of 'my' life not only cannot survive the other upon whom I depend in order to survive (beyond my death) but moreover cannot survive at or in the heart of the other (*au cœur de l'autre*). This adds a crucial clarification to the account of the passive decision in *Politiques de l'amitié* as being 'delivered over to the other' (88/69). The ambiguity in *La peine de mort* points to a paradox: I cannot survive beyond life, in a life-after-death, except by being carried in the heart of the other and yet to the extent that I am incorporated or encysted in the heart of the other it is not the same 'I' that lives on. And again, when Derrida speaks of '*l'affirmation et la préférence de ma vie*', there is a double sense, objective and subjective: it is both the affirmation and preference *for* my life, putting my life before the lives of others – that is, the very crime that warrants the moral reimbursement of the death penalty – but it also refers to that which my life affirms and prefers, which is the friend whom I esteem more than myself without reciprocity or equivalence, whose life I thereby put before my own.

This is why democracy, in its rhythmic pulsation, is the deconstruction of sovereignty, but this preferential character of friendship, which prefers one friend over another and thus leads to aristocracy (37/19–20), gives rise to the question of arithmetic that vexes *Politiques de l'amitié* (how many friends is too many?), of the 'quantum' of democracy, defined as 'the decided and declared approbation of the greatest number' (124/102). Critically, the heartbeat of the other cuts across the decision of wilful subjects and the calculability on which the greatest number is premised. Accordingly, even the syntax in this passage from *La peine de mort* dispossesses me of 'my' life, making me an exception and the recipient of 'its' decision. It is on the basis of this heteronomy that Derrida can claim for *la démocratie à venir* an 'infinite alterity' in which '*tout autre est tout autre*' and which, far from contradicting the 'scansion' of friendship's preferential or 'dissymmetrical curving', would follow from it without this 'infinite heterogeneity' collapsing into the hierarchical difference of socio-political inequality or the equality of birth (259/232).

Finally, nested in the *faire passer* is the simpler sense of spending my life, passing the time of my life, before I die, but Derrida points out that I can only spend my life in a state of openness to the surprise of other, to the uncertainty of when my death might other. The death penalty puts an end to the existence that I call 'my' life, but it moreover puts an end to the very chanciness and potential for surprise, including the surprise of the moment of my death, that makes a life worthy of the name. A life in which the moment of death is calculable, in deciding (on) my life, 'exonerates me' of happenstance.[15]

> Where the anticipation of my death becomes the anticipation of a calculable instant, there is no longer any future, there is thus no longer any event to come, nothing to come, no longer any other, even no more heart of the other, and so forth. So that where 'my life,' be it originarily granted by the heart of the other, is 'my life,' it must keep this relation to the coming of the other as coming of the to-come [*venue de l'à-venir*] in the opening of the incalculable and the undecidable. 'My life,' and especially my life insofar as it depends on the [*tient au*] heart of the other, cannot affirm itself and affirm its preference except over against this, which is not so much death as calculation and decision, the calculable decidability of what puts an end to it.[16]

It is this incalculability of decision that defines the event of democracy in *Politiques de l'amitié* where the figure of the perhaps names the excess of what happens over its conditions of possibility (35/18).

By contrast with both the death penalty and abolitionism in the name of a priceless life, to be *for life* – this preference *for* life – can only be understood in the substitutive sense of *for* that Derrida highlights in his analysis of Hélène Cixous's art of replacement in *H. C. pour la vie*, where the *pro* of the prolegomenon put before everything is at once the dativity of the gift and the prostheticity of arriving in the place of the other, taking and displacing the place of the other.[17] In that text, the speed with which a moving body is displaced from one point to another is, before all being, 'the animation and elation, the rhythm of a sentence, its pulse and heartbeat, its breathing or its tachycardia'.[18]

In *La peine de mort*, just as in the passage on the passive decision in *Politiques de l'amitié*, it likewise transpires that the relation to the heart of the other has an expressly rhythmic character. In a multiple wordplay, the life drive (*pulsion*) is figured literally as a beating of the heart.

> When I say 'my life,' or even my 'living present,' here, I have already named the other in me, the other greater, younger, or older than me, the other of my sex or not, the other who nonetheless lets me be me, the other whose heart is more interior to my heart than my heart itself, which means that I protect my heart, I protest in the name of my heart when I fight [*en me battant*] so that the heart of the other will continue to beat [*battre*] – in me before me, after me, or even without me. Where else would I find the strength and the drive [*pulsion*] and the interest to fight [*me battre*] and to struggle [*me débattre*], with my whole heart, with the beating [*battant*] of my heart against the death penalty? I can do it, me, as me, only thanks to the other, by the grace of the other heart that affirms life in me.[19]

The common (fraternal?) interest shared by proponents and abolitionists, by contrast, is to put to death the lively undecidability of the perhaps that renders incalculable the moment at which the grim reaper will strike. It is to liberate life from finitude, to infinitise life by giving and receiving death in a calculated fashion precisely so as to indemnify life against an aneconomic death. Later in the tenth session, Derrida once again locates this interest in the scene of fraternity. Reading Benveniste, he points out that the penalty to which one is condemned is the price paid to redeem a familial, filial, tribal or national crime or debt and thus to acquit a duty of fraternity. But not unlike friendship, the price paid is incommensurate to the punishment fitting the crime. Besides paying what is owed, this reimbursement or indemnification pays *interest* 'as the incalculable surplus value of capital'.[20] Capital punishment is a 'capitalization': the calculating drive becomes vertiginous 'when death without return is a part of the market there where it cannot be part of the market, where it ought to remain incalculable'.[21]

At this point, one can see why democracy's passive decision is furthermore an 'absolutely cutting [*coupante*] [. . .] heartrending [*déchirante*]' (97/79) *incision* – much as the death penalty paradoxically consists in the phantasm of 'an infinite survival assured by interruption itself'.[22] But when it comes to interest defined otherwise, as dissymmetrical pulsation, this cut is never straightforwardly a single strike. Rather, as Derrida puts it in his reading of Blanchot's *L'arrêt de mort*, when J. dies, twice, 'her pulse [. . .] scattered like sand', she gives herself 'a death sentence, in an instant as elusive as the last grain of sand in the time of hourglasses, death also as the result of the dissemination of the rhythm of life [*rythme de vie*] without a finishing stroke [*coup d'arrêt*], unbordered and unbounded arhythmy [*arythmie sans bord*] on a beach that is a continuation of the sea'.[23] The affirmation of life reveals itself to be a double blow, an *arrêt de mort* that syncopates itself – anticipating the discussion of the passive decision of *Politiques de l'amitié* – with a suspensive *arrêt* that defers and holds back death beating against, one might say, a decisive *arrêt* that decides, decrees, gives, and hence hastens death. These two temporalities of *arrêt*, each interrupting the other, also interrupt themselves, yielding an 'arhythmic pulsation of its syntax' on the point of scattering into sand,[24] exonerating or acquitting life of finitude only by multiplying and dispersing it.

This incision might usefully be compared to the radically undecidable and incalculable cut that severs the Gordian knot of entangled 'differential vibrations of time and rhythm' in Derrida's account of stricture.[25] This incision beyond all decision – perhaps beyond even that of the passive decision that comes from the heartbeat of the other – is a condition for all politics. But it might just be the way in which democracy re-marks itself: neither a single immutable regime nor one constitutional form among others, democracy, as Derrida gestures in *Voyous*, just is that dissemination of multiple political forms *and* an example of that indeterminate openness to diversity and transformation.[26]

If there is no one *type* of democracy, if it is also a double or multiple strike, democracy is the rhythm of arrhythmia. Its incision is the cruel flow of blood (*cruor*) and the staunching that interrupts that measure of life, the syncopation of diastole and systole. Whereas the death penalty reaches back to infect all of life with the stroke of death, what makes both of these temporalities possible is a more originary temporal dispersal, an originary differential rhythm that scatters moments of time not into self-identical instants but as a more or less shattered dissemination that will always already have cut across every 'now'.

This incision is not simply the interior mechanical interruption of an infinite fluidity of circulation and/or the punctuating articulation of an auto-affecting vibration of the kind that David Wills highlights in Hegel's conception of blood-flow.[27] Rather, in a deconstructive analysis, the blood-letting that stops the heart, scattering its beat like sand, entails '*blood pulsating on the outside*', to the originary prostheticisation of the rhythmic pulse of life,[28] and hence to a political life that does not simply flow out into a dispersed multiplicity but is always somewhat staunched, beating against itself. The rhythm of life is not something that takes its cue from the vibration of blood pumped around the inside of the body but rather is the pulsation of time that technologises blood from the outside as prosthesis, as if from the heartbeat of the other that cuts across and syncopates 'mine'.

It is on account of a certain type of rhythm that there is 'no deconstruction without democracy, no democracy without deconstruction' (128/105). Democracy is deconstructive self-delimitation not in the name of perfectibility but each and every singular time. Its syncopated pulsation is what separates blood from its nationalistic or xenoracist reference. The indifference of equality, Derrida concedes, 'certainly can impose homogenizing calculability while exalting land and blood, and the risk is as terrifying as it is inevitable – it is the risk today, more than ever' (129/106). But the flow of blood can also pulsate outside itself – and that would be the chance and the risk of democracy, its syncopated rhythm of best against worst.

Notes

1. Jacques Derrida, *Politiques de l'amitié: suivi de L'Oreille de Heidegger* (Paris: Galilée, 1994); Jacques Derrida, *Politics of Friendship*, trans. George Collins (London: Verso, 1997). Hereafter, page references to the French/English translation are given in parenthesis in the text (*PF*).
2. Carl Schmitt, *Der Begriff des Politischen* (Berlin: Duncker and Humblot, 1991 [1932]), p. 104.
3. Jacques Derrida, *Geschlecht III*, ed. Geoffrey Bennington, Katie Chenoweth and Rodrigo Therezo (Paris: Seuil, 2018), pp. 38–9; Jacques Derrida, *Geschlecht III: Sex, Race, Nation, Humanity*, trans. Katie Chenoweth and Rodrigo Therezo, ed. Geoffrey Bennington, Katie Chenoweth and Rodrigo Therezo (Chicago: University of Chicago Press, 2020), pp. 6–7.
4. Jacques Derrida, *La dissémination* (Paris: Seuil, 1972), p. 204; Jacques Derrida, *Dissemination*, trans. Barbara Johnson (Chicago: University of Chicago Press, 1981), p. 178.
5. Derrida, *Geschlecht III*, p. 35/1.
6. Ibid. pp. 41n/8–9n10.
7. Geoffrey Bennington, '*Geschlecht pollachos legetai*: Translation, Polysemia, Dissemination', *Philosophy Today*, 64.2 (2020), 423–39.
8. Derrida, *La dissémination*, p. 251/222.
9. Jacques Derrida, 'Désistance', in *Psyché: Inventions de l'autre II* (Paris: Galilée, 2003 [1987]), p. 238. Jacques Derrida, 'Désistance', in *Psyche: Inventions of the Other, Vol. 2*, ed. Peggy Kamuf and Elizabeth Rottenberg (Stanford: Stanford University Press, 2008), p. 230.
10. Geoffrey Bennington, 'The Democricy to Come', *The Oxford Literary Review*, 39.1 (2017) (pp. 120, 129).

11. Jacques Derrida, *Séminaire La peine de mort, Vol. I (1999–2000)*, ed. Geoffrey Bennington, Marc Crépon and Thomas Dutoit (Paris: Galilée, 2012), p. 345; Jacques Derrida, *The Death Penalty, Vol. I*, trans. Peggy Kamuf (Chicago: University of Chicago Press, 2014), pp. 254–5.
12. Ibid. p. 345/255.
13. Ibid. p. 346/255.
14. Ibid. p. 380/283.
15. Ibid. p. 349/258.
16. Ibid. p. 347/256.
17. Jacques Derrida, *H. C. pour la vie, c'est-a-dire . . .* (Paris: Galilée, 2002), p. 78; Jacques Derrida, *H. C. for Life, That Is to Say . . .*, trans. Laurent Milesi and Stefan Herbrechter (Stanford: Stanford University Press, 2006), p. 87.
18. Ibid. p. 66/73.
19. Derrida, *La peine de mort I*, p. 348/257.
20. Ibid. p. 353/261.
21. Ibid. p. 355/262.
22. Ibid. p. 349/258.
23. Jacques Derrida, 'Survivre: journal de bord', in Derrida, *Parages* (Paris: Galilée, 1986), p. 165; Jacques Derrida, 'Living On / Borderlines', trans. Kames Hulbert, in Harold Bloom, Paul de Man, Jacques Derrida, Geoffrey H. Hartman and J. Hillis Miller, *Deconstruction and Criticism* (London and New York: Continuum, 2004), p. 121.
24. Ibid. pp. 159–60/114–15.
25. Jacques Derrida, *Negotiations: Interventions and Interviews*, ed. and trans. Elizabeth Rottenberg (Stanford: Stanford University Press, 2002), pp. 29–31.
26. Jacques Derrida, *Voyous: Deux essais sur la raison* (Paris: Galilée, 2003), pp. 47–9; Jacques Derrida, *Rogues: Two Essays on Reason*, trans. Pascale-Anne Brault and Michael Naas (Stanford: Stanford University Press, 2005), p. 26.
27. David Wills, 'The Future Anterior of Blood', *Killing Times* (New York: Fordham University Press, 2018), pp. 106ff.
28. Ibid. p. 116.

17

Derrida, Democracy and the State of Education: Learning, by Design, Perchance

Allan Parsons

Will we ever be finished with this law and this secret police between us?
Jacques Derrida, 'Envois'[1]

This chapter, in exploring the implications of Derrida's admission of the example of the Clipper chip into the book version of *Politics of Friendship*, desacralises the notion of *chōra*, as 'the place of possible substitution', and as 'third genus' between the intelligible and the sensible.[2] This opens up a 'spectrology' of the in-between in which the importance of design education, design practices and designed entities emerges, as media for formal and informal public education, by extension from Derrida's emphasis on the role of literature and the humanities in the university.[3] In doing so, it acknowledges Derrida's emphasis on secrecy or confidentiality for his conception of the relation between the educational and the political. For Derrida, reflection upon the Kantian ethics and politics of friendship should organise itself around the concept of secrecy (*PF*, 257).[4] The secret is 'that which one *thinks* [. . .] *must* remain secret because an engagement has been entered upon and a promise made in certain non-natural conditions' (259). It is the in(ter)vention of the third party as witness, however, that prevents the jealous narcissism of the dual, or the n+1, relation of the secret from sinking into abyssal self-reflection, opening the possibility of a moral and a political friendship that nevertheless remains, even for Kant's friend of humankind, within the horizon of cosmopolitics as phratrocentrism, a horizon that Derrida affirmatively deconstructs.[5]

It is argued that design pedagogies, design practices and design production may only begin to deliver on their promise in respect of justice and democracy if they are practised as forms of *inventio*, not only in the rhetorical sense of 'an activity of invention concerned with the indeterminate' but also, more importantly, in the Derridean sense of opening to the other, of allowing a space for the in-coming of the other through a deconstructive inventiveness that destabilises structures that foreclose, letting the other come by preparing for its coming.[6] Design practices are obliged in the name of justice, if justice is taken as a concern for an otherness that cannot either be foreseen or totalised and which addresses itself to the singularity of the other, to keep open the possibility of the surprise of the 'invention' of the other.[7] Such invention, which may unveil what was already there or produce what was not already there from an existing stock of elements, implies 'both a first time and every time, the inaugural event and iterability'.[8] Furthermore, if the other is no longer simply another human being, equal to me as a 'brother', but includes other human beings unlike me as well as the non-human others, the outputs of design may then be seen to exhibit agential in-betweenness, where agency lies in the interrelationship of humans with the material world, constituting realities that interweave the human, non-human and more-than-human.[9] Design then becomes a place where the law one gives to oneself and the position one is given in the order of the other conspire or confide, a place to which the 'altogether other, and every other (one) is every (bit) other, comes [. . .] to upset the order of phenomenology' and ideality (232). The invention of design education, design practice and designed produce may then be capable of enacting public education in the form of a deconstructive inventiveness or an affirmative deconstruction 'that is not simply positive, not simply conservative, not simply a way of repeating the given institution'.[10]

Necessarily absent from the 1988 and 1993 texts, the Clipper chip is admitted into the book despite Derrida's reservations about the use of such examples to illustrate or actualise his analyses (272).[11] The Clipper chip existed as a designed, socio-technical invention in 1993–6. The Clinton administration in the United States proposed the Clipper chip in April 1993 as a way to give the National Security Agency (NSA) a key to decrypt the content of any telecommunication. Opponents argued that the Clipper chip would eradicate the Fourth Amendment protecting people's right to privacy and freedom from unreasonable governmental intrusions. By 1996 the White House had backed down and the Clipper chip was never implemented. Nonetheless, soon afterwards, the NSA began anticipating and thwarting encryption tools before they became mainstream, setting up a clandestine programme allowing them to circumvent many of the virtual security systems intended to protect digital telecommunications. By the 2010s, the NSA had accomplished in secret what it had failed to do through political persuasion in the 1990s.[12]

As an invention, the Clipper chip marks, on the one hand, a continuation in thinking about *the political*: 'there is nothing new here, despite the leap of technological mutation which also produces structural effects' (144). On the other hand, acknowledging the *political difference or political paradox*, the Clipper chip represents a break in *politics*: 'the novelty of these structural effects must not be neglected; this is the entirety of the "concrete" in politics' (144).[13] These effects, had the device been implemented, would have altered digital encryption-decryption in telecommunications systems in such a way as to ensure there could be no 'equiveillance' between citizen and state, thereby undermining liberal defences of the security state which argue that citizens are able to restrain the state from becoming overbearing.[14]

For Derrida, the example of the Clipper chip is intended only to recall that 'a reflection on the politics of friendship should not be distinguishable from a meditation on secrecy, on the "meaning", the "history", and the "techniques" of [. . .] [the] secret' (145). Montaigne, for example, placed the law of secrecy, the sovereign fraternity of secrecy between two, above the law of the city, the brotherhood of political secrecy, which begins with three; while, moreover, the Kantian ethics and politics of friendship organises itself around the concept of secrecy, marking the ideal of friendship as communication or egalitarian sharing (184, 257). Unlike aesthetic friendship, which is based solely on feelings of love, Kant argues that moral friendship, articulating love (attachment) and respect (detachment), demands absolute confidence, such that two people share not just their impressions but their secret judgements. True friends ought to be able to say anything to each other, a potentially dangerous situation, as there are few 'who are able to renounce all public profit, all political or institutional consequence, to the possession or circulation of this secret' (258). Such friends, although rare and improbable, may nonetheless may come along.

This tension between two confidentialities draws the double bind of friendship as fraternity out to its limit. Kantian cosmopolitan democracy could not be promised or realised without the figure of the brother: cosmopolitical democracy is cosmo-phratrocentism (264). Hence, the categorical imperative not to betray humanity means not to betray one's brother, which is another way of saying that only the brother can be betrayed (273). Secrecy is implicated in the oppositions within friendship, with the secret-private-invisible-illegible-apolitical, on one side, and the manifest-public-testimonial-political, on the other (277). Fraternal friendship thus appears alien to the *res publica* and could never found a politics. Nevertheless, the canonical philosophical discourses on friendship explicitly tie the friend as brother to virtue and justice and to moral and political reason (277).

Derrida's deconstruction of friendship as brotherhood, (con)founding the ethical and the political, is extended here to consider the relationships between the ethical-political subject and the pedagogical-educational subject. This extension is based on the recognition that at the beginnings of the Western philosophical canon both the political and the educational are intimately intertwined with *philos* and *philia*. Plato's reflections on friendship, begun in the dialogue *Lysis*, form the core of a theory of politics that treats the *politeia* as principally an educational force.[15] The political is identified with *paideia*, the moral and cultural education of the members of the *polis*, as a public space linked to national territory and autochthony.[16] *Paideia* 'is not primarily a matter of books and academic credits. First and foremost, it involves becoming conscious that the *polis* is also oneself and that its fate also depends upon one's mind, behaviour, and decisions; [. . .] it is participation in political life'.[17]

Rather than placing *philos*, as masculine homosociality, at the heart of political-educational association within a unitary, autochthonous *polis*, Derrida offers the promise of a non-foundational, non-dialectical, relational *philoxenia*, derived from the 'Athenian political philosophy of hospitality [. . .] which commanded one to receive the stranger, the *xenos*, and treat him as a friend, an ally, a *philos*'.[18] Thus, for Derrida, 'there is no politics without [. . .] an open hospitality to the guest as *ghost*, whom one holds, just as he [*sic*] holds us, hostage'.[19]

Assumptions about the close relationship between the political and the educational in *paideia* have long persisted in European thought.[20] Thus, in the eighteenth century, it was a fundamental assumption that 'the overall goal of pedagogy should be the production of a moral and civic-minded citizenry', while in the nineteenth century, 'classical liberal theory sees democracy not just as a system of government, but also as a system of education'.[21] This educational humanism and political liberalism, with their implicit masculine homosociality, is deconstructed by Derrida when he insists that the humanities should create a culture that questions and resists 'all the powers that limit democracy to come'.[22] The university should be a place where nothing is beyond question, so as to become 'a vital public sphere for critical learning, ethical deliberation, and civic engagement', wherein 'a social commitment to the notion and the practices of justice is instilled'.[23] This does not, however, imply a pedagogisation of politics such that, as proposed by Heidegger in his 1933 rectoral address, the university provides the spiritual leadership that guides the nation's political leadership, a conception of the education–politics relation that joins Heidegger with Plato, Fichte with Nietzsche.[24]

Notwithstanding the importance of the university for democracy, Giroux points out that the sites of education and pedagogy in the contemporary world extend far beyond those of formal education, to include 'a range of other spheres such as advertising, television, film, the Internet, video game culture, and the popular press', broadening and deepening the meaning and importance of public pedagogy.[25] Reflexively, those sites of public education must become a central concern for formal education, so that 'students can be educated to understand, engage critically, and transform those dominant spheres of public pedagogy that are largely shaping their beliefs and sense of agency'.[26] For these reasons, design pedagogy in higher education must put the progeny of design practices, as major elements of the *res publica*, into question.

When Derrida talks of artifactuality and actuvirtuality, it is initially mass media outputs to which he refers.[27] Actuality, Derrida argues, is actively 'sorted, invested and performatively interpreted by a range of hierarchising and selective procedures – factitious or artificial procedures which are always subservient to various powers and interests of which their 'subjects' and agents [. . .] are never sufficiently aware. The "reality" of "actuality" [. . .] only reaches us through fictional devices', that is, technical and poematic inventions.[28] This calls for 'a work of resistance, of vigilant counter-interpretation', and a responsibility to develop 'a critical culture, a kind of education'.[29] Crucially, such deconstruction of artifactuality must not 'be used to neutralise every danger by means of [. . .] a denial of events, by which everything – even violence and suffering, war and death – is said to be constructed and fictive, and constituted by and for the media, so that nothing really ever happens, only images, simulacra, and delusions'. Actuvirtuality implies that 'Virtuality now reaches right into the structure of the eventual event and imprints itself there; it affects [. . .] everything which connects us to actuality, to the unappeasable reality of its supposed present.'[30]

If it is through artifactual, actuvirtual inventions that the 'reality' of 'actuality' reaches us, then, it is argued here, it is not simply in the form of literary, textual and media resources, 'writing' in the narrow sense, but rather through 'inventions', some in textual form, but many more in the form of designs, from symbols to artefacts and from actions to systems – 'writing' in Derrida's extended sense of *différance*. Since public education is enacted through active engagement with such designed outputs, design pedagogy, while acknowledging the necessity of qualification (practical knowledge and skills) and socialisation (competent action in the socio-cultural world), must foreground additionally 'subjectification': the ways in which qualified, socialised educands 'invent' their own, highly conditioned and conditional, personhood.[31] Such educational 'inventionalism', by breaking through the 'order of socialization, the order of the present and the same', opens up design education as a practice of affirmative deconstruction.[32]

Through a critically intimate engagement with the liberal, humanist, educational-political subject, human being is shown to be incomplete, bearing 'the character of not being closed': open to contingent historicity.[33] Sloterdijk argues, inventively misreading Heidegger, that, 'Being-in designed spaces constitutes our fundamental condition'; in other words, 'Dasein is Design'.[34] For Latour, 'we are enveloped, entangled, surrounded; we are never outside without having recreated another more artificial, more fragile, more engineered envelope. We move from envelopes to envelopes, from folds to folds, never from one private sphere to the Great Outside'.[35] The countless overlapping and interacting webs we have created have enveloped the planet with design as a geological layer, such that design has become the world.[36] In being communicative, intersubjective and dialogic as well as objective, substantial and impedimentary, designs articulate the two great alternative narratives of modernity: 'one of emancipation, detachment, modernization, progress and mastery, and the other, [. . .] of attachment, precaution, entanglement, dependence and care'.[37]

By considering design in this way, Heideggerian *Dasein*, *Mitsein* and *Mit-da-sein*, as thrownness and being between, is translated into Sloterdijkian situated existence, a being-in-the-media that characterises our 'radical mediocrity'.[38] For Sloterdijk, we are thrown into situations, mediated by designs of various orders. Situations are 'forms of coexistence of someone with someone and something in something', where collectives at different scales are caught up in shared immersive environments.[39] In seeking a grounding for its own value, human being as situated ek-sistence may become 'an unceasing attempt to give a decisive turn to our state of thrownness in the world by moving together to design a society'.[40] To free ourselves from the givenness of the world, 'We must *ont-werpen* our lives [the Dutch word for 'design' can also be read as 'un-throw' – Tr.] [. . .] Thrownness-unthrowing: there you have the human condition'.[41]

Design pedagogy and design practice as un- or over-throwing thrownness is far from the common-sense understanding of design as a positive, technical art (*ars/technê*). Design becomes a discipline that deals with possible worlds and with opinions about what the parts as well as the whole of the human environment could be, while not predetermining, on its own terms, what they should be. So, while 'the moral imperative falls to leaders in governments, institutions, and corporations to enact radical policy changes', design may nevertheless take part in public education about complex policies, while also urging and inspiring people to put pressure on those in positions of authority to enact justice through restitutive, restorative and reparative design.[42]

The Clipper chip, from the days prior to the infiltration of the World Wide Web into all aspects of social existence, remains a pertinent example because, of all the political binaries that permeate Western democratic life, it is secrecy–revelation that is currently in most need of political theorising and historicisation within political thought.[43] This is, first, because human subjects, no longer conceivable as sovereign but rather as networked, are incentivised to give away their privacy (confidences) in exchange for perceived health or financial benefits; and, second, because a hyper-informed citizenry is paralysed by being simultaneously overwhelmed by information and unable to trust any of it and therefore to act confidently on it. This secrecy–revelation dynamic became all the more conspicuous during the coronavirus pandemic. Existing fault lines, notably between totalitarian surveillance and citizen empowerment, on the one hand, and between nationalist isolation and global solidarity, on the other hand, have been exacerbated and, while there is a good case for more intrusive policing and surveillance measures, there is a danger that such temporary responses may become permanent, implying a major reduction in civil liberties.[44] In the society of control into which we have been thrown, we might well find ourselves uttering and citing the quite possibly apocryphal apostrophe, in both its canonical and recoil versions, 'O my friends, there is no friend!', while perhaps not yet having confidently overthrown, or being able to overthrow, anything in our own name.[45]

Notes

1. Jacques Derrida, 'Envois', in Derrida, *The Post Card: From Socrates to Freud and Beyond*, trans. Alan Bass (Chicago: University of Chicago Press, 1987), pp. 1–256 (p. 50).
2. Jacques Derrida, 'Khora', in Derrida, *On the Name*, ed. Thomas Dutoit, trans. Ian McLeod (Stanford: Stanford University Press, 1995), pp. 89–127 (p. 89); Henk Oosterling, 'ICTology and Local Inter-Esse: Desacralizing Derrida's Chora', in *Essays zu Jacques Derrida and Gianni Vattimo, Religion*, ed. Ludwig Nagl (Frankfurt am Main: Peter Lang, 2001), pp. 109–29.
3. Jacques Derrida, *Specters of Marx: The State of the Debt, the Work of Mourning and the New International* (New York: Routledge, 1994).
4. Jacques Derrida, *Politics of Friendship*, trans. George Collins (London: Verso, 1997); Jacques Derrida, *Politiques de l'amitié: suivi de L'Oreille*

de Heidegger (Paris: Galilée, 1994). Hereafter, page references to the English translation are given in parenthesis in the text.

5. Jacques Derrida, 'The Politics of Friendship', *Journal of Philosophy*, 85.11 (1988), 632–44 (pp. 640–1).
6. Richard Buchanan, 'Rhetoric, Humanism, and Design', in *Discovering Design: Explorations in Design Studies*, ed. Richard Buchanan and Victor Margolin (Chicago: University of Chicago Press, 1995), pp. 23–66 (p. 27); Jacques Derrida, *Psyche: Inventions of the Other, Vol. I*, ed. Peggy Kamuf and Elizabeth Rottenberg (Stanford: Stanford University Press, 2007) (p. 45).
7. Jacques Derrida, 'Force of Law: The "Mystical Foundation of Authority"', *Cardozo Law Review*, 11.5/6 (1990), 920–1045; Gert Biesta, 'Education after Deconstruction: Between Event and Invention', in Michael A. Peters and Gert Biesta, *Derrida, Deconstruction, and the Politics of Pedagogy* (New York: Peter Lang, 2009), pp. 97–113.
8. Derrida, *Psyche: Inventions of the Other, Vol. I*, p. 24.
9. Candace R. Kuby, 'Why a Paradigm Shift of "More than Human Ontologies" Is Needed: Putting to Work Poststructural and Posthuman Theories in Writers' Studio', *International Journal of Qualitative Studies in Education*, 30.9 (2017), 877–96 (p. 878).
10. Jacques Derrida, *Deconstruction in a Nutshell: A Conversation with Jacques Derrida*, ed. John D. Caputo (New York: Fordham University Press, 1997), p. 5.
11. Jacques Derrida, 'The Politics of Friendship', *Journal of Philosophy*, 85.11 (1988), 632–44; Jacques Derrida, 'Politics of Friendship', *American Imago*, 50.3 (1993), 353–91.
12. Nicole Perlroth, Jeff Larson and Scott Shane, 'N.S.A. Able to Foil Basic Safeguards of Privacy on Web', *New York Times*, 5 September 2013.
13. Oliver Marchart, *Post-Foundational Political Thought: Political Difference in Nancy, Lefort, Badiou and Laclau* (Edinburgh: Edinburgh University Press, 2007); Paul Ricoeur, 'The Political Paradox', in Ricoeur, *History and Truth*, trans. Charles Andrew Kelbley (Evanston: Northwestern University Press, 1965), pp. 247–70.
14. Lawrence Quill, *Secrets and Democracy* (Basingstoke: Palgrave Macmillan, 2014).
15. Werner Jaeger, *Paideia: The Ideals of Greek Culture. Vol. II: In Search of the Divine*, trans. Gilbert Highet (Oxford: Oxford University Press, 1986), p. 174.
16. Sheldon S Wolin, *Politics and Vision: Continuity and Innovation in Western Political Thought* (Princeton: Princeton University Press, 2016), p. 67;

Jacques Derrida and Jean Birnbaum, *Learning to Live Finally: The Last Interview*, trans. Pascale-Anne Brault and Michael Naas (Basingstoke: Palgrave Macmillan, 2007).

17. Cornelius Castoriadis, 'The Greek Polis and the Creation of Democracy', in *The Castoriadis Reader*, ed. and trans. David Ames Curtis (Oxford: Blackwell, 1997), pp. 267–89 (p. 281).
18. Jacques Derrida, 'Unconditionality or Sovereignty: The University at the Frontiers of Europe', *Oxford Literary Review*, 31.2 (2009), 115–31 (p. 117).
19. Jacques Derrida, *Aporias*, trans. Thomas Dutoit (Stanford: Stanford University Press, 1993), p. 36.
20. Martin Heidegger, 'Letter on "Humanism"', in Heidegger, *Pathmarks*, trans. Frank A. Capuzzi (Cambridge: Cambridge University Press, 1998), pp. 239–76; Jacques Derrida, 'The Ends of Man', *Philosophy and Phenomenological Research*, 30.1 (1969), 31–57.
21. G. Felicitas Munzel, 'Menschenfreundschaft: Friendship and Pedagogy in Kant', *Eighteenth-Century Studies*, 32.2 (1998), 247–59 (p. 248); Robert Friedrich, 'Liberal Education and Liberal Politics. Phi Beta Kappa Oration, Theta Chapter of Pennsylvania', *Phi Beta Kappa, Franklin & Marshall College*, 2009.
22. Jacques Derrida, 'The Future of the Profession or the University without Condition (Thanks to the "Humanities", What Could Take Place Tomorrow)', in *Jacques Derrida and the Humanities: A Critical Reader*, ed. Tom Cohen (Cambridge: Cambridge University Press, 2001), pp. 24–57 (p. 26).
23. Derrida, 'The Future of the Profession', p. 26; Henry A. Giroux, 'Critical Pedagogy and the Postmodern/Modern Divide: Towards a Pedagogy of Democratization', *Teacher Education Quarterly*, 31.1 (2004), 31–47 (p. 38); Henry A. Giroux, 'Higher Education and Democracy's Promise: Jacques Derrida's Pedagogy of Uncertainty', in *Deconstructing Derrida*, ed. Peter Pericles Trifonas and Michael A. Peters (New York: Palgrave Macmillan, 2005), pp. 53–81 (p. 53).
24. Martin Heidegger, 'The Self-Assertion of the German University: Address, Delivered on the Solemn Assumption of the Rectorate of the University Freiburg the Rectorate 1933/34: Facts and Thoughts', trans. Karsten Harries and Hermann Heidegger, *Review of Metaphysics*, 38.3 (1985), 467–502.
25. Henry A. Giroux, 'Public Pedagogy and the Politics of Neo-Liberalism: Making the Political More Pedagogical', *Policy Futures in Education*, 2.3–4 (2004), 494–503 (p. 498).

26. Giroux, 'Public Pedagogy', p. 498.
27. Jacques Derrida, 'The Deconstruction of Actuality', *Radical Philosophy*, 68 (1994), 28–41 (p. 28).
28. Derrida, 'The Deconstruction of Actuality', p. 28; Derrida, *Psyche: Inventions of the Other, Vol. I*, p. 34.
29. Derrida, 'The Deconstruction of Actuality', p. 8.
30. Ibid. p. 29.
31. Gert Biesta, 'No Education without Hesitation: Exploring the Limits of Educational Relations', *Philosophy of Education*, 2012, 1–13 (p. 2).
32. Biesta, 'Education after Deconstruction', p. 104; Gayatri Chakravorty Spivak, 'The Setting to Work of Deconstruction', in Spivak, *A Critique of Postcolonial Reason: Toward a History of the Vanishing Present* (Cambridge: Harvard University Press, 1999), pp. 423–31 (p. 425).
33. Martin Heidegger, *Being and Time*, trans. Joan Stambaugh (Albany: SUNY Press, 1996), p. 125.
34. Peter Sloterdijk, 'Architecture as an Art of Immersion', *Interstices*, 12 (2011), 105–9 (p. 109); Bruno Latour, 'A Cautious Prometheus? A Few Steps toward a Philosophy of Design (with Special Attention to Peter Sloterdijk)', in *Networks of Design: Proceedings of the 2008 Annual International Conference of the Design History Society*, ed. Fiona Hackney, Jonathan Glynne and Viv Minto (Boca Raton: Universal Publishers, 2009), p. 7.
35. Latour, 'A Cautious Prometheus?', p. 8.
36. Beatriz Colomina and Mark Wigley, *Are We Human?: Notes on an Archaeology of Design* (Zurich: Lars Muller, 2016), p. 9.
37. Vilem Flusser, 'Design: Obstacle for/to the Removal of Obstacles', in *Shape of Things: A Philosophy of Design* (London: Reaktion Books, 1999), pp. 58–61 (p. 59); Latour, 'A Cautious Prometheus?', p. 2.
38. Heidegger, *Being and Time*, pp. 112, 127, 343; Henk Oosterling, 'Dasein as Design or: Must Design Save the World?', *Premselalecture*, 2009, 1–20 (p. 3). Henk Oosterling, 'Interest and Excess of Modern Man's Radical Mediocrity: Rescaling Sloterdijk's Grandiose Aesthetic Strategy', *Cultural Politics*, 3.3 (2007), 357–80 (p. 360).
39. Sloterdijk, 'Architecture as an Art of Immersion', p. 107.
40. Oosterling, 'Dasein as Design or: Must Design Save the World?', p. 3.
41. Ibid. p. 3.
42. Suzanne Labarre and Paola Antonelli, 'MoMA Curator: "[Humanity] Will Become Extinct. We Need to Design an Elegant Ending"', *FastCompany* (2019).
43. Quill, *Secrets and Democracy*.

44. Yuval Noah Harari, 'The World after Coronavirus', *Financial Times Weekend, Life and Arts*, 21 March 2020, pp. 1–2; Kenan Malik, 'Yes, Expect More Surveillance during a Crisis, but Beware It Once the Danger Has Passed', *Observer*, 12 April 2020; Stephen Bush, 'Johnson and Starmer Both Know a True Exit Plan Means Reducing Our Freedoms', *Observer*, 10 May 2020, p. 41.
45. Gilles Deleuze, 'Postscript on the Societies of Control', *October*, 59 (1992), 3–7.

18

The Law of Autoimmunity

Chris Lloyd

Introduction

Politics of Friendship is a seminal text within the apparent 'ethical turn' in Jacques Derrida's work, in which it has been argued that 'the social and the political', and the 'ethical and juridical', became the focus of his attention.[1] However, Derrida's own thoughts on this 'turn' render it dubious as an accurate description of his *oeuvre*.[2] And yet, contestation over the 'ethical turn' aside,[3] *Politics of Friendship* does illustrate Derrida's thoughts on various juridico-political concepts: in particular, his critical account of 'the political' (in French, *le politique*) which was so prominent in his work of the 1980s.[4] This chapter concentrates on this aspect of Derrida's work.

The chapter also reads the works published under the name *Politics of Friendship* as representing Derrida's entire, 'collected',[5] 1988–9 seminar series *Politiques de l'amitié*.[6] Whilst this is *perhaps* an unorthodox reading of Derrida's work – which will be explored below – it provides initial support for this chapter's two theses (*PF*, vii).[7] The first is that *Politics of Friendship*, qua the 1988–9 seminar series *Politiques de l'amitié*, houses the inaugural appearances of the concept of 'autoimmunity' in Derrida's work. The second thesis is then that these appearances are best explained not by reference to 'biological or physiological' readings of autoimmunity but rather by readings which acknowledge the juridico-political themes which have, for millennia, been attached to the concept of immunity.[8]

With the context set, and the reading undertaken explained, we can now move to unearth autoimmunity's inaugural appearances in Derrida's 1980s work on *le politique*.

Politiques de l'amitié and le politique: The 'Re-treat'

In the fourth session of *Politiques de l'amitié* Derrida builds upon his argument from previous sessions which had focused on Friedrich Nietzsche's rereading of Aristotle's habitual phrase, 'O my friends, there is no friend!' This leitmotif of *Politiques de l'amitié* is reread by Nietzsche in *Human All Too Human*, becoming:

> Perhaps to each of us there will come the more joyful hour when we exclaim:
> 'Friends, there are no friends!' thus said the dying sage;
> 'Foes, there are no foes!' say I, the living fool.[9]

For Derrida, this rereading is a 'seismic revolution in [Aristotle's] political concept of friendship' (27). Specifically, it revolutionises the Aristotelian conception of '*the political*', as per the distinction in French between *le* and *la politique*: 'the political' and 'politics' (8). The differences illustrated between these two variations of the noun *politique* establish the juridico-political scene for all which follows in this chapter. 'The political', *le politique* (or *du politique*, as per *Politiques de l'amitié*),[10] 'is endowed with a dignity superior to that of politics, either because it is distinguished from everyday politics, or [. . .] is the specific object of philosophy and grand theory',[11] whereas 'politics', *la politique*, encompasses 'everything that concerns public debate, competition for access to power, and thus the "domain in which various *politiques* [in the sense of 'policy'] compete or oppose each other"'.[12] It is upon this distinction that Derrida deploys Nietzsche's rereading in order to disrupt Aristotelian metaphysics, whereby 'the *very work of the political* [*du politique*]' is a '*properly* political act or operation' which 'amounts to creating (to producing, to making, etc.) the most friendship possible' (8). Derrida then 'ups the ante' of this disruption – *surenchère*[13] – by utilising the Nietzschean '*perhaps*' featured in the rereading.[14] Nietzsche's thought becomes an 'antithesis' against 'the "metaphysician of all ages"' and structural accounts of *le politique*, thus aligning with the openness of other Derridean concepts such as the '*á venir*',[15] or '*la démocratie a venir*'(34).[16] As Derrida explains, Nietzsche's critique of metaphysics combats the rigidity of the Aristotelian *le politique* with the '[u]nheard-of, totally new, that very experience which no metaphysician might have dared to think' (29).

This critical account of *le politique* draws on Derrida's earlier work which had been so influential for Philippe Lacoue-Labarthe and Jean-Luc Nancy's complete rethinking of *le politique*.[17] They opposed a totalised metaphysical schema of *le politique* and were influenced by Derrida's call for 'a kind of retreat',[18] thus 'think[ing] in terms of *re-treating the political*': a 're-tracing,' a 're-marking' of *le politique* opposing totalisation.[19] Lacoue-Labarthe endorsed Derrida's critique as ethos and Nancy acknowledged a debt to Derrida's thinking.[20] Thus, autoimmunity's appearance in *Politiques de l'amitié*, as a critique of a totalised metaphysical schema of *le politique*, matched other aspects of Derrida's hugely influential earlier work: 'one recalls Lacoue-Labarthe and Nancy's remarks [. . .] what is at stake is the "traversing and displacing of the 'political' and its 'meaning.'" And it is precisely this traversal and displacement that, following Derrida, they call the retreat.'[21] At this point, with the juridico-political context set, we can return to the fourth session of *Politiques de l'amitié* to unearth the inaugural appearances of autoimmunity.

The Appearance of Autoimmunity

First Appearance

After Derrida deploys the Nietzschean '*perhaps*' to oppose the Aristotelian account of *le politique*, he then 'ups the ante' again by introducing the concept of autoimmunity. Derrida states: 'The modality of the possible, the unquenchable *perhaps*, would, implacably, destroy everything, by means of a sort of self-immunity' (75–6). The English here is found in George Collins's 1997 translation. However, in the original French publication of *Politiques de l'amitié* from 1994, the same sentence reads as follows: 'La modalité du possible, l'insatiable *peut-être* détruirait tout, implacablement, par une sorte d'auto-immunité.'[22] Here, the original French supports the argument that the English translation *should have* featured the word 'auto-immunity,' not 'self-immunity'.[23] Consequently, it is argued that this is the first appearance, in Derrida's *oeuvre*, of the concept of autoimmunity. This is contra to, for example, Francesco Vitale's argument whereby autoimmunity does not appear until some five years later.[24] Instead, it is argued that *Politiques de l'amitié*'s fourth session of 1988–9 houses the first appearance of autoimmunity, illustrating the radical, unconditional potential through which an entity or a concept – such as *le politique* – *could* entirely reinvent itself, even to the point of self-destruction, via an openness to radical alterity: 'a sort of auto-immunity from which no region of being, *phúsis* or history would be exempt' (76).[25]

Second Appearance

Then, on the same page in the original French, there is a second appearance of autoimmunity. There, Derrida uses '*d'auto-immunité*' to further critique the Aristotelian conception of *le politique*.[26] Again, Collins's English translation does not feature the word 'autoimmunity' but the argument above carries with regards to this second appearance. Thus, via the modified English translation offered by this author, Derrida states: 'The imminence of a self-destruction by the infinite development of a madness of autoimmunity' (76).[27] It is argued that this sentence more accurately translates Derrida's original French: 'Imminence d'une autodestruction par développement infini d'une folie d'auto-immunité'.[28] This second appearance of autoimmunity continues to develop Derrida's radical reimaging of *le politique*. Autoimmunity is utilised to complicate 'a cool, directly logical analysis' of the Aristotelian account of *le politique* (76).

Then, the fourth session of *Politiques de l'amitié* also includes a third appearance of autoimmunity. However, this third appearance in the 1988–9 seminar series can only be unearthed *ex post facto*, in an operation conducted some fifteen years after the seminar was originally penned and presented.

Third Appearance (ex post facto)

Later in the fourth session Derrida asserts: 'no deconstruction without democracy, no democracy without deconstruction' (105). Accordingly, democracy is only *democratic* – thus subject to 'question, to criticism' (105) – *if* it oscillates between two fundamental positions. The first is 'the conditional', 'enclosing the effective practice of democracy', and the second is 'the unconditional', 'inscrib[ing] a self-deconstructive force in the very motif of democracy' (105). In detailing this oscillation, Derrida's original French describes the second position with reference to '*une force auto-déconstructrice dans le motif même de la démocratie*' and thus lacks the word autoimmunity.[29] Rather, the French contains '*auto-déconstructrice*', rendered as 'self-deconstruction' by Collins in the English translation (105). This suggests an act whereby 'the self, the *autos*' of a given entity is subject to deconstruction.[30] However, this is *not* the last word on this account of democracy's self-deconstruction, because, nearly fifteen years after this account was originally penned in *Politiques de l'amitié's* fourth session, Derrida revisited this passage in a 2002 lecture.

Derrida's lecture – published in 2003 in French in *Voyous: Deux Essais sur la Raison* and in 2005 in English in *Rogues: Two Essays on Reason* –

re-evaluated his argument pertaining to democracy's 'self-delimitation' ('*auto-déconstructrice*' in the French) (105).[31] In his re-evaluation, as Haddad has superbly shown, Derrida 'cites himself from *Politics of Friendship*' but with some small amendments:[32] 'no deconstruction without democracy, no democracy without deconstruction. [. . .] the unconditional, which, from the outset, will have inscribed a self-deconstructive force [I could have in fact said "autoimmune" force] in the very motif of democracy'.[33] In rereading and self-citing himself, Derrida comments that in *Politics of Friendship* he 'could have in fact said' 'autoimmunity': '[*j'aurais pu alors dire "auto-immunitaire"*]'.[34] Here, Derrida's rereading is not unexpected: given that he *had already* utilised autoimmunity, *twice over*, in the original French in the *same session* of *Politiques de l'amitié*, it is unsurprising that he believes he could have replaced 'self-deconstructive' ('*auto-déconstructrice*') [35] with 'autoimmunity' (105). As Haddad argues, this 'interjection' suggests 'that at the time of writing *Politics of Friendship* Derrida could have just as easily used "autoimmune" instead of self-deconstructive – that this vocabulary was then available to him. And in fact it was'.[36] Here, whilst I am in overall agreement with Haddad's insightful thesis, it may not be as accurate as it could be, in light of this chapter's reading of *Politiques de l'amitié*. For Haddad argues that autoimmunity was 'available' for Derrida to use because he had *already* used the concept prior to the 1994 French publication of *Politiques de l'amitié*.[37] Here Haddad cites Derrida's 1993 publication, *Spectres de Marx: L'État de la dette, le travail du deuil, et la nouvelle Internationale*, published one year prior to *Politiques de l'amitié*, in which Derrida stated: 'Le moi vivant est auto-immune, ils ne veulent pas le savoir'.[38] In the 1994 English publication, *Specters of Marx: The State of the Debt, the Work of Mourning and the New International*, Peggy Kamuf's accurate translation renders this as follows: 'The living ego is auto-immune, which is what they do not want to know'.[39] In *either* French (1993) *or* English (1994), this text contains the first appearance *in print* of autoimmunity, as Haddad notes.[40] This I agree with. But contra Haddad it is submitted that autoimmunity was 'available' in Derrida's 2002 *ex post facto* rereading[41] *not* because of *Spectres de Marx*'s use of the concept but because Derrida *had already* utilised autoimmunity, *twice over*, in the original French for the *same session* of *Politiques de l'amitié*, in 1988–9, to describe the deconstructive critique of *le politique*: '*Imminence d'une autodestruction par développement infini d'une folie d'auto-immunité.*'[42]

Recall that this chapter reads the works published under the name *Politics of Friendship* as the 'collected' 1988–9 seminar series *Politiques de l'amitié*, 'writ[ten by Derrida] [. . .] from the first word to the last'[43] – whether by 'typescripts, with manuscript annotations and corrections' ('1970 to 1988') or by 'electronic files and printouts' ('1988 to 2003')[44] – to read in the seminars.[45] Consequently, the material in the seminar series *is* the material in the latter publications, as evidenced by Derrida's 1988 publications and presentations containing the material later found in *Politics of Friendship*.[46] Thus, it is the strong presence of the autoimmunity in the fourth session of *Politiques de l'amitié*, and *not* its singular lacklustre appearance in *Spectres de Marx*, which explains the concept's 'availability' to Derrida in his 2002 rereading. As argued above, the fourth session features Derrida's critique of *le politique* in which autoimmunity features in 'the reconstruction of the political' (104). This involves a '*genealogical* deconstruction of the political' (104) which is necessary in order to 'think, interpret and implement another politics, another democracy' (104). It is not – as Haddad argues on the one hand – that the concept's appearances in *Politiques de l'amitié* were 'brief mentions' and thus unimportant but rather – as he argues on the other hand – that their extreme political intensity regarding *le politique* elevates their status, ensuring that they are 'the proper point of reference for all subsequent uses'.[47]

Having now unearthed the inaugural appearances of autoimmunity appearing in the *Politiques de l'amitié* 1988–9 seminar series, we can now move to decipher the significance of this 'strange and paradoxical revolution' in Derrida's thought.[48]

The General Law of Autoimmunity

Within Derrida's *oeuvre*, autoimmunity appears with increased frequency following his self-declared attempt to 'formalize the general law of this autoimmune process in "Faith and Knowledge" [The Two Sources of "Religion" at the Limits of Reason Alone]'.[49] In that essay – written and presented in 1994,[50] published in French in 1996,[51] and thereafter in English in 1998[52] – Derrida defined autoimmunity as a process by which 'a living organism [. . .] protect[s] itself against its self-protection by destroying its own immune system'.[53] As brilliantly argued by Eszter Timár, Derrida's definition is not entirely aligned with the definitions offered by immunologists: 'autoimmunity here is not identified in the way biomedical discourse discusses autoimmunity, that is, as a process in which the immune system attacks components and tissues of the organism it ought to protect, but rather as the very opposite'.[54]

However, notwithstanding Derrida's '[mistake] regarding the medical meaning of the term',[55] 'Faith and Knowledge' nevertheless contains his most 'substantial' account of autoimmunity and has received lavish attention from scholars.[56] Derrida draws on immunological, philosophical and juridico-political registers to theorise a 'general logic of autoimmunization', culminating in a general law of radical alterity.[57] Derrida shows that an entity – or 'self' – which immunises absolutely against all other entities – all that is 'non-self' – guarantees itself only death, without the chance of survival. He explains that 'life can only subsist beyond the present living being' and that an 'auto-immune and self-sacrificial supplementarity' which 'ruin[s] the principle of self-protection' is 'silently at work in every community, every *auto-com-immunity*'; 'Community as *com-mon auto-immunity*: no community <is possible> that would not cultivate its own auto-immunity'.[58]

Derrida's work convincingly argues that an entity's survival beyond any given present moment is dependent upon its 'open[ness] to something other and more than itself'.[59] Accordingly, *only* an autoimmune entity *can* survive through the 'chance and threat, threat as chance' of the other,[60] whereas an absolutely immune entity *cannot* survive and would consequently cease to exist: 'Without autoimmunity, with absolute immunity nothing would ever happen or arrive.'[61] Consequently, Derrida posits laws of autoimmunity which apply to *all life*: first, 'autoimmunity is not an absolute ill or evil',[62] and second, it is '. . . the self, the *ipse*, the *autos* that finds itself infected [by autoimmunity]'.[63] Said somewhat differently, *everything is autoimmune by necessity*: '[w]ithout autoimmunity, the organism would have, in short, no future before it'.[64] This is Derrida's theorisation of a 'general law' of autoimmunity.[65]

Conclusion: Juridico-political Rather Than Bio-physiological

Most contemporary Derridean scholarship focuses on how autoimmunity, qua immunological, operates within Derrida's philosophical *oeuvre*.[66] It is argued that this methodology is, overall, an error. Indeed, Derrida explicitly warned against such biologically themed musings:

> Why did I think it necessary [. . .] to formalize this strange and paradoxical revolution to privilege today something that might look like a [. . .] biological or physiological model, namely, autoimmunity? It is not, you might well imagine, out of some excessive biologistic or geneticist proclivity on my part.[67]

In fact, given Derrida's declared connections between autoimmunity and the *pharmakon*,[68] and the *pharmakon* and *différance*,[69] autoimmunity is evidently another lynchpin concept[70] within an infinite chain of 'Derrideophemes or deconstructo-nyms' critiquing the metaphysics of presence.[71] This accords with autoimmunity's appearance in *Politiques de l'amitié* where it de-totalised the Aristotelian account of *le politique*: 'auto-immunity from which no region of being, *phúsis* or history would be exempt' (76, translation modified). From this conceptual framing of autoimmunity, and aligned with the status it holds as a 'general law', we can now fully comprehend it as a *juridico-political*, and *not biological*, concept within *Politiques de l'amitié*.[72]

In utilising autoimmunity in *Politiques de l'amitié* Derrida wielded a concept which, prior to its appropriation by the natural sciences in the nineteenth century, had been a juridico-political concept for a millennium before.[73] The entire *oeuvre* of the Italian philosopher Roberto Esposito explores this: *Communitas*, *Immunitas* and *Bíos*.[74] And it is also clear that Derrida knew this.[75] In his radical critique of the Aristotelian (and Schmittian) significance of 'friend' and 'enemy' within *le politique*, Derrida – via *surenchère* – utilised a juridico-political concept known to keep entities *inviolate and separate* to achieve precisely the opposite, by way of an 'illogical logic' (83–106).[76] Thus, immunity turns against its *raison d'être* and contributes to *complication and contamination*: 'slippage and inversion: the friend (*amicus*) can be an enemy (*hostis*)' (88).

Consequently, autoimmunity *should* be understood, first and foremost, as an intensely juridico-political concept, strongly aligning with the thematics of *Politiques de l'amitié* (arguably the first text it appeared in). Therein, Derrida's critique of *le politique* was so radical precisely because it inverted the trajectory of a juridico-political concept, 'think[ing] the limit of the concept',[77] to posit the 'thesis' of 'moving out *beyond this* politics' and enacting a 'de-naturalization of fraternal authority' (159).

Notes

1. Peter Salmon, *An Event, Perhaps: A Biography of Jacques Derrida* (London: Verso, 2020), pp. 222, 229.
2. Jacques Derrida, *Rogues: Two Essays on Reason*, trans. Pascale-Anne Brault and Michael Naas (Stanford: Stanford University Press, 2005), p. 39: 'there never was in the 1980s or 1990s, as has sometimes been claimed, a *political turn* or *ethical turn* in "deconstruction," at least not as I experience it'.
3. See Pheng Cheah and Suzanne Guerlac, 'Introduction: Derrida and the Time of the Political', in *Derrida and the Time of the Political*, ed. Pheng Cheah and Suzanne Guerlac (Durham, NC: Duke University Press, 2009), pp. 1–37.

4. Philippe Raynaud, 'Politics', in *Dictionary of Untranslatables: A Philosophical Lexicon*, ed. Barbara Cassin (Princeton: Princeton University Press, 2014), pp. 803–4.
5. Salmon, *An Event, Perhaps*, p. 229.
6. Jacques Derrida, *Politics of Friendship*, trans. George Collins (London: Verso, 1997); Jacques Derrida, *Politiques de l'amitié: suivi de L'Oreille de Heidegger* (Paris: Galilée, 1994). Hereafter, page references to the English translation are given in parenthesis in the text.
7. Derrida, *Politics of Friendship*, p. vii: 'an address [. . .] [of] *only the first session of a seminar* conducted with this title, "Politics of Friendship", in 1988–89'.
8. Derrida, *Rogues*, p. 109.
9. Friedrich Nietzsche, *Human, All Too Human: A Book for Free Spirits*, trans. R. J. Hollingdale (Cambridge: Cambridge University Press, 1996), p. 149.
10. Derrida, *Politiques de l'amitié*, p. 25: 'Cette opinion concerne l'*œuvre même du politique*.'
11. Raynaud, 'Politics', p. 804.
12. Ibid. p. 803. Raynaud quotes Raymond Aron, *Democracy and Totalitarianism*, trans. Valence Ionescu (London: Weidenfeld & Nicolson, 1968), pp. 3–4.
13. See Samuel Weber, 'La Surenchère – (Upping the Ante)', in *Le Passage des Frontières: Autour du travail de Jacques Derrida* (Paris: Galilée, 1994), pp. 141–9.
14. Friedrich Nietzsche, *Beyond Good and Evil: Prelude to a Philosophy of the Future*, trans. Marion Faber (Oxford: Oxford University Press 1998), p. 6: 'Perhaps! [. . .] We must wait for a new category of philosophers to arrive [. . .] they will be in every sense philosophers of the dangerous Perhaps.'
15. Jacques Derrida, *The Other Heading: Reflections on Today's Europe*, trans. Pascale-Anne Brault and Michael Naas (Bloomington: Indiana University Press, 1992), p. 78.
16. Jacques Derrida, 'Autoimmunity: Real and Symbolic Suicides', in *Philosophy in a Time of Terror: Dialogues with Jürgen Habermas and Jacques Derrida*, ed. Giovanna Borradori (Chicago: University of Chicago Press, 2003), pp. 85–136 (p. 120).
17. Philippe Lacoue-Labarthe and Jean-Luc Nancy, *Les Fins de l'homme: À partir du travail de Jacques Derrida* (Paris: Galilée, 1981), and Philippe Lacoue-Labarthe and Jean-Luc Nancy, *Retreating the Political*, ed. Simon Sparks (London: Routledge, 1997).

18. Lacoue-Labarthe and Nancy, *Les Fins de l'homme*, p. 527: 'Il a indiqué, par une espèce de retrait . . .'
19. Philippe Lacoue-Labarthe and Jean-Luc Nancy, 'Opening Address to the Centre for Philosophical Research on the Political', trans. Simon Sparks, in Lacoue-Labarthe and Nancy, *Retreating the Political*, pp. 107–21 (p. 112).
20. Lacoue-Labarthe and Nancy, *Les Fins de l'homme*, p. 494; Jean-Luc Nancy, 'The Political and/or Politics', trans. Christopher Sauder, *Oxford Literary Review*, 36.1 (2014), 5–17 (p. 7).
21. Simon Sparks, 'Introduction: *Politica ficta*', in Lacoue-Labarthe and Nancy, *Retreating the Political*, pp. xiv–xxviii (p. xxvii).
22. Derrida, *Politiques de l'amitié*, p. 94.
23. Michael Naas, *Derrida From Now On* (New York: Fordham University Press, 2009), p. 129n10: 'in 1994 in *PF*, Derrida wrote: "The modality of the possible, the unquenchable perhaps, would, implacably, destroy everything, by means of a sort of autoimmunity [auto-immunité]".' And see Samir Haddad, 'Derrida and Democracy at Risk', *Contretemps*, 4.29 (2004), 29–44 (p. 31n10): 'In *Politics of Friendship*, Derrida speaks of the "modality of the possible, the unquenchable perhaps, would, implacably, destroy everything, by means of a sort of self-immunity [auto-immunité]"'.
24. Francesco Vitale, *Biodeconstruction: Jacques Derrida and the Life Sciences*, trans. Mauro Senatore (Albany: SUNY Press, 2018), p. 173: 'The first occurrence of the term can be found in *Specters of Marx* (1993).' Vitale references Jacques Derrida, *Spectres de Marx: L'État de la dette, le travail du deuil, et la nouvelle Internationale* (Paris: Galilée, 1993), p. 224: 'Le moi vivant est auto-immune, ils ne veulent pas le savoir.'
25. Translation modified.
26. Derrida, *Politiques de l'amitié*, p. 94.
27. Translation modified.
28. Derrida, *Politiques de l'amitié*, p. 94.
29. Ibid. p. 129.
30. Derrida, *Rogues*, p. 45.
31. Jacques Derrida, *Voyous: Deux essais sur la raison* (Paris: Galilée, 2003), pp. 17–161, 'La raison du plus fort (Y a-t-il des États voyous?).'
32. Samir Haddad, 'Reading Derrida Reading Derrida: Deconstruction as Self-Inheritance', *International Journal of Philosophical Studies*, 14.4 (2006), 505–20 (p. 510).
33. Derrida, *Rogues*, p. 90. Here Derrida cites Derrida, *Politics of Friendship*, p. 105, with his comments added via the square brackets.

34. Derrida, *Voyous*, p. 130.
35. Derrida, *Politiques de l'amitié*, p. 129.
36. Haddad, 'Reading Derrida', p. 512.
37. Jacques Derrida, *Politiques de l'amitié* (Paris: Galilée, 1994).
38. Derrida, *Spectres de Marx*, p. 224.
39. Jacques Derrida, *Specters of Marx: The State of the Debt, the Work of Mourning and the New International*, trans. Peggy Kamuf (London: Routledge Classics, 2006), p. 177.
40. Haddad, 'Reading Derrida', p. 513.
41. Recall Derrida stating: 'j'aurais pu alors dire "auto-immunitaire"' ('I could have in fact said "autoimmune" force'). Derrida, *Voyous*, p. 130.
42. Derrida, *Politiques de l'amitié*, p. 94.
43. Benoît Peeters, *Derrida: A Biography*, trans. Andrew Brown (Cambridge: Polity, 2013), p. 443.
44. Jacques Derrida, *The Beast and the Sovereign, Vol. 1*, trans. Geoffrey Bennington (Chicago: University of Chicago Press, 2009), p. x.
45. Derrida, *The Beast and the Sovereign*, p. xi: 'the *text* of the seminar, as *written* by Jacques Derrida *with a view* to speech . . .'
46. Jacques Derrida, 'The Politics of Friendship', *The Journal of Philosophy*, 85.11 (1988), 632–44; Jacques Derrida, 'The Politics of Friendship', lecture delivered at Cornell University, Ithaca, NY, 3 October 1988, and 'The Politics of Friendship', conference paper delivered at 85th Annual Meeting of the American Philosophical Association, Eastern Division, Sheraton Washington Hotel, Washington, DC, 30 December 1988.
47. Haddad, 'Reading Derrida', pp. 513, 515.
48. Derrida, *Rogues*, p. 109.
49. Ibid. p. 35.
50. Michael Naas, *Miracle and Machine: Jacques Derrida and the Two Sources of Religion, Science, and the Media* (New York: Fordham University Press, 2012), p. 1.
51. Jacques Derrida, 'Foi et savoir', in *La religion*, ed. Jacques Derrida and Gianni Vattimo (Paris: Seuil, 1996), pp. 9–86.
52. This chapter references the most recent English publication: Jacques Derrida, 'Faith and Knowledge: The Two Sources of "Religion" at the Limits of Reason Alone', trans. Samuel Weber, in *Acts of Religion*, ed. Gil Anidjar (London: Routledge, 2002), pp. 40–101.
53. Derrida, 'Faith and Knowledge', p. 80n27.
54. Eszter Timár, 'Derrida's Error and Immunology', *The Oxford Literary Review*, 39.1 (2017), 65–81 (p. 67).
55. Timár, 'Derrida's Error and Immunology', p. 66.

56. Samir Haddad, *Derrida and the Inheritance of Democracy* (Bloomington: Indiana University Press, 2013), p. 54; Naas, *Derrida From Now On*, p. 131; Naas, *Miracle and Machine*, pp. 206–9; Timár, 'Derrida's Error and Immunology', pp. 77–8; and Haddad, 'Derrida and Democracy at Risk', p. 31.
57. Derrida, 'Faith and Knowledge', p. 80n27.
58. Ibid. p. 87. Note the French contains 'auto-immunitaire', '*auto-co-immunité*' and '*auto-immunité*'. See Jacques Derrida, 'Foi et Savoir: Les deux sources de la "religion" aux limites de la simple raison', in Jacques Derrida, *Foi et Savoir suivi de Le Siècle et le Pardon* (Paris: Seuil, 2000), pp. 9–100 (p. 79).
59. Derrida, 'Faith and Knowledge', p. 87.
60. Derrida, *Rogues*, p. 52.
61. Ibid. p. 152.
62. Ibid. p. 152.
63. Ibid. p. 109.
64. Naas, *Miracle and Machine*, p. 82.
65. Derrida, *Rogues*, p. 35.
66. See Vitale, *Biodeconstruction*, p. 173: 'Derrida's turn to the autoimmunitarian lexicon is neither metaphorical nor merely formal but refers instead to the biological conditions of the organization of the living as they are reproduced without limits beyond the living itself according to the law of general textuality'. As an exception, see Martin Hägglund, *Radical Atheism: Derrida and the Time of Life* (Stanford: Stanford University Press, 2008), p. 9: 'I want to point out that I am not concerned with the relation between how Derrida uses the term "autoimmunity" and how it is employed in biological science.'
67. Derrida, *Rogues*, p. 109.
68. Derrida, 'Autoimmunity: Real and Symbolic Suicides', p. 124: 'The pharmakon is another name, an old name, for this autoimmunitary logic.'
69. Jacques Derrida, 'Différance', trans. Alan Bass, in Jacques Derrida, *Margins of Philosophy* (Chicago: University of Chicago Press, 1982), pp. 1–27 (p. 12): '. . . the chain in which différance lends itself to a certain number of nonsynonymous substitutions [. . .] to the pharmakon . . .'
70. See Vicki Kirby, 'Autoimmunity: The Political State of Nature', *Parallax*, 23.1)(2017), 46–60 (p. 54): '[in] Rogues, [. . .] the term "autoimmunity" is deployed in a way that resonates with his use of other neologisms, such as "supplementarity" or "différance", terms (or non-concepts) that defy precise definition . . .'

71. Naas, *Derrida From Now On*, p. 135.
72. Derrida, *Rogues*, p. 35.
73. See Alfred I. Tauber, *The Immune Self: Theory or Metaphor?* (Cambridge: Cambridge University Press, 1994) and Ed Cohen, *A Body Worth Defending: Immunity, Biopolitics, and the Apotheosis of the Modern Body* (Durham, NC: Duke University Press, 2009).
74. Roberto Esposito, *Communitas: The Origin and Destiny of Community*, trans. Timothy Campbell (Stanford: Stanford University Press, 2010); Roberto Esposito, *Immunitas: The Protection and Negation of Life*, trans. Zakiya Hanafi (Cambridge: Polity, 2011); Roberto Esposito, *Bíos: Biopolitics and Philosophy*, trans. Timothy Campbell (Minneapolis: University of Minnesota Press, 2008).
75. Derrida, 'Faith and Knowledge', p. 80n27: 'The "immune" (*immunis*) is freed or exempted from the charges, the service, the taxes, the obligations (*munus*, root of the common of community). This freedom or this exemption was subsequently transported into the domains of constitutional or international law (parliamentary or diplomatic immunity) . . .'
76. Derrida, *Rogues*, p. 123.
77. Jacques Derrida, *For What Tomorrow . . . A Dialogue*, trans. Jeff Fort (Stanford: Stanford University Press, 2004), p. 5.

19

The Other That Accompanies Me

Nicole Anderson

> Is it possible to think and to implement democracy, that which would keep the old name 'democracy', while uprooting from it all these figures of friendship [. . .] which prescribe fraternity: the family and the androcentric ethnic group? Is it possible [. . .] to open out to the future, or rather, to the 'come', of a certain democracy?
>
> Jacques Derrida, *Politics of Friendship*[1]

> Instead of simply giving speech back to the animal, or giving to the animal what the human deprives it of [. . .] [the strategy would be] marking that the human is, [. . .] similarly 'deprived' [. . .]. There you have it. That would presume a radical reinterpretation of what is living, naturally, but not in terms of the 'essence of the living,' of the 'essence of the animal'.
>
> Jacques Derrida, *The Animal That Therefore I Am*[2]

Introduction

Both these epigraphs, located on the last page of their respective books, are calls to rethink the concepts of 'democracy' and 'friendship', on the one hand, and the 'animal' and the 'human', on the other. Two different topics in two different books, so it seems. And yet, what both these calls to think differently return us to are the ways in which Derrida employs deconstructive moves to expose the contingent, contextual, constructed, and hence political, relations between concepts across all his works.[3] In both books he does this in multiple and various ways, but one way, for example, is through a '*genealogical* deconstruction' that works to reveal tensions and contradictions within a given concept brought about via various historical interpretations, as well as through their interrelations to other seemingly unrelated concepts[4] – this, without rejecting them or necessarily waging 'war on them and to see evil therein, but to think and live a politics, a friendship, a justice which begin by breaking with their naturalness or their homogeneity' (*PF*, 105). Unable to entirely reject the political or social-psychological relations that structures all our concepts, Derrida provokes us to 'radically reinterpret' and to think differently about these concepts, and calls on us to dispense with our comfortable, traditional androcentric and anthropocentric assumptions that tend to fetishise 'all these figures of friendship [. . .] which prescribe fraternity', and which work to maintain a strong distinction and boundary between the 'Animal' and the 'Human' (306).[5] The question, though, is how does one 'radically reinterpret' or think differently when as humans we have been constructed in and by a language; by this inherited conceptual apparatus, that renders a logocentric perspective: one that 'apprehends' and understands the world in particular ways?

While there are no obvious prescriptive answers offered to the questions and calls that Derrida makes in these epigraphs, I would argue that there are unprescriptive and oblique ones offered in and through the performative deconstructive moves that both books undertake. If, as Derrida claims in the epigraph from *The Animal That Therefore I Am*, he wants to pluralise and multiply the 'as such' (i.e., ipseity) in order to undermine the constructed essential boundary between animal and human, and thus break all ipseity apart, then the varying deconstructive moves he makes are a means of performing this multiplicity. This is because his performance works to reveal the tensions, contradictions and aporias not only between concepts (such as friendship, fraternity, democracy, or the animal and the human), but within the concepts themselves; contradictions which then deconstruct the ways in which all concepts are politically constructed to maintain certain notions and definitions of the human; and a deconstruction that works to show how the 'other', in fact, operates within these concepts. To deconstruct the conceptual apparatus is not to abandon concepts or their historical formation. I would rather argue that Derrida's notion of responsibility discussed in *Politics of Friendship* becomes key to thinking about the connection between the seemingly unrelated concepts of 'democracy to come', friendship, and the animal. That is, responsibility is key to thinking about how the animal, as other, accompanying us as friend, might enable us to be open 'to the "come", of a certain democracy'.

Canonical Concepts

Derrida demonstrates how 'friendship' is one of those concepts that is foundational to both our notions and practices of the family, sovereignty, war, politics, gender, death, love, ethics, decision, consciousness, reason, brothers, men and democracy, and, as I will argue later, it is foundational to our relations with animals. He exposes the structural complexity and interrelation that 'friendship' has with all these other concepts through a '*genealogical* deconstruction' of the phrase attributed to Aristotle, 'O my friends, there is no friend', on which hang the common conceptions and interpretations of friendship we know today (105). But this is no simple genealogical analysis (which Derrida says he also deconstructs). This is because, as David Wills argues, in a performative deconstructive move Derrida iteratively 'turns', and 'returns' to, this phrase over and over again in relation to the various interpretations of key philosophical thinkers throughout the Western philosophical tradition. In doing so, he not only deconstructs the linear or teleological-historical notion of time (proximity and distance) underpinning the conventional concept of friendship, but performatively reveals 'the ways in which this phrase not only deconstructs notions of "friendship", but itself'.[6]

In drawing out the multiple readings of, and aporias in, the phrase 'O my friends, there is no friend', Derrida argues that there are two dominant interpretations that continually recur throughout our history, and that model our current conceptions of friendship and democracy. The first is the canonical version first articulated by Aristotle and Cicero, and characterised by linking the values of reciprocity, symmetry and equality to primary fraternal friendship (one that can only occur between brothers). The second is what Derrida calls the recoil version, which he argues is more subtle and interprets the phrase in terms of *number*, thereby putting into question the number of friends one can have before symmetry and reciprocity break down. That is, primary fraternal friendship and therefore reciprocity and symmetry between friends takes *time*. How much time is needed to develop this symmetry with one potential friend, let alone many? In a nutshell, the interpretation of the canonical version of this famous phrase hinges on the question of the 'existence of the friend in general', while the recoil version hinges on the question of 'the number of friends, on their suitable number': that is, 'he who has too many [friends] has none' (209). In both versions, the question of what constitutes a democracy is raised; the answer is provided by the link made between friendship and democracy: if friendship is based on equality (symmetry and reciprocity), and the *demos* is made up of fraternal friends (that is, all citizens are friends), then the problem of equality and symmetry in friendship, raised by both versions, extends to the problem of equality in democracy. So, the problem of how many friends one can have, and still retain equality, extends to the problem of how many friends can make up a democracy (what is the magic number that would sustain democracy as a society of equal friends?). But any equality among friends or with a primary friend can only be achieved, as we will see, by the exclusion of the 'other'.

While it seems that these two interpretations are different in their emphasis and therefore meaning, Derrida argues that it is not a matter of playing 'off the two great competing mythical phrases against a "speech act" theory' (214). Rather his aim is to demonstrate that they are not in opposition but rather form a chiasmus, which is evident in the fact that however the phrase is interpreted and whatever aspect is emphasised, the phrase itself, and thus both interpretations, conjoin in a simultaneous reportative and performative address (the significance of which I will return to shortly) (213).[7] That is, both versions performatively *name* the friend ('O my friends'), and in doing so both question the existence of the 'one' primary friend, and at the same time, the amount or number of friends one can have in order to establish reciprocity (22). Both versions therefore sustain and perpetuate a belief and idea in the symmetry and equality between friends (those who are like oneself), and, as mentioned above, form the basis of the ancient Greek notion of *demos* (democracy) (despite Plato and Aristotle attempting to re-examine and recast friendship as something more subtle and 'other' than simply an affinity of like for like or even a like for unlike). In other words, this notion of friendship is based on the 'reciprocal association of ego and alter ego or, even more generally, in terms of a symmetrical affinity of like to like'.[8] According to Derrida, what we have inherited from Greek ancient dominant culture, then, is a notion that the friend is 'our own ideal image'; the friend is the 'same' as me, and thus 'the true friend, it is his ideal double, his other self, the same as self but improved' (4). Consequently, friendship involves loving the friend (who is other but also the 'same'), and it is this *act* of 'loving' that defines the worth of friendship rather than the being loved: 'Aristotle recalls not only that it is more worthwhile *to love*, but that you had better love *in this way*, and *not in that way*; and hence *it is more worthwhile to love* than *to be loved*' (7). The uniqueness and the rarity of a certain kind of friendship (one privileged as fraternal) involves, supposedly, a symmetrical operation between true friends, where both do the loving: 'One can love to be loved – or to be lovable – but one must first know how to love, and know what loving means by loving' (11).

More could be said about Derrida's complicated arguments; however, to summarise: if the principle of friendship is 'to love before being loved', then to love is to 'act' rather than passively receive (being beloved is equated with passivity, non-knowing, lifelessness) (8). To act means one can 'know' what it means to love rather than being known. To know engenders decision and reflection (autonomy, self-presence), which leads to the stability and reliability of love and friendship through time, which in turn is, and must be, beyond 'nature', and this, for Aristotle, as Derrida argues, is what defines the 'virtue of friendship':

> There may well be other forms of friendship, those whose name is thereby derived from primary friendship (for example, says Aristotle, with children, animals, and the wicked), but they never imply virtue, nor equality in virtue. For if all the species of friendship (the three principal ones, according to virtue, to usefulness or to pleasure) imply equality or equity (*isótēs*), only primary friendship demands an equality of virtue between friends, in what assigns them reciprocally to one another. (23)

Not only democracy, but political and individual sovereignty (that is, a humanist subject) are built on, and sustained through, this notion of friendship, precisely because of 'this logic that friendship (*philia*) is first accessible on the side of its subject, who thinks and lives it, not on the side of its object, who can be loved or lovable' (9–10). Democracy, being made up of the equality of virtue between friends, is based on the exclusion of the other: women, children, animals. This, of course, begs the obvious questions: how would one apply these canonical concepts and values of friendship to animals? Is this even possible without anthropomorphising the animal especially given that friendship for the ancient Greeks is androcentric (more of this below): it is the 'relation of brothers', and '[b]etween the political as such, fraternity, and democracy, their co-implication or mutual appurtenance would be quasi-tautological' (viii, 197–8). That is, the canonical notion of friendship that we moderns have inherited from Aristotle is overwhelmingly associated with a fraternity on which democracy has been formed, and which also serves to create the sovereignty of the (humanist) subject (197).

The Paradox Within

If for Derrida both the conventional and recoil interpretations of the phrase, 'O my friends, there is no friend', have in common the perpetuation of the phrase's internal contradiction generated by its simultaneous reportative and performative address, then 'it suffices that the concept of perfect friendship be contradictory for someone to raise his voice and say "O my friends, there is no friend"' (213, 224). Because '[h]ow will you affirm non-contradictorily that having some friends is to have no friend?' (234). Furthermore, as Derrida argues:

> [I]t is impossible to address only one person ['O my friends'] [. . .] such an address would have to be *each time one single time* [. . .]. Now, for only one person to receive a single mark once, the mark must be, however minimally, identifiable, hence iterable, hence interiorally multiple and divided in its occurrence [. . .]. This drama or this chance of a singular multiplicity is witnessed in both versions, if only in the divide, within each of them, of singular and plural [. . .] both say that there is not *a* friend, a sole friend, some friend, no friend; both say *a* friend is not (*oudeis philos*). And both declare as much against a backdrop of multiplicity ('O friends,' or for him who has 'friends'). (215)

If it is impossible to address only one person, then the fraternal and symmetrical notion of a singular friendship trembles and crumbles under the weight of this internal contradiction; under the weight of this multiplicity. And therefore, any idea that friendship can be founded on pure symmetry and reciprocity (equality) will always be unsuccessful, which is why democracy is always 'to come' (something that is not here and now but to be continually worked on); it is why the question of number will undermine any attempt at this pure 'primary' friendship. So not only does Derrida reveal through this contradiction that fraternal friendship is based on the exclusion of the other, 'woman, animal, and gods', but that the phrase itself, and thus 'friendship' in general, is structured by the other (*différance*, iterability, undecidability), by the thought of multiple others, including animal others.[9] Even a primary friendship (in the Aristotelian sense) is structured by *différance* and alterity. And once Derrida has introduced the other into this notion of friendship, he is able to start to tear apart the conventional and perceived 'natural' and homogeneous association between the subject and sovereignty; friendship and fraternity; and fraternity and democracy.[10] This does not mean that Derrida abandons symmetry (a relation of like to like) altogether and simply privileges the dissymmetrical, non-reciprocal and unequal (214, 237). Rather, for Derrida, just as there is no presence without absence, there is no symmetrical, reciprocal friendship without 'dissymmetry, separation and infinite distance' or *différance* (232). And if friendship is *différance* then there can never be a symmetrical relation, only the never-ending ideal of symmetry: a friendship always 'to come'. If we agree this to be the case, then perhaps friendship is only ever a 'relation without relation' (which is not the same as 'non-relation', but always already one of *différance*).[11]

The Animal That Accompanies Me[12]

We have seen how fraternity (brotherhood) is elevated above what has been considered lesser kinds of friendships that might take place between men and women, or between humans and animals. And fraternal friendship perpetuates the belief in the absolute autonomy and unity of the subject, which, in turn, is also elevated above the animal. The 'politics of friendship', then, is not only founded on androcentrism, but also on 'an anthropocentric – one could say humanist – concept'. 'To man alone, in so far as he is neither animal nor god, is appointed the primary and highest friendship' (197–8). This is because predominantly throughout Western metaphysical history, from the ancient Greeks to today, there is no symmetry, reciprocity and equality in what we might loosely call friendship or companionship between human and animal.[13]

And yet, as Derrida demonstrates, friendship is inherently a dissymmetrical relationship. It is structured by *différance*. If there is any such thing as friendship, it cannot exist, and neither can the 'self', without the thought of the other, an 'other' that always already produces dissymmetry:

> Translated into the language of a human and finite *cogito*, this gives the formula: I think, therefore I am the other; I think, therefore I need the other (in order to think); I think, therefore the possibility of friendship is lodged in the movement of my thought in so far as it demands, calls for, desires the other, the necessity of the other, the cause of the other at the heart of the *cogito*. (224)

Undermining the Cartesian 'I think Therefore I Am', and as the title of the book *The Animal That Therefore I Am* indicates, Derrida deconstructs the ipseity (the autonomy) of the human as that which is *purely* distinct from the animal as other. As Derrida explains in *The Animal*, this belief in ipseity is maintained by two dominant assumptions. First, that as humans we seek to think ourselves 'before and without the animal'; second, and at the same time, we construct an opposition between Human and Animal, an opposition achieved by distancing the animal as other and thereby retaining our assumed superiority.[14] Yet the problem with this, as Derrida articulates it in the epigraph, is not so much that we deny animals certain characteristics (i.e., the 'likenesses' and thus proximity we share with each other), such as speech, or response, in order to maintain our superiority and our 'humanness', but that we do not acknowledge that we may be just as much 'deprived' of these characteristics as the animal. Ironically, our assumed superiority is maintained by a dissymmetrical opposition, an opposition we create that works to construct the animal (the other) as an essential structure of being human.[15]

Consequently, being similarly deprived as well as creating a dissymmetrical (i.e., hierarchical) opposition, puts a symmetrical, equal friendship into question. So, in the same way that Derrida in *The Animal* turns what is assumed to be only human characteristics against the human itself, his deconstruction of friendship and democracy in *Politics* takes a similar turn. By revealing that friendship contains dissymmetry and a paradox, Derrida questions the assumption that we have access to a pure symmetrical, reciprocal, and hence equitable, relation with another human being; that we have all the *human* characteristics (defined by ipseity) that founds our conception of friendship, and that the only friendship worth having is one that supports, acknowledges and reciprocates this ipseity. And so long as we don't acknowledge this dissymmetry and this similar deprivation, then the model of fraternal, humanistic friendship that we have inherited will continue to exclude the other such as the animal (the consequences of which has included species extinction and various forms of cruelty on our part and suffering on the animal's).

What would happen to our relation with the animal as other if we acknowledged this potential deprivation and this dissymmetry? Can we only claim our society is a democracy by not making this acknowledgement? It is impossible in the space of this chapter to provide a discussion of the multiplicity of kinds of physical friendships and relations that humans have with animals (such as domestic, farm or wild). There is also no space to rigorously unpack all the problems that would come with a friendship with the animal, such as an anthropomorphism that, no matter how necessary, even inadvertently, reduces the radical otherness of the animal to the same and thereby sustaining the characteristics of the human. Therefore, I want to conclude this chapter with two thoughts: first, that the animal as other always already accompanies us (either in thought, or structurally through opposition, and/or physically), and second, because this accompaniment (a 'relation without relation') will always involve dissymmetry, then 'responsibility' is key to thinking how the animal, as other, accompanying us as friend, might enable us to be open 'to the "come", of a certain democracy'.

Derrida's notion of responsibility is not metaphysical (that is, it is not only about a universal ethics and law applied to the many: here the question of 'number' returns, but it is also not a rejection of ethics and a universal commensurable responsibility). Rather it is what Derrida calls, in *The Gift of Death*, an 'absolute responsibility', which works to question the priority that a metaphysical notion of ethics and responsibility gives to the subject (as ipseity) over the other. Absolute responsibility for the other is therefore not only about ethical and lawful duty, but exceeds our expectation of reciprocity (286). To put it another way, being answerable, being responsible *to* and *for* the other, entails dissymmetry. And it is dissymmetrical precisely because the call or demand to respond responsibly is excessive: it means putting my friend's needs before mine. It means sacrificing myself, which in turn requires the dissolution of my ipseity in order, ironically, to respond. Now I want to suggest that the 'absolute responsibility' for the animal is hyper-excessive, precisely because there can never be reciprocity in the humanist and canonical sense of friendship in any relation with the animal, not because this is a question about whether or not the animal responds, but because, I would argue, the animal represents an absolute alterity that no analogical appresentation (or anthropomorphism) can successfully explain.[16] Given this, what, then, 'would being-with-the-animal mean? What is the company of the animal?'[17] Perhaps the company of the animal would be that which entails a responsibility that opens towards a democracy to come? Or perhaps 'democracy to come' can be defined as that 'absolute responsibility' to the other that is absolute difference (alterity)? In the following quote Derrida hints at this, and he also makes clear that 'democracy to come' is not some ideal political utopian future state that can eventually be achieved. Rather it is because of democracy's internal division and dissymmetry that Derrida can claim that democracy is only ever 'to come':

> It would now be a matter of suggesting that a democracy to come – still not given, not thought; indeed, put down or repressed – not only would not contradict this dissymmetrical curving and this infinite heterogeneity, but would in truth be demanded by them.
>
> Such a dissymmetry and infinite alterity would have no relation to what Aristotle would have called inequality or superiority. They would indeed be incompatible with all socio-political hierarchy *as such*. *It would therefore be a matter of thinking an alterity without hierarchical difference at the root of democracy*. (232)

Responsibility for the other entails dissymmetry, precisely because I don't respond or 'act' and thus affirm my superiority in doing so, and I can't affirm my reason, autonomy and control. Instead, in and through responsibility I elevate the other; I give the other power over me: and this is an attempt to think '*an alterity without hierarchical difference*'. As a result, the absolute alterity of the animal that cannot be reduced to the same puts into question the democracy we have inherited based on a fraternal friendship, that is, it breaks our notion of our own sovereignty and ipseity that founds our current and historical notions of democracy.[18] Responsibility *to* and *for* the animal as absolute other is to enact and to put in place, in the here and now, a 'democracy to come'.[19] For Derrida, it is 'the structure of a promise – *and thus the memory of that which carries the future, the to-come, here and now*' (232) that defines 'democracy to come', and not some 'in-principle possible but not yet achieved constitutional state'.[20] As Paul Patton argues, 'this reference to the here and now suggests, the concept of "democracy to come" is supposed to play an immediate and active role in the present [. . .]. In effect, the phrase is not simply constative but also performative: it is both an open-ended descriptive function and a demand for more democracy'.[21]

As mentioned at the start of this chapter, Derrida's genealogical deconstruction does exactly this: it performs an endless responsibility on, and for, philosophy, and in the performance itself enacts a 'democracy to come'. Perhaps responsibility is the desire for symmetry, equality, reciprocity – hoping that in giving oneself over to the other human, overturning the hierarchy, we also receive in equitable form a response from the other, perhaps a gratitude thus reaffirming and maintaining our ipseity. And yet, this desire is always already thwarted in the absolute responsibility called for by the animal that accompanies us. Because, regardless of whether or not the animal responds (which is not the issue as many Western philosophers have problematically claimed: Descartes, Kant, Heidegger, Lacan, Levinas, for instance), the otherness of the animal is that to which I am answerable. In being answerable, I am answerable also to the other in myself (the animal that therefore I am). And it is in the company of the animal to which I am responsible that I open to a democracy to come: not by rejecting the inherited concepts of friendship, democracy and ipseity, but by 'radically interpreting them'; by deconstructing the privilege given to the 'self' (as ipseity) that is perpetually sustained by the marginalisation of the other (in this case the animal). A question I posed in the introduction to this chapter is how might one do that given we are constituted by a logocentric apparatus? What I would tentatively suggest is that acknowledging and accepting that we are always already accompanied by the animal as other might perhaps contribute to lessening the domination and marginalisation of the other; it may serve as an example of how in taking responsibility for the absolute other we model, and welcome and contribute to, a 'democracy to come' in the *here and now*.

Notes

1. Jacques Derrida, *Politics of Friendship*, trans. George Collins (London: Verso, 1997), p. 306; Jacques Derrida, *Politiques de l'amitié: suivi de L'Oreille de Heidegger* (Paris: Galilée, 1994). Hereafter, page references to the English translation are given in parenthesis in the text (*PF*).
2. Jacques Derrida, *The Animal That Therefore I Am*, trans. David Wills (New York: Fordham University Press, 2008), p. 160. My thanks and gratitude to the editors for their editing of this chapter. I particularly want to thank Cillian Ó Fathaigh for his endless patience.
3. Michael Naas, *The End of the World and Other Teachable Moments: Jacques Derrida's Final Seminar* (New York: Fordham University Press, 2015).
4. See Paul Patton, 'Derrida, Politics and Democracy to Come', *Philosophy Compass*, 2.6 (2007), 766–80 (p. 768).
5. Also, Derrida, *The Animal That Therefore I Am*, p. 160.
6. David Wills, 'Full Dorsal: Derrida's Politics of Friendship', *Postmodern Culture*, 15.3 (2005) (para. 7 of 32).
7. See also Wills, 'Full Dorsal: Derrida's Politics of Friendship', para 11 of 32.
8. Peter Fenves, 'Politics of Friendship, Once Again', *Eighteenth-Century Studies*, 32.2 (1998), 133–55 (p. 141).
9. Friendship with these others, the possibility of which is not denied, is simply categorised as less than fraternal friendship. Derrida shows how these categories of friendship slide, blur and undermine its whole political configuration.
10. See Wills, 'Full Dorsal: Derrida's Politics of Friendship'.
11. Fenves, 'Politics of Friendship, Once Again', p. 142.
12. This is a play on the title of chapter seven ('He Who Accompanies Me') in *Politics of Friendship*.
13. See Derrida, *The Animal That Therefore I Am*.
14. Derrida, *The Animal That Therefore I Am*, pp. 79–80.
15. Ibid. pp. 79–80.
16. If there were space, I would make a detailed connection between philosophers throughout our history claiming that the animal cannot respond, and the notion of responsibility.
17. Derrida, *The Animal That Therefore I Am*, pp. 79–80.
18. Patton, 'Derrida, Politics and Democracy to Come', p. 777.
19. Jacques Derrida, *Rogues: Two Essays on Reason*, trans. Pascale-Anne

Brault and Michael Naas (Stanford: Stanford University Press, 2005), pp. 85–6.

20. Patton, 'Derrida, Politics and Democracy to Come', p. 772.
21. Ibid. p. 773.

20

Companionship, Kinship, Friendship, Readership – and 'the Possibility of Failure'

Thomas Clément Mercier

My contribution to this volume – a volume which functions as a sort of 'companion' to Jacques Derrida's *Politics of Friendship* – will consist in taking a small step aside in order to analyse something which has been called 'companionship' in the field of animal studies, especially in the work of Donna J. Haraway. This might look like a step aside because, certainly, it would be an overstatement to claim that *Politics of Friendship* is a book *on* animality. Derrida's book is chiefly concerned with the powerful, multilayered logic of fraternal friendship inasmuch as it provides the philosophical undergirding of Western humanist ethics and onto-politics. And, sure enough, there are not many non-human animals crowding the pages of *Politics of Friendship*, give or take Nietzsche's passing frogs, owls or serpents, and Kant's elusive black swans. Nevertheless, my claim is that Derrida's overall line of enquiry, as well as many elements in the book, could be interpreted as prefiguring several of his later works in which the 'question of animality' is raised more explicitly.

The animal 'question' appears a few times in *Politics of Friendship* in the course of Derrida's analyses of canonical Western discourses on friendship. Every time the question is raised, usually in the form 'Are non-human animals capable of friendship?', the tradition's answer is a resounding 'No'. What we call 'friendship' – especially in the form of a non-natural brotherhood, which predicates that I love my friend *like* a 'brother', *as if* he were my brother, in a way that seems to *both* transcend *and* confirm 'natural' kinship – is chiefly conceived by Aristotle and the subsequent tradition as the 'proper' of humankind, and as the privilege of male men rather than female friends or sisters. In this way, Derrida's book pursues the work of deconstruction of the familialist schema of kinship governing Western carnophallogocentric politics – a work that was already initiated in previous texts, such as 'Plato's Pharmacy' and *Glas*. Everything thus happens as if the canonical representation of friendship as a certain relation to the fraternal, and therefore to a certain (mono-)genealogical drive for sameness and homogeneity, perhaps a racial or specic homogeneity, were by definition exclusive of sexual and animal differences – or, at best, inclusive of those differences to the extent that they can be appropriated or assimilated within the great discourse of universal fraternity. If that is true, Derrida's deconstructive analysis of canonical Western discourses on friendship and fraternity also involves a radical attention to multiple effects of intersectional exclusions and forceful inclusions fostered by those discourses.

Failed Encounters – Of Texts

This short essay – which I see as an incision, a cut sample, biopsy or *prélèvement* on the body of *Politics of Friendship* – will start from a parenthesis (what we call, in French, *une incise*) that intervenes at page 149, in the middle of the chapter titled 'Oath, Conjuration, Fraternization or the "Armed" Question'. The parenthesis seems to enclose a dialogue between two voices – two voices calling each other 'friend'. It starts with the following question: 'But, I ask you, what is a brother?' In only a few lines, the two friends jump abruptly from one subject to another, *passent du coq à l'âne*. The voices discuss differences between nature and culture, the role of political-juridical oaths in shaping our representations of family, kinship and birth, the status of the mother, and bring out the questions of animality, of species and sexual differences. In the context of the book, this parenthesis is singular in both its *form* and *content*. First, in its *form*: the bracket signs seem to represent curtains surrounding a theatre stage, opening and closing a short dialogical scene between two nondescript characters – *who* or *what* are they? What is their gender? Their species?[1] Second, in its *content*: those curtains interrupt the course of Derrida's argument and raise the question of animal kinship, somewhat anticipating his later writings on animality, notably *The Animal That Therefore I Am* and the two volumes of the seminar *The Beast and the Sovereign*. The animal 'question' comes and interrupts anthropological questions raised by Derrida with respect to the ethics and politics of friendship and fraternity. What of the animal in the sarabande of discourses on friendship and fraternity that make up Western thought? In the same pseudo-dialogical scene, Derrida immediately associates the animal question with that of sexual difference. The scene ends with the following questions: 'And the sister? Would she be in the same situation? Would she be a case of fraternity?' (*PF*, 149).[2] Curtain.

How does one *read* such a scene? What rules can we or should we follow in order to make sense of this text-within-the-text? What will be the index of a legitimate, *successful* reading? How should we interpret this specific incision within the overall dispositive of *Politics of Friendship*, inasmuch as the book as a whole also stages the scene of an impossible address to the friend, to the reader?

Following the work of Anne Emmanuelle Berger and Marta Segarra, Elissa Marder, Lynn Turner and others,[3] my claim is that these matters of text, interpretation and reading – in other words, the *differantial* structure mobilised by the trace – are crucial to approach the 'question of animality' as described by Derrida in 2001:

> The 'question of animality' is not one question among others, of course. I have long considered it to be decisive (as one says), in itself and for its strategic value; and that's because, while it is difficult and enigmatic in itself, it also represents the limit upon which all the great questions are formed and determined, as well as all the concepts that attempt to delimit what is 'proper to man', the essence and future of humanity, ethics, politics, law, 'human rights', 'crimes against humanity', genocide, etc.[4]

Derrida then connects this 'question' to the general structure of the trace:

> Beginning with *Of Grammatology*, the elaboration of a new concept of the *trace* had to be extended to the entire field of the living, or rather to the life/death relation, beyond the anthropological limits of 'spoken' language (or 'written' language, in the ordinary sense), beyond the phonocentrism or the logocentrism that always trusts in a simple and oppositional limit between Man and the Animal. (63)

The claim I want to pursue here is that the problematic of the trace, inasmuch as it troubles the humanist-anthropocentric logic and exceeds any simple delimitation between humankind and animality, can also be followed in *Politics of Friendship* as a condition for thinking friendship, kinship or companionship as non-strictly anthropological categories, and for accounting for a certain principle of failure or fallibility at the very heart of the 'encounter' with the other – human or non-human. As we will see, such fallibility is inseparable from a certain legibility *and* illegibility of friendship, kinship and companionship, from their dependence on the trace-structure, which suggests that they do not have strict ontological consistency but are structurally *differantial* and heterogeneous, and therefore remain to be read, interpreted, attested, translated, perhaps in view of transformative deconstruction. Furthermore, taken from the perspective of the exegesis of deconstruction, what I am trying to gesture towards here also implies that the problematic of the trace-structure, which is virtually limitless in Derrida's corpus, presupposes *everywhere it appears* – for example, but this is perhaps more than an example, in *Politics of Friendship* – the interrogation of the anthropological machine, of human exceptionalism, and raises the 'question of animality' even when this 'question' does not seem to be formulated *as such*, in these terms, and even when the so-called 'animal' does not seem to be named *as such*.

By contrast, Donna Haraway's engagements with Derrida on animality, in her book *When Species Meet*, are strictly limited to some of Derrida's texts that are most directly and explicitly dedicated to the 'animal question'.[5] In that book, Haraway only refers to '"Eating Well", or the Calculation of the Subject', and to the lectures collected in *The Animal That Therefore I Am*. She doesn't mention any other texts by Derrida – such as *Of Grammatology*, *Politics of Friendship*, or anything in between or beyond. In the first chapter of *When Species Meet*, Haraway reads and cites Derrida's first lecture from *The Animal That Therefore I Am*. She zooms in on a famous scene: Derrida's depiction of his 'encounter' with his 'little cat', one morning, naked in his bedroom. Haraway offers a long interpretation of this scene, of what interests her in it, of what it does to a certain philosophical discourse, and so on. However, Haraway declares, somewhat peremptorily: 'with his cat, Derrida *failed* a simple obligation of companion species'.[6] This is an indubitably violent, authoritative verdict, made in the declarative form: you failed. You failed to be a companion. Bad companion. Before we get into this scene of judgement and the specifics of Haraway's accusation, let me raise my main question. I would like to ask Haraway, in the friendliest possible way, the following: What is companionship without failure? Isn't there, perhaps, some fundamental violence in thinking of companionship, kinship or friendship according to what I would call an *ontology of success*?[7] And shouldn't such ontology itself presuppose the *possibility*, the *irreducible* possibility of a radical interruption and failure – possibilities that are essential to *reading* – as the very condition of friendship, kinship, companionship?

We'll soon return to these questions through the analysis of what Derrida names, in *Politics of Friendship*, 'the possibility of failure'. Before we get there, let's go back to the first chapter of *When Species Meet*. It is an extraordinary, multilayered scene: text on text on text. Haraway *reads* Derrida's 'scene' – the now famous 'nude-Derrida-and-cat' scene, a scene which has become canonical, almost a trope, perhaps a meme – and she *believes* him: she *says* she believes everything Derrida writes about that little cat, about that bedroom, that bathroom, about that 'encounter', one morning. She's probably right to – at least, it is her right to believe. Certainly, in his lecture, Derrida 'himself' – or, at least, a certain signature: a narrative voice that says 'I', 'je', and seems to speak in the name of 'Jacques Derrida' – implored the listener or reader to *believe* him, explicitly and quasi-performatively:

> I must immediately make it clear, the cat I am talking about is a real cat, truly, believe me, *a little cat*. It isn't the *figure* of a cat. It doesn't silently enter the bedroom as an allegory for all the cats on the earth, the felines that traverse our myths and religions, literature and fables.[8]

Let's pretend, at least for a moment, that we *believe* Derrida's autobiographical tale, as Haraway seems to do. She says she believes Derrida, and we can believe her. She also believes that there is something 'shocking' about that scene. Here's the 'shocking' part: Derrida 'did not become curious about what the cat might actually be doing, feeling, thinking, or perhaps making available to him in looking back at him that morning. [. . .] Incurious, he missed a possible invitation, a possible introduction to other-worlding.'[9]

Derrida 'failed' and 'missed' – the cat-other. According to Haraway, Derrida's failure or fault is to have ignored, at least 'explicitly', knowledge produced by 'ethologists and other behavioral scientists'.[10] Certainly, Haraway agrees with Derrida that there is always a risk of violent classification and homogenisation in curiosity and knowledge-production, and that the other's singularity (human or non-human) ultimately resists being 'conceptualized'.[11] Nevertheless, she also wants to believe that '[p]ositive knowledge of and with animals might just be possible, knowledge that is positive in quite a radical sense if it is not built on the Great Divides'.[12] Haraway holds onto another 'kind of truth', one that involves 'dancing'.[13] This reference to dancing or to 'ontological choreography' (an expression borrowed from Charis Thompson) sustains a relational ontology of being-with, of becoming-with, a multiplicity of multispecies, naturalcultural entanglements, situated worldings, and proteiform companionships predicated on 'actual encounters'.[14] Haraway's ontology of kinship and companionship, of 'beings-in-encounter',[15] produces more or less stable commonalities, worlds-in-common – it *makes* kin[16] – but it is not infallible, of course. It is *messy*: 'I am who I become with companion species, who and which make a mess out of categories in the making of kin and kind. Queer messmates in mortal play, indeed.'[17]

But, if there's no such thing as infallible 'kin-making', if dancing can always involve 'tripping', what justifies Haraway's judgement on Derrida's 'failure'? How is Derrida's 'encounter' illegitimate *as* companionship? I'm not even sure what indexes or rules to follow to answer this question, and if it can actually be answered in all rigour. My goal, here, is certainly not to oppose Haraway's and Derrida's discourses on animality. In fact, my feeling is that they are more in agreement than Haraway seems to suggest in several passages of *When Species Meet*.[18] They agree on at least two crucial aspects: first, they share similar concerns about deconstructing the 'great divides' (nature/culture, animality/humanity, reaction/response, and so on) that undergird traditional Western philosophical discourses on 'the animal', and which continue to enable and legitimise violences against non-human animals, and beyond; second, Derrida would certainly agree on the necessity to read, decipher, analyse and, perhaps, deconstruct biological, ethological, behavioural and other scientific discourses, but also literature, diaries, and any other texts, practices, or systems of traces mobilising and/or mobilised by non-human animals. Derrida, like Haraway, encourages us to read and read again philosophical, scientific or literary discourses, and to read them otherwise – to read, track and retrace the multitude of intersectional marks, footprints, semiotic-materialities, border-crossing traces and crisscrossing figurations that make up bastardised assemblages and heterogeneous heritages across disciplines, naturecultures, sexes and species: across multiple worlds, *other* worlds, worlds/others. On all of this, Derrida would certainly agree with Haraway, although, as we will now see, the problematic of 'reading' in relation to knowledge, truth and being would certainly be developed differently by him and by her – 'differently', and in a way that might irreducibly affect concepts *and* experiences of kinship, companionship and friendship. At least, thus goes my reading. Because, yes, I *believe* he would agree with her up to a certain point, a point where she herself seems to disagree with him – and this *point*, which, admittedly, cannot easily be located, is perhaps the point of a certain *failure*. This point is where Haraway finds the resources for her accusative judgement: 'Derrida *failed* a simple obligation of companion species.' As always, the scene of judgement is predicated on a claim to ontological truth and legitimacy.

After this step aside, by which we followed the tracks of Haraway following Derrida and his cat, let's now return to *Politics of Friendship*. In the pseudo-dialogical scene we started with, one of the voices emphasises the non-natural character of kinship, and hypothesises that it is 'never found in an experience of perception'; to approach kinship, one must 'start from memory's injunction, and thus from some oath' (149). In another interruptive parenthesis, Derrida associates this oath-like structure with what Joyce calls a 'legal fiction'. Derrida writes: 'a genealogical tie will never be simply real; its supposed reality never gives itself in any intuition, it is always posed, constructed, induced' (92–3). The consequences are very different for Derrida and Haraway: while Haraway also emphasises the 'constructed' or 'composed' character of kin and companionship, she predicates them on an onto-logic of success, one that confirms that the 'construction' can be effectively attested *as companionship*. In contrast, Derrida's trace-structure implies that the tie, the bond to the other, starting with the other in me, before me, remains entrusted to the inappropriable other, which supposes a recourse to 'belief' and 'faith' for anyone that says 'I' or 'we' – 'my' companion, 'our' companionship – and thus a certain insistence of fictionality which troubles any claim to ontological truth on the subject. In the same pages, Derrida evokes the always-present risk of renaturalising kin by confirming, in good conscience, its supposed reality – and isn't that what Haraway does? Even though she emphasises the naturalcultural, composed or constructed, choreographic character of kin-making, she also confirms its ontological reality *as such*.

In another passage of *Politics of Friendship* – one which I consider particularly important – Derrida associates the oath-like, promissory structure of friendship, kinship, companionship with the trace. He deploys the hypothesis ('the temptation') that the structure of the trace, of the mark, could provide the foundation for a 'hyperbolical' and 'invincible' concept of friendship, an *aimance* on which an authentic 'politics of friendship' could be founded – at last! – one exceeding Western representations of kin, traditional conceptions of fraternal friendship, anthropo-phallogocentric politics, and so on (214–20). *La belle tentation*: inasmuch as all trace implies the possibility that it finds a reader, as it is structurally open to the other, it could indicate a hyperbolical friendship without opposite, some irreducible tendency to accord and harmony – perhaps a 'dancing' worthy of the name, finally. But Derrida immediately adds that this temptation *must be resisted*, precisely by virtue of the trace-structure, which involves 'the possibility of failure':

> for the accord of hyperbolic *aimance* to be possible [. . .] it is necessary [*il faut*] that the possibility of failure not be simply an accidental edge, but a haunting. And that this haunting leaves its imprint right on the body it seems to threaten, to the point of being indissociable from it, as inseparable as its essence or its essential attribute. (218–19, translation modified)

In the same passage, Derrida *insists* that the necessity of *resisting* 'the temptation' is not meant 'to deny, exclude or oppose, but precisely to preserve the chance of temptation, so that it is not taken for an assurance or a programme' (218, translation modified). The resistance of a certain fallibility is mandated by the trace, which remains entrusted to the other, to some reader's countersigning response, with the irreducible risk that it never finds a reader and never arrives at destination. Particularly interesting is the fact that this insisting resistance is marked, or marks itself, in several places on the text-body of *Politics of Friendship* – and particularly in another of those interruptive parentheses we have been tracking in this essay:

> In speaking like this, saying that love or friendship is improbable, I am saying nothing, I am neither stating nor describing anything. [. . .]
>
> And yet my saying, the declaration of love or the call to the friend, the address to the other in the night, the writing that does not resign itself to this non-said – who could swear that they return to nothingness as soon as nothing said could exhaust them?
>
> The response no longer belongs to me – that is all I wanted to say to you, my friend the reader. (70, translation modified)

In this way – and in parentheses – the book 'itself' presents 'itself' as an offering, a somewhat friendly gift, but one that remains irreparably marked, scarred or haunted by 'the possibility of failure': the necessary possibility of a (self-)interruption marked in the text, and affecting the very idea of 'encountering' the other, the reader, with irreducible undecidability.

Undecidable Addresses

To conclude, *un jeu d'adresse*: Derrida too had an interest in 'choreographies'.[19] In a sense, a dancing 'worthy of the name' should not be the repetition of any ontological framework: it should materialise the invention of impossible forms, incalculable differences, beyond the dual logics of sexual difference or speciesism. But, how are we to be sure that the dance of beings 'we' perform every day does not already repeat immemorial choreographies, programmatic codes or gestures that prevent 'us' from encountering 'the other'? All 'choreography' would thus include, incorporate, the possibility or risk of such failure, and a certain undecidability as to what is happening in the very dance. Shouldn't we assume that the dance cannot (and should not) *not* take that risk, the risk of this very failure – in the name of the other's im-possible affirmation?

This suggests an essential difference between ontologies of companionship and Derrida's affirmative deconstruction of friendship: deconstruction does not refuse friendship, companionship or kinship, of course, but points to the irreducible undecidability marking these as well as what constitutes an 'actual encounter' with the other, human or non-human. Put in motion by the trace-structure, this haunting 'possibility of failure' starts from within the ipseity of a self, before any 'I' or 'we', resisting its closure as its condition of im-possibility. It beckons to a *non-negative* impossibility, a transformative deconstructibility mobilised by a generative force of self-resistance, an affirmative *envoi* provoking stories and readings, a propulsive fallibility in the 'perhaps' of an address – before and beyond ontological stabilisations of self, kin, companionship or friendship, before and beyond all 'good conscience' that would manifest itself in the presence of the present.[20]

O my friends – animal-dancers, queer messmates and sexual partners, cosmopolitical dwellers, lovers, readers and translators – yet another effort to 'encounter' the other!

Notes

1. In the French original, the two 'voices' seem to address each other in the masculine form – although it could also be the mark of an indefinite neutral form. There are other occurrences of such short parentheses in the rest of the book, which seem to operate by interrupting and pluralising the traditional narrative voice of the lone philosopher, marking the intervention of another voice or narrative instance, maybe that of a potential friend or lover, a 'who' or 'what' which at once disrupts the flow of the argument, opens a window and breaks a digressive path, thus relaunching the discussion otherwise.
2. Jacques Derrida, *Politics of Friendship*, trans. George Collins (London: Verso, 1997); Jacques Derrida, *Politiques de l'amitié: suivi de L'Oreille de Heidegger* (Paris: Galilée, 1994). Hereafter, page references to the English translation are given in parenthesis in the text.
3. See Anne Emmanuelle Berger and Marta Segarra (eds), *Demenageries: Thinking (of) Animals after Derrida* (Amsterdam: Rodopi, 2011); Lynn Turner (ed.), *The Animal Question in Deconstruction* (Edinburgh: Edinburgh University Press, 2013); Elissa Marder, 'Insex', *Parallax*, 25.2 (2019), 228–39.
4. Jacques Derrida and Elisabeth Roudinesco, *For What Tomorrow . . . A Dialogue*, trans. Jeff Fort (Stanford: Stanford University Press, 2004), pp. 62–3.
5. Donna J. Haraway, *When Species Meet* (Minneapolis: University of Minnesota Press, 2008).
6. Haraway, *When Species Meet*, p. 20, my emphasis.

7. I analysed what I call 'ontology of success' in previous works, notably: Thomas Clément Mercier, 'Resisting Legitimacy: Weber, Derrida, and the Fallibility of Sovereign Power', *Global Discourse*, 6.3 (2016), 374–91.
8. Jacques Derrida, *The Animal That Therefore I Am*, ed. Marie-Louise Mallet, trans. David Wills (New York: Fordham University Press, 2008), p. 6.
9. Haraway, *When Species Meet*, p. 20.
10. Ibid. p. 21.
11. Ibid. p. 22.
12. Ibid. p. 21.
13. Ibid. pp. 26–7. Let's note that Derrida does not, either, abandon the notion of truth, but inscribes it within a certain experience of *fallibility* – as he often writes: 'Il *faut* la vérité' – exceeding the ontological discourse inasmuch as this discourse presents itself as authoritative judgement on the truth of being, and as a decision on performative success and/or failure. In *Politics of Friendship*, this truth-fallibility (*il faut* . . .) is bound to Nietzsche's 'dangerous perhaps' (p. 30). It beckons, perhaps, to another type of 'dancing' than the one advocated by Haraway.
14. Haraway, *When Species Meet*, p. 67.
15. Ibid. p. 5.
16. In re-elaborating 'kinship' or *parenté*, Haraway preserves an 'old' name to give it new meaning. Haraway wants to think 'kin' or 'kind' beyond genealogical-arboreal motifs of lineage, engendering and homogeneity. Question: can one keep the word 'kin' to make it mean something drastically different from what it means traditionally or etymologically? It is true, however, that Haraway's 'kin-making' remains embedded in an ontology of *production*, *creation* and *generation*. Are these only 'metaphors'? But has 'kin' ever been pure from metaphoricity? These difficult questions of old-words/new-meanings, of differential heritages and transformative memory-traces across generations, are raised by Derrida in *Politics of Friendship*, p. 297. On the 'intersextuality' of words, families, kin/kinds, genders-and-generations, see Elissa Marder's wonderful 'intervention' 'Insex' (pp. 233–6).
17. Haraway, *When Species Meet*, p. 19. Haraway continued exploring new forms of kin-making indexed on pluriversal-cosmopolitical ontologies and other-world-makings in *Staying with the Trouble: Making Kin in the Chthulucene* (Durham, NC: Duke University Press, 2016). For an exploration of the cosmo-ontology of the pluriverse in Latour, de la Cadena, Haraway, Viveiros de Castro and others, see Thomas Clément

Mercier, 'Uses of "the Pluriverse": Cosmos, Interrupted – or the Others of Humanities', *Ostium*, 15.2 (2019), 1–15.

18. While Haraway strongly marks her disagreement with Derrida on epistemic-ontological grounds, she's more amenable to the ethical implications of his reflections on animality, notably around the motifs of sacrifice and 'eating well'. In 'Critical Companions', Lynn Turner discusses how Haraway and Derrida can fruitfully be read together (also with Anna Tsing, Cary Wolfe, John Mowitt and many others), and offers several exciting avenues for reflection in the combined fields of feminism, animal studies, environmentalism and psychoanalysis. Lynn Turner, 'Critical Companions: Derrida, Haraway, and Other Animals', in *Introducing Criticism in the 21st Century*, 2nd edn, ed. Julian Wolfreys (Edinburgh: Edinburgh University Press, 2015), pp. 63–80.
19. See e.g. Jacques Derrida, 'Choreographies', trans. Christie V. McDonald, in Derrida, *Points . . . Interviews, 1974–1994*, ed. Elisabeth Weber, trans. Peggy Kamuf *et al.* (Stanford: Stanford University Press, 1995), pp. 89–108.
20. On 'good conscience', see *Politics of Friendship*'s chapter 2, 'Loving in Friendship: Perhaps – the Noun and the Adverb' (pp. 26–48). See also Jacques Derrida, *Aporias*, trans. Thomas Dutoit (Stanford: Stanford University Press, 1993), p. 19: 'How to justify the choice of *negative form* (*aporia*) to designate a duty that, through the impossible or the impracticable, nonetheless announces itself in an affirmative fashion? Because one must avoid good conscience at all costs.' The affirmativeness of the im-possible is also marked, 'haunted' by 'the possibility of failure', in Jacques Derrida, *Negotiations: Interventions and Interviews, 1971–2001* ed. and trans. Elizabeth Rottenberg (Stanford: Stanford University Press, 2002), p. 362.

Acknowledgments: The author would like to thank ANID FONDECYT for their support (ANID FONDECYT/ POSTDOCTORADO/ N° 3200401).

21

Interruption and Responsibility: Derrida's Passive Decision

Mauro Senatore

> My decision is, in fact, the other's decision. This does not exempt or exonerate me from responsibility. My decision can never be mine; it's always the other's decision in me, and in a way I am passive in the decision-making. For my decision to be an event, for it to disrupt my power, my ability, my possibility, for it to disrupt the normal course of history, I must undergo my decision, which is evidently logically unacceptable.
>
> Jacques Derrida, 'A Certain Impossibility of Saying the Event'[1]

The Aporia of Classical Decision

In the concluding pages of the Foreword to *Politics of Friendship*, Derrida announces as one of the main tasks of his book (and of his subsequent work, from the late 1980s on) an exploration of the status of decision and the deciding subject: 'We will then ask *ourselves* what a decision is and *who* decides. And if a decision is – as we are told – active, free, conscious and willful, sovereign. What would happen if we kept this word and this concept, but changed these last determinations?' (*PF*, xi).[2] As I aim to demonstrate in my chapter, Derrida responds to this task by developing the thought of a decision worthy of the name, which he designates as a passive decision or the other's decision in me. This thought consists in the two-step deconstructive re-elaboration of the classical conception of decision that is sketched in the aforementioned passage. On one hand, Derrida sheds light on the aporia of classical decision, that is, the contradiction between the two mutually exclusive meanings inscribed in the word and the concept of *decision*: interruptive decision and the decision of a free and conscious subject. Building on this aporia, Derrida argues that classical discourses do not account for decision at all, that is, for a decision worthy of the name.[3] As we see later, interruptive decision bears within itself an experience of freedom from knowledge and consciousness and of the delivery over to the other or the undecidable, which anticipates subjectivation, that is, the constitution of the free and conscious subject, and thus prevents decision from being reappropriated by this subject. Therefore, on the other hand, Derrida unfolds a new conception of decision, this time worthy of the name: namely, a responsible or just decision, which draws together the meanings of interruptive decision and responsibility. In this case, decision is passive and unconscious, as it retains the experience of freedom evoked above. Furthermore, the deciding subject is affected originarily, that is, before its subjectivation, or lets itself be affected by its decision. In what follows, I shall put my overall hypothesis to the test through a close reading of the two contemporary versions of his response that Derrida offers in the short treatise on decision placed in *Politics of Friendship* and in the analysis of the aporias concerning the relationship between justice and right developed in 'Force of Law'. In the final paragraph of this chapter, I shall highlight the implications of my reading for Derrida's subsequent work.

The Decision of the Other

Derrida responds to the task announced in *Politics of Friendship* in a couple of pages from chapter 3 of the same book, which I have designated above as his short treatise on decision. He unfolds therein his thought of a decision worthy of the name along the lines summarised in the previous section, as a two-step deconstructive re-elaboration of the classical conception of decision. First, Derrida uncovers the aporia that makes classical decision unworthy of the name, that is, the fact that the subjectivation presupposed by this decision annuls the meaning of interruptive decision implicit in the name and the experience of freedom attached to it. To this end, he shows how this aporia is interwoven together with the aporia of the event:

> There is no event, to be sure, that is not preceded and followed by its own perhaps, and that is not as unique, singular and irreplaceable as the decision with which it is frequently associated, notably in politics. But can one not suggest without a facile paradox, that the eventness of an event remains minimal, if not excluded, by a decision? Certainly the decision makes the event, but it also neutralizes this happening that must surprise both the freedom and the will of every subject – surprise, in a word, the very subjectivity of the subject, affecting it wherever the subject is exposed, sensitive, receptive, vulnerable and fundamentally passive, before and beyond any decision – indeed, before any subjectivation or objectivation. (68)

The event is traditionally associated to decision, especially, in politics, since it shares with the latter the experience of a certain unconditionality, that is, of an interruption of and freedom from knowledge and consciousness, an experience that comes before subjectivation and thus cannot be reappropriated by the free and conscious subject.[4] However, the event, namely, the experience of interruption and freedom that it carries with itself, is neutralised by decision so long as the latter also presupposes subjectivation.[5] Building on the double aporia of event and decision, interruption and subjectivation, Derrida argues for the inability of the classical conception of decision (including Schmittian decisionism, which is under scrutiny in *Politics of Friendship*) and of the underpinning theory of the subject to account for the meaning of interruptive decision and thus for decision at all. In other words, nothing happens to the free and conscious subject, not even that for which it believes that it decides. Derrida unfolds his argument as follows:

> Undoubtedly the subjectivity of a subject, already, never decides anything; its identity in itself and its calculable permanence make every decision an accident which leaves the subject unchanged and indifferent. A *theory of the subject is incapable of accounting for the slightest decision*. But this must be said *a fortiori* of the event, and of the event with regard to the decision. For if nothing ever happens to a subject, nothing deserving the name 'event,' the schema of decision tends regularly [. . .] to imply the instance of the subject, a classic, free, and willful subject, therefore a subject to whom nothing can happen, not even the singular event for which he believes to have taken and kept the initiative. (68)

At this point, Derrida takes a second step in his deconstructive re-elaboration of classical decision. He sketches his conception of decision – a passive decision or the other's decision in me – which takes account of the experience of unconditionality and freedom inscribed in interruptive decision at the same time as for the responsibility of the deciding subject. Derrida begins by wondering if another decision can be thought that entails another experience of freedom, the freedom of the event and not that of the self-present and conscious subject. 'But should one imagine, for all that, a "passive" decision,' he asks, 'as it were, without freedom, without that freedom? Without that activity, and without the passivity that is mated to it? But not, for all that, without responsibility?'[6] From this suggestion, he unfolds the thought of a decision that is passive or of the other in me, which, on one hand, retains the experience of the interruption and freedom (from knowledge and consciousness) that it shares with the event and that prevents it from being the decision of the free and conscious subject; and, on the other hand, remains a responsible decision. Furthermore, the deciding subject is affected originarily, namely, before any self-reappropriation, or lets itself be affected by its decision. Let us read Derrida's thought:

> The passive decision, condition of the event, is always in me, structurally, another event, a rending decision as the decision of the other. Of the absolute other in me, the other as the absolute that decides on me in me. Absolutely singular in principle, according to its most traditional concept, the decision is not only always exceptional, *it makes an exception for/of me*. In me. I decide, I make up my mind in all sovereignty – this would mean: the other than myself, the me as other and other than myself, *he makes* or I *make* an exception of the same. This normal exception, the supposed norm of all decision, exonerates from no responsibility. Responsible for myself before the other, I am first of all and also *responsible for the other before the other*. (68)

Therefore, for Derrida, this other freedom or the freedom of the other, which resists the classical conception of decision and the related theory of the subject, does not exclude a responsible decision but makes it possible. 'This heteronomy, which is undoubtedly rebellious against the decisionist conception of sovereignty or of the exception (Schmitt),' Derrida explains, 'does not contradict; it opens autonomy on to itself.' Finally, 'it matches the decision to the gift, if there is one, as the other's gift'(68–9). In a subsequent paragraph, Derrida offers an explicit elaboration of the experience of interruption and freedom that, on his view, is at work in a responsible decision and makes the latter into a passive decision. He places this experience in the act of suspending knowledge and consciousness and being exposed or delivered over to the other, which is implicit in the act of decision. This act comes before subjectivation and thus no free and conscious subject can reappropriate it. Ultimately, the act of a decision worthy of the name, which, by definition, includes that act, is not passive or unconscious as it rejects knowledge and consciousness (we know that it is still a responsible decision). Rather, it is so as it must pass the test of the aforementioned experience of interruption and freedom and consequently it bears within itself the trace of the act corresponding to that experience.[7] Derrida writes:

> For yet again, one *must* certainly *know, one must know it*, knowledge is necessary if one is to assume responsibility, but the decisive or deciding

> moment of responsibility supposes a leap by which an act takes off, ceasing in that instant to follow the consequence of what is – that is, of that which can be determined by science or consciousness – and thereby *frees itself* (this is what is called freedom), by the act of its act, of what is therefore heterogeneous to it, that is, knowledge. *In sum, a decision is unconscious* – insane as that may seem, it involves the unconscious and nevertheless remains responsible. And we are hereby unfolding the classic concept of decision. It is this act of the act that we are attempting here to think: 'passive,' delivered over to the other, suspended over the other's heartbeat. (69)

We can draw some conclusions from this exploration of Derrida's short treatise on decision. In contrast to classical decision, a responsible decision is passive as it presupposes an experience of freedom that is other than subjective freedom, namely the freedom from knowledge and consciousness or the freedom of the other. This experience, which allows for a responsible decision, also prevents the latter from being reappropriated by the free and conscious subject. For this reason, to rephrase a Sartrean expression, the deciding subject *must* be free but only to let itself be affected by its decision.[8]

The Test of the Undecidable

It is time to look into the other version of his thought of decision that Derrida offers in the same year, in 'Force of Law'. In this text, he develops his thought within the framework of the three aporias of justice and right. This time, Derrida conceives of the decision worthy of the name as a just decision. In what follows, I trace Derrida's elaboration of his thought as it develops through the three aporias, from the exploration of the conditions for a just decision to the definition of decision as both passive and unconscious. Once again, like in the short treatise, Derrida's thought of decision unfolds as the two-step deconstructive re-elaboration of the classical conception of decision and of the underpinning conception of subjectivation.

In the first aporia, Derrida explains that a just decision must be free or responsible and thus cannot merely follow from the application of a rule. He acknowledges that a just decision entails a certain experience of unconditionality and freedom that suspends knowledge and subjectivation. However, Derrida goes on, this decision must also be recognised as such and thus must follow a rule. For this reason, he suggests that a just decision, worthy of the name as it draws together the meaning of interruption and justice, must amount to the reinstitution and not the application of a rule.

'To be just,' Derrida observes, 'the decision of a judge, for example, must not only follow a rule of law or a general law [*loi*] but must also assume it [. . .] by a reinstituting act of interpretation, as if, at the limit, the law [*loi*] did not exist previously, as if the judge himself invented it in each case.'[9] Here Derrida does not unfold the implications that such a proposal has on the status of decision and the deciding subject. However, we can observe that the difference between reinstitution and application already entails a passive decision, which includes a certain presubjective experience of interruption and freedom, and an autoheteroaffective deciding subject, which is originarily affected by its decision.[10]

In the second aporia, Derrida starts by recalling that a decision worthy of the name includes the meaning of interruptive decision, which, as we know, exceeds the application of a rule or of knowledge, and more generally, the reappropriation of the free and conscious subject. 'No justice is exercised,' he remarks, '. . . no justice becomes effective nor does it determine itself in the form of law, without a decision that cuts and divides [*une decision qui tranche*].' And, he adds, 'if calculation is calculation, the decision to calculate is not of the order of the calculable'.[11] Derrida identifies that meaning with the experience of the undecidable, that is, the suspension of the rule and knowledge, presubjective freedom, and so forth. As Derrida points out, this experience is not opposite but heterogeneous or excessive with regard to the rule, namely, the non-rule. A just decision must pass the test of this experience, which makes it impossible, that is, irreducible to subjectivation or to what is possible and in the power of the free and conscious subject. Derrida writes:

> Undecidable – this is the experience of that which, though foreign and heterogeneous to the order of the calculable and the rule, must [*doit*] nonetheless – it is of duty [*devoir*] that one must speak – deliver itself over to the impossible decision while taking account of law and rules. A decision that would not go through the test and ordeal of the undecidable would not be a free decision; it would only be the programmable application or the continuous unfolding of a calculable process.[12]

At this point, Derrida marks a radical shift between his thought of a just decision and the classical conception of decision that hinges on subjectivation. He affirms again that the free and conscious subject annuls the experience of presubjective freedom implicit in the meaning of interruptive decision, and thus nothing for which it decides finally happens to it. As Derrida puts it, 'a subject can never decide anything: a subject is even that to which a decision cannot come or happen [*arriver*] otherwise than as a marginal accident that does not affect the essential identity and the substantial presence-to-self'.[13] Now, it is worth remarking that, to be just, a decision cannot remain stuck at the undecidable and therefore it must follow a rule: 'the decision has again followed a rule, a given, invented or reinvented, and reaffirmed rule'.[14] But this does not mean that the test of the undecidable has been overcome, in the dialectical sense of the term, and has been reappropriated. Derrida explains:

> The test and ordeal of the undecidable, of which I have just said it must be gone through by any decision worthy of this name, is never past or passed [*passée ou depassée*], it is not a surmounted or sublated [*relevé*] (*aufgehoben*) moment of the decision. The undecidable remains caught, lodged, as a ghost at least, but an essential ghost, in every decision, in every event of decision.[15]

It is precisely this ghost that the deconstructive thought of a responsible or just decision aims to take into account, while demarcating itself from classical discourses. This thought casts light on the test of the undecidable, namely, the experience of presubjective freedom, which constitutes the condition and excess of a just decision.

In the third aporia, Derrida develops the implications of the first two aporias for the status of decision and the deciding subject, thus unfolding his conception of a passive and unconscious decision and an autoheteroaffective deciding subject. He starts again by recalling that a just decision draws together interruption and responsibility. For this reason, the moment of decision must be finite; it must include the suspension of knowledge and the rule, which we have identified as the experience of presubjective freedom and the test of the undecidable that the free and self-present subject cannot reappropriate. As Derrida points out, even if one has all the time and all the necessary knowledge about the matter, a just decision cannot do without a moment that makes it as such, which is the moment of interruption or of the test of the undecidable: in Derrida's words, 'a finite moment of urgency and precipitation'.[16] As we know, this moment is irreducible; otherwise we would relapse into the classical conception of decision, for which the decision consists in the consequence or the effect of knowledge and consciousness and the deciding subject is free and conscious.

From this, it follows that the moment of decision must retain something heterogeneous and excessive with regard to knowledge and the rule and, more generally, to subjectivation: it must be a moment of non-knowledge, unconsciousness and madness. Finally, Derrida reveals that a just decision must be passive and unconscious, and thus that the deciding subject takes this decision to the extent that it is affected by it originarily:

> The instant of decision is a madness, says Kierkegaard. This is particularly true of the instant of the just decision that must rend time and defy dialectics. It is a madness; a madness because such decision is both hyperactive and suffered [*sur-active et subie*], it preserves something passive, even unconscious, as if the deciding one was free only by letting himself be affected by his own decision and as if it came to him from the other.[17]

In the subsequent paragraph, Derrida offers another memorable elaboration of the act of presubjective freedom that he had discovered in the decisive and deciding moment of decision described in *Politics of Friendship*. He places this act 'in the night of nonknowledge and nonrule'.[18] As we know, this night does not just account for the absence of knowledge and the rule, but for an order excessive to subjectivation and subjective reappropriation. It is the retention of this order, its trace within a decision, that makes the latter worthy of the name, namely, not the application of a rule and a subjective decision but the reinstitution of a rule and thus a passive decision or the decision by which a deciding and responsible subject lets itself be affected.

To conclude, I would like to suggest in a schematic fashion two ways in which, on my view, the analyses of decision and the deciding subject that I have examined in this chapter influence Derrida's subsequent work, throughout and beyond *Politics of Friendship*. These analyses pave the way for a new thinking of democracy that no longer rests on classical and decisionist theories of decision and the deciding subject. They provide Derrida with a new concept of freedom, such as the freedom of the other or, as he calls it later, the freedom (or unconditionality) without sovereignty, which unleashes a new exploration of political subjectivity and sovereignty. Besides the treatment of democracy in *Politics of Friendship*, think of the two seminars on *The Beast and the Sovereign* (2001–3) and of *Rogues: Two Essays on Reason* (2003). Furthermore, Derrida builds on these analyses to develop his deconstructive re-elaboration of the humanist and oppositional history of life that modern philosophy since Descartes has told us and that has undergirded the cruelties perpetrated in our society against animals. In *The Animal That Therefore I Am (Following)* (presented in 1998 and published posthumously in 2006), Derrida calls into question the axiom of this history – namely, the abyss between the animal in general and the self-referent and responsible human subject – by resorting to a two-step argument.[19] On one hand, by drawing on the results of contemporary ethology, he explains that self-referentiality is not merely human. On the other, by tracing self-reference and self-referentiality back to his conception of decision and auto-heteroaffection, he calls for a differential rather than oppositional account of living beings, that is, for a history that accounts for life in a differential way.

Acknowledgement

I thank Felipe Quinteros for our quarantine conversations on my manuscript.

Notes

1. Jacques Derrida, 'A Certain Impossibility of Saying the Event' [2003], trans. Gia Walker, *Critical Inquiry*, 33 (2007), 455.
2. The earliest explorations of decision in Derrida's work can be found in 'Force of Law', first presented in 1989 and published in 1990 in Jacques Derrida, *Acts of Religion*, trans. Gil Anidjar (London: Routledge, 2002), pp. 228–98; and *Politics of Friendship* (based on the three-year seminar taught between 1988 and 1991, and published in 1994). As I show in the subsequent footnotes, more or less developed traces of Derrida's thought about decision are disseminated throughout his later work. For Derrida scholarship, see the following important readings: Geoffrey Bennington, *Scattered 1: The Politics of Politics in Foucault, Heidegger, and Derrida* (New York: Fordham University Press, 2016), pp. 159–86; François Raffoul, 'Heidegger and Derrida on Responsibility', in *A Companion to Derrida*, ed. Zeynep Direk and Leonard Lawlor (Oxford: Wiley Blackwell, 2014), pp. 412–29. Jacques Derrida, *Politics of Friendship*, trans. George Collins (London: Verso, 1997); Jacques Derrida, *Politiques de l'amitié: suivi de L'Oreille de Heidegger* (Paris: Galilée, 1994). Hereafter, page references to the English translation are given in parenthesis in the text (*PF*).
3. On Derrida's use of the expression 'worthy of the name', see Geoffrey Bennington, *Not Half Not End: Militantly Melancholic Essays in Memory of Jacques Derrida* (Edinburgh: Edinburgh University Press, 2010), pp. 35–46.
4. For the meaning of interruptive decision, a few sentences later Derrida writes: 'It would thus recall the type or the silhouette of the classic concept of decision, which must interrupt and mark an absolute beginning' (86). For other exemplary explanations of this meaning, see Derrida,

'Force of Law', p. 41 ('its very moment of foundation or institution, besides, is never a moment inscribed in the homogeneous fabric [*tissu*] of a story or history, since it rips it apart with one decision') and Jacques Derrida, *Rogues: Two Essays on Reason*, trans. Pascale-Anne Brault and Michael Naas (Stanford: Stanford University Press, 2005), p. 35 ('the event of the interruptive decision').

5. For a description of the event as the experience of originary or hetero-affection prior to the subjectivation presupposed by classical decision, see Derrida, *Rogues*, p. xiv: 'Through certain experiences that will be central to this book, and, more generally, through the experience that lets itself be affected by what or who comes [*(ce) qui vient*], by what happens or by who happens by, by *the other to some*, a certain unconditional renunciation of sovereignty is required a priori. Even before the act of a decision.'
6. For Derrida's discovery of the experience of freedom, as a certain dependency on the other, alternative to the freedom of the self-present and conscious subject, see his reading of Nietzsche's *Gay Science* §44 (63–4), and Mauro Senatore, 'In the Night of Nonknowledge: Derrida on Freedom', *Enrahonar. An International Journal of Theoretical and Practical Reason*, 66 (2021), 49–70.
7. For a later elaboration of this experience of freedom (as freedom from knowledge) retained in a decision worthy of the name, see Jacques Derrida, *Le parjure et le pardon. Vol. I (1997–98)*, ed. Ginette Michaud and Nicholas Cotton (Paris: Seuil, 2019), p. 255: 'Act, doing, decision, responsibility, freedom are heterogeneous to knowledge. We never *know* what we do, not as we close our eyes or remain ignorant or unconscious on this subject, but because doing and the decision to do presuppose a rupture or a heterogeneity, a hiatus between knowing and acting, knowledge and freedom, and so forth.'
8. For Derrida's rewriting of Sartre's conception of freedom, see Jacques Derrida and Elizabeth Roudinesco, *For What Tomorrow . . . A Dialogue* (2001), trans. Jeff Fort (Stanford: Stanford University Press, 2004), pp. 47–61.
9. Derrida, 'Force of Law', p. 251.
10. On my view, this autoheteroaffection does not merely overlap the notion of autoaffection elaborated by Derrida in earlier works such as *Voice and Phenomenon*, in which the movement of *différance* (namely, the trace) is already implicated. This later notion takes account of the experience of presubjective freedom that does not seem to occupy the foreground of Derrida's work until the late 1980s. See Jacques Derrida,

Voice and Phenomenon, trans. Leonard Lawlor (Evanston: Northwestern University Press, 2011), pp. 60–74.

11. Derrida, 'Force of Law', p. 252.
12. Ibid. p. 252.
13. Ibid. p. 253.
14. Ibid. p. 254.
15. Ibid. p. 254.
16. Ibid. p. 255.
17. Derrida, 'Force of Law', p. 255. On the legacy of Kierkegaard in Derrida's reference to madness, see Bennington, *Scattered 1*, pp. 159–86. For a later version of the aforementioned account of a just decision, see Derrida and Roudinesco, *For What Tomorrow*, p. 53.
18. Derrida, 'Force of Law', p. 255.
19. Jacques Derrida, *The Animal That Therefore I Am (Following)*, trans. David Wills (New York: Fordham University Press, 2008), pp. 94–5.

22

The Phantasmatic Fiction: Derrida on the Ground of Politics

Gavin Rae

This chapter will focus on one response that Derrida gives in *Politics of Friendship* to the question of what grounds politics.[1] To do so, I first outline Derrida's critical engagement with Carl Schmitt's insistence that the political is grounded in the friend/enemy distinction, to show that, on Derrida's telling, it not only leaves out a number of important aspects that it actually depends upon, namely the question of language, but is also based on a problematic logic of opposition. Although I would ideally critically evaluate Derrida's analysis of Schmitt, space constraints mean that I bracket that issue to simply follow Derrida to determine what he does with his reading of Schmitt.[2] Specifically, I argue that Derrida implicitly reaffirms the fundamental importance of his earlier concept of *différance*,[3] before delving into the problem of what grounds politics. Whereas political theory has traditionally grounded politics in a singular legitimating source, whether this is the divine right, the will of the populace, or some other foundational identity, Derrida's claim that the ground 'is' *différance* generates a different conception of politics, one that rejects the notion of an absolute foundation. However, if this is so, the questions arise as to how 'order' or 'stability' are achieved, and how political systems generate and sustain themselves.

I respond that in *Politics of Friendship*, specifically chapter 4, 'The Phantom Friend Returning (in the Name of Democracy)' (*PF*, 75–111),[4] Derrida offers a particularly innovative response to these issues that accepts that there is a ground to politics, but rejects the traditional claim that the ground is an ahistoric, substantial one. Instead, he affirms a post-foundational account that maintains that all political systems are premised on a phantasmatic fictional story or discourse that is performatively created by the community, with this fictional ground generating, binding and structuring both the community's sense of identity and its politics. So, although it might be thought that its fictional status renders it unimportant, Derrida claims that this fictive ground is actually fundamentally important because it is the necessary condition of the community and its politics.

This *conceptual* argument is supported by and also highlights a *hermeneutical* one that demonstrates that *Politics of Friendship* occupies an important place within Derrida's *oeuvre*, insofar as it depends on the notions of *différance* and 'mysticism' as well as the critique of the logic of binary oppositions developed in the earlier works 'Différance', 'Force of Law'[5] and *Dissemination*[6] respectively, while its emphasis on the relationship between politics and symbolism paves the way for his late seminars *The Beast and the Sovereign*[7] and *The Death Penalty*,[8] which return to discuss the relationship between symbolic fictions and sovereignty. With this, I highlight a little discussed aspect of *Politics of Friendship*, show the necessary and foundational role that symbolic fictions play in Derrida's notion of politics, and demonstrate that this theme binds different texts within Derrida's *oeuvre*.

The Political: Critiquing Carl Schmitt

The figure of Carl Schmitt plays a fundamental role throughout *Politics of Friendship*.[9] In *The Concept of the Political*, Schmitt attempts to ascertain the nature of the political to determine the 'true' nature and scope of politics. To do so, he claims that it is necessary to examine the concept of the political in a manner that distinguishes it from the economic, aesthetic, moral and so on. As a consequence, Schmitt contends that 'the political has its own criteria which express themselves in a characteristic way'.[10] Whereas 'in the realm of morality the final distinctions are between good and evil, in aesthetics beautiful and ugly, in economics profitable and unprofitable',[11] he suggests that '[t]he specific political distinction to which political actions and motives can be reduced is that between friend and enemy'.[12]

Although recognising that it is dangerous to reduce Schmitt's thinking to this distinction, Derrida nevertheless focuses on and praises the 'originality' of its two theses: (1) we need to pay attention to the 'political difference' between everyday *politics* and the *political*, with the latter describing the transcendental conditions of possibility of the former, and (2) the political is defined through the friend/enemy opposition (83–5). However, given that (1) depends upon (2), insofar as identifying what the political entails takes place through an analysis of the friend/enemy distinction, Derrida focuses his critical comments on (2). These take at least three forms: first, Schmitt's dichotomy depends upon the capacity of the sovereign State to know the intentions of the one before it (106). Only then can the other be designated as friend or enemy. The problem, for Derrida, appears to be that the

Schmittian other is always separated from the sovereign by an unbridgeable gulf. As such, for the sovereign to know the intention of the other would require that the other be transparent to both itself and the sovereign. For Derrida, however, this appears to depend upon the metaphysics of (self-) presence that he otherwise rejects,[13] insofar as such transparency requires that the enemy-other be only as it is presented. As a consequence, Derrida claims that the unbridgeable gulf between the two means that it is simply not possible for one to know the intentions of the other. Any judgement about the other necessarily requires that the sovereign impose its interpretation on to the other; an action that reduces the other to the sovereign to, in so doing, undermine the distinction between them that conditions and necessitates the political decision in the first place.

Derrida ties this to his second line of critique, which is orientated towards the logic of binary opposition that informs the friend/enemy distinction. According to Derrida, Schmitt maintains that political identity is generated from an *opposition* to an other, who can only ever be classified as 'friend' or 'enemy'.[14] In *Dissemination*, from 1972, Derrida points to a 'Crisis of *versus*', which I want to suggest is both a description of and a prescription for contemporary thought.[15] *Politics of Friendship* contributes to this by putting into question the logic of binary opposition that Schmitt's distinction depends upon. The overall aim is to '*oppose opposition*' (122). So, whereas, for Schmitt, the other can only be 'friend' *or* 'enemy', Derrida posits the possibility that the same figure can be both friend *and* enemy: 'the friend (*amicus*) can be an enemy (*hostis*); I can be hostile towards my friend, I can be hostile towards him publicly, and conversely I can, in privacy, love my enemy' (88). Rather than strictly oppositional, '[t]he two concepts (friend/enemy) consequently intersect and ceaselessly change places'. We have not the friend or the enemy, but '[t]he enemy the friend, the friend the enemy' (72).

This critique of logical opposition continues in and underpins Derrida's third line of critique, which refers to the linguistic dimension of Schmitt's analysis. There are two aspects to this: first, Derrida questions Schmitt's reliance on the distinction found in Latin and Greek between *hostis/amicus* and *polemios/echthros*, 'as though the distinction of the political could not be properly formulated in more than two idioms; as if other languages, even the German language, could not have as clear as access to the distinction', which would prevent them from having the concept of the political and, as such, being so (87). In other words, Schmitt's definition of the political is supposed to be universal, but yet it is linguistically reductionist by virtue of only adhering to two languages. This reductionism is compounded by the second problem inherent in Schmitt's analysis: language is not an isolatable phenomenon, but always 'belongs to a culture, to structures of ethnic, social and political organization in which language is irreducible' (89). In other words, not only is the linguistic dimension of Schmitt's account problematically reductionist, but so also is its lack of consideration for the wider role that the symbolic system as a 'whole' plays in structuring language and, by extension, the political decision. Derrida's own account aims to remedy this by giving the symbolic realm a fundamental place in the political generally and the question of sovereignty specifically.

The Symbolic Ground of Politics

Derrida's most schematic outline of his account of the symbolic takes place in the famous 1972 essay 'Différance'. The basic idea of this essay is to criticise the metaphysics of presence that he diagnoses as subtending Western thinking, which reduces thought to an originary presenting unity or identity. To counter this, Derrida introduces the notion of '*différance*', which in English combines 'defer' and 'differ',[16] to undercut the unitary ahistoric claims of the dominant metaphysics. Space constraints prevent a detailed discussion,[17] but, very simply, Derrida takes over Ferdinand de Saussure's claim that meaning is relational,[18] with the consequence that a signifier and its meaning are never monadic, and combines it with the notion that such relationality also prevents closure; as relations alter, so must being and meaning. The combination of 'deferment' and 'difference' ensures that the singular unity subtending the metaphysics of presence is a mirage, underpinned by a constantly changing field of differential and deferring relations.

However, if, as Derrida claims, the primordiality of *différance* undermines Schmitt's claim that the political is defined by the friend/enemy opposition, the question arises as to what grounds or founds a notion of the political thought from *différance*, which, in turn, generates the further one regarding the process(es) through which the homogeneity or order of the community is based.[19] Before turning to Derrida's responses, it will be helpful to situate them within a contemporary debate – to which Derrida was one of the early contributors – regarding the conceptual apparatus of 'foundations' and, in particular, the distinction between foundationalism, anti-foundationalism and post-foundationalism.

'Foundationalism' is based on the idea that there exists a solid, ahistoric, transcendent foundation to ground existent beings, including their actions, activities and truth-claims. The problem of foundationalism, from a Derridean perspective, is, of course, its appeal to a single, ahistoric, transcendent ground; all of which are rejected by Derrida's notion of *différance*. It might therefore be thought that Derrida affirms an anti-foundationalist stance that simply rejects the existence of grounds. Although this might appear, on first glance, to accord with Derrida's account of *différance*, there are at least two problems with such a conclusion: first, anti-foundationalism is premised on the negation of foundationalism. It is therefore inherently negative. In itself that is not necessarily problematic, but it becomes so for Derrida when that negativity is constricted within the restricted economy of the binary opposition between 'foundationalism' and its negative, 'anti-foundationalism'. Here, Derrida's critique is informed by Martin Heidegger's claim that 'the reversal of a metaphysical statement remains a metaphysical statement'.[20] By remaining within the logic of binary opposition, anti-foundationalism remains tied to the logical structures that Derrida diagnoses as governing Western metaphysics and which *différance* aims to overcome.

For this reason, second, Derrida does not simply adopt the binary logic that affirms or rejects foundationalism; rather, as Mathew Dinnon points out, 'he affirms the need for foundations, but aims to interrupt our expectation that foundations be stable and certain'.[21] For this reason, I want to suggest that Derrida affirms a post-foundational account, where

> What distinguishes [post-foundationalism] from [anti-foundationalism] is that it does not assume the absence of *any* ground; what it assumes is the absence of an *ultimate* ground, since it is only on the basis of such absence that grounds, in the plural, are possible. The problem is therefore posed not in terms of *no* foundations (the logic of all-or-nothing) but in terms of *contingent* foundations.[22]

At least two issues arise here. First, Derrida accepts the necessary existence of foundations but claims that these are constructed and contingent. As James Martel points out in a discussion of Derrida's analysis of the archive ('*arkheion*') in *Archive Fever*,[23] this ensures that 'the archeon, archism can take many forms; it can be liberal, it can be neoliberal, it can be fascist, monarchist, or just about any other form that is based on rule and projection of authority over others'.[24] Second, no system of foundations can ever claim to be ahistoric, 'true' or 'foundational' per se. Any foundation established is precisely that, established, rather than fixed and immutable, with the process of establishment being both a result of contestation amongst competing possibilities *and* always threatened with dissolution by that ongoing contestation.[25]

Having introduced this conceptual schema and claimed that Derrida adopts a post-foundationalist position, the task now is to show the implications for the political. Chapter 4 of *Politics of Friendship*, titled 'The Phantom Friend Returning (in the Name of "Democracy")', is particularly important here. To develop his response, Derrida engages with Schmitt's justification for basing his definition of the friend/enemy distinction on the Greek distinction between *polemios* and *echthros*. Noting that Schmitt briefly ties it to Plato's *Republic*, Derrida challenges Schmitt's reading by claiming that Plato does not actually operate with such an opposition but 'opposes war strictly speaking (*pólemos*) to civil war, to rebellion or to uprising (*stásis*)' (89).

Having undermined the interpretation of Plato supposedly supporting Schmitt's analysis, Derrida goes on to challenge the *logic* supporting it, claiming that it is based on the affirmation of a binary opposition that is also not found in Plato, who rather than 'being satisfied with the opposition on which Schmitt relies so heavily [. . .] *prescribes* its erasure' (90). Specifically, 'it is [. . .] recommended that the Greeks behave towards their enemies – the barbarians – as they behave today among themselves' (90). This, however, depends upon a particular conception of 'Greekness', including how one acts as a 'Greek', that is linked to the question of what it is to be 'naturally' Greek, which in turn is always held to be distinct from the 'barbarian' (92).

From this, Derrida makes two points. First, within Plato's discourse, there is a latent appeal to a logic of (political) purity grounded on a natural foundation, one that comes to find expression in Schmitt's claim regarding the 'purity' of the categories 'friend' and 'enemy' and against which, as previously noted, Derrida sets himself. Nevertheless, from Plato's text, Derrida draws the general conclusion that

> as in every racism, every ethnocentrism – more precisely, in every one of the nationalisms throughout history – a *discourse* on birth and on nature, a *phúsis* of genealogy (more precisely, a discourse and a phantasm on the genealogical *phúsis*) regulates, in the final analysis, the movement of each opposition: repulsion and attraction, disagreement and accord, war and peace, hatred and friendship. This *phúsis* comprises everything – language, law, politics, etc. (91)

Second, the ways in which Greeks were able to reconcile themselves after civil war with other Greeks 'ha[d] no other cause than actual kinship, *suggénia*, which produces a solid friendship founded on *homogeneity*, on *homophilia*, on a solid and firm affinity (*bébaion*) stemming from birth, from native community'. As Derrida points out, '[p]rovided that it is real – and not only spoken or set by convention – this syngenealogy durably guarantees the strength of the social bond in life and according to life'. The key critical part of this for Derrida resides in the initial clause 'Provided that it is real', which brings him to discuss the nature of 'real' and, by extension, the nature of 'nature' (92).

The basic question that Derrida claims this passage throws up relates to the role of identity and, in particular, the way in which identity is often held to be founded on a fixed and pure 'natural' substratum that sharply delineates those included within that identity from those excluded. As noted, Derrida's affirmation of *différance* is aimed squarely against such a notion of identity and, indeed, aims to show that identity per se is a problematic concept without ontological ground. *Différance* is ontologically primordial, with the consequence that identity is, at best, a second order phenomenon and, indeed, is never 'really' an identity because of the differential–deferred structure of *différance* which prevents the fixed signification inherent in identity from arising. However, although this allows Derrida to cast doubt on any simplistic appeal to a natural ground for politics, it does throw up the issue of how the perception of such identity arises in the first place and, relatedly, the 'nature' of the homogeneity that binds political communities.

It is here that Derrida offers his account of both the ground of politics and, by implication, the political that emphasises the important role of the symbolic. Specifically, he claims that the identity of the political community, while held to be 'real', is, in fact, 'a *dreamt* condition', 'a phantasm', and that, far from being grounded in a fixed natural substratum, 'a genealogical tie will never be simply real; its supposed reality never gives itself in any intuition, it is always posed, constructed, induced, it always implies a symbolic effect of discourse'. More specifically, it entails the construction of a 'legal fiction' that generates a particular founding narrative regarding the constitution of the political entity (92–3). This founding fiction sets the norms and parameters that define the identity of each community.

Two further points can be made. First, the construction of the legal fiction of an originary political homogeneity is a performative that is constantly created through the symbolic actions of the populace.[26] It is, in other words, 'a matter of a people insofar as it can *identify itself*, insofar as it is what it is or would wish to be' (103). It is this performative self-creation that creates a '*determined politics*, which, be it left- or right-wing, alleges a real fraternity or regulates spiritual fraternity, fraternity in the figurative sense, on the symbolic projection of a real or natural fraternity' (93). Crucially, however, the populace as community does not precede the founding political act, but only comes to be through that act. The founding act is then paradoxical: it depends upon the existence of the community that it actually creates.

Second, the basis of this performative legal fiction is not 'natural', in the sense of a fixed, non-symbolic realm that could and should be accurately symbolically represented to bind the heterogeneous parts, but is premised on 'mere' belief or faith in the existence and power of that binding: 'All politics and all policies, all political discourses on "birth", misuse what can in this regard be only a belief, some will say: what can only remain a belief; others: what can only tend towards an act of faith' (93). Why a belief takes hold, or is structured in a particular way, is and must remain an open one. As a performative construction, there is no way to identify before the event which belief will take hold to structure the community. Mirroring his earlier claim regarding the mystical source of authority,[27] Derrida explains that the 'bond between two structurally heterogeneous ties will always remain obscure, *mystical*, essentially foreign to rationality – which does not mean simply irrational, in the equally modern sense of the term'. As a symbolic performative, '[i]t will always be exposed, to say the least, to the "sophistications," mystifications, and perversions of rhetoric' (99). In many respects, for Derrida, the key aspect of the political – and, by extension, politics – is the ongoing contestation to establish the founding, mystical, (symbolic) fictional discourse that will structure both politics and the community.

So, although Derrida recognises that it is entirely possible that a populace may 'choose' 'homogenenizing calculability while exalting land and blood'– a possibility that he claims has unfortunately tended to be realised historically – it does not have to (106). After all, the lack of *a priori* foundations and the symbolic construction of identity always permits alternatives – including Derrida's affirmation of 'democracy to come' – although whatever is chosen will continuously have to be reaffirmed (104). Indeed, Derrida explains that the question as to whether it is necessary that the mystical aspect of the political be tied to xenophobic or ethnocentric forms of politics is precisely 'the question we are concerned with here' (100). With this, he notes that while his rejection of the logic of binary opposition and claim that enmity is fundamentally important for the political, might, on a Schmittian reading, appear to affirm 'an essential and necessary depoliticization' (104) – precisely that which Schmitt warns us about – in reality any depoliticisation is only a depoliticisation of the Schmittian conception of the political (based on a logic of opposition and a threatening other), with such a movement permitting the thinking, interpreting and implementation of 'another politics, another democracy' orientated from and around 'the social bond, of community, of friendship' (104). As I have argued, however, such a notion would continue to entail the performative creation of grounding (symbolic) fictions.

Conclusion

With this, Derrida (1) proposes a multidimensional critique of Schmitt, (2) offers a post-foundational account of the construction of political identity based on contestation and the ongoing creation of symbolic fictions, and (3) claims that the creation of any symbolic identity is grounded in a mystical performative process constituted by nothing other than belief and faith in the validity of a particular symbolic fiction. Furthermore, to do so, he draws on his earlier works, specifically the essays 'Différance' and 'The Force of Law', and *Dissemination*, all the while, by highlighting the importance of symbolic fictions for the political, setting the scene for his two final seminars – *The Beast and the Sovereign* and *The Death Penalty* – where he returns to the relationship between symbolic fictions and sovereignty.[28] *Politics of Friendship* is, then, an important work, not only because of its contents regarding the symbolic construction of the political, but also because it is a key mediating moment in Derrida's *oeuvre*, one that binds his earlier and later texts.

Notes

1. I would like to thank Emma Ingala and the editors – Luke Collison, Cillian Ó Fathaigh and Georgios Tsagdis – for their helpful comments on an original version of this chapter. This chapter forms part of the activities for the following research projects: (1) 'Agency and Society: An Inquiry through Poststructuralism' (PR108/20-26); (2) 'Differential Ontology and the Politics of Reason,' funded by the Government of the Region of Madrid, as part of line 3 of the multi-year agreement with the Universidad Complutense de Madrid: V PRICIT Excellence Program for University Professors (Fifth Regional Plan for Scientific Investigation and Technological Innovation); and (3) 'The Politics of Reason' (PID2020-117386GA-I00), financed by the Ministry of Science and Innovation, Government of Spain.
2. For a critical discussion of Derrida's reading of Schmitt, see Gavin Rae, *The Problem of Political Foundations in Carl Schmitt and Emmanuel Levinas* (Basingstoke: Palgrave Macmillan, 2016), pp. 69–74.
3. Jacques Derrida, 'Différance', in Derrida, *Margins of Philosophy*, trans. Alan Bass (Chicago: University of Chicago Press, 1982), pp. 3–27.
4. Jacques Derrida, *The Politics of Friendship*, trans. George Collins (London:

Verso, 1997); Jacques Derrida, *Politiques de l'amitié: suivi de L'Oreille de Heidegger* (Paris: Galilée, 1994). Hereafter, page references to the English translation are given in parenthesis in the text (*PF*).

5. Jacques Derrida, 'Force of Law: "The Mystical Foundation of Authority"', in Derrida, *Acts of Religion*, ed. Gil Anidjar (New York: Routledge, 2002), pp. 230–98.
6. Jacques Derrida, *Dissemination*, trans. Barbara Johnson (London: Continuum, 2004), p. 21.
7. Jacques Derrida, *The Beast and the Sovereign: Vol. 1*, trans. Geoffrey Bennington (Chicago: University of Chicago Press, 2009); Jacques Derrida, *The Beast and the Sovereign: Vol. 2*, trans. Geoffrey Bennington (Chicago: University of Chicago Press, 2011).
8. Jacques Derrida, *The Death Penalty: Vol. 1*, trans. Peggy Kamuf (Chicago: University of Chicago Press, 2014); Jacques Derrida, *The Death Penalty: Vol. 2*, trans. Elizabeth Rottenberg (Chicago: University of Chicago Press, 2017).
9. Derrida's interest in Schmitt was part of – and a major stimulus for – the turn to Schmitt and, by extension, the political that marked political theory at the turn of the millennium. See, for example, Chantal Mouffe (ed.), *The Challenge of Carl Schmitt* (London: Verso, 1993); Ellen Kennedy, *Constitutional Failure: Carl Schmitt in Weimar* (Durham, NC: Duke University Press, 2004); Andreas Kalyvas, *Democracy and the Politics of the Extraordinary: Max Weber, Carl Schmitt, and Hannah Arendt* (Cambridge: Cambridge University Press, 2008). For a critique of the turn to the political in contemporary theory, see Lois McNay, *The Misguided Search for the Political* (Cambridge: Polity, 2014).
10. Carl Schmitt, *The Concept of the Political: Expanded Edition*, trans. George Schwab (Chicago: University of Chicago Press, 2007), p. 26.
11. Ibid. p. 26.
12. Ibid. p. 26.
13. Derrida, 'Différance', pp. 16–17.
14. I have previously argued that this reading downplays the relationality inherent in Schmitt's analysis of the onto-genesis of political identity. See Rae, *The Problem of Political Foundations in Carl Schmitt and Emmanuel Levinas*, pp. 83–94.
15. Derrida, *Dissemination*, p. 21.
16. Derrida, 'Différance', pp. 7–8.
17. A detailed analysis can be found in Gavin Rae, 'Disharmonious Continuity: Critiquing Presence with Sartre and Derrida', *Sartre Studies International*, 23.2 (2017), 58–81.

18. Ferdinand de Saussure, *Course in General Linguistics*, ed. Charles Bally and Albert Sechehaye with the collaboration of Albert Riedlinger, trans. Roy Harris (Chicago: Open Court, 1986), p. 118.
19. In chapter 1 of *The Politics of Friendship*, Derrida explains that although democracy is based on singularity, these singularities must also be based in a sense of community (22).
20. Martin Heidegger, 'Letter on Humanism', trans. Frank A. Capuzzi in collaboration with J. Glenn Gray, in *Basic Writings*, ed. David Farrell Krell (London: Harper, 2008), pp. 217–65 (p. 232). On Derrida's relationship to Heidegger, see Gavin Rae, 'Authoritarian and Anthropocentric: Examining Derrida's Critique of Heidegger', *Critical Horizons: A Journal of Philosophy and Social Theory*, 16.1 (2015), 27–51.
21. Mathew D. Dinnon, 'Keeping the Old Name: Derrida and the Deconstructive Foundations of Democracy', *European Journal of Political Theory*, 13.1 (2016), 61–77 (p. 62).
22. Oliver Marchart, *Post-Foundational Political Thought: Political Difference in Nancy, Lefort, Badiou and Laclau* (Edinburgh: Edinburgh University Press, 2007), p. 14.
23. Jacques Derrida, *Archive Fever: A Freudian Impression*, trans. Eric Prenowitz (Chicago: University of Chicago Press, 1996), pp. 1–3.
24. James Martel, 'Walter Benjamin and the General Strike: Non-Violence and the Archeon', in *The Meanings of Violence: From Critical Theory to Biopolitics*, ed. Gavin Rae and Emma Ingala (New York: Routledge, 2019), pp. 13–30 (p. 16).
25. Interestingly, Michael Marder, in *Groundless Existence: The Political Ontology of Carl Schmitt* (London: Continuum, 2010), argues that Schmitt also affirms a post-foundational account of the political. Although I cannot explore this issue further here, it does point to an interesting overlap between Derrida's and Schmitt's thought regarding the question of political foundations.
26. It might be thought that, in *Constitutional Theory* (ed. and trans. Jeffrey Seitzer [Durham, NC: Duke University Press, 2008], p. 131), Schmitt argues for something similar when he introduces and depends upon the notion of 'acclamation' to explain the way(s) in which a particular political decision gains or loses popular support. Again, space constraints prevent a detailed discussion, but the key difference between Derrida's and Schmitt's performative accounts seems to be that in the latter, the moment of acclamation is premised on a binary yes/no response to a political decision presented to the populace by the sovereign in the face of a perceived threatening other. In contrast, the performative

moment in Derrida's account does not take place through a simple yes/no response to a pregiven proposal regarding a threatening other, but refers to a far more open-ended, positive and expressive moment in which the populace (which, it will be remembered, only comes into existence through its actions) becomes and expresses itself through its 'choice' of founding symbolic fiction.

27. Derrida, 'Force of Law', pp. 230–98.
28. For an analysis of the role that symbolic fictions play in the former, see Gavin Rae, 'The Wolves of the World: Derrida on the Political Symbolism of the Beast and the Sovereign', in *Seeing Animals after Derrida*, ed. James Tink and Sarah Bezan (Lanham, MD: Lexington Books, 2018), pp. 3–19; and on the role that they play in the latter, see Gavin Rae, *Critiquing Sovereign Violence: Law, Biopolitics, Biojuridicalism* (Edinburgh: Edinburgh University Press, 2019), ch. 7.

23

Modal Aporias: Derrida on the *reale Möglichkeit* of Friends and Enemies in Schmitt

Luke Collison

> It is all a matter of seeing correctly where this capacity for myth and this vital strength are really alive today.
>
> Carl Schmitt, *The Crisis of Parliamentary Democracy*[1]

In Derrida's *Politics of Friendship*, both friendship and the political are characterised by two irreconcilable demands: the demand for stability and reliability; and the demand for openness to renewal. This aporetic matrix of politics and friendship is approached in various ways, but a recurrent one, which provides the theme for this chapter, is through the category of modality. If the classical taxonomy of actuality, possibility and necessity forms the basis for Derrida's conception of modality, this set is regularly expanded to include the modality of the spectre or phantom (developed in *Specters of Marx*), as well as a multiplicity of modalities: talking to, speaking of, questioning, promising, but also befriending, whether in a reliable, faithful, *bébaios*, unstable or always renewed manner, as well as writing, scientifically or polemically, calculating the possible or the impossible, and even failing. Nonetheless, in Derrida's engagement with Carl Schmitt in *Politics of Friendship* he fixes on a specific modality that pervades Schmitt's *The Concept of the Political*, the modality of 'real possibility' or '*reale Möglichkeit*'. Schmitt's incessant repetition of the phrase reaches the intensity of an exorcising chant. Identifying the foundational status of this peculiar modality for 'the political', Schmitt writes that 'concepts of friend, enemy, and combat receive their real meaning precisely because they refer to the *real possibility* of physical killing'.[2] The political is inseparable from the 'ever present possibility' of war, the 'real possibility of a friend–enemy grouping'.[3] Derrida describes this constant appeal as an attempt to 'resist the return of the spectral', an attempt 'to exercise, to conjure, to "repress" the returning ghost' (*PF*, 132).[4]

The object of this chapter is Derrida's deconstruction of this modality of 'real possibility'. After elaborating his conception of the modality of spectral, I retrace his engagement with Schmitt on the topic of the real possibility of war. I argue that Derrida attempts a 'spectral inversion' of Schmitt's political concepts, but relies on a dubious equation of the exception and the improbable. I identify certain problems with Derrida's reading of Schmitt, particularly his ambivalence to the energetic themes of 'intensity' in *The Concept of the Political.* In my concluding remarks, I offer an alternative reading emphasising the influence of Georges Sorel's 'energetic politics' on Schmitt and suggest that this might trouble the modal assumptions of Derrida's *hauntology*.

Derrida and Modality

Derrida begins from Aristotle's canonical distinction between potentiality and act, *dynamis* and *energeia*, virtuality and actuality, translating these (with the addition of necessity) into the respective Kantian alternatives used by Schmitt: possibility, actuality and necessity, or *Möglichkeit*, *Wirklichkeit* and *Nötwendigkeit* (230). However, as he noted in *Specters of Marx*, there is a tendency for new categories to appear, like ghosts or spectres between possibility and actuality. Between the usual pair of modal ontological categories – being and non-being, actuality and non-actuality (possibility, or virtuality) the living and the dead – lies another 'paradoxical incorporation'.[5] In the earlier work, this realm is exemplified by money. The spectral modality is a 'hauntology' of ghostly objects which are present/but not present. It is a social or relational modality: 'All phenomena of friendship, all things and all beings to be loved, belong to spectrality' (288). Between these two lies a modality of 'failure, inadequation, disjunction, disadjustment, being "out of joint"'.[6] However, rejecting Marx's attempts to exorcise the spectral, Derrida defends this in-between realm as a 'messianic opening to what is coming': the event, the other, democracy to come.[7] The 'specter [. . .] is the frequency of a certain visibility. But the visibility of the invisible'.[8]

Derrida draws Schmitt's conception of the political towards this 'logic of spectrality', aiming to perform a vertiginous 'inversion' of Schmitt's categories, thus demonstrating the 'effect of haunting'. The logic of spectrality induces an 'inversion of signs' such that the 'purely concrete starts to resemble a ghost'. In Schmitt's case, the inversion involves the terms 'politicisation' and 'depoliticisation'. Undermining Schmitt's polemic against liberal 'depoliticisation', Derrida argues that Schmitt's own logic demands a kind of oscillation between the two. For Derrida, the key to this inversion lies in Schmitt's use of real possibility, which represents not a traditional 'actualisation', but '*Realisierung*', a passage to the act by way of intensification. Derrida claims that Schmitt's categories lead to the 'unavoidable consequence' – via a logic of 'rarefaction' or scarcity – that depoliticisation is in fact over-politicisation, or 'hyperpoliticization' (129, 138–40). Schmitt's political modality thus re-enacts Nietzsche's inversion of the friend and enemy. However, there are certain difficulties with Derrida's treatment that deserve a more thorough investigation – in particular, Schmitt's category of *real possibility* and its philosophical precursors.

Schmitt and War

We can identify various precursors to these spectral modalities in the history of political thought. In Hobbes's *Leviathan*, for instance, he writes that the modality of war is to be found, 'not in actual fighting, but in the known disposition thereto'.[9] For Hobbes, war is not entirely 'actual'. He does not identify war with actual 'battle' or 'the act of fighting' and instead displaces it to a modality of the known possibility. Invoking meteorological uncertainty, he notes that war is like the threat of 'foul weather' and that 'war consisteth not in battle only, or the act of fighting, but in a tract of time wherein the will to contend by battle is sufficiently known'.[10] War need not precipitate actual fighting. The threat of battle, like the threat of rain, remains an effective influence on behaviour. In agriculture, the imminent possibility of rain, evident in visible signs, is effective in guiding the actions of the farmer.

For both Hobbes and Schmitt, the *possibility* of fighting is the decisive factor. A contrast is offered in Walter Lippmann's *Public Opinion*, a text Schmitt was familiar with and which also points to the role of war in accomplishing the '*union sacrée*'. However, Lippmann limits war's effectiveness to those periods of active combat, the '*middle phases of war* when fear, pugnacity, and hatred have secured complete domination of the spirit'. The confrontation with the enemy and war function only as 'symbols of public opinion', whereas in Schmitt we find a 'structuring enemy' (84).[11]

Schmitt's spur for the figure of the enemy can be traced to the Hegelian-Marxist image of bourgeoisie.[12] Shortly after the publication of *History and Class Consciousness*, in reference to the political potential of Marxism, Schmitt writes, that '[b]oth Russian and proletarian saw now in the bourgeois the incarnation of everything that sought to enslave their way of life in a deadly mechanism'. Foreshadowing his developed conception of the enemy, Schmitt continues that, in Marxism, the 'Hegelian dialectic has served to create an image of the enemy [*Gegner*] that was capable of intensifying all the emotions of hatred and contempt'.[13] In the *Tagebücher* in 1926, Schmitt returns to this formulation in a passage suggesting that the friend/enemy distinction is imagined as a generalisation of a Hegelian-Marxist conception of 'negation'. 'The proletariat in Marx is *negatively* determined; [. . .] the *people* as well negatively determined; the negative (hence the equality [*Gleichheit*]!).'[14] Schmitt pairs this Hegelian 'negative' with a paraphrase of Aristotle's remarks on equality and distributive justice: '[e]very actual [*wirkliche*] democracy rests on the principle that not only are equals equal, but rather, and with necessary consequences, the unequal will not be treated equally'.[15]

Derrida's deconstruction of Schmitt centres on this modality of conflict. Schmitt's constant references to *wirklich* (actual) and *real possibility* indicate the 'the most obscure zone of difficulty' which concerns the 'passage from possibility to eventuality' (86). Attesting to its obscurity, Derrida makes two distinct approaches to the problem.[16]

The first focuses on the eventuality [*Eventualität*] of war. However, Derrida's line of thought is difficult to unravel. Initially, he appears to suggest that Schmitt confuses *possibility* with a weak form of *necessity*. But this argument would turn on a rather forced interpretation of *Eventualität* as that which will 'eventually occur'. In German, like in French, the term *eventuell* does not ordinarily imply a sense of necessity. A common translation of *eventuell* is in fact 'perhaps'. More likely, Derrida's focus lies on the transition between a '*quasi-transcendental* modality of the possible and the *historico-factual* modality of the eventual' (86).

The problem Derrida identifies is the passage between the quasi-transcendental and the concrete. Schmitt does not admit the distinction between the conditions of possibility of the political and the historically determinant form of the meaning of the political and the subsequent political groupings. The passage from eventuality, the historical-factual appearance of the enemy, to a 'synthetic *a priori*' construction of the 'very concept of the political' leads Schmitt to an 'eidetic reduction' and need for a phenomenological purification of 'the political'. Derrida claims that this leads Schmitt to distinguish the political from '[a]ll other regional disciplines, all other knowledge – economic, aesthetic, moral, military, even religious knowledge – must be suspended'. A 'border' is constructed between 'the political' and all other spheres of life (86–8).[17] For Derrida, Schmitt's construction of the political thus resembles something like Hannah Arendt's strict borders between the *polis* and the *oikos*.[18]

However, Derrida ignores a key aspect of Schmitt's account: the transformation of 'the political' into a kind of elastic, mutable opposition, into a 'degree of intensity'. The enemy 'need not' [*braucht nicht*] be morally evil, but 'psychologically the enemy is easily treated as being evil and ugly, because every distinction, most of all the political, as the strongest and most intense of the distinctions and categorizations, draws upon other distinctions for support'.[19] In contrast to Arendt's strictly delimited political sphere, from which, for example, the 'social question' is excluded, Schmitt depicts the political as a kind of energy or intensity that is parasitic on another domain, but, like a formless amoeba, it can spread and infect all regions of human life. All collective gatherings, demonstrations, public festivals, the audiences of theatres and sporting events, 'every popular assembly, even one that initially appears nonpolitical, intrinsically contains unexpected political possibilities'.[20] For Schmitt, the marker of 'the political' is collective participation and collective goals, rather than those of an individual. One reason for Derrida's difficulty with *real possibility* is thus his misreading of the *intensification* of the political in *The Concept of the Political.*

In Derrida's second approach to this difficulty, the modality of *real possibility*, he focuses on the passage from the possible to the actual, which he insists Schmitt renders a kind of radicalisation, a 'hyperbolization'. He notes that, for Schmitt, the real possibility of war is not an 'actualization' of something possible but a 'radicalisation of a possible reality' (a *Realisierung*). And importantly for Derrida, *Realisierung* breaks with the Aristotelian dichotomy of potentiality and actuality, *dynamis* and *energeia* (124, 239). Derrida divides the radicalisation into two moments.

The first moment consists of a play or oscillation of the political between two 'stratifications'. One is particular and concrete while the other is general. Any fixed sense of the modality of the political is displaced by an oscillation between these two stratifications. The political appears first as a 'a concrete particular form' but shifts to a general form that 'invades the entire fundamental grounding stratum of existence'. Schmitt's modality thus exhibits paradoxical qualities, appearing both as a particular political opposition or polemic and as a general form which acts as a 'supplementary and overdetermining determination cutting through all other regions of the human world or of the cultural, symbolic or "spiritual" communities'. Derrida does not explicitly refer to Schmitt's text, but the likely reference is Schmitt's transformation of the political into a 'degree of intensity' discussed above.

According to Derrida, the second moment of Schmitt's passage of radicalisation relies on a 'classic' transcendental-ontological philosophical strategy. Like Leo Strauss and Heinrich Meier, Derrida is attentive to Schmitt's use of the 'presupposition [*Voraussetzung*]'. But he eschews Meier's interpretation of it as a substitute for revelation, exemplified in Meier and Strauss's claim that Schmitt's presupposition of man's dangerousness is an 'anthropological confession of faith' (124–6).[21] Instead, Derrida draws attention to the way a presupposed political decision (on an enemy) displaces the meaning of war. War becomes 'the political's condition of possibility without it being for all that, in any respect, the aim, the finality or even the content of the political!' (126) For Schmitt, war is the condition of possibility of the political, precisely because it 'creates a specifically political behaviour'.[22] War is not the aim of politics, but rather '[t]he enemy "was already there"' (172). It was decisively predetermined, through a decision, an 'exceptional' decision.

With this connection between the modality of 'real possibility' and the exception established, the aim of Derrida's argument emerges. The final move is to turn Schmitt on himself, by showing that depoliticisation is itself a means of intensifying the 'specifically political tension' produced by the possibility of actual/effective combat. Pushing the concept of the 'exception' towards that of the 'extreme possibility' and a logic of scarcity or 'rarefaction', Derrida suggests, 'one must conclude that *rarefaction* intensifies the political tension and the revealing power'.[23] Derrida's conclusion: 'the less war there is, the more the hostility, etc.'. Thus Schmitt's logic 'inevitably leads [. . .] to having to measure politicization in terms of the degree of depoliticization' (129). Inverting Schmitt's categories, Derrida claims that depoliticisation is a form of politicisation, thus confirming the spectral modality of the Schmittian political. It is indeed a vertiginous inversion for anyone familiar with Schmitt's work. Is the political really subject to a logic of rarity?

Tracing Derrida's account closely, however, the ground for this strategy was developed a few paragraphs earlier. Derrida makes a kind of a synonymic sleight of hand, in which the 'exception' is equated with the 'improbable'. On the question of killing, Derrida writes, 'one might say, the more exceptional, unusual, *improbable* it is the more it weighs decisively on decision'. Based on this quasi-synonymic transition from the exceptional, to the unusual, to the improbable, Derrida equates 'the improbable situation' and 'the exceptional case' (128–9). But we should be suspicious of this synonymic transition from the *exceptional* to the *improbable*. The Schmittian exception, the *Ausnahme*, is not an improbable occurrence; it is an exception to a given system of law or set of rules. As Schmitt writes, the exception 'cannot be circumscribed factually and made to conform to a preformed law'.[24]

Contrary to Derrida's synonymic illusion, I claim it is the *unpredictability* that is important to Schmitt. The distinction between the *improbable* and *unpredictable* is clearly exemplified in Brownian motion: the random and unpredictable movement of gaseous molecules occurring at every moment in the air around us. Like the fluctuations of stock market prices, these events are not improbable, since they occur constantly. The 'random walk' of such entities was the object of a new field of mathematics developed in the twentieth century: stochastic analysis. It sought to put measurable limits and bounds on these fluctuations. Without making them absolutely predictable, they could be contained and limited, much as law – in particular, constitutional law – aims to set boundaries and limits to the actions of political actors. While both law and stochastic analysis remain incomplete sciences, the difficulty is not so much one of probability but multiplicity. There are simply too many things that could happen.

Perhaps aware of the difficulty, Derrida supplements this line of thought with an alternative, in which the improbable and a 'logic of scarcity' are introduced through the *extreme* nature of combat (131). But again, the introduction is forced. Combat is only or primarily *extreme* due to its proximity to death, not its improbability.

Why is Derrida so determined to equate war with the improbable? Is it a demand for symmetry between the enemy and the friend? In the later chapters, discussing Kant and the black swan, the theme of scarcity returns. 'Rarity is the virtue of friendship' (212). Against the enemy and the modality of real possibility, Derrida constructs its corrected alternatives: friendship and the perhaps. The 'event of friendship' is shown to be 'random and improbable, but not excluded', unlike Schmitt's excluded 'exceptional, unusual, improbable' enemy. Kant's ideal friend also 'actually exists here and there in its perfection' (259). The 'perhaps' and the 'real possibility of combat' face one another as two modes of experience of the event. One welcomes it and the other fears it.

From the modality of the perhaps, which Derrida tentatively defends, one accepts friendship from the point of view of possibility, uncertainty. There is a certain risk, but also the chance for 'friendship with an open heart' (29–30). Derrida conjures an alternative political based in shared enjoyment and an alternative conception of responsibility that is 'exercised only in silence' (52).[25] But if 'a perhaps always delivers itself to chance' then would a politics of friendship take chance as its guiding principle? The theme of 'chance' plays a central role in Schmitt's analysis of the mode of legitimation of the Weimar constitution, *Legality and Legitimacy*. According to Schmitt, insofar as legality could legitimate a political system, this required adherence to the principle of 'equal chance'. The 'substantive principle of justice' of the Weimar constitution is the 'principle that there is an unconditional equal chance for all conceivable opinions, tendencies, and movements to achieve a majority'.[26]

Derrida does not cite this text and refers little, if at all, to the historical situation to which Schmitt's work responds. Writing in 1932 in *Legality and Legitimacy*, Schmitt's advice to Weimar's parliament entailed that, in order to survive, the Weimar republic must admit its political nature and ban its enemies, the 'National-Socialists, Communists, [and] the godless'.[27] Instead, they largely upheld the doctrine of an 'equal chance' and accepted the 'risk of instability' and the 'dangerous perhaps', with disastrous results (28–9).

Energy, Sorel and Schmitt

To conclude, I want to suggest an alternative reading of Schmitt's *reale Möglichkeit*, one which might address some of these difficulties. If there is a lacuna in Derrida's engagement with Schmitt, it would be Georges Sorel. Why does Derrida avoid this *fin de siècle* figure of revolutionary violence? Even in *Force of Law*, Derrida only mentions Sorel briefly and in passing.[28] Instead of a Sorelian politics of myth, in *Politics of Friendship* Derrida returns to Montaigne and the mystical foundations of law. By contrast, in Schmitt's writings of the 1920s there are signs of an extended engagement with Sorel. Schmitt writes that Sorel's 'theory of myth', when joined with the 'energy of nationalism', will form a means of 'establishing the foundation of another authority, [. . .] based on the new feeling for order, discipline and hierarchy'.[29] Putting aside the question of myth, I suggest the reference of 'political energy' which appears occasionally in Schmitt's writings offers a key to this puzzle of the modal tension of 'actual possibility [*reale Möglichkeit*]'.[30]

The nationalist political writings of *fin de siècle* Europe contain extensive rhetorical use of 'energy'. We could cite Maurice Barrès's trilogy *Roman de l'énergie nationale* or Futurist Marinetti's references to 'energy'. Hippolyte Taine complained that in the nineteenth century '*energy*, formerly ridiculous, becomes fashionable and is used on every occasion'.[31] However, for Sorel, energy is not simply a rhetorical reference to enthusiasm. Instead, Sorel depicts physics and the natural sciences as the source of the models and concepts on which political institutions are based. According to Sorel, the realm of spectrality, as Derrida describes it, is governed by the concepts of physics.[32]

What is the modality of energy? A curiously abstract, unconditioned thing, energy is infinitely mutable and transformable, elastic and convertible, but undestroyable. Despite this abstract convertibility, energy can only exist in the world in a particular concrete form. It can stand as a reserve in a latent, potential form, which can later be put to 'work', and transformed into heat or movement (kinetic energy). Resembling Schmitt's conception of 'the political' as a degree of intensity, energy oscillates between the particular and the general. It wasn't until late nineteenth-century thermodynamics that 'energy' became a general term for all forms of 'ordinary motion and mechanical power [work], chemical action, heat, light, electricity, magnetism, and all other powers, known or unknown, which are convertible or commensurable with these'.[33] Based on these theories, the precondition of all 'work', all effectivity, was the possession of a quantity of energy.

In the juxtaposition of Sorel and Derrida, the question that emerges is what spectral energy is 'put to work [. . .] to produce [. . .] a forever errant surplus value' in acts of conjuration?[34] Sorel's interest in Brownian motion, the spontaneous movement of molecules, is paired with his interest in spontaneous political action.[35] Sorel thought Brownian motion demonstrated the existence of a 'new and unknown energy [*énergie nouvelle et inconnue*]' that defies the doctrine of the conservation of energy.[36] Thus it offered a model for the violence of the general strike as a 'creative energy [*énergie créatrice*]' that escaped the laws of entropy. In addition, Sorel saw in the physics of friction, a model for a kind of energy that in the political field appeared between oppositional forces. In *Reflections*, class division (*scission*) is identified as a source of energy for both parties involved. Class conflict and the violence of the proletariat will also 'restore to the bourgeoisie something of its energy'.[37] The 'line of cleavage [*scission*]' between classes generates the energy and excitation, without which 'socialism cannot fulfil its historic role'.[38]

There has been a growing interest in the topic of 'energy' in recent years.[39] In particular, among new work on Marx, there is a strand focused on energy connecting it to 'labour power' as the reserve capacity of an individual to work, to produce.[40] Given the scientific developments of the nineteenth century, it is curious that Derrida derives from Marx the idea of the ghost as a model for an alternative modality, rather than thermodynamic theories of energy. However, if we consider the context of *fin de siècle* Europe, there was a strange traffic between these fields, demonstrated in the scientific interest in 'paranormal phenomena'. For instance, various philosophers and scientists – Henri Bergson, Étienne Marey, Marie and Pierre Curie – all participated in studies of psychic phenomena.[41] Instead of the ghost, I suggest the implicit model for Schmitt's intensified politics is drawn from Sorel and the modality of post-thermodynamic energy.[42]

Notes

1. Carl Schmitt, *The Crisis of Parliamentary Democracy*, trans. Ellen Kennedy (Cambridge, MA: MIT Press, 1988 [1923]), p. 68.

2. Carl Schmitt and Leo Strauss, *The Concept of the Political, Expanded Edition*, ed. and trans. George Schwab (Chicago: University of Chicago Press, 2007 [1927, 1932]), p. 33. Translation modified, my italics. Hereafter '*CP*'.
3. Schmitt and Strauss, *CP*, pp. 34–5.
4. Jacques Derrida, *Politics of Friendship*, trans. George Collins (London: Verso, 1997); Jacques Derrida, *Politiques de l'amitié: suivi de L'Oreille de Heidegger* (Paris: Galilée, 1994). Hereafter, page references to the English translation are given in parenthesus in the text (*PF*).
5. Jacques Derrida, *Specters of Marx: The State of the Debt, the Work of Mourning and the New International* (London: Routledge, 2012), pp. 5, 12.
6. Derrida, *Specters of Marx*, p. 81.
7. Ibid. p. 82.
8. Ibid. p. 125. Curiously, Derrida does not discuss the affinities between 'spectrality' and the concepts of 'visibility' and 'representation' in Schmitt's 1920s writings. Anticipating Derrida, Schmitt writes that social institutions 'must be rooted in the invisible and appear in the visible'. Carl Schmitt, *Roman Catholicism and Political Form*, ed. George Schwab and G. L. Ulmen, trans. G. L. Ulmen (London: Greenwood Press, 1996 [1923]), pp. 20–1, 52–3.
9. Thomas Hobbes, *Leviathan, with Selected Variants from the Latin Edition of 1668*, ed. Edwin Curley (Cambridge: Hackett, 1994), ch. 13.[8].
10. Hobbes, *Leviathan*, ch. 13.[8].
11. Walter Lippmann, *Public Opinion* (New York: The Macmillan Company, 1929 [1922]), p. 11.
12. Derrida specifically notes the influence of Gyorgy Lukács on Schmitt's concept of the enemy (84, 141).
13. Schmitt, *Crisis*, pp. 73–4.
14. Carl Schmitt, *Tagebücher 1925 bis 1929*, ed. Martin Tielke and Gerd Giesler (Berlin: Duncker & Humblot, 2018), p. 347, 16r. underlined in original. The notes in the 'Parallel Tagebuch' are not dated, but from the surrounding notes, this fragment may have been written in early 1926.
15. Schmitt, *Crisis*, p. 9. Translation modified.
16. These appear in chapters 4 and 5 respectively.
17. Gavin Rae, *The Problem of Political Foundations in Carl Schmitt and Emmanuel Levinas* (London: Palgrave Macmillan, 2016), p. 72.
18. See for instance Hannah Arendt, 'What Is Authority?', in Arendt, *Between Past and Future* (New York: Viking Press, 1961), pp. 104–5.

19. Schmitt and Strauss, *CP*, pp. 26–7.
20. Carl Schmitt, *Constitutional Theory*, ed. and trans. Jeffrey Seitzer (London: Duke University Press, 2008 [1928]), p. 272.
21. Heinrich Meier, *Carl Schmitt and Leo Strauss: The Hidden Dialogue* (Chicago: University of Chicago Press, 1995), pp. 50–9; Schmitt and Strauss, *CP*, p. 105.
22. Schmitt and Strauss, *CP*, p. 34.
23. My italics.
24. Carl Schmitt, *Political Theology: Four Chapters on the Concept of Sovereignty*, trans. George Schwab (Chicago: University of Chicago Press, 2005 [1922]), p. 6.
25. In the background here is possibly Schmitt's demand that only 'public acclamation' can guarantee responsibility (*Verantwortlichkeit*).
26. Carl Schmitt, *Legality and Legitimacy*, trans. Jeffrey Seitzer (London: Duke University Press, 2004 [1932]), p. 28. Hereafter *L&L*.
27. Schmitt, *L&L*, p. 48.
28. Jacques Derrida, 'Force of Law: The "Mystical Foundation of Authority"', *Cardozo Law Review*, 11.5–6 (1990), 919–1046 (pp. 996, 1016, 1026).
29. Schmitt, *Crisis*, pp. 75, 76.
30. There are a number of references to 'political energy' in Schmitt's published and unpublished writings: Carl Schmitt, *Dictatorship: From the Origin of the Modern Concept of Sovereignty to Proletarian Class Struggle*, trans. Michael Hoelzl and Graham Ward (Cambridge: Polity, 2014 [1921]), p. 6; Schmitt and Strauss, *CP*, p. 69n36; Schmitt, *L&L*, pp. 32–3.
31. Hippolyte A. Taine, *The Ancient Regime*, *Trans*, trans. J. Durand (New York: Henry Holt & Company, 1876), p. 295.
32. Georges Sorel, *Sorel: Reflections on Violence* (Cambridge: Cambridge University Press, 1999), pp. 12–13, 54; Georges Sorel, *The Illusions of Progress*, trans. John and Charlotte Stanley (Berkeley: University of California Press, 1969), pp. 158–9. On Sorel and energy, see Luke Collison, 'Georges Sorel's Political Energy', *History of European Ideas*, 48 (2021).
33. Peter Michael Harman, *Energy, Force and Matter: The Conceptual Development of Nineteenth-Century Physics* (Cambridge: Cambridge University Press, 1982), p. 58.
34. Derrida, *Specters of Marx*, p. 49.
35. Ernest Coumet, 'Écrits épistémologiques de Georges Sorel (1905): H. Poincaré, P. Duhem, E. Le Roy', *Mil neuf cent. Revue d'histoire intellectuelle (Cahiers Georges Sorel)*, 6.1 (1988), 5–51 (pp. 43–4).

36. Coumet, 'Écrits épistémologiques', sec. Annex pp. 42–5.
37. Sorel, *Reflections*, p. 85.
38. Ibid. pp. 125, 182.
39. Loosely described as the 'energy humanities', this field is often traced to Bruce Clarke, *Energy Forms: Allegory and Science in the Era of Classical Thermodynamics* (Ann Arbor: University of Michigan Press, 2001).
40. See Allan Stoekl, 'Marxism, Materialism, and the Critique of Energy', in *Materialism and the Critique of Energy*, ed. Brent Ryan Bellamy and Jeff Diamanti (Chicago: MCM, 2018), pp. 1–28.
41. Lynn Ann Badia, 'A Universe of Forces: Energy in Early Twentieth-Century Theory and Literature' (PhD, Chapel Hill, 2014), pp. 30–3.
42. In Schmitt's Sorelian reading of Hobbes's mythical image of the leviathan, we find a passage juxtaposing (1) the potential of myth for the 'restoration of the vital energy and political unity' of a state, with (2) its perception 'in a ghostly light' by which the leviathan became 'a grotesque horror picture'. Carl Schmitt, *The Leviathan in the State Theory of Thomas Hobbes: Meaning and Failure of a Political Symbol* (Chicago: University of Chicago Press, 2008 [1938]), p. 81.

Index